Differential Equations and Inverse Problems

Differential Equations and Inverse Problems

Guest Editors

Tao Liu
Qiang Ma
Songshu Liu

Basel • Beijing • Wuhan • Barcelona • Belgrade • Novi Sad • Cluj • Manchester

Guest Editors

Tao Liu
College of Sciences
Northeastern University
Shenyang
China

Qiang Ma
Department of Mathematics
Harbin Institute of
Technology
Harbin
China

Songshu Liu
School of Mathematics and
Statistics
Northeastern University at
Qinhuangdao
Qinhuangdao
China

Editorial Office
MDPI AG
Grosspeteranlage 5
4052 Basel, Switzerland

This is a reprint of the Special Issue, published open access by the journal *Axioms* (ISSN 2075-1680), freely accessible at: https://www.mdpi.com/journal/axioms/special_issues/UX61E6N6E1.

For citation purposes, cite each article independently as indicated on the article page online and as indicated below:

Lastname, A.A.; Lastname, B.B. Article Title. *Journal Name* **Year**, *Volume Number*, Page Range.

ISBN 978-3-7258-3067-1 (Hbk)
ISBN 978-3-7258-3068-8 (PDF)
https://doi.org/10.3390/books978-3-7258-3068-8

© 2025 by the authors. Articles in this book are Open Access and distributed under the Creative Commons Attribution (CC BY) license. The book as a whole is distributed by MDPI under the terms and conditions of the Creative Commons Attribution-NonCommercial-NoDerivs (CC BY-NC-ND) license (https://creativecommons.org/licenses/by-nc-nd/4.0/).

Contents

About the Editors vii

Preface ix

Zhiwei Wang, Guilai Zhang and Yang Sun
Convergence of Collocation Methods for One Class of Impulsive Delay Differential Equations
Reprinted from: *Axioms* 2023, 12, 700, https://doi.org/10.3390/axioms12070700 1

Dan Wu, Yuezan Tao and Honglei Ren
The Laplace Transform Shortcut Solution to a One-Dimensional Heat Conduction Model with Dirichlet Boundary Conditions
Reprinted from: *Axioms* 2023, 12, 770, https://doi.org/10.3390/axioms12080770 15

Rian Yan and Yige Zhao
Positive Solutions for Periodic BoundaryValue Problems of Fractional Differential Equations with Sign-Changing Nonlinearity and Green's Function
Reprinted from: *Axioms* 2023, 12, 819, https://doi.org/10.3390/axioms12090819 29

Yingchun Li, Zhengjie Zhou, Cheng Chen, Peng Wu and Zhiquan Zhou
An Efficient Convolutional Neural Network with Supervised Contrastive Learning for Multi-Target DOA Estimation in Low SNR
Reprinted from: *Axioms* 2023, 12, 862, https://doi.org/10.3390/axioms12090862 42

Mingzhu Li, Lijuan Chen and Yongtao Zhou
Sinc Collocation Method to Simulate the Fractional Partial Integro-Differential Equation with a Weakly Singular Kernel
Reprinted from: *Axioms* 2023, 12, 898, https://doi.org/10.3390/axioms12090898 56

Gui-Lai Zhang, Zhi-Wei Wang, Yang Sun and Tao Liu
Asymptotical Stability Criteria for Exact Solutions and Numerical Solutions of Nonlinear Impulsive Neutral Delay Differential Equations
Reprinted from: *Axioms* 2023, 12, 988, https://doi.org/10.3390/axioms12100988 71

Songshu Liu, Tao Liu and Qiang Ma
On a Backward Problem for the Rayleigh–Stokes Equation with a Fractional Derivative
Reprinted from: *Axioms* 2024, 13, 30, https://doi.org/10.3390/axioms13010030 93

Liangyu Wang and Hongyu Li
Solvability Criterion for a System Arising from Monge–Ampère Equations with Two Parameters
Reprinted from: *Axioms* 2024, 13, 175, https://doi.org/10.3390/axioms13030175 105

Yang Li, Yingmei Xu, Qianhai Xu and Yu Zhang
New Simplified High-Order Schemes for Solving SDEs with Markovian Switching Driven by Pure Jumps
Reprinted from: *Axioms* 2024, 13, 190, https://doi.org/10.3390/axioms13030190 120

Ioannis K. Argyros, Santhosh George, Samundra Regmi and Michael I. Argyros
On the Kantorovich Theory for Nonsingular and Singular Equations
Reprinted from: *Axioms* 2024, 13, 358, https://doi.org/10.3390/axioms13060358 140

Feixiang Yang, Tinglei Wang and Yun Huang
An Accelerated Dual-Integral Structure Zeroing Neural Network Resistant to Linear Noise for Dynamic Complex Matrix Inversion
Reprinted from: *Axioms* 2024, 13, 374, https://doi.org/10.3390/axioms13060374 153

Jiaxin Hu, Feixiang Yang and Yun Huang
An Efficient Anti-Noise Zeroing Neural Network for Time-Varying Matrix Inverse
Reprinted from: *Axioms* **2024**, *13*, 540, https://doi.org/10.3390/axioms13080540 . . . . **172**

About the Editors

Tao Liu

Tao Liu is an Associate Professor at the College of Sciences, Northeastern University. He received a Ph.D. in Mathematics and an M.S. in Applied Mathematics from Harbin Institute of Technology and Harbin Engineering University, respectively. He was a Post-Doctoral Research Fellow at the School of Electrical and Electronic Engineering, Nanyang Technological University, from 2022 to 2023. His research interests include deep learning, reinforcement learning, multiscale methods (multigrid and wavelet), homotopy methods, inverse and ill-posed problems, computational mathematics, and applied mathematics. In related subjects, he has published more than 40 SCI journal papers and more than 30 EI conference papers. His work was awarded the Outstanding Project of Nature Science Foundation of Hebei Province of China in 2019. His research is funded by the Natural Science Foundation of Hebei Province of China and the Marine Ecological Restoration and Smart Ocean Engineering Research Center of Hebei Province of China, among others. Furthermore, he serves as a reviewer for *Mathematical Reviews*, a journal of the American Mathematical Society, is an Editorial Board Member and Topical Advisory Panel Member for several academic journals indexed in SCI, and had been invited as a speaker and member of many international technical committees for several conferences indexed in EI.

Qiang Ma

Qiang Ma is an Associate Professor at the Department of Mathematics, Harbin Institute of Technology. He received a Ph.D. in Basic Mathematics and an M.S. in Computational Mathematics from Harbin Institute of Technology. His interests, in both research and teaching, include structure-preserving algorithms for differential equations and numerical methods for stochastic differential equation. He has published over 50 papers in prestigious international journals such as *International Journal of Computer Mathematics*, *Numerical Methods for Partial Differential Equations*, *Mathematical Methods in the Applied Sciences*, *Calcolo*, *Numerical Algorithms*, and so on. He has presided over one National Natural Science Foundation of China Youth Science Foundation Project, one National Key Research and Development Special Sub-Project, and one Shandong Provincial Natural Science Foundation General Project.

Songshu Liu

Songshu Liu is an Associate Professor at the School of Mathematics and Statistics, Northeastern University, Qinhuangdao. He received a Ph.D. in Basic Mathematics and an M.S. in Computational Mathematics from Harbin Institute of Technology and Heilongjiang University, respectively. His main research areas include ill-posed problems, regularization methods, inverse source problems, backward problems, parabolic equations, elliptic equations, fractional diffusion equations, and convergence analysis. He has published over 20 papers in prestigious international journals such as *Taiwanese Journal of Mathematics*, *Bulletin of the Malaysian Mathematical Sciences Society*, *Computational and Applied Mathematics*, *Journal of Computational and Applied Mathematics*, *Inverse Problems in Science and Engineering*, *Journal of Inverse and Ill-Posed Problems*, *Complex Variables and Elliptic Equations*, and so on. His research is funded by the Natural Science Foundation of Hebei Province of China and the Fundamental Research Funds for the Central Universities, among others.

Preface

Differential equations and inverse problems have become a rapidly growing topic because of the new techniques developed recently and the amazing achievements in computational sciences. With the progress of science and technology, differential equations and inverse problems have quickly developed, and new waves have been successively set off in a broad range of disciplines, such as mathematics, physics, engineering, business, economics, earth science, biology, etc.

This reprint features a selection of 12 distinguished papers that present groundbreaking findings in theoretical studies, along with the latest advancements in addressing practical scientific and technological challenges.

This reprint brought together mathematicians with physicists, engineers, and other scientists to share their findings. Topics covered in this reprint include the following:

Impulsive delay differential equations;
Fractional differential equations;
Rayleigh–Stokes equation with a fractional derivative;
Monge–Ampère equation;
One-dimensional heat conduction;
Dynamic complex matrix inversion;
Collocation methods;
Runge–Kutta method;
Tikhonov regularization method;
Convolution neural networks;
Supervised contrastive learning;
Zeroing neural networks.

Tao Liu, Qiang Ma, and Songshu Liu
Guest Editors

Article

Convergence of Collocation Methods for One Class of Impulsive Delay Differential Equations

Zhiwei Wang, Guilai Zhang * and Yang Sun

College of Sciences, Northeastern University, Shenyang 110819, China; 2172045@stu.neu.edu.cn (Z.W.); 2101906@stu.neu.edu.cn (Y.S.)
* Correspondence: zhangguilai@neuq.edu.cn

Abstract: This paper is concerned with collocation methods for one class of impulsive delay differential equations (IDDEs). Some results for the convergence, global superconvergence and local superconvergence of collocation methods are given. We choose a suitable piecewise continuous collocation space to obtain high-order numerical methods. Some illustrative examples are given to verify the theoretical results.

Keywords: impulsive delay differential equations; collocation methods; convergence; superconvergence

MSC: 65L03

1. Introduction

Impulsive differential equations appear to represent models of several real-life phenomena. In recent decades, systems with impulse effects have arisen in control theory, medicine, biotechnology, economics, population growth, etc. Some work on these systems was presented [1–5]. In recent years, there has been increasing attention on the initial value problem of IDDEs. The corresponding theory of the exact solutions of IDDEs has been studied from different angles (see [6–12]): oscillation, stability, asymptotic stability and exponential stability in some specific classes of IDDEs.

Collocation methods as numerical methods have a wide range of applications in the treatment of integral–algebraic equations [13–16], Volterra integral equations [17–19] and delay differential equations [20–22]. Specifically, the convergence of the collocation methods has received a lot of attention, such as the convergence of collocation methods for weakly singular Volterra integral equations [23], the superconvergence of collocation methods for first-kind Volterra integral equations [24], the convergence of collocation methods for Volterra integral equations [25], the convergence of multistep collocation methods for integral–algebraic equations [16], etc. But to the best of our knowledge, there are no articles referring to the convergence of the collocation method for IDDEs.

In this paper, we consider the following impulsive delay differential equation with collocation methods:

$$\begin{cases} y'(t) = p(t)y(t) + q(t)y(t-\tau), & t \neq k\tau, k = 1, 2, \cdots, t \in I, \\ \triangle y = B_k y, & t = k\tau, k = 1, 2, \cdots, \\ y(t) = \phi(t), & t \in [-\tau, 0], \end{cases} \quad (1)$$

where $I := [0, T]$, $\triangle y = y(t^+) - y(t)$, $y(t^+)$ is the right limit of $y(t)$, $p : I \to \mathbb{R}, q : I \to \mathbb{R}$ are two given functions and sufficiently smooth, $\tau > 0$ is a positive constant, ϕ is a continuous function on $[-\tau, 0]$ and $y'(t)$ denotes the left-hand derivative of $y(t)$.

The rest of the present paper is organized as follows: Firstly, the existence and uniqueness of collocation methods are presented in Section 2. In Section 3, the global convergence of collocation methods is analytically derived. Following that, Section 4 gives the global and local superconvergence of properties. Finally, two numerical experiments are given in Section 5.

Definition 1 (Jurang Yan [8]). *The function $y : I \to R$ is said to be a solution of system (1) when the following conditions are satisfied:*
1. $y(t) = \phi(t), t \in [-\tau, 0]$;
2. for $t \in I, t \neq k\tau$, the function $y(t)$ is differentiable and $y'(t) = p(t)y(t) + q(t)y(t - \tau)$;
3. the function $y(t)$ is left-continuous in I, and if $t \in I$ and $t = k\tau$, then $y(t^+) = (1 + B_k)y(t)$, $y(t^-) = y(t)$;
4. $B_k \in (-\infty, -1) \cup (-1, +\infty)$ are constants, $k = 1, 2, \cdots$.

2. Collocation Methods

For ease of notation, we assume that $T = N\tau$, N is a positive integer. All $k\tau$, $k = 1, 2, \cdots, N$, are chosen as numerical nodes to ensure the convergence of collocation methods. Define a positive integer $p \geqslant 1$ and the stepsize $h = \frac{\tau}{p}$ corresponding to the given intervals (t_n, t_{n+1}). $t_n = nh$ are fixed time. The global mesh I_h on I is defined by

$$I_h := \{t_n : 0 = t_0 < t_1 < \cdots < t_{Np} = T\}.$$

Firstly, we will choose the collocation points as follows:

$$X_h := \{t_{n,i} = t_n + c_i h : 0 < c_1 < \cdots < c_m \leqslant 1\},$$

where $\{c_i\}$ indicates a series of collocation parameters. Define $\sigma_n := (t_n, t_{n+1}]$. The exact solution can be approximated by a collocation solution in the piecewise polynomial space

$$\widetilde{S_m^{(0)}}(I_h) := \left\{ v : v|_{\sigma_n} \in \pi_m, \begin{cases} \triangle v = 0, & \text{if } t \neq k\tau, t \in I \\ \triangle v = B_k v, & t = k\tau \end{cases} \right\},$$

where π_m denotes the space of all real polynomials of degree not exceeding m (see [17,21]), and $\triangle v = v(t^+) - v(t)$. The collocation solution u_h is the element of the piecewise polynomial space that satisfies the following equation:

$$\begin{cases} u_h'(t) = p(t)u_h(t) + q(t)u_h(t - \tau), & t \neq k\tau, t \in X_h, \\ \triangle u_h(t_{kp}) = B_k u_h(t_{kp}), & k = 1, 2, \cdots, \\ u_h(t) = \phi(t), & t \in [-\tau, 0], \end{cases} \quad (2)$$

where $u_h(t)$ and $u_h'(t)$ are left-continuous.

Setting $Y_{n,j} := u_h'(t_n + c_j h)$, we have

$$u_h'(t_n + vh) = \sum_{j=1}^{m} L_j(v) Y_{n,j}, \quad (3)$$

where $L_j(v)$ denotes the following Lagrange fundamental corresponding to the collocation parameters $\{c_i\}$ (see [17,21]):

$$L_j(v) = \prod_{i=1, i \neq j}^{m} \frac{v - c_i}{c_j - c_i}.$$

Integrating (3), we can obtain

$$u_h(t_n + vh) = u_h(t_n^+) + h \sum_{j=1}^{m} \beta_j(v) Y_{n,j}, v \in (0, 1], \quad (4)$$

where

$$\beta_j(v) = \int_0^v L_j(s)ds.$$

According to the definition of $\widetilde{S_m^{(0)}}(I_h)$, we have

$$u_h(t_n^+) = \begin{cases} u_h(t_n), & t_n \neq k\tau, k = 1, 2, \cdots, \\ (1+B_k)u_h(t_n), & t_n = k\tau. \end{cases} \quad (5)$$

By (2) and (4), we obtain

$$\begin{aligned} Y_{n,i} &= p(t_{n,i})u_h(t_{n,i}) + q(t_{n,i})u_h(t_{n,i} - \tau) \\ &= p(t_{n,i})\left[u_h(t_n^+) + h\sum_{j=1}^m \beta_j(v)Y_{n,j}\right] \\ &\quad + q(t_{n,i})\left[u_h(t_{n-p}^+) + h\sum_{j=1}^m \beta_j(v)Y_{n-p,j}\right], \end{aligned} \quad (6)$$

where $a_{ij} := \beta_j(c_i)$. Let

$$\widetilde{P}_n := \mathrm{diag}(p(t_{n,i})), A = (a_{ij}) \in L(\mathbb{R}^m), P_n := \widetilde{P}_n A,$$

$$\widetilde{Q}_n := \mathrm{diag}(q(t_{n,i})), A = (a_{ij}) \in L(\mathbb{R}^m), Q_n := \widetilde{Q}_n A,$$

$$\beta(v) := (\beta_1(v), \beta_2(v), \cdots, \beta_m(v))^T, Y_n := (Y_{n,1}, Y_{n,2}, \cdots, Y_{n,m})^T, e := \underbrace{\left(1, \cdots, 1\right)^T}_{m}.$$

Then

$$[I_{m \times m} - hP_n]Y_n = \left[\widetilde{P}_n u_h(t_n^+) + \widetilde{Q}_n u_h(t_{n-p}^+)\right]e + hQ_n Y_{n-p}. \quad (7)$$

When the solution Y_n has been found by (6), the collocation solution on the interval $(t_n, t_{n+1}]$ is determined by

$$u_h[(t_n + vh)] = u_h(t_n^+) + h\beta^T(v)Y_n, v \in (0,1]. \quad (8)$$

According to [17], the following theorem is given without proof.

Theorem 1. *There exists an $\bar{h} > 0$ such that for the mesh diameter h belonging to the interval $(0, \bar{h})$, (7) has unique solutions $Y_n \in \mathbb{R}^m$. Then, the collocation solution $u_h \in \widetilde{S_m^{(0)}}(I_h)$ for impulsive delay differential Equation (1) is unique and is given by (8) on the subinterval $(t_n, t_{n+1}]$.*

3. Global Convergence

In the following section, the global convergence of the collocation solution for IDDEs will be analyzed.

Theorem 2. *If $p, q \in C^m(I)$ and the collocation solution u_h for (1) is defined by (2), then there exists two constants C_0 and C_1 which are independent of h, satisfying*

$$\|y - u_h\|_\infty := \max_{t \in I}|y(t) - u_h(t)| \leqslant C_0\left\|y^{(m+1)}\right\|_\infty h^m, \quad (9)$$

$$\|y' - u_h'\|_\infty := \sup_{t \in I}|y'(t) - u_h'(t)| \leqslant C_1\left\|y^{(m+1)}\right\|_\infty h^m, \quad (10)$$

for $h \in (0, \bar{h})$ and any collocation parameters with $0 < c_1 < \cdots < c_m \leqslant 1$.

Proof. Assume that $p, q \in C^m(I)$ implies $y \in C^{m+1}(\sigma_n)$ and $y' \in C^m(\sigma_n)$. The collocation error $e_h(t) := y(t) - u_h(t)$ satisfies the equation

$$e'_h(t) = p(t)e_h(t) + q(t)e_h(t - \tau), \quad t \neq k\tau, \quad t \in X_h, \tag{11}$$

with $e_h(t) = 0, t \leqslant 0$. By Peano's theorem [17], we can obtain that

$$y'(t_n + vh) = \sum_{j=1}^{m} L_j(v) Z_{n,j} + h^m R^{(1)}_{m+1,n}(v), \quad v \in (0, 1], \tag{12}$$

where

$$R^{(1)}_{m+1,n}(v) := \int_0^1 K_m(v, z) y^{(m+1)}(t_n + zh) dz,$$

$$K_m(v, z) := \frac{1}{(m-1)!} \left\{ (v - z)_+^{m-1} - \sum_{k=1}^{m} L_k(v)(c_k - z)_+^{m-1} \right\}, v \in (0, 1],$$

and $Z_{n,j} := y'(t_{n,j})$. Integrating (12), we have

$$y(t_n + vh) = y(t_n^+) + h \sum_{j=1}^{m} \beta_j(v) Z_{n,j} + h^{m+1} R_{m+1,n}(v), v \in (0, 1], \tag{13}$$

where

$$R_{m+1,n}(v) := \int_0^v R^{(1)}_{m+1,n}(v) dv,$$

and

$$y(t_n^+) = \begin{cases} y(t_n), & t_n \neq k\tau, k = 1, 2, \cdots, \\ (1 + B_k)y(t_n), & t_n = k\tau. \end{cases}$$

Let $\varepsilon_{n,j} := Z_{n,j} - Y_{n,j}$. Comparing (4) and (13), we obtain

$$e_h(t_n + vh) = e_h(t_n^+) + h \sum_{j=1}^{m} \beta_j(v) \varepsilon_{n,j} + h^{m+1} R_{m+1,n}(v), v \in (0, 1], \tag{14}$$

where

$$e_h(t_n^+) = \begin{cases} e_h(t_n), & t_n \neq k\tau, k = 1, 2, \cdots, \\ (1 + B_k)e_h(t_n), & t_n = k\tau. \end{cases} \tag{15}$$

Due to (3) and (12), we can obtain that

$$e'_h(t_n + vh) = \sum_{j=1}^{m} L_j(v) \varepsilon_{n,j} + h^m R^{(1)}_{m+1,n}(v), v \in (0, 1]. \tag{16}$$

By the definition of $\varepsilon_{n,j}$ and (14), we obtain

$$\begin{aligned}\varepsilon_{n,i} &= y'(t_{n,i}) - u'_h(t_{n,i}) \\ &= p(t_{n,i})e_h(t_n + vh) + q(t_{n,i})e_h[(t_n + vh) - \tau] \\ &= p(t_{n,i})e_h(t_n + vh) + q(t_{n,i})e_h[(t_{n-p} + vh)] \\ &= p(t_{n,i})\left[e_h(t_n^+) + h\sum_{j=1}^m a_{ij}\varepsilon_{n,j} + h^{m+1}R_{m+1,n}(c_i)\right] \\ &\quad + q(t_{n,i})\left[e_h(t_{n-p}^+) + h\sum_{j=1}^m a_{ij}\varepsilon_{n-p,j} + h^{m+1}R_{m+1,n-p}(c_i)\right],\end{aligned}$$ (17)

i.e.,

$$\begin{aligned}[I_{m\times m} - hP_n]\varepsilon_n &= \left[\widetilde{P}_n e_h(t_n^+) + \widetilde{Q}_n e_h(t_{n-p}^+)\right]e + h^{m+1}\widetilde{P}_n R_{m+1,n} \\ &\quad + hQ_n\varepsilon_{n-p} + h^{m+1}\widetilde{Q}_n R_{m+1,n-p},\end{aligned}$$ (18)

where $R_{m+1,n} := (R_{m+1,n}(c_1),\ldots,R_{m+1,n}(c_m))^T$ and $\varepsilon_n := (\varepsilon_{n,1},\varepsilon_{n,2},\ldots,\varepsilon_{n,m})^T$. For ease of notation, we assume $n = pk + l (l = 1, 2,\ldots,p)$, then $t_n = t_{pk+l} \in (k\tau, (k+1)\tau]$. By (14) and (15),

$$\begin{aligned}e_h(t_n^+) &= e_h\left(t_{pk+l}^+\right) = W_{k+1}e_h\left(t_{pk+l}\right) = W_{k+1}e_h\left(t_{pk+l-1} + h\right) \\ &= W_{k+1}\left[e_h\left(t_{pk+l-1}\right) + h\sum_{j=1}^m b_j\varepsilon_{pk+l-1,j} + h^{m+1}R_{m+1,pk+l-1}(1)\right] \\ &= \cdots = W_{k+1}\left[e_h\left(t_{pk}^+\right) + \sum_{i=pk}^{n-1} h\sum_{j=1}^m b_j\varepsilon_{i,j} + \sum_{i=pk}^{n-1} h^{m+1}R_{m+1,i}(1)\right] \\ &= W_{k+1}\left[(1+B_k)e_h\left(t_{pk}\right) + \sum_{i=pk}^{n-1} h\sum_{j=1}^m b_j\varepsilon_{i,j} + \sum_{i=pk}^{n-1} h^{m+1}R_{m+1,i}(1)\right] \\ &= \cdots = W_{k+1}\prod_{d=1}^k (1+B_d)\left[\sum_{i=0}^{p-1} h\sum_{j=1}^m b_j\varepsilon_{i,j} + \sum_{i=0}^{p-1} h^{m+1}R_{m+1,i}(1)\right] \\ &\quad + W_{k+1}\prod_{d=2}^k (1+B_d)\left[\sum_{i=p}^{2p-1} h\sum_{j=1}^m b_j\varepsilon_{i,j} + \sum_{i=p}^{2p-1} h^{m+1}R_{m+1,i}(1)\right] \\ &\quad + \cdots + W_{k+1}(1+B_k)\left[\sum_{i=(k-1)p}^{kp-1} h\sum_{j=1}^m b_j\varepsilon_{i,j} + \sum_{i=(k-1)p}^{kp-1} h^{m+1}R_{m+1,i}(1)\right] \\ &\quad + W_{k+1}\left[\sum_{i=kp}^{pk+l-1} h\sum_{j=1}^m b_j\varepsilon_{i,j} + \sum_{i=kp}^{pk+l-1} h^{m+1}R_{m+1,i}(1)\right],\end{aligned}$$

where $b_j := \beta_j(1), e_h(0^+) = 0$, and

$$W_k := \begin{cases} 1 + B_k, & \text{if } l = p, \\ 1, & l \neq p. \end{cases}$$ (19)

Hence,

$$
\begin{aligned}
e_h\left(t_{n-p}^+\right) &= e_h\left(t_{p(k-1)+l}^+\right) = W_k e_h\left(t_{p(k-1)+l}\right) = W_k e_h\left(t_{p(k-1)+l-1} + h\right) \\
&= \cdots = W_k \prod_{d=1}^{k-1}(1+B_d)\left[\sum_{i=0}^{p-1} h \sum_{j=1}^{m} b_j \varepsilon_{i,j} + \sum_{i=0}^{p-1} h^{m+1} R_{m+1,i}(1)\right] \\
&\quad + W_k \prod_{d=2}^{k-1}(1+B_d)\left[\sum_{i=p}^{2p-1} h \sum_{j=1}^{m} b_j \varepsilon_{i,j} + \sum_{i=p}^{2p-1} h^{m+1} R_{m+1,i}(1)\right] \\
&\quad + \cdots + W_k(1+B_{k-1})\left[\sum_{i=(k-2)p}^{kp-p-1} h \sum_{j=1}^{m} b_j \varepsilon_{i,j} + \sum_{i=(k-2)p}^{kp-p-1} h^{m+1} R_{m+1,i}(1)\right] \\
&\quad + W_k\left[\sum_{i=kp-p}^{pk-p+l-1} h \sum_{j=1}^{m} b_j \varepsilon_{i,j} + \sum_{i=kp-p}^{pk-p+l-1} h^{m+1} R_{m+1,i}(1)\right],
\end{aligned}
\tag{20}
$$

where $b := (b_1, b_2, \cdots, b_m)^T$. In view of Theorem 1, we can easily obtain that the matrices $(I_m - hP_n - hQ_n)$ have bounded inverses whenever $h \in (0, \bar{h})$, and there exists a constant $D_0 < \infty$ such that

$$\left\|(I_m - hP_n - hQ_n)^{-1}\right\|_1 \leqslant D_0, n = 0, 1, 2, \cdots.$$

By (18),

$$
\begin{aligned}
\|\varepsilon_n\|_1 \leqslant D_0 \| & h^{m+1} \widetilde{P}_n R_{m+1,n} + h^{m+1} \widetilde{Q}_n R_{m+1,n-p} \\
&+ \tilde{P}_n e W_{k+1} \prod_{d=1}^{k}(1+B_d)\left[\sum_{i=0}^{p-1} h \sum_{j=1}^{m} b_j \varepsilon_{i,j} + \sum_{i=0}^{p-1} h^{m+1} R_{m+1,i}(1)\right] \\
&+ \tilde{P}_n e W_{k+1} \prod_{d=2}^{k}(1+B_d)\left[\sum_{i=p}^{2p-1} h \sum_{j=1}^{m} b_j \varepsilon_{i,j} + \sum_{i=p}^{2p-1} h^{m+1} R_{m+1,i}(1)\right] \\
&+ \cdots + \tilde{P}_n e W_{k+1}(1+B_k)\left[\sum_{i=(k-1)p}^{kp-1} h \sum_{j=1}^{m} b_j \varepsilon_{i,j} + \sum_{i=(k-1)p}^{kp-1} h^{m+1} R_{m+1,i}(1)\right] \\
&+ \tilde{P}_n e W_{k+1}\left[\sum_{i=kp}^{pk+l-1} h \sum_{j=1}^{m} b_j \varepsilon_{i,j} + \sum_{i=kp}^{pk+l-1} h^{m+1} R_{m+1,i}(1)\right] \\
&+ \tilde{Q}_n e W_k \prod_{d=1}^{k-1}(1+B_d)\left[\sum_{i=0}^{p-1} h \sum_{j=1}^{m} b_j \varepsilon_{i,j} + \sum_{i=0}^{p-1} h^{m+1} R_{m+1,i}(1)\right] \\
&+ \tilde{Q}_n e W_k \prod_{d=2}^{k-1}(1+B_d)\left[\sum_{i=p}^{2p-1} h \sum_{j=1}^{m} b_j \varepsilon_{i,j} + \sum_{i=p}^{2p-1} h^{m+1} R_{m+1,i}(1)\right] \\
&+ \cdots + \tilde{Q}_n e W_k (1+B_{k-1})\left[\sum_{i=(k-2)p}^{kp-p-1} h \sum_{j=1}^{m} b_j \varepsilon_{i,j} + \sum_{i=(k-2)p}^{kp-p-1} h^{m+1} R_{m+1,i}(1)\right] \\
&+ \tilde{Q}_n e W_k\left[\sum_{i=kp-p}^{pk-p+l-1} h \sum_{j=1}^{m} b_j \varepsilon_{i,j} + \sum_{i=kp-p}^{pk-p+l-1} h^{m+1} R_{m+1,i}(1)\right] \|_1.
\end{aligned}
$$

Because $|B_i|(i=1,2,\ldots,k)$ is finite, there exists a constant $R(R>1)$, satisfying $\left|\prod_{d=1}^{k}(1+B_d)\right| \leqslant R(d=1,2,\cdots,k)$. Let

$$P_0 := \|p(t)\|_\infty, Q_0 := \|q(t)\|_\infty, M_{m+1} := \left\|y^{(m+1)}\right\|_\infty,$$

$$K_m := \max_{v \in [0,1]} \int_0^v |K_m(v,z)| dz, \bar{b} := \max_{(j)} |b_j|.$$

Consequently, we have

$$\|\varepsilon_n\|_1 \leqslant D_0 |W_{k+1}|R| \|\tilde{P}_n e\|_1 \left[\sum_{i=0}^{n-1} h |b^T \varepsilon_i| + \sum_{i=0}^{n-1} h^{m+1} |R_{m+1,i}(1)| \right] + D_0 h^{m+1} \|\tilde{P}_n R_{m+1,n}\|_1$$

$$+ D_0 |W_k|R| \|\tilde{Q}_n e\| \left[\sum_{i=0}^{n-p-1} h |b^T \varepsilon_i| + \sum_{i=0}^{n-p-1} h^{m+1} |R_{m+1,i}(1)| \right] + D_0 h^{m+1} \|\tilde{Q}_n R_{m+1,n-p}\|_1$$

$$\leqslant D_0 |W_{k+1}|R| \|\tilde{P}_n e\|_1 \left[\sum_{i=0}^{n-1} h |b^T \varepsilon_i| + \sum_{i=0}^{n-1} h^{m+1} |R_{m+1,i}(1)| \right] + D_0 h^{m+1} \|\tilde{P}_n R_{m+1,n}\|_1$$

$$+ D_0 |W_k|R| \|\tilde{Q}_n e\|_1 \left[\sum_{i=0}^{n-1} h |b^T \varepsilon_i| + \sum_{i=0}^{n-1} h^{m+1} |R_{m+1,i}(1)| \right] + D_0 h^{m+1} \|\tilde{Q}_n R_{m+1,n-p}\|_1$$

$$\leqslant D_0 \max\{|W_k|,|W_{k+1}|\} m (P_0 + Q_0) R \bar{b} \sum_{i=0}^{n-1} h \|\varepsilon_i\|_1$$

$$+ D_0 \max\{|W_k|,|W_{k+1}|\} m (P_0 + Q_0) R \left(\sum_{i=0}^{n-1} h \right) K_m M_{m+1} h^m$$

$$+ D_0 m (P_0 + Q_0) m K_m M_{m+1} h^{m+1}$$

$$\leqslant D_0 m (P_0 + Q_0) R^2 \bar{b} \sum_{i=0}^{n-1} h \|\varepsilon_i\|_1$$

$$+ \left(D_0 m (P_0 + Q_0) R^2 T K_m + D_0 m (P_0 + Q_0) m K_m T \right) M_{m+1} h^m$$

$$=: \gamma_0 \sum_{i=0}^{n-1} h \|\varepsilon_i\|_1 + \gamma_1 M_{m+1} h^m,$$

with obvious meaning of γ_0, γ_1. Due to the discrete Gronwall inequality [17], we obtain

$$\|\varepsilon_n\|_1 \leqslant \gamma_1 M_{m+1} h^m \exp(\gamma_0 T) =: B M_{m+1} h^m, n = 0, 1, \cdots,$$

and

$$|e_h(t_n^+)| \leqslant R|W_{k+1}| \bar{b} \sum_{i=0}^{n-1} h \|\varepsilon_i\|_1 + R|W_{k+1}| h^m \left(\sum_{i=0}^{n-1} h \right) K_m M_{m+1}.$$

By (14) and (16),

$$|e_h(t_n + vh)| \leqslant |e_h(t_n^+)| + h \bar{\beta} \|\varepsilon_n\|_1 + h^{m+1} K_m M_{m+1}$$

$$\leqslant R|W_{k+1}| \bar{b} \sum_{i=0}^{n-1} h \|\varepsilon_i\|_1 + R|W_{k+1}| \left(\sum_{i=0}^{n-1} h \right) K_m M_{m+1} h^m$$

$$+ h \bar{\beta} \|\varepsilon_n\|_1 + h^{m+1} K_m M_{m+1}$$

$$\leqslant \left[R|W_{k+1}| \left(\sum_{i=0}^{n-1} h \right) \bar{b} B + R|W_{k+1}| \left(\sum_{i=0}^{n-1} h \right) K_m + h \bar{\beta} B + h K_m \right] M_{m+1} h^m$$

$$\leqslant \left[R^2 T \bar{b} B + R^2 T K_m + T \bar{\beta} B + T K_m \right] M_{m+1} h^m =: C_0 M_{m+1} h^m,$$

and

$$|e_h'(t_n + vh)| \leqslant \Lambda B M_{m+1} h^m + h^m K_m M_{m+1}$$

$$= (\Lambda B + K_m) M_{m+1} h^m \qquad (21)$$

$$=: C_1 M_{m+1} h^m,$$

where
$$\bar{\beta} := \max_{(j)} \|\beta_j\|_\infty, \Lambda := \max_{(j)} \|L_j\|_\infty.$$

The proof of Theorem 2 is complete. □

4. Global Superconvergence and Local Superconvergence

In this part, the global superconvergence of the collocation solution is discussed first and the local superconvergence is analyzed later.

Theorem 3. *Let the given function in (1) satisfy $p, q \in C^d(I), \phi \in C^{d+1}[-\tau, 0]$, $d \geqslant m+1$. Assume that the m collocation parameters $\{c_i\}$ are subject to the orthogonality condition*

$$J_0 := \int_0^1 \prod_{i=1}^m (s - c_i) ds = 0. \tag{22}$$

Then, the corresponding collocation solution u_h on I satisfies the following conditions:

$$\|y - u_h\|_\infty \leqslant C_2 h^{m+1}, \tag{23}$$

$$\|y' - u_h'\|_\infty \leqslant C_3 h^m, \tag{24}$$

where $h \in (0, \bar{h})$, C_2 and C_3 are two constants which are independent of h.

Proof. The (24) can be obtained with (21). The following discussion is for (23). We define the defect $\delta_h(t)$ by

$$\delta_h(t) := -u_h'(t) + p(t)u_h(t) + q(t)u_h(t-\tau), t \in I. \tag{25}$$

By (1), we can easily obtain the following form:

$$\delta_h(t) := e_h'(t) - p(t)e_h(t) - q(t)e_h(t-\tau), t \in I, \tag{26}$$

and $\delta_h(t) = 0$ for all $t \in X_h$. Due to Theorem 2, we can obtain that

$$\|\delta_h\|_\infty \leqslant C_1 M_{m+1} h^m + P_0 C_0 M_{m+1} h^m + Q_0 C_0 M_{m+1} h^m =: D_1 M_{m+1} h^m, \tag{27}$$

for any c_i in $\{c_i : i = 1, 2, \cdots, m, 0 < c_i \leqslant 1\}$.

Here, $e_h(t)$ can be treated as the solution of the following equation:

$$\begin{cases} e_h'(t) = p(t)e_h(t) + q(t)e_h(t-\tau) + \delta_h(t), & t \neq k\tau, t \in I, \\ e_h(t^+) = (1 + B_k)e_h(t), & t = k\tau, \\ e_h(t) = 0, & t \in [-\tau, 0]. \end{cases} \tag{28}$$

Let $r(t, s)$ denote the resolvent of (1)

$$r(t, s) := \exp\left(\int_s^t p(v) dv\right), r \in C^{m+1}(D),$$

where $D := \{(t, s) : 0 \leqslant s \leqslant t \leqslant T\}$. So, for $t \in (0, \tau]$, we have

$$e_h(t) = \int_0^t r(t, s)(q(s)e_h(s-\tau) + \delta_h(s)) ds,$$

for $t \in (\tau, 2\tau]$, we obtain

$$e_h(t) = (1 + B_1)r(t, \tau) \int_0^\tau r(\tau, s)(q(s)e_h(s - \tau) + \delta_h(s))ds$$
$$+ \int_\tau^t r(t, s)(q(s)e_h(s - \tau) + \delta_h(s))ds,$$

for $t \in (2\tau, 3\tau]$, we can obtain that

$$e_h(t) = (1 + B_2)r(t, 2\tau)\left[(1 + B_1)r(2\tau, \tau) \int_0^\tau r(\tau, s)(q(s)e_h(s - \tau) + \delta_h(s))ds \right.$$
$$\left. + \int_\tau^{2\tau} r(t, s)(q(s)e_h(s - \tau) + \delta_h(s))ds\right] + \int_{2\tau}^t r(t, s)(q(s)e_h(s - \tau) + \delta_h(s))ds,$$

for $t \in (k\tau, (k+1)\tau]$, $e_h(t)$ can be expressed by

$$e_h(t)$$
$$= r(t, k\tau) \prod_{d=1}^k (1 + B_d) \prod_{\mu=2}^k r(\mu\tau, (\mu - 1)\tau) \int_0^\tau r(\tau, s)(q(s)e_h(s - \tau) + \delta_h(s))ds$$
$$+ r(t, k\tau) \prod_{d=2}^k (1 + B_d) \prod_{\mu=3}^k r(\mu\tau, (\mu - 1)\tau) \int_\tau^{2\tau} r(2\tau, s)(q(s)e_h(s - \tau) + \delta_h(s))ds$$
$$+ \cdots$$
$$+ r(t, k\tau)(1 + B_k) \int_{(k-1)\tau}^{k\tau} r(k\tau, s)(q(s)e_h(s - \tau) + \delta_h(s))ds$$
$$+ \int_{k\tau}^t r(t, s)(q(s)e_h(s - \tau) + \delta_h(s))ds.$$

For ease of notation, we assume that $n = pk + l$, $(l = 1, 2, \ldots, p)$ and $t = t_n + vh = t_{pk+l} + vh \in (k\tau, (k+1)\tau]$, $v \in (0, 1]$. Obviously, there exists a constant $\tilde{R}$ such that

$$\left|\prod_{\mu=1}^{k+1} r(\mu\tau, (\mu - 1)\tau)\right| \leqslant \tilde{R}.$$

From the above analysis, we have the following inequality:

$$|e_h(t)| \leqslant R\tilde{R} \int_0^t |r(t, s)(q(s)e_h(s - \tau) + \delta_h(s))|ds, \qquad (29)$$

where $\int_0^t |r(t, s)(q(s)e_h(s - \tau) + \delta_h(s))|ds$ can be expressed as

$$\int_0^t |r(t, s)(q(s)e_h(s - \tau) + \delta_h(s))|ds$$
$$= \sum_{i=0}^{n-1} h \int_0^1 |r(t, t_i + sh)(q(t_i + sh)e_h(t_i + sh - \tau) + \delta_h(t_i + sh))|ds$$
$$+ h \int_0^v |r(t, t_n + sh)(q(t_n + sh)e_h(t_n + sh - \tau) + \delta_h(t_n + sh))|ds$$
$$=: \sum_{i=0}^{n-1} h \int_0^1 \phi_n(t_i + sh)ds + h \int_0^v \phi_n(t_n + sh)ds.$$

Now, using an interpolatory m-point quadrature formula with collocation parameters $\{c_i\}$ to approximate $\int_0^1 \phi_n(t_i + sh)ds$, we have

$$\int_0^1 \phi_n(t_i + sh)ds = \sum_{j=1}^m b_j \phi_n(t_i + c_j h) + E_n^i(v) = E_n^i(v), \quad (30)$$

where $v \in (0,1] (l < n)$ and E_n^i indicates quadrature errors. So, we have

$$\int_0^t |r(t,s)(q(s)e_h(s-\tau) + \delta_h(s))| ds$$
$$= \sum_{i=0}^{n-1} h E_n^i(v) + h \int_0^v \phi_n(t_n + sh)ds. \quad (31)$$

By the orthogonality condition (22) and the Peano theorem, it is obvious that quadrature errors satisfy

$$\left| E_n^{(i)}(v) \right| \leq Q_i h^{m+1}, v \in [0,1], i \leq n-1, \quad (32)$$

where Q_i are constants. According to (29), (31) and (32), we can obtain

$$|e_h(t)|$$
$$\leq R\tilde{R} \sum_{i=0}^{n-1} h E_n^i(v) + R\tilde{R}h \int_0^v \phi_n(t_n + sh)ds$$
$$\leq R\tilde{R} \sum_{i=0}^{n-1} h E_n^i(v) + R\tilde{R}h \int_0^v |r(t, t_n + sh)\delta_h(t_n + sh)|ds$$
$$+ R\tilde{R}h \int_0^v |r(t, t_n + sh)q(t_n + sh)e_h(t_n + sh - \tau)|ds$$
$$\leq R\tilde{R} \sum_{i=0}^{n-1} h Q_i h^{m+1} + R\tilde{R}h r_0 \|\delta_h\|_\infty + R\tilde{R}h r_0 \tilde{r}_0 C_0 M_{m+1} h^m,$$

where $r_0 = \max\limits_{t \in I} \int_0^t |r(t,s)|ds, \tilde{r}_0 = \max\limits_{t \in I} |q(t)|$. By (27), we have

$$|e_h(t)| \leq R\tilde{R}Q \left(\sum_{i=0}^{n-1} h \right) h^{m+1} + R\tilde{R} r_0 D_1 M_{m+1} h^{m+1} + R\tilde{R}h r_0 \tilde{r}_0 C_0 M_{m+1} h^m$$
$$\leq \left(R\tilde{R}QT + R\tilde{R} r_0 D_1 M_{m+1} + R\tilde{R} r_0 \tilde{r}_0 C_0 M_{m+1} \right) h^{m+1}$$
$$=: C_2 h^{m+1}.$$

Here, $Q := \max\{Q_i : 0 \leq i \leq n-1\}$. The estimation (24) follows from (26). The proof is completed. □

Theorem 4. *Assume that the solution of (1) lies in $C^{m+k}(I)(1 \leq k \leq m)$ and the m distinct collocation parameters $\{c_i\}$ are selected such that the general orthogonality condition (33) holds, with $J_k \neq 0$,*

$$J_v := \int_0^1 s^v \prod_{i=1}^m (s - c_i) ds = 0, v = 0, 1, .., k-1. \quad (33)$$

Then, for all meshes $I_h := \{t_0, t_1, \ldots\}$ with $h \in (0, \bar{h})$, the collocation solution u_h with the above collocation parameters $\{c_i\}$ satisfies

$$\max\{|y(t) - u_h(t)| : t \in I_h\} \leq C_4 h^{m+k}, \quad (34)$$

where C_4 is a constant and independent of h.

Proof. When $v = 0$, (31) is changed into

$$\int_0^t |r(t,s)(q(s)e_h(s-\tau) + \delta_h(s))|ds = \sum_{i=0}^{n-1} hE_n^i(0). \tag{35}$$

Due to the general orthogonality condition (33) and the Peano theorem for quadrature, we can obtain

$$\left|E_n^{(i)}(0)\right| \leqslant Q_i h^{m+k}, i \leqslant n-1. \tag{36}$$

Then, on meshes I_h, by (31), we have

$$\begin{aligned}
|e_h(t)| &\leqslant R\tilde{R} \int_0^t |r(t,s)(q(s)e_h(s-\tau) + \delta_h(s))|ds \\
&= R\tilde{R} \sum_{i=0}^{n-1} hE_n^i(0) \leqslant R\tilde{R} \sum_{i=0}^{n-1} hQ_i h^{m+k} \\
&\leqslant R\tilde{R}Q \left(\sum_{i=0}^{n-1} h\right) h^{m+k} \leqslant R\tilde{R}QTh^{m+k} \\
&:= C_4 h^{m+k}.
\end{aligned} \tag{37}$$

The proof is completed. □

5. Numerical Experiments

In the last section, two examples are given to illustrate the conclusions. Consider two IDDEs as follows:

$$\begin{cases} y'(t) = -2y(t) + y(t-1), & t \neq k, t \in I, \\ \triangle y = 0.2(-1)^k y, & t = k, \\ y(t) = 1, & t \in [-1,0], \end{cases} \tag{38}$$

$$\begin{cases} y'(t) = -2ty(t) + ty(t-1), & t \neq k, t \in I, \\ \triangle y = -0.2y, & t = k, \\ y(t) = 1, & t \in [-1,0]. \end{cases} \tag{39}$$

In Figure 1, the image of the 2-Lobatto IIIA collocation solution with $p = 2$ for (38) is drawn. In Figure 2, we use the same method to draw the image for (39).

Tables 1 and 2 illustrate the ratios of the absolute errors between $p = 8$ and $p = 16$ at non-impulsive nodes and impulsive nodes using four different collocation methods for (38). Tables 3 and 4 illustrate the ratios of the absolute errors between $p = 8$ and $p = 16$ at non-impulsive nodes and impulsive nodes using four different collocation methods for (39). We can obtain that the convergence orders of the 2-Lobatto IIIA, 2-Radau IIA , 2-Gauss methods and 3-Gauss methods are 2, 3, 4 and 6, respectively. The ratios indicate that our numerical process can preserve the convergence order of collocation methods for IDDEs.

Table 1. The absolute error of 2-Lobatto IIIA and 2-Gauss methods for (38).

p	2-Lobatto IIIA		2-Gauss	
	t = 0.5	t = 1	t = 0.5	t = 1
2	1.7240×10^{-2}	1.2168×10^{-2}	2.7472×10^{-4}	2.0228×10^{-4}
4	3.9397×10^{-3}	2.8676×10^{-3}	1.4879×10^{-5}	1.0948×10^{-5}
8	9.3972×10^{-4}	7.0782×10^{-4}	1.0017×10^{-6}	7.3700×10^{-7}
16	2.3991×10^{-4}	1.7640×10^{-4}	6.2500×10^{-8}	4.6000×10^{-8}
Ratio	3.9170	4.0125	16.0272	16.0217

Table 2. The absolute error of 2-Radau IIA and 3-Gauss methods for (38).

p	2-Radau IIA		3-Gauss	
	t = 0.5	t = 1	t = 0.5	t = 1
2	2.1397×10^{-3}	1.5676×10^{-3}	1.8968×10^{-6}	1.3955×10^{-6}
4	2.3972×10^{-4}	1.6764×10^{-4}	2.8791×10^{-8}	2.1183×10^{-8}
8	3.7523×10^{-5}	2.7605×10^{-5}	4.4659×10^{-10}	3.2858×10^{-10}
16	4.8319×10^{-6}	3.5550×10^{-6}	6.9650×10^{-12}	5.1240×10^{-12}
Ratio	7.7657	7.7651	64.1195	64.1261

Table 3. The absolute error of 2-Lobatto IIIA and 2-Gauss methods for (39).

p	2-Lobatto IIIA		2-Gauss	
	t = 0.5	t = 1	t = 0.5	t = 1
2	1.0600×10^{-2}	1.6060×10^{-2}	1.6962×10^{-4}	2.6848×10^{-4}
4	2.7996×10^{-3}	3.8603×10^{-3}	1.0462×10^{-5}	1.5195×10^{-5}
8	6.9520×10^{-4}	9.6125×10^{-4}	6.5040×10^{-7}	9.2360×10^{-7}
16	1.7417×10^{-4}	2.3971×10^{-4}	4.0600×10^{-8}	5.7300×10^{-8}
Ratio	3.9915	4.0101	16.0197	16.1187

Table 4. The absolute error of 2-Radau IIA and 3-Gauss methods for (39).

p	2-Radau IIA		3-Gauss	
	t = 0.5	t = 1	t = 0.5	t = 1
2	1.4042×10^{-3}	1.5269×10^{-3}	3.1785×10^{-7}	4.0601×10^{-6}
4	1.9795×10^{-4}	2.1244×10^{-4}	8.6487×10^{-9}	6.6899×10^{-8}
8	2.5980×10^{-5}	2.8380×10^{-5}	1.4918×10^{-10}	1.0551×10^{-9}
16	3.3200×10^{-6}	3.6800×10^{-6}	2.3850×10^{-12}	1.6521×10^{-11}
Ratio	7.8253	7.7120	62.5489	63.8865

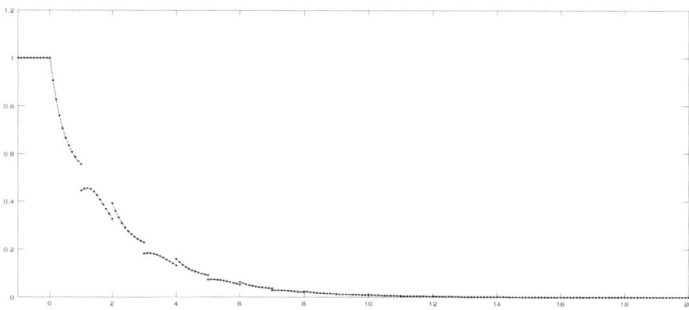

Figure 1. Two-stage Lobatto IIIA for (38).

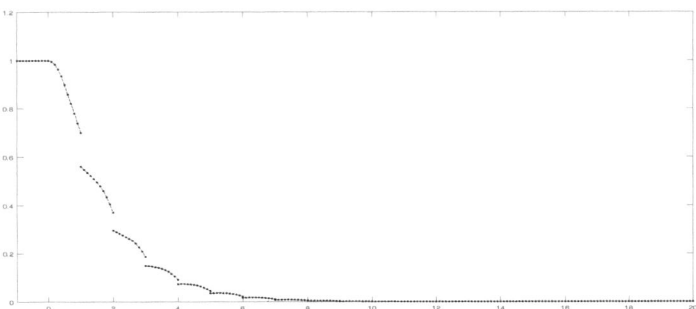

Figure 2. Two-stage Lobatto IIIA for (39).

Author Contributions: Conceptualization, Z.W.; Methodology, Z.W. Software, Z.W.; Validation, Z.W.; Formal analysis, Z.W.; Resources, G.Z.; Data curation, Z.W.; Writing—original draft, Z.W.; Writing—review&editing, Z.W. and G.Z.; Visualization, Z.W.; Supervision, G.Z.; Project administration, G.Z. and Y.S. All authors have read and agreed to the published version of the manuscript.

Funding: This research received no external funding.

Data Availability Statement: Not applicable.

Conflicts of Interest: The authors declare no conflicts of interest.

References

1. Akgöl, S.D. Oscillation of impulsive linear differential equations with discontinuous solutions. *Bull. Aust. Math. Soc.* **2023**, *107*, 112–124. [CrossRef]
2. Liu, M.Z.; Liang, H.; Yang, Z.W. Stability of Runge-Kutta methods in the numerical solution of linear impulsive differential equations. *Appl. Math. Comput.* **2007**, *192*, 346–357. [CrossRef]
3. Liu, X.; Zhang, G.L.; Liu, M.Z. Analytic and numerical exponential asymptotic stability of nonlinear impulsive differential equations. *Appl. Numer. Math.* **2014**, *81*, 40–49. [CrossRef]
4. Stamova, I.M.; Stamov, T.G. Impulsive effects on global stability of models based on impulsive differential equations with "supremum" and variable impulsive perturbations. *Appl. Math. Mech.* **2014**, *35*, 85–96. [CrossRef]
5. Wen, Q.; Wang, J.R.; O'Regan, D. Stability analysis of second order impulsive differential equations. *Qual. Theory Dyn.* **2022**, *21*, 54. [CrossRef]
6. Agarwal, R.P.; Karakoç, F. Oscillation of impulsive linear differential equations with discontinuous solutions. *Comput. Math. Appl.* **2010**, *60*, 1648–1685. [CrossRef]
7. Bainov, D.D.; Dimitrova, M.B.; Dishliev, A.B. Oscillation of the solutions of a class of impulsive differential equations with deviating argument. *J. Appl. Math. Stoch. Anal.* **1998**, *11*, 95–102. [CrossRef]
8. Yan, J.R. Stability for impulsive delay differential equations. *Nonlinear Anal. Theory Methods Appl.* **2005**, *63*, 66–80. [CrossRef]
9. Yan, J.; Kou, C. Oscillation of solutions of impulsive delay differential equations. *J. Math. Anal. Appl.* **2001**, *254*, 358–370. [CrossRef]
10. You, Z.L.; Wang, J.R. Stability of impulsive delay differential equations. *J. Appl. Math. Comput.* **2018**, *56*, 253–268. [CrossRef]
11. You, Z.L.; Wang, J.R.; O'Regan, D. Asymptotic stability of solutions of impulsive multi-delay differential equations. *Trans. Inst. Meas. Control* **2018**, *40*, 4143–4152. [CrossRef]
12. Zhang, G.L.; Song, M.H.; Liu, M.Z. Exponential stability of the exact solutions and the numerical solutions for a class of linear impulsive delay differential equations. *J. Comput. Appl. Math.* **2015**, *285*, 32–44. [CrossRef]
13. Gao, H.C.; Liang, H. Discontinuous piecewise polynomial collocation methods for integral-algebraic equations of hessenberg type. *Comput. Appl. Math.* **2022**, *41*, 291. [CrossRef]
14. Liang, H.; Brunner, H. Integral-algebraic equations: Theory of collocation methods I. *SIAM J. Numer. Anal.* **2013**, *51*, 2238–2259. [CrossRef]
15. Liang, H.; Brunner, H. Integral-algebraic equations: Theory of collocation methods II. *SIAM J. Numer. Anal.* **2016**, *54*, 2640–2663. [CrossRef]
16. Zhang, T.T.; Liang, H.; Zhang, S.J. On the convergence of multistep collocation methods for integral-algebraic equations of index 1. *Comput. Appl. Math.* **2020**, *39*, 294. [CrossRef]
17. Brunner, H. *Collocation Methods for Volterra Integral and Related Functional Differential Equations*; Cambridge University Press: Cambridge, UK, 2004.
18. Li, Y.P.; Yang, Z.W.; Liang, H. Analysis of collocation methods for a class of third-kind auto-convolution Volterra integral equations. *Math. Comput. Simul.* **2022**, *199*, 341–358. [CrossRef]

19. Zhang, R.; Liang, H.; Brunner, H. Analysis of collocation methods for generalized auto-convolution Volterra integral equations. *SIAM J. Numer. Anal.* **2016**, *54*, 899–920. [CrossRef]
20. Brunner, H.; Liang, H. Stability of collocation methods for delay differential equations with vanishing delays. *BIT Numer. Math.* **2010**, *50*, 693–711. [CrossRef]
21. Liang, H.; Brunner, H. Collocation methods for differential equations with piecewise linear delays. *Commun. Pure Appl. Anal.* **2012**, *11*, 1839–1857. [CrossRef]
22. Yi, L.J.; Wang, Z.Q. A legendre-gauss-radau spectral collocation method for first order nonlinear delay differential equations. *Calcolo* **2016**, *53*, 691–721. [CrossRef]
23. Liang, H.; Brunner, H. The convergence of collocation solutions in continuous piecewise polynomial spaces for weakly singular Volterra integral equations. *SIAM J. Numer. Anal.* **2019**, *57*, 1875–1896. [CrossRef]
24. Liang, H.; Brunner, H. Discrete superconvergence of collocation solutions for first-kind Volterra integral equations. *J. Integral Equ. Appl.* **2012**, *24*, 359–391. [CrossRef]
25. Liang, H.; Brunner, H. On the convergence of collocation solutions in continuous piecewise polynomial spaces for Volterra integral equations. *BIT Numer. Math.* **2016**, *56*, 1339–1367. [CrossRef]

Disclaimer/Publisher's Note: The statements, opinions and data contained in all publications are solely those of the individual author(s) and contributor(s) and not of MDPI and/or the editor(s). MDPI and/or the editor(s) disclaim responsibility for any injury to people or property resulting from any ideas, methods, instructions or products referred to in the content.

Article

The Laplace Transform Shortcut Solution to a One-Dimensional Heat Conduction Model with Dirichlet Boundary Conditions

Dan Wu [1], Yuezan Tao [2,*] and Honglei Ren [2]

[1] School of Urban Construction and Transportation, Hefei University, Hefei 230601, China; wudan@hfuu.edu.cn
[2] School of Civil Engineering, Hefei University of Technology, Hefei 230009, China; renhonglei2021@163.com
* Correspondence: 2005800093@hfut.edu.cn

Abstract: When using the Laplace transform to solve a one-dimensional heat conduction model with Dirichlet boundary conditions, the integration and transformation processes become complex and cumbersome due to the varying properties of the boundary function $f(t)$. Meanwhile, if $f(t)$ has a complex functional form, e.g., an exponential decay function, the product of the image function of the Laplace transform and the general solution to the model cannot be obtained directly due to the difficulty in solving the inverse. To address this issue, operators are introduced to replace $f(t)$ in the transformation process. Based on the properties of the Laplace transform and the convolution theorem, without the direct involvement of $f(t)$ in the transformation, a general theoretical solution incorporating $f(t)$ is derived, which consists of the product of $erfc(t)$ and $f(0)$, as well as the convolution of $erfc(t)$ and the derivative of $f(t)$. Then, by substituting $f(t)$ into the general theoretical solution, the corresponding analytical solution is formulated. Based on the general theoretical solution, analytical solutions are given for $f(t)$ as a commonly used function. Finally, combined with an exemplifying application demonstration based on the test data of temperature $T(x, t)$ at point x away from the boundary and the characteristics of curve $T(x, t) - t$ and curve $\partial T(x, t)/\partial t - t$, the inflection point and curve fitting methods are established for the inversion of model parameters.

Keywords: one-dimensional heat conduction; Laplace transform; general theoretical solution; common function; inflection point method; curve fitting method

MSC: 35A22; 35F15; 35K05

Citation: Wu, D.; Tao, Y.; Ren, H. The Laplace Transform Shortcut Solution to a One-Dimensional Heat Conduction Model with Dirichlet Boundary Conditions. *Axioms* **2023**, *12*, 770. https://doi.org/10.3390/axioms12080770

Academic Editors: Tao Liu, Qiang Ma, Songshu Liu and Florin Felix Nichita

Received: 20 June 2023
Revised: 18 July 2023
Accepted: 7 August 2023
Published: 9 August 2023

Copyright: © 2023 by the authors. Licensee MDPI, Basel, Switzerland. This article is an open access article distributed under the terms and conditions of the Creative Commons Attribution (CC BY) license (https://creativecommons.org/licenses/by/4.0/).

1. Introduction

The one-dimensional heat conduction model in a half-infinite domain with Dirichlet boundary conditions is a classical heat conduction model [1]. In this model, the boundary function $f(t)$ is assumed to be a known constant ΔT_0 (representing an instantaneous change ΔT_0 in the initial temperature and remaining constant). An analytical solution for the model can be directly obtained using Laplace and Fourier transforms [1–3].

In practical problems, the expression of $f(t)$ is often complex and variable. As the boundary function type of $f(t)$ changes or the same function type has different expressions, complex and tedious integral transform operations are needed to obtain the solution to the problem [3]. For some complex boundary functions, specific solution methods have been proposed, such as the thermal equilibrium integral method [4–7] and the boundary value method [8,9]. To effectively deal with complex and varied boundary functions, some of the literature has extensively investigated the impact of boundary conditions on model solutions [10], as well as methods for handling boundaries in specific problems [10–14]. Among the studies of similar problems based on the one-dimensional heat conduction model, such as groundwater seepage in a semi-infinite aquifer under the control of river and channel boundaries, the literature [15–22] provides a detailed investigation of a seepage model under changing river and channel water level characteristics. The solution methods in these studies are too complex, making their application difficult, or the treatment of boundary conditions is difficult to generalize in practical applications. However, there are still cases where the model is difficult to solve directly when common function types are used as boundary functions in one-dimensional heat conduction models. For instance, when $f(t)$ is an exponentially decaying function $\Delta T_0\, e^{-\lambda t}$ after the Laplace transform, the inverse problem of the combined product of the model's general solution and the function-like $f(t)$ becomes difficult to solve directly.

In practical problems, the function type of $f(t)$ is complex and variable [20,21]. To avoid the complex and tedious process of integral transform operations mentioned above, the literature [21] proposed a shortcut Fourier transform method for $f(t)$ as the Lagrange linear interpolation equation when solving unsteady-flow models near river and canal boundaries. This method exploits the properties of the Fourier transform and the convolution theorem, enabling $f(t)$ to participate in the transformation process indirectly. When $f(t)$ is an exponentially decaying function, the one-dimensional heat conduction model is difficult to solve directly using Laplace and Fourier transforms. To address this problem, research on the fast solution method based on the feature that $f(t)$ does not directly participate in the transformation process is carried out in the literature [22,23].

The shortcut solution for the Laplace and Fourier transforms provides a general theoretical solution approach for models of this type by replacing $f(t)$ with operators and performing calculations in the transformation process without directly computing the transformation of $f(t)$. This approach is based on the differential properties of the transform and the convolution theorem. Given the conditions for determining $f(t)$ in practical problems, the general theoretical solution is applied by substituting $f(t)$ to obtain the actual solution to the problem [19–21]. This solving approach does not need complex and cumbersome integral transformation processes, making it a fast, concise, and convenient alternative to traditional solving methods.

This paper systematically describes the process of establishing the Laplace transform shortcut solution method and provides the analytical solutions of several common function types using the general theoretical solution. Combined with the exemplifying research, the establishment and application of the inflection point and curve fitting methods for calculating model parameters using temperature-based dynamic monitoring data are demonstrated.

2. Basic Model

As illustrated in Figures 1 and 2, the one-dimensional heat conduction problem in the semi-infinite domain under Dirichlet boundary control assumes:

(1) A homogeneous thin plate extending infinitely in the x-direction, with a heat source at the boundary ($x = 0$) that varies with time as $f(t)$. $f(t)$ must meet the basic requirements of the Laplace transform.
(2) The temperature at any point within the thin plate can be represented as $T(x,t)$, and the initial temperature is uniformly zero: $T(x,0) = 0$.
(3) The outer surface of the thin plate is insulated, indicating that there is no heat exchange between the thin plate and the external environment, and the one-dimensional heat conduction only occurs within the thin plate due to the boundary heat source.

The above problem can be represented as a mathematical model (I):

$$\frac{\partial T}{\partial t} = a\frac{\partial^2 T}{\partial x^2} \qquad (0 < x < +\infty, t > 0), \tag{1}$$

$$T(x,t)|_{t=0} = T(x,0) \qquad (x > 0), \tag{2}$$

$$T(x,t)|_{x=0} = T(0,0) + f(t) \qquad (t \geq 0), \tag{3}$$

where a (m^2/s) represents the thermal diffusivity or thermal conductivity of the solid material.

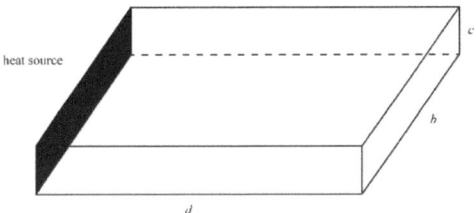

Figure 1. Schematic diagram corresponding to the physical model.

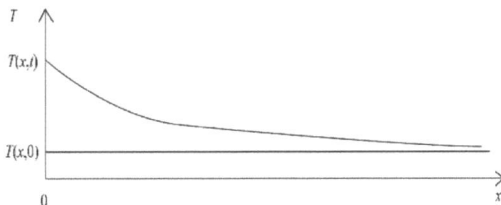

Figure 2. The spatial variations in the temperature field near the boundaries.

3. General Theoretical Solution

By defining $u(x, t) = T(x, t) - T(x, 0)$, the mathematical model (I) can be rewritten as (II):

$$\frac{\partial u}{\partial t} = a\frac{\partial^2 u}{\partial x^2} \quad (0 < x < +\infty, \ t > 0), \tag{4}$$

$$u(x, t)|_{t=0} = 0 \quad (x > 0), \tag{5}$$

$$u(x, t)|_{x=0} = f(t) \quad (t \geq 0), \tag{6}$$

The right end of Formula (5) is 0, which is convenient for the later formula derivation and expression simplification.

Taking the Laplace transform of model (II) with respect to t yields model (III):

$$\frac{d^2 \bar{u}}{dx^2} - \frac{s}{D}\bar{u} = 0, \tag{7}$$

$$\bar{u}|_{x=0} = L[f(t)], \tag{8}$$

where $\bar{u}$ represents the Laplace transform of u with respect to t, s is the Laplace operator, and L and L^{-1} denote the Laplace transform operator and the inverse transform operator, respectively.

In the aforementioned process, during the transformation of boundary condition (6) to boundary condition (8), $f(t)$ does not directly participate in the transformation process. That is, the transformation operation does not involve calculating the image function of $f(t)$. Instead, $f(t)$ is treated as an operator in the direct transformation process.

The general solution to Equation (7) in Part (III) is

$$\bar{u}(x, s) = c_1 \exp\left(\sqrt{\frac{s}{a}}x\right) + c_2 \exp\left(-\sqrt{\frac{s}{a}}x\right), \tag{9}$$

where c_1 and c_2 are undetermined constants. With the boundary conditions (8), considering the mathematical meaning of the solution as x approaches infinity ($u(x,t)|_{x\to\infty} = 0$, $\overline{u}|_{x\to\infty} = 0$), the specific solution for model (III) is

$$\overline{u}(x,s) = L[f(t)]\exp\left(-\sqrt{\frac{s}{a}}x\right), \tag{10}$$

Applying the inverse Laplace transform to Equation (10) yields the solution to the problem. When the Laplace transform is used to solve the one-dimensional heat conduction model, the image function of $L[f(t)]$ is usually obtained and substituted into Equation (10). Then, the inverse Laplace transform is applied to Equation (10), and the solution to the problem can be obtained.

When the form of $f(t)$ is complicated or $f(t)$ is of a special function type, it is difficult to find the solution to the problem using the above method. If $f(t)$ is an exponentially decaying function $\Delta T_0\, e^{-\lambda t}$, where $\lambda > 0$, and the image function of $L[f(t)]$ is $\Delta T_0/(s+\lambda)$, the right-hand side of the above Equation becomes $\Delta T_0 \exp(-\sqrt{s/a}x)/(s+\lambda)$. The convolution of this product combination during the inverse transformation makes it challenging to obtain the solution directly [3]. Therefore, it is difficult to obtain the solution to the problem by directly using the Laplace transform.

To avoid the above tedious or even solution-free inverse process, under the condition that the image function of $f(t)$ is not sought and the inverse of the product of the image function and the general solution is not sought, $L[f(t)]$ is used as an operator on the Laplace inverse transform process to establish the Laplace transform general theoretical solution, provided that $f(t)$ satisfies the basic requirements of the Laplace transform.

According to the "convolution theorem for Laplace inversions" [3], we have

$$\begin{aligned} u(x,t) = L^{-1}[\overline{u}(x,s)] &= L^{-1}\left[L(f(t))\exp\left(-\sqrt{\tfrac{s}{a}}x\right)\right], \\ &= L^{-1}[L(f(t))] * L^{-1}\left[\exp\left(-\sqrt{\tfrac{s}{a}}x\right)\right] \\ &= f(t) * L^{-1}\left[\exp\left(-\sqrt{\tfrac{s}{a}}x\right)\right], \end{aligned} \tag{11}$$

where $*$ represents the convolution operator.

The inverse Laplace transform function of the complementary error function "$erfc(u)$" [3] is

$$L^{-1}\left[\frac{1}{s}\exp\left(-\sqrt{\frac{s}{a}}x\right)\right] = \frac{2}{\sqrt{\pi}}\int_{\frac{x}{2\sqrt{at}}}^{+\infty} e^{-\zeta^2}d\zeta = erfc\left(\frac{x}{2\sqrt{at}}\right), \tag{12}$$

The left-hand side $L^{-1}\left[\frac{1}{s}\exp\left(-\sqrt{\frac{s}{a}}x\right)\right]$ of Equation (12) and the right-hand side $L^{-1}\left[\exp\left(-\sqrt{\frac{s}{a}}x\right)\right]$ of Equation (11) have a differential relationship in the context of the inverse Laplace transform. For Equation (11), according to the "differential property" of the inverse Laplace transform [3], we have

$$\begin{aligned} L^{-1}\left[\exp\left(-\sqrt{\tfrac{s}{a}}x\right)\right] &= L^{-1}\left\{s\left[\tfrac{1}{s}\exp\left(-\sqrt{\tfrac{s}{a}}x\right)\right]\right\} \\ &= \tfrac{d}{dt}\left\{L^{-1}\left[\tfrac{1}{s}\exp\left(-\sqrt{\tfrac{s}{a}}x\right)\right]\right\}, \end{aligned} \tag{13}$$

Substituting Equation (12) into (13) yields

$$L^{-1}\left[\exp\left(-\sqrt{\frac{s}{a}}x\right)\right] = \frac{d}{dt}\left[erfc\left(\frac{x}{2\sqrt{at}}\right)\right] \tag{14}$$

Substituting Equation (14) into (11) yields

$$\begin{aligned}u(x,t) &= L^{-1}[\overline{u}(x,s)] \\ &= L^{-1}[L(f(t))] * L^{-1}[\exp(-\sqrt{\tfrac{s}{a}} \cdot x)] \\ &= f(t) * \tfrac{d}{dt}[erfc(\tfrac{x}{2\sqrt{at}})],\end{aligned} \quad (15)$$

The "convolution differentiation" [3] property of the Laplace transform implies that

$$\begin{aligned}&f(t) * \tfrac{d}{dt}\left[erfc\left(\tfrac{x}{2\sqrt{at}}\right)\right] + f(t)\left[erfc(\tfrac{x}{2\sqrt{at}})\right]\Big|_{t=0} \\ &= erfc\left(\tfrac{x}{2\sqrt{at}}\right) * \tfrac{d[f(t)]}{dt} + f(t)|_{t=0} erfc\left(\tfrac{x}{2\sqrt{at}}\right),\end{aligned} \quad (16)$$

Because $erfc\left(\tfrac{x}{2\sqrt{at}}\right)\Big|_{t=0} = 0$, through Equations (15) and (16), after rearrangement, we have

$$\begin{aligned}u(x,t) &= f(t) * \tfrac{d}{dt}\left[erfc\left(\tfrac{x}{2\sqrt{at}}\right)\right], \\ &= f(t)|_{t=0} erfc\left(\tfrac{x}{2\sqrt{at}}\right) + erfc\left(\tfrac{x}{2\sqrt{at}}\right) * \tfrac{d[f(t)]}{dt},\end{aligned} \quad (17)$$

Note that $u(x, t) = T(x, t) - T(x, 0)$ and $T(x, 0) = 0$. According to the commutative property of convolution, the above Equation can be written in the following integral form:

$$T(x,t) = f(t)|_{t=0} erfc\left(\tfrac{x}{2\sqrt{at}}\right) + \int_0^t \tfrac{d[f(t)]}{dt} erfc\left(\tfrac{x}{2\sqrt{a(t-\tau)}}\right) d\tau. \quad (18)$$

Equation (18) represents a model solution obtained under the condition that $f(t)$ is not directly involved in the transformation process. The solution contains $f(t)$. It is worth noting that $T(x, 0) = 0$, but $f(0)$ is not necessarily equal to 0. In practical applications, it is necessary to substitute the known $f(t)$ and further expand the Equation to obtain the solution to the actual problem. Therefore, for any given $f(t)$, Equation (18) represents the general theoretical solution of the model.

4. Solution for Boundary Functions of Commonly Used Function Types

Based on the general theoretical solution, this paper provides solutions for boundary functions of commonly used function types for ease of reference in practical applications.

In engineering and technology, commonly used function types include constant functions, polynomial functions, and elementary functions.

4.1. Constant Function

A constant function indicates that $f(t)$ is a constant, and $f(t) = \Delta T_0$. The physical significance of this condition is that as t approaches 0^+, the boundary temperature undergoes an instantaneous change of ΔT_0 and remains constant after that. This constitutes the classical one-dimensional heat conduction model.

In this case, based on Equation (18), we have $d[f(t)]/dt = d[\Delta T_0]/dt = 0$ and $f(0) = \Delta T_0$, which leads to

$$T(x,t) = \Delta T_0 \, erfc\left(\tfrac{x}{2\sqrt{at}}\right). \quad (19)$$

Equation (19) is the solution to the classical model [1–3].

4.2. Linear Interpolation Function

For the one-dimensional heat conduction problem with Dirichlet boundary conditions, although many variables vary continuously with time, actual observation processes are often discrete. For example, boundary temperature measurement data, even self-recorded test data, are mostly collected at a certain time interval from the previous test, so it is necessary to make extractions. Therefore, to express the variations in variables over time based on discrete measured data, piecewise function types are commonly used [24].

When a variable has a complex variation process, it is common to discretize $f(t)$ based on the measured data using methods such as linear interpolation, including the Lagrange linear interpolation equation.

$$f(t) = \Delta T_0 + \sum_{i=2}^{n}[f(t_i)-f(t_{i-1})]\frac{t-t_{i-1}}{t_i-t_{i-1}}\cdot\delta(t-t_{i-1}). \tag{20}$$

where $\delta(t-t_{i-1})$ is the Heaviside function and has the following properties [25]: when $t < t_{i-1}$, $\delta(t-t_{i-1}) = 0$, and when $t \geq t_{i-1}$, $\delta(t-t_{i-1}) = 1$.

Substituting Equation (20) into (18), considering the properties of the $\delta(t-t_{i-1})$ function, we have

$$T(x,t) = \Delta T_0 erfc\left(\frac{x}{2\sqrt{at}}\right) + \sum_{i=2}^{n}\frac{f(t_i)-f(t_{i-1})}{t_i-t_{i-1}}\cdot\int_{t_{i-1}}^{t}erfc\left(\frac{x}{2\sqrt{at}}\right)dt. \tag{21}$$

Note that ΔT_0 represents the interval during which the temperature remains constant starting from $t\to 0^+$, and this constant period is from t_1 to t_0 (Figure 3). Therefore, the summation part in Equation (20) is for $i = 2 - n$. When establishing an interpolation equation for $f(t)$ based on the definition of ΔT_0, it is important to consider the expression of each time interval in the function [26].

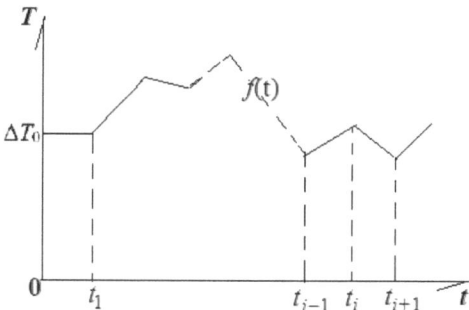

Figure 3. Discretization of boundary function $f(t)$.

4.3. Step Function

For the boundary temperature $f(t_i, t_{i+1})$ in the segment between $t_i - t_{i+1}(i \geq 2)$, the average value of the temperature $[f(t_i)+f(t_{i+1})]/2$ in the time period is used, or the increase $f(t_{i+1})-f(t_i)$ in the time period after t_1 is used. The step function of $f(t)$ can be written as

$$f(t) = \Delta T_0 + \sum_{i=2}^{n}[(f(t_i)-f(t_{i-1})]\cdot\delta(t-t_{i-1}) \quad (t > t_{i-1}, i \in N^*), \tag{22}$$

Substituting Equation (22) into (18), considering the properties of $\delta(t-t_{i-1})$ and $f(0) = \Delta T_0$, we have

$$T(x,t) = \Delta T_0 erfc\left(\frac{x}{2\sqrt{at}}\right) + \sum_{i=2}^{n}[f(t_i)-f(t_{i-1})]erfc\left(\frac{x}{2\sqrt{a(t-t_{i-1})}}\right). \tag{23}$$

4.4. Exponential Function

When there is a Newtonian cooling boundary [27,28], i.e., $f(t)$ is an exponential function ($\lambda > 0$, and $e^{\lambda t}$ does not satisfy the requirements of the Laplace transform existence theorem, which will not be discussed here), substituting $f(t) = \Delta T_0 \, e^{-\lambda t}$ into Equation (18) yields [20–22]

$$T(x,t) = \Delta T_0 \, erfc\left(\frac{x}{2\sqrt{at}}\right) - \lambda \Delta T_0 \int_0^t e^{-\lambda \tau} erfc\left(\frac{x}{2\sqrt{a(t-\tau)}}\right) d\tau. \tag{24}$$

4.5. Trigonometric Function

When the boundary function $f(t)$ is a trigonometric function (take the sine function as an example), substituting $f(t) = \Delta T_0 \sin(t)$ into Equation (18) yields

$$T(x,t) = \Delta T_0 \int_0^t \cos(\tau) erfc\left(\frac{x}{2\sqrt{a(t-\tau)}}\right) d\tau. \tag{25}$$

When the boundary function $f(t)$ is a cosine function, substituting $f(t) = \Delta T_0 \cos(t)$ into Equation (18) yields

$$T(x,t) = \Delta T_0 \, erfc\left(\frac{x}{2\sqrt{at}}\right) - \Delta T_0 \int_0^t \sin(\tau) erfc\left(\frac{x}{2\sqrt{a(t-\tau)}}\right) d\tau. \tag{26}$$

Based on the above descriptions, once the boundary function $f(t)$ is determined, it is convenient and efficient to substitute $f(t)$ into the general solution of the theory to obtain the corresponding solution to the specific problem. The provided solutions for different function types and their corresponding interpretations facilitate practical references and applications. Of course, after the specific $f(t)$ is determined, stepwise integration can be employed to expand the aforementioned solution further. Additionally, it is possible to establish numerical algorithms for analytical solutions based on the obtained solutions [23], which will be beneficial for frequent applications in practical scenarios.

5. Application of the Solution

5.1. Specific Solutions and Their Mathematical Significance

Discussing the model's specific solution and its mathematical significance helps to not only further understand the rationality of its assumptions but also verify the correctness of its solution.

In the following, based on Formula (21) of the model solution whose boundary function is Lagrange linear interpolation, taking the application of $i = 2$ as an example, the specific solution and its mathematical and physical significance are discussed.

When $i = 2$, Equation (21) is transformed into

$$T(x,t) = \Delta T_0 \, erfc\left(\frac{x}{2\sqrt{at}}\right) + \lambda \int_{t_1}^t erfc\left(\frac{x}{2\sqrt{at}}\right) dt. \tag{27}$$

where $\lambda = (f_2 - f_1)/(t_2 - t_1)$, corresponding to the slope of the boundary temperature change during the period of $t_2 - t_1$.

5.1.1. When $\lambda = 0$

When $\lambda = 0$, Equation (27) is transformed into

$$T(x,t) = \Delta T_0 \, erfc\left(\frac{x}{2\sqrt{at}}\right). \tag{28}$$

Equation (28) shows the solution of the classical model. Therefore, the classical model is a special solution of Equation (27).

5.1.2. When $\Delta T_0 = 0$

When $\Delta T_0 = 0$, Equation (27) is transformed into

$$T(x,t) = \lambda \int_{t_1}^{t} erfc\left(\frac{x}{2\sqrt{at}}\right) dt. \tag{29}$$

The physical meaning of Equation (29) is that if the initial temperature of the temperature field is consistent with the boundary temperature, the boundary temperature remains unchanged. If the temperature of the temperature field changes at a rate of λ because of other factors (such as noninsulating surface materials with vertical heat exchange), the thermal motion within the material is still affected by the boundary even if the boundary temperature remains constant.

5.1.3. When $x \to \infty$

Because $erfc(z)|_{z \to \infty} = 0$, then $T(x,t)|_{x \to \infty} = 0$.

The boundary temperature has no effect on ∞, which is consistent with the general law of heat conduction problems.

5.2. Methods for Calculating Model Parameters

According to the model's interpretation, one of the most important objectives of studying such problems is to exploit the temperature-based dynamic monitoring data of the temperature field to calculate the model parameters. Because the solution contains an integral term, to facilitate the application of the solution, it is convenient to establish a method for the inversion of model parameters by using temperature-field dynamic monitoring data based on the variation in temperature $T(x, t)$ with time $T(x, t) - t$, or the variation in the temperature change rate at a point with time $\partial T(x, t)/\partial t - t$ [27–35].

Then, based on the model solution (21) with the boundary function as Lagrange linear interpolation, taking the instance of $i = 2$ as an example, the method for establishing and applying the finite-difference approximation $\partial T(x, t)/\partial t - t$ is demonstrated to estimate the model parameter "a".

The main methods for calculating the model parameter a with the measured curves of the variables over time are the inflection point and the curve fitting methods.

5.2.1. The Inflection Point Method

The inflection point method solves parameter a by plotting the inflection points on the curve based on actual measured data.

From Equation (24), taking the derivative with respect to t, the temperature variation rate at a distance x from the boundary, denoted as $\varphi(x, t) = \partial T(x, t)/\partial t$, is represented as

$$\varphi(x,t) = \Delta T_0 \cdot \frac{2^{-3/2}}{2\sqrt{\pi a}} \exp\left(\frac{x^2}{4at}\right) + \sum_{i=2}^{n} \frac{f_i - f_{i-1}}{t_i - t_{i-1}} erfc\left(\frac{x}{2\sqrt{a(t-t_{i-1})}}\right), \tag{30}$$

When $n = 2$, Equation (30) can be written as

$$\varphi(x,t) = \Delta T_0 \frac{t^{-3/2}}{2\sqrt{\pi a}} \exp\left(\frac{x^2}{4at}\right) + \lambda erfc\left(\frac{x}{2\sqrt{at}}\right). \tag{31}$$

In the Equation, $\lambda = (f_2 - f_1)/(t_2 - t_1)$, where λ represents the slope of the boundary temperature change in the time interval of $t_2 - t_1$.

To further differentiate Equation (31) with respect to t, we have

$$\frac{\partial \varphi(x,t)}{\partial t} = \frac{1}{2\sqrt{\pi a t^5}} e^{-\frac{x^2}{4at}} \left[\Delta T_0 \left(-\frac{3}{2} + \frac{x^2}{4at}\right) + \lambda t\right] \tag{32}$$

At the inflection point of the curve $\partial \varphi(x,t)/\partial t - t$, the right side of Equation (32) is equal to zero. Let t_g be the time at the inflection point. By solving the Equation inside the square brackets on the right side, two roots can be obtained, among which the one with reasonable mathematical and physical significance is [20]:

$$t_g = \frac{\Delta T_0}{2\lambda}\left[\frac{3}{2} - \sqrt{\left(\frac{3}{2}\right)^2 - \frac{\lambda x^2}{a\Delta T_0}}\right] \quad (33)$$

Based on Equation (33), the model parameter a can be directly obtained from the inflection point on the measured curve of x with respect to t (at this point, ΔT_0, λ, and x are all known):

$$a = x^2/[2t_g(3 - 2\lambda t_g/\Delta T_0)] \quad (34)$$

When $\lambda = 0$, according to Equation (34), we have

$$t_g = x^2/6a \quad \lambda = 0. \quad (35)$$

Equation (32) is also the calculation formula for finding the model parameter a for the classical heat conduction model by using the inflection point of the curve $\varphi(x,t) - t$ when the boundary temperature changes instantaneously by ΔT_0 from the initial temperature and remains constant [1–3].

5.2.2. The Curve Fitting Method

When ΔT_0 can be maintained long enough, the temperature field formed by ΔT_0 at point x changes as indicated by Equation (19).

For the measurement point at a distance x from the boundary (x is a definite value), $T(x,t)$ at moment t is calculated according to Equation (19), from which a family of $T(x,t) - t$ theoretical curves corresponding to different values of a is produced; from the measured temperature $T(x,t)$ at the measurement point, the real curve of $T(x,t) - t$ can be drawn.

When the value of a for the actual material is equal to that for one of the curves in the family of theoretical curves $T(x,t) - t$, the measured curve $T(x,t) - t$ and the same a-value of the theoretical curve should have the same form and completely overlap; according to this principle, through the above-measured curve and the theoretical curve family of the appropriate line, the a-value of the aquifer can be determined.

Similarly, the line fitting method to calculate the a-value based on the temperature change rate curve can also be given, i.e., $\varphi(x,t) - t$. The line fitting method to calculate the a-value based on the $T(x,t) - t$ curve, which is relatively more direct and convenient.

Under different boundary conditions, the calculation method differs. Specifically, under a constant boundary temperature, $\lambda = 0$, the a-value can be calculated based on the $T(x,t) - t$ curve by matching; under the variable boundary temperature condition, $\lambda \neq 0$, the $\varphi(x,t) - t$ curve inflection point can be used to calculate the a-value. Of course, under the constant temperature boundary condition with $\lambda = 0$, the $\varphi(x,t) - t$ curve inflection point can also be used to calculate the a-value based on Equation (29).

5.3. The Case Study

In the case study, a silty mudstone core drilled by a ground source heat pump in Hefei, Anhui Province, was processed into a test piece with d = 3.0 m/b = 1.5 m/c = 0.3 m (see Figure 1) and conduct protective and thermal insulation treatment on the test piece referring to the standard "Thermal insulation-determination of steady-state thermal resistance and related properties-guarded hot plate apparatus (GB10294)". For the test, the "steady-state method" was adopted, and the temperature measurement point was set 0.2~0.5 m away from the steel pipe in the middle of the test piece to test the temperature of the test piece continuously.

5.3.1. Calculation Example of the Variable-Temperature-Boundary Inflection Point Method

In a continuous 2D experiment, the initial temperature of the specimen was 18.06 °C. In the initial stage of the experiment, hot water at 36 °C was rapidly injected into the steel pipe, and then the water temperature was slowly decreased at an approximately constant rate using a resistance heater. At the end of the experiment, the water temperature reached 35.5 °C. Thus, in the experiment, ΔT_0 was 17.94 °C and λ was -0.25 °C/d.

In the test, considering the influence of size, in the material with a length of 3.0 m, temperature measurements were recorded 0.5 m away from the heating device. The results are presented in Table 1. Note that the first two hours of the experiment have been excluded because the temperature readings in this period were not sensitive enough.

Table 1. Temperature measurements at $x = 0.5$ m with variable temperature boundary.

t/h	3	4	5	6	8	10	12	16	20	24	36	48
$T(x,t)$/°C	17.96	17.97	18.03	18.14	18.35	18.53	18.7	18.98	19.24	19.49	20.17	20.81
$\varphi(x,t)$/(°C/h)	0.007	0.010	0.060	0.110	0.105	0.090	0.085	0.070	0.065	0.063	0.057	0.053

As shown in Figure 4, at the inflection point on the curve of $\varphi(x, t) - t$, $t_g = 6.3$ h. According to Equation (28), the value of a is determined to be 1.85×10^{-6} m²/s. In the process of determining the inflection point from the measured temperature, this paper uses the forward-interpolation method based on the measured temperature to find the temperature change velocity $\varphi(x, t)$, as listed in Table 1. According to the excerpting process of 1 h, the inflection point appears at around 6.3 h; if the calculation accuracy is not high enough, the encryption excerpt can be made near the inflection point. Additionally, using forward or backward interpolation to find the temperature change velocity $\varphi(x, t)$ also has some influence on the determination of the inflection point time; however, this influence can be effectively avoided by employing multiple encryptions [36].

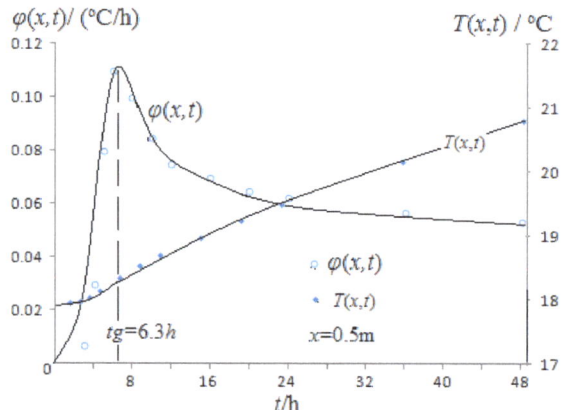

Figure 4. The inflection point method for finding a.

5.3.2. Calculation Example of Constant Temperature Boundary

In another continuous 2D test, the initial temperature of the specimen was 18.00 °C. At the initial stage of the test, hot water at 36 °C was rapidly injected into the steel pipe, and then the water temperature was kept approximately constant through the resistance heater until the end of the test when the water temperature reached 36.0 °C. The test data under this condition are presented in Table 2.

Table 2. Temperature measurements at x = 0.5 m with constant temperature boundary.

t/h	2	3	4	6	8	10	12	16	20	24	36	48
$T(x,t)$/°C	22.1	23.85	25.09	26.83	27.94	28.69	29.23	30.16	30.75	31.16	32	32.58

In the experiment, ΔT_0 was 18 °C and λ was 0 °C/d.

Figure 5 shows that the actual measured $T(x, t)$ point is located between the curve of $a = 0.16 - 0.18 \text{ m}^2/\text{d}$, and the value of a for the test material is approximately $0.17 \text{ m}^2/\text{d}$, which is $1.98 \times 10^{-6} \text{ m}^2/\text{s}$.

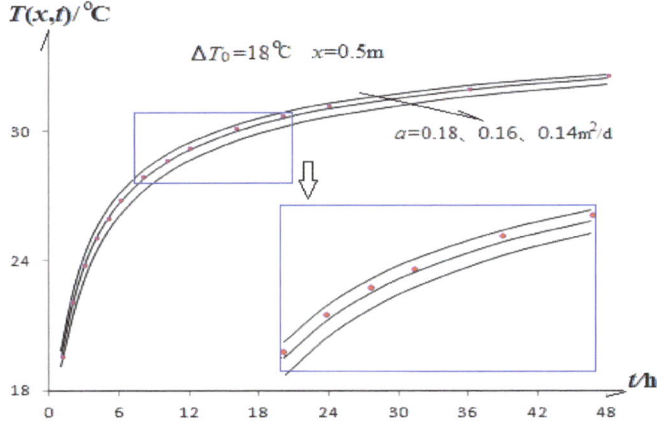

Figure 5. $T(x,t) - t$ curve fitting method for a.

The results obtained by the inflection point method and the wiring method are in general agreement with those of [22], which found a result of $1.94 \times 10^{-6} \text{ m}^2/\text{s}$.

In the case study, in the calculation using the inflection point method, when drawing the graph, determining the time t_g at which the inflection point appears has a greater impact on the calculation of the a-value, and if the measurement time density interval of the temperature in the experiment is large, it may lead to a large error in the calculation of the a-value due to the inaccuracy of the determined t_g. It is worth noting that in the existing literature, the $\varphi(x, t) - t$ inflection point method is mostly used to find the a-value, and the curve fitting method is rarely studied. The curve fitting method, which can apply all the test data to the curve fitting process, requires the prior establishment of a theoretical curve family, and the workload is relatively large. Additionally, the influence of manual human judgment in the curve-fitting process is obvious; the self-applicable curve-fitting method can be adopted to avoid this influence effectively [36]. Alternatively, it is also possible to draw on some computational methods [37,38] or numerical algorithms [39] for building the solution to facilitate application.

5.3.3. Application in Engineering

For this work to have meaning, the solution must allow its application in engineering. The experimental method we proposed can be used to determine the thermal diffusivity. For example, in the design of a ground-source heat pump, due to the difficulty and high cost of testing the thermal physical parameters of the formation in the field, rock samples can be selected at the engineering site, and the steady-state method is used. Then the inflection point method and the curve fitting method are used to calculate thermal diffusivity or thermal conductivity of the actual drill core samples.

The steady-state method is to establish a stable temperature distribution inside the material, measure the temperature gradient and heat flux density inside the material, and then obtain the thermal conductivity of the measured material. The thermal diffusivity or thermal conductivity coefficient a is calculated according to the "steady-state method test"; generally, the boundary temperature $f(t)$ needs to remain stable during the test. However, in the actual test process, it is difficult to keep $f(t)$ unchanged due to the long test time of the "steady-state method". The calculation method established in this paper can be effectively applied to the actual situation where $f(t)$ has a certain range of slow change in the test.

6. Conclusions

The following conclusions were obtained in this paper by proposing a Laplace transform shortcut solution method for a one-dimensional heat conduction model with Dirichlet boundary conditions:

(1) For the one-dimensional heat conduction model with the Dirichlet boundary function $f(t)$, according to the differential properties of the Laplace transform and the convolution theorem, a general theoretical solution can be obtained as a product of $erfc(t)$ and $f(0)$, as well as $erfc(t)$ and $f(t)$. The general theoretical solution is derived for this type of model.

(2) By substituting the boundary function $f(t)$ into the general theoretical solution, the solution to practical problems can be obtained quickly. This shortcut solution method does not directly involve the transformation of $f(t)$ and does not require a complex and cumbersome Laplace transform process.

(3) With the temperature-based dynamic monitoring data and the time variation curve of the temperature change rate $\varphi(x, t) - t$, the model parameter "a" can be determined based on the fitting between the measured curve and the theoretical curve.

(4) When calculating the temperature change rate $\varphi(x, t)$ based on the measured temperature, using forward or backward interpolation has a certain influence on the results; when determining the time of the inflection point based on the self-recorded data, it is advisable to appropriately encrypt the data extraction time near the inflection point to avoid this influence.

Note that although the image function of $f(t)$ with respect to the Laplace transform and the inverse function of the specific solution $L[f(t)]\exp(-\sqrt{s/a} \cdot x)$ are not directly obtained in the solving process, they are essentially involved in the Laplace transform process [40]. Therefore, $f(t)$ must satisfy the basic requirements of the Laplace transform; it should be piecewise continuous on any interval for $t \geq 0$ and have finite growth as $t \to \infty$ [3,41]. Most functions in engineering and technology satisfy this requirement.

In this paper, the Laplace transform shortcut solution to a one-dimensional heat transfer conduction model is presented. In engineering applications, the calculation of thermophysical parameters (i.e., thermal diffusivities or thermal conductivity coefficients in the model) of the test materials based on the methodology of this paper by using data from dynamic monitoring of the temperature field is one of the important purposes of the study of such problems. Thermal diffusivity is crucial to determine the dimension of the systems in civil engineering and initial investment. Considering the assumptions and the parameters that are used in deriving the analytical solution, and in order to use the analytical solution in this paper to determine all model parameters accurately, it is necessary to propose a more detailed field and indoor experimental approach to determine and measure all the physical parameters with precision. This is for further research.

Author Contributions: Conceptualization, D.W. and Y.T.; methodology, D.W.; validation, D.W.; formal analysis, D.W. and Y.T.; investigation, D.W.; resources, Y.T.; data curation, D.W.; writing—original draft preparation, D.W.; writing—review and editing, Y.T.; visualization, D.W.; supervision, Y.T.; project administration, H.R.; funding acquisition, H.R. All authors have read and agreed to the published version of the manuscript.

Funding: This research was funded by the National Natural Science Foundation of China (grant number 42107082, 42107162) and the National Key Research and Development Program of China (grant number 2018YFC1802700).

Institutional Review Board Statement: Not applicable.

Informed Consent Statement: Not applicable.

Data Availability Statement: Not applicable.

Acknowledgments: I would like to thank the editors, the referees and the editorial staff for all the help.

Conflicts of Interest: The authors declare no conflict of interest.

Nomenclature

a	thermal diffusivity, m^2/s
f	boundary temperature, °C
L	Laplace transform operator
L^{-1}	inverse Laplace transform operator
$\bar{u}$	image function for Laplace transform
s	Laplace operator
$erfc(u)$	the complementary error function
$\delta(t - t_{i-1})$	Heaviside function
t	time, d
φ	temperature variation rate of the calculation point, °C/h
λ	boundary temperature variation rate, °C/d
t_g	appearance of inflection point, h
T	temperature of calculation point, °C
ΔT_0	instantaneous change in boundary temperature, °C
x	distance of the calculation point from the boundary, m
$*$	convolution operator

References

1. Tao, W.Q. *Heat Transfer Theory*, 5th ed.; Higher Education Press: Beijing, China, 2019; pp. 75–77.
2. Gu, C.H.; Li, D.Q.; Chen, S.X. *Mathematical Physical Equation*, 3rd ed.; Higher Education Press: Beijing, China, 2012; pp. 148–150.
3. Zhang, Y.L. *Integral Transformation*, 4th ed.; Higher Education Press: Beijing, China, 2012; pp. 96–97.
4. Hu, X.; Deng, S.; Wang, Y.; Chen, J.; Zhang, L.; Guo, W.; Han, Y. Study progress on analytical solution of static temperature field with artificial ground freezing. *Mine Constr. Technol.* **2015**, *36*, 1–9.
5. Fabrea, A.; Hristov, J. On the integral-balance approach to the transient heat conduction with linearly temperature-dependent thermal diffusivity. *Heat Mass Transf.* **2016**, *53*, 177–204. [CrossRef]
6. Falta, R.W.; Wang, W.W. A semi-analytical method for simulating matrix diffusion in numerical transport models. *J. Contam. Hydrol.* **2017**, *197*, 39–49. [CrossRef] [PubMed]
7. Zhou, Q.; Oldenburg, C.M.; Rutqvist, J. Revisiting the analytical solutions of heat transport in fractured reservoirs using a generalized multirate memory function. *Water Resour. Res.* **2019**, *55*, 1405–1428. [CrossRef]
8. BniLam, N.; Al-Khoury, R.; Shiri, A.; Sluys, L.J. A semi-analytical model for detailed 3D heat flow in shallow geothermal systems. *Int. J. Heat Mass Transf.* **2018**, *123*, 911–927. [CrossRef]
9. Li, Y.; Shu, L.; Xiao, R.; Tao, Y.; Niu, S.; Wang, Z. Effect of pumping-recharge well structures on heat transfer characteristics of double-well groundwater heat pump systems considering hydrothermal coupling. *Energy Convers. Manag.* **2021**, *249*, 114871. [CrossRef]
10. Povstenko, Y.; Klekot, J. Fractional heat conduction with heat absorption in a sphere under Dirichlet boundary condition. *Comput. Appl. Math.* **2018**, *37*, 4475–4483. [CrossRef]
11. Hua, Y.C.; Zhao, T.; Guo, Z.Y. Optimization of the one-dimensional transient heat conduction problems using extended entransy analyses. *Int. J. Heat Mass Transf.* **2018**, *116*, 166–172. [CrossRef]
12. Huang, D.; Li, Y.; Pei, D. Identification of a time-dependent coefficient in heat conduction problem by new iteration method. *Adv. Math. Phys.* **2018**, *2018*, 4918256. [CrossRef]
13. Kot, V.A. Integral method of boundary characteristics: The Dirichlet condition. Principles. *Heat Transf.Res.* **2016**, *47*, 1035–1055. [CrossRef]
14. Chen, H.L.; Liu, Z.L. Solving the inverse heat conduction problem based on data driven model. *Chin. J. Comput. Mech.* **2021**, *38*, 272–279.
15. Sa, M.; Rw, Z. Laplace transform inversion for late-time behavior of groundwater flow problems. *Water Resour. Res.* **2003**, *39*, 1283.
16. Sedghi, M.M.; Zhan, H. Groundwater dynamics due to general stream fluctuations in an unconfined single or dual-porosity aquifer subjected to general areal recharge. *J. Hydrol.* **2019**, *574*, 436–449. [CrossRef]

17. Zhao, Y.; Zhang, Y.K.; Liang, X. Analytical solutions of three-dimensional groundwater flow to a well in a leaky sloping fault-zone aquifer. *J. Hydrol.* **2016**, *539*, 204–213. [CrossRef]
18. Bansal, R.K. Groundwater flow in floping aquifer under localized transient recharge: Analytical study. *J. Hydraul. Eng.* **2013**, *139*, 1165–1174. [CrossRef]
19. Saeedpanah, I.; Azar, R.G. Solution of unsteady flow in a confined aquifer interacting with a stream with exponentially decreasing stream stage. *J. Hydrol. Eng.* **2019**, *24*, 1–11. [CrossRef]
20. Saeedpanah, I.; Azar, R.G. Modeling the river-aquifer via a new exact model under a more general function of river water level variation. *Appl. Water Sci.* **2023**, *13*, 95. [CrossRef]
21. Wu, D.; Tao, Y.Z.; Lin, F. Application of unsteady phreatic flow model and its solution under the boundary control of complicated function. *J. Hydraul. Eng.* **2018**, *49*, 725–731.
22. Wei, T.; Tao, Y.Z.; Ren, H.L.; Wu, D. The solution to one- dimensional heat conduction problem bounded by the exponential decay condition and its application. *Chin. J. Appl. Mech.* **2022**, *39*, 1135–1139,1202.
23. Ren, H.L.; Tao, Y.Z.; Lin, F.; Wei, T. Analytical Solution to the One-Dimensional Unsteady Temperature Field near the Newtonian Cooling Boundary. *Axioms* **2023**, *12*, 61. [CrossRef]
24. Zhang, J.P. Principles and methods of expressing segmented functions as a single equation using unit step functions. *Teach. Res.* **1994**, *1*, 24–26.
25. Tang, Z.H.; Wang, R.Q. On Definitions and Natures of Dirac Function. *J. Liuzhou Voc. Tech. Coll.* **2009**, *9*, 76–78.
26. Hu, C.J.; Wang, Y.Z. The Laplace transform problem related to series of functions. *Eng. Math.* **1991**, *3*, 165–717.
27. Silva, S. Newton's cooling law in generalised statistical mechanics. *Phys. A Stat. Mech. Appl.* **2021**, *565*, 125539. [CrossRef]
28. Zhang, S.C. The available range of Newton's law of cooling. *Coll. Phys.* **2000**, *19*, 36–37.
29. Zhang, W.Z. *Calculation of Unsteady Flow of Groundwater and Evaluation of Groundwater Resources*; Science Press: Beijing, China, 1983; pp. 69–75.
30. Alim, T.; Zhou, Z.F.; Mutalip, I. A universal solution to unstable groundwater movement in vicinity of canals. *J. Hohai Univ.* **2003**, *31*, 649–651.
31. Yang, H.P.; Xie, X.Y.; Zhang, J.F. Analytical solution of one-dimensional transient phreatic flow and its application. *Adv. Water Sci.* **2004**, *24*, 82–86.
32. Tang, Z.H.; Qian, G.H.; Qian, W.Q. Estimation of temperature-dependent function of thermal conductivity for a material. *Chin. J. Comput. Mech.* **2011**, *28*, 377–382.
33. Li, Z.J.; Fu, X.; Shi, L.Q. Inversely identified natural ice thermal diffusivity by using measured vertical ice temperature profiles: Recent advancement and considerations. *J. Glaciol. Geocryolo.* **2023**, *45*, 599–611.
34. Dominic, G. Analytical solution to the unsteady one-dimensional conduction problem with two time-varying boundary conditions: Duhamel's theorem and separation of variables. *Heat Mass Transf.* **2010**, *46*, 707–716.
35. Tadue, A.; Chen, C.S.; Antonio, J. A boundary meshless method for solving heat transfer problems using the Fourier transform. *Adv. Appl. Math. Mech.* **2011**, *3*, 572–585. [CrossRef]
36. He, L.X.; Li, B.J.; Long, Y.; Zhang, Z. Intelligent Optimization Curve Fitting of the Newman Model for the Unsteady Flow of Submerged Aquifer. *Haihe Water Resour.* **2023**, *5*, 60–65.
37. Akbıyık, M.; Yamaç Akbıyık, S.; Karaca, E.; Yılmaz, F. De Moivre's and Euler Formulas for Matrices of Hybrid Numbers. *Axioms* **2021**, *10*, 213. [CrossRef]
38. Nichita, F.F. Unifification Theories: Rings, Boolean Algebras and Yang–Baxter Systems. *Axioms* **2023**, *12*, 341. [CrossRef]
39. Batiha, I.M.; Abubaker, A.A.; Jebril, I.H.; Al-Shaikh, S.B.; Matarneh, K. A Numerical Approach of Handling Fractional Stochastic Differential Equations. *Axioms* **2023**, *12*, 388. [CrossRef]
40. Ma, S.H. Laplace transformation the uniqueness of primitive function and inverse image function. *J. Xi'an Aero. Tech. Coll.* **2002**, *2*, 47–48.
41. Teng, Y.M. Some problems in integeral transform. *Coll. Math.* **2015**, *31*, 105–109.

Disclaimer/Publisher's Note: The statements, opinions and data contained in all publications are solely those of the individual author(s) and contributor(s) and not of MDPI and/or the editor(s). MDPI and/or the editor(s) disclaim responsibility for any injury to people or property resulting from any ideas, methods, instructions or products referred to in the content.

Article

Positive Solutions for Periodic Boundary Value Problems of Fractional Differential Equations with Sign-Changing Nonlinearity and Green's Function

Rian Yan [1,*] and Yige Zhao [2,*]

1. School of Mathematics and Computer Science, Hunan City University, Yiyang 413000, China
2. School of Mathematical Sciences, University of Jinan, Jinan 250022, China
* Correspondence: yanrian89@163.com or yanrian@hncu.edu.cn (R.Y.); sms_zhaoyg@ujn.edu.cn or zhaoeager@126.com (Y.Z.)

Abstract: In this paper, a class of nonlinear fractional differential equations with periodic boundary condition is investigated. Although the nonlinearity of the equation and the Green's function are sign-changing, the results of the existence and nonexistence of positive solutions are obtained by using the Schaefer's fixed-point theorem. Finally, two examples are given to illustrate the main results.

Keywords: fractional differential equation; sign-changing; periodic boundary condition; fixed-point theorem

MSC: 34A08; 34B10

1. Introduction

Fractional differential equations (FDEs) have attracted great interests in the past several decades as FDEs are widely used in many fields, see [1–5]. In recent years, many papers have investigated the existence, multiplicity and non-existence of solutions for initial value problems (IVPs) or boundary value problems (BVPs) of various classes of FDEs (conformable FDEs [6], impulsive FDEs [7], coupled system of FDEs [8–10], hybrid FDEs [11–13], fractional relaxation DEs [14], variable-order FDEs [15]); also see the references therein.

BVPs with positive solutions have played a very important role in the study of mathematical physics problems; see [16–19]. There are some very recent interesting results on this topic; see [16,20–25], and the references therein. Bai and Lü [26] studied the existence of positive solutions of the BVP

$$D_{0+}^{\alpha} u(t) + f(t, u(t)) = 0, \quad t \in (0,1), \tag{1}$$

$$u(0) = u(1) = 0, \tag{2}$$

where $1 < \alpha \leq 2$, D_{0+}^{α} is the Riemann–Liouville fractional differentiation, $f : [0,1] \times [0,\infty) \to [0,\infty)$ is a continuous function, and $u : [0,1] \to [0,+\infty)$ is the positive solution of (1) and (2). By using the techniques of fixed-point theorems, they obtained some existence results under the conditions that the nonlinearity f and the corresponding Green's function are non-negative. Li et al. [27] considered a class of FDEs with four point boundary condition. By means of the Avery-Peterson theorem, they derived the existence result of positive solutions based on the assumption that the nonlinearity is non-negative.

To the best of our knowledge, in most of the existing studies found in the literature, the non-negative conditions of the nonlinearity or the Green's function are fundamental to obtaining the positive solutions [28]. Hence, a natural question is what would happen if the nonlinearity or the Green's function is sign-changing. Several papers have considered

the positive solutions for BVPs with sign-changing nonlinearity and sign-changing Green's function [28–34]. Ma [29] studied the BVP with sign-changing Green's function:

$$u''(t) + a(t)u(t) = \lambda b(t)f(u(t)), \quad t \in (0, T), \tag{3}$$

$$u(0) = u(T), \quad u'(0) = u'(T), \tag{4}$$

f, a and b are given functions, and λ is a parameter. Some suitable assumptions of f, a and b are imposed, wherein they obtained the existence and nonexistence of positive solutions for the above problem.

Motivated by the above works, this paper considers the periodic BVP with sign-changing nonlinearity and Green's function:

$$(^C D_{0+}^\alpha u)(t) - Mu(t) - \lambda g(t)f(u(t)) = 0, \quad t \in (0, 1), \tag{5}$$

$$u(0) = u(1), \quad u'(0) = u'(1), \tag{6}$$

where $1 < \alpha < 2$, $^C D_{0+}^\alpha$ is the Caputo fractional derivative (FD), $M > 0$ is a constant, λ is a parameter and $g : [0, 1] \to [0, \infty)$ is a continuous function, $f : [0, \infty) \to \mathbb{R}$ is a continuous function and $f(0) > 0$. In [3] (Equation (9.37)), Podlubny pointed out, with $\alpha = 1.0315$, the FDE of (5) and (6) is good at depicting the model of a re-heating furnace. The most remarkable feature of the paper is its capability to obtain the results of the existence and nonexistence of positive solutions under the conditions that the nonlinearity f and the Green's function are sign-changing.

The paper is organized as follows. In Section 2, some notations and definitions of fractional calculus are introduced, and a lemma is proven. In Section 3, some useful criteria of existence and nonexistence for the BVPs of (5) and (6) are established. In Section 4, two examples are presented to illustrate the main results. Finally, a conclusion of the paper is presented.

2. Preliminaries

Definition 1 ([2] (p. 69, Equation (2.1.1)). *Let $[a, b]$ be a finite interval on the real axis $\mathbb{R}$. The Riemann–Liouville fractional integral $I_{a+}^\alpha f$ of order α is defined by*

$$(I_{a+}^\alpha f)(x) = \frac{1}{\Gamma(\alpha)} \int_a^x (x - t)^{\alpha - 1} f(t) dt, \quad x > a; \ \alpha > 0. \tag{7}$$

Definition 2 ([2] (p. 70, Equation (2.1.5))). *The Riemann–Liouville fractional derivative $D_{a+}^\alpha y$ of order α is defined by*

$$(D_{a+}^\alpha y)(x) = \left(\frac{d}{dx}\right)^n I_{a+}^{n-\alpha} y(x) = \frac{1}{\Gamma(n-\alpha)} \left(\frac{d}{dx}\right)^n \int_a^x (x-t)^{n-\alpha-1} y(t) dt, \quad n = [\alpha] + 1; x > a, \tag{8}$$

where $[\alpha]$ means the integral part of α.

Definition 3 ([2] (pp. 90–91, Equation (2.4.1))). *The Caputo fractional derivative $^C D_{a+}^\alpha y(x)$ of order α on $[a, b]$ is defined via the above Riemann–Liouville fractional derivatives by*

$$(^C D_{a+}^\alpha y)(x) = \left(D_{a+}^\alpha \left[y(t) - \sum_{k=0}^{n-1} \frac{y^{(k)}(a)}{k!}(t-a)^k\right]\right)(x), \tag{9}$$

where $n = [\alpha] + 1$ for $\alpha \notin \mathbb{N}_0$; $n = \alpha$ for $\alpha \in \mathbb{N}_0$, $\mathbb{N}_0 = \{0, 1, \cdots\}$.

Lemma 1 ([2] (p. 230)). *The Cauchy problem*

$$(^C D_{a+}^\alpha y)(x) - My(x) = f(x) \ (a < x < b; \ n - 1 < \alpha < n; \ n \in \mathbb{N}; \ M \in \mathbb{R}; \ f(x) \in C[a, b]), \tag{10}$$

$$y^{(k)}(a) = b_k \ (b_k \in \mathbb{R}; \ k = 0, 1, \cdots, n - 1), \tag{11}$$

has a unique solution

$$y(x) = \sum_{j=0}^{n-1} b_j (x-a)^j E_{\alpha,j+1}(M(x-a)^\alpha) + \int_a^x (x-t)^{\alpha-1} E_{\alpha,\alpha}(M(x-t)^\alpha) f(t) dt, \quad (12)$$

where $E_{\alpha,\beta}(z) = \sum_{k=0}^{\infty} \frac{z^k}{\Gamma(\alpha k + \beta)}$ is the Mittag-Leffler (ML) function.

Next, we shall prove a lemma which is very useful in proving our main results.

Lemma 2. *Assume that $M > 0$ satisfies*

$$(1 - E_{\alpha,1}(M))^2 \neq \frac{1}{\alpha} E_{\alpha,\alpha}(M) E_{\alpha,2}(M) \quad (13)$$

Then, the BVP

$$(^C D_{0+}^\alpha u)(t) - Mu(t) = f(t), \quad t \in (0,1), \quad 1 < \alpha < 2, \quad f(t) \in C[0,1], \quad (14)$$

$$u(0) = u(1), \quad u'(0) = u'(1), \quad (15)$$

has a unique solution

$$u(t) = \int_0^1 G(t,s) f(s) ds, t \in [0,1], \quad (16)$$

where

$$G(t,s) = \begin{cases} \frac{(1-E_{\alpha,1}(M))E_{\alpha,1}(Mt^\alpha) + \frac{t}{\alpha}E_{\alpha,\alpha}(M)E_{\alpha,2}(Mt^\alpha)}{F(M)} (1-s)^{\alpha-1} E_{\alpha,\alpha}(M(1-s)^\alpha) \\ + \frac{E_{\alpha,2}(M)E_{\alpha,1}(Mt^\alpha) + t(1-E_{\alpha,1}(M))E_{\alpha,2}(Mt^\alpha)}{F(M)} (1-s)^{\alpha-2} E_{\alpha,\alpha-1}(M(1-s)^\alpha) \\ +(t-s)^{\alpha-1} E_{\alpha,\alpha}(M(t-s)^\alpha), \qquad\qquad\qquad s \leq t, \\ \frac{(1-E_{\alpha,1}(M))E_{\alpha,1}(Mt^\alpha) + \frac{t}{\alpha}E_{\alpha,\alpha}(M)E_{\alpha,2}(Mt^\alpha)}{F(M)} (1-s)^{\alpha-1} E_{\alpha,\alpha}(M(1-s)^\alpha) \\ + \frac{E_{\alpha,2}(M)E_{\alpha,1}(Mt^\alpha) + t(1-E_{\alpha,1}(M))E_{\alpha,2}(Mt^\alpha)}{F(M)} (1-s)^{\alpha-2} E_{\alpha,\alpha-1}(M(1-s)^\alpha), \quad t < s, \end{cases} \quad (17)$$

and

$$F(M) = (1 - E_{\alpha,1}(M))^2 - \frac{1}{\alpha} E_{\alpha,\alpha}(M) E_{\alpha,2}(M). \quad (18)$$

Proof. By Lemma 1, we can obtain the solution for the problem of (14), subject to the following initial conditions:

$$u(0) = b_0, \quad u'(0) = b_1 \quad (19)$$

is

$$u(t) = b_0 E_{\alpha,1}(Mt^\alpha) + b_1 t E_{\alpha,2}(Mt^\alpha) + \int_0^t (t-s)^{\alpha-1} E_{\alpha,\alpha}(M(t-s)^\alpha) f(s) ds. \quad (20)$$

Using the properties of the ML function (see p. 42 of [2]):

$$\frac{d}{dt}(t^{\beta-1} E_{\alpha,\beta}(Mt^\alpha)) = t^{\beta-2} E_{\alpha,\beta-1}(Mt^\alpha), \quad \beta = 2, \alpha, \quad (21)$$

$$\frac{d}{dt}(E_{\alpha,1}(Mt^\alpha)) = E_{\alpha,1+\alpha}^2(Mt^\alpha) = \frac{1}{\alpha} E_{\alpha,\alpha}(Mt^\alpha), \quad (22)$$

we have

$$u'(t) = b_0 \frac{1}{\alpha} E_{\alpha,\alpha}(Mt^\alpha) + b_1 E_{\alpha,1}(Mt^\alpha) + \int_0^t (t-s)^{\alpha-2} E_{\alpha,\alpha-1}(M(t-s)^\alpha) f(s) ds. \tag{23}$$

From (15), (20) and (23), it implies that:

$$u(1) = b_0 = b_0 E_{\alpha,1}(M) + b_1 E_{\alpha,2}(M) + \int_0^1 (1-s)^{\alpha-1} E_{\alpha,\alpha}(M(1-s)^\alpha) f(s) ds, \tag{24}$$

$$u'(1) = b_1 = b_0 \frac{1}{\alpha} E_{\alpha,\alpha}(M) + b_1 E_{\alpha,1}(M) + \int_0^1 (1-s)^{\alpha-2} E_{\alpha,\alpha-1}(M(1-s)^\alpha) f(s) ds. \tag{25}$$

Since (13) holds, it implies $F(M) \neq 0$. Thus:

$$\begin{aligned} u(t) &= \frac{(1 - E_{\alpha,1}(M)) E_{\alpha,1}(Mt^\alpha) + \frac{t}{\alpha} E_{\alpha,\alpha}(M) E_{\alpha,2}(Mt^\alpha)}{F(M)} \int_0^1 (1-s)^{\alpha-1} E_{\alpha,\alpha}(M(1-s)^\alpha) f(s) ds \\ &+ \frac{E_{\alpha,2}(M) E_{\alpha,1}(Mt^\alpha) + t(1 - E_{\alpha,1}(M)) E_{\alpha,2}(Mt^\alpha)}{F(M)} \int_0^1 (1-s)^{\alpha-2} E_{\alpha,\alpha-1}(M(1-s)^\alpha) f(s) ds \\ &+ \int_0^t (t-s)^{\alpha-1} E_{\alpha,\alpha}(M(t-s)^\alpha) f(s) ds \\ &= \int_0^1 G(t,s) f(s) ds. \end{aligned} \tag{26}$$

□

Remark 1. *If $f(\cdot) \in \mathbb{C}[0,1]$, then the improper integral in Lemma 2 is:*

$$\int_0^1 (1-s)^{\alpha-2} E_{\alpha,\alpha-1}(M(1-s)^\alpha) f(s) ds < \infty. \tag{27}$$

3. Main Results

Lemma 3. *Let*

$$E_{\alpha,1}(M) > E_{\alpha,2}(M) + 1, \quad E_{\alpha,1}(M) > \frac{1}{\alpha} E_{\alpha,\alpha}(M) + 1 \tag{28}$$

holds. Suppose that
(i) $h: \mathbb{R} \to \mathbb{R}$ *is a continuous function and* $|h(\cdot)| \leq N$ *for some constant* $N > 0$.
(ii) $g: [0,1] \to [0,\infty)$ *is a continuous function.*
Then, for every $\lambda \in \mathbb{R}$, the BVP

$$({}^C D_{0+}^\alpha u)(t) - Mu(t) - \lambda g(t) h(u(t)) = 0, \quad t \in (0,1), \tag{29}$$

$$u(0) = u(1), \quad u'(0) = u'(1), \tag{30}$$

has a solution $u_\lambda \in \mathbb{X}$, where $\mathbb{X}$ is the Banach space $\mathbb{C}[0,1]$ with the norm $\|u\| = \max\limits_{0 \leq t \leq 1} |u(t)|$.

Proof. Consider the operator $\Lambda_\lambda : \mathbb{X} \to \mathbb{X}$ defined by:

$$\Lambda_\lambda u(t) = \lambda \int_0^1 G(t,s) g(s) h(u(s)) ds, \quad t \in [0,1]. \tag{31}$$

From Lemma 2, we can obtain and determine that the solutions of the BVPs (29) and (30) are fixed points of Λ_λ. Next, we will prove that all the fixed points of Λ_λ are solutions of the BVPs (29) and (30). In fact, Let $u(t) = \Lambda_\lambda u(t)$. Then

$$u(t) = b_0 E_{\alpha,1}(Mt^\alpha) + b_1 t E_{\alpha,2}(Mt^\alpha) + \int_0^t (t-s)^{\alpha-1} E_{\alpha,\alpha}(M(t-s)^\alpha) \lambda g(s) h(u(s)) ds, \quad (32)$$

where

$$b_0 = \frac{(1-E_{\alpha,1}(M))\int_0^1 (1-s)^{\alpha-1} E_{\alpha,\alpha}(M(1-s)^\alpha) \lambda g(s) h(u(s)) ds + E_{\alpha,2}(M) \int_0^1 (1-s)^{\alpha-2} E_{\alpha,\alpha-1}(M(1-s)^\alpha) \lambda g(s) h(u(s)) ds}{F(M)}, \quad (33)$$

$$b_1 = \frac{\frac{1}{\alpha} E_{\alpha,\alpha}(M) \int_0^1 (1-s)^{\alpha-1} E_{\alpha,\alpha}(M(1-s)^\alpha) \lambda g(s) h(u(s)) ds + (1-E_{\alpha,1}(M)) \int_0^1 (1-s)^{\alpha-2} E_{\alpha,\alpha-1}(M(1-s)^\alpha) \lambda g(s) h(u(s)) ds}{F(M)}. \quad (34)$$

Hence, from Lemma 1, we know that $u(t)$ satisfies the problem of (29), subject to the following conditions:

$$u(0) = b_0, \quad u'(0) = b_1. \quad (35)$$

Moreover, through (32)–(34), together with the properties of the ML function (21) and (22), we can obtain $u(t)$, which satisfies (30). Thus, $u(t)$ is a solution of the BVPs (29) and (30).

Next, we use the Schaefer's fixed-point theorem to consider the fixed points of Λ_λ. Here, (a) we will prove that Λ_λ is a continuous operator. Denote $\{u_n\}$ to be a sequence, which satisfy $u_n \to u$,

$$\begin{aligned}
|\Lambda_\lambda u_n(t) - \Lambda_\lambda u(t)| &\leq |\lambda| \int_0^1 |G(t,s)| g(s) |h(u_n(s)) - h(u(s))| ds \\
&\leq |\lambda| \int_0^1 \frac{2E_{\alpha,1}(M)-1}{(\alpha-1)F(M)} \left((E_{\alpha,1}(M)-1)(1-s) + E_{\alpha,2}(M)(\alpha-1) \right) \\
&\quad \cdot (1-s)^{\alpha-2} E_{\alpha,\alpha-1}(M(1-s)^\alpha) g(s) |h(u_n(s)) - h(u(s))| ds \\
&\leq |\lambda| \cdot \frac{2E_{\alpha,1}(M)-1}{(\alpha-1)F(M)} (E_{\alpha,1}(M) - 1 + E_{\alpha,2}(M)) \\
&\quad \cdot \int_0^1 (1-s)^{\alpha-2} E_{\alpha,\alpha-1}(M(1-s)^\alpha) g(s) |h(u_n(s)) - h(u(s))| ds.
\end{aligned} \quad (36)$$

From the definition of the ML function, it achieves

$$\int_0^1 (1-s)^{\alpha-2} E_{\alpha,\alpha-1}(M(1-s)^\alpha) ds = \int_0^1 (1-s)^{\alpha-2} \sum_{k=0}^\infty \frac{M^k (1-s)^{\alpha k}}{\Gamma(\alpha k + \alpha - 1)} ds = E_{\alpha,\alpha}(M) \quad (37)$$

is bounded. Note that h and g are both continuous, and so we obtain

$$\|\Lambda_\lambda u_n - \Lambda_\lambda u\| \to 0, \quad n \to \infty. \quad (38)$$

Thus, Λ_λ is a continuous operator.

(b) We shall show that Λ_λ is uniformly bounded in $\mathbb{X}$. For each $u \in \mathbb{X}$,

$$\begin{aligned}
|\Lambda_\lambda u| &\leq |\lambda| \int_0^1 |G(t,s)| g(s) |h(u(s))| ds \\
&\leq |\lambda| \cdot \frac{(2E_{\alpha,1}(M)-1)(E_{\alpha,1}(M)-1+E_{\alpha,2}(M))}{(\alpha-1)F(M)} \|g\| E_{\alpha,\alpha}(M) N
\end{aligned} \quad (39)$$

This implies that Λ_λ is uniformly bounded.

(c) We will verify that Λ_λ is equicontinuous in $\mathbb{X}$. For each $t_1, t_2 \in [0,1]$, $t_1 < t_2$:

$$|\Lambda_\lambda u(t_2) - \Lambda_\lambda u(t_1)|$$

$$\leq |\lambda \int_0^1 G(t_2, s) g(s) h(u(s)) ds - \lambda \int_0^1 G(t_1, s) g(s) h(u(s)) ds|$$

$$\leq |\lambda| \frac{(E_{\alpha,1}(M) - 1)(E_{\alpha,1}(Mt_2^\alpha) - E_{\alpha,1}(Mt_1^\alpha)) + \frac{1}{\alpha} E_{\alpha,\alpha}(M)(t_2 E_{\alpha,2}(Mt_2^\alpha) - t_1 E_{\alpha,2}(Mt_1^\alpha))}{F(M)}$$

$$\cdot \int_0^1 (1-s)^{\alpha-1} E_{\alpha,\alpha}(M(1-s)^\alpha) g(s) h(u(s)) ds$$

$$+ |\lambda| \frac{E_{\alpha,2}(M)(E_{\alpha,1}(Mt_2^\alpha) - E_{\alpha,1}(Mt_1^\alpha)) + (E_{\alpha,1}(M) - 1)(t_2 E_{\alpha,2}(Mt_2^\alpha) - t_1 E_{\alpha,2}(Mt_1^\alpha))}{F(M)}$$

$$\cdot \int_0^1 (1-s)^{\alpha-2} E_{\alpha,\alpha-1}(M(1-s)^\alpha) g(s) h(u(s)) ds$$

$$+ |\lambda| \int_0^{t_2} (t_2 - s)^{\alpha-1} E_{\alpha,\alpha}(M(t_2-s)^\alpha) g(s) h(u(s)) ds$$

$$- |\lambda| \int_0^{t_1} (t_1 - s)^{\alpha-1} E_{\alpha,\alpha}(M(t_1-s)^\alpha) g(s) h(u(s)) ds. \qquad (40)$$

Note that

$$\int_0^{t_2} (t_2-s)^{\alpha-1} E_{\alpha,\alpha}(M(t_2-s)^\alpha) ds - \int_0^{t_1} (t_1-s)^{\alpha-1} E_{\alpha,\alpha}(M(t_1-s)^\alpha) ds$$

$$= \int_0^{t_2} \sum_{k=0}^\infty \frac{M^k (t_2-s)^{\alpha k+\alpha-1}}{\Gamma(\alpha k+\alpha)} ds - \int_0^{t_1} \sum_{k=0}^\infty \frac{M^k (t_1-s)^{\alpha k+\alpha-1}}{\Gamma(\alpha k+\alpha)} ds$$

$$= \sum_{k=0}^\infty \frac{M^k}{\Gamma(\alpha k+\alpha)} \int_0^{t_2} (t_2-s)^{\alpha k+\alpha-1} ds - \sum_{k=0}^\infty \frac{M^k}{\Gamma(\alpha k+\alpha)} \int_0^{t_1} (t_1-s)^{\alpha k+\alpha-1} ds \qquad (41)$$

$$= \sum_{k=0}^\infty \frac{M^k}{\Gamma(\alpha k+\alpha+1)} t_2^{\alpha k+\alpha} - \sum_{k=0}^\infty \frac{M^k}{\Gamma(\alpha k+\alpha+1)} t_1^{\alpha k+\alpha}$$

$$= t_2^\alpha E_{\alpha,\alpha+1}(Mt_2^\alpha) - t_1^\alpha E_{\alpha,\alpha+1}(Mt_1^\alpha).$$

Therefore, the right hand side of (40) $\to 0$ as $t_1 \to t_2$. Then, Λ_λ is equicontinuous in $\mathbb{X}$. Due to (a), (b), (c) and the Arzela–Ascoli theorem, we can determine that Λ_λ is completely continuous.

(d) It remains to show that the set $\Omega = \{u \in \mathbb{X} | u = \mu \Lambda_\lambda u, 0 < \mu < 1\}$ is bounded. Let $u \in \Omega$. Then, $u = \mu \Lambda_\lambda u$, $0 < \mu < 1$. For each $t \in [0,1]$, we have

$$|u(t)| = |\mu \Lambda_\lambda u(t)| \leq |\lambda| \frac{(2E_{\alpha,1}(M) - 1)(E_{\alpha,1}(M) - 1 + E_{\alpha,2}(M))}{(\alpha-1) F(M)} \|g\| E_{\alpha,\alpha}(M) N. \qquad (42)$$

Hence, Ω is bounded. Through the Schaefer's fixed-point theorem, we can discern that Λ_λ has a fixed point. □

Remark 2. *The function $G(\cdot,\cdot)$ defined by (17) may change sign on $(0,1) \times (0,1)$.*

In fact, for $s \leq t$:

$$G(t,s) = \frac{(1 - E_{\alpha,1}(M)) E_{\alpha,1}(Mt^\alpha) + \frac{t}{\alpha} E_{\alpha,\alpha}(M) E_{\alpha,2}(Mt^\alpha)}{F(M)} (1-s)^{\alpha-1} E_{\alpha,\alpha}(M(1-s)^\alpha)$$

$$+ \frac{E_{\alpha,2}(M) E_{\alpha,1}(Mt^\alpha) + t(1 - E_{\alpha,1}(M)) E_{\alpha,2}(Mt^\alpha)}{F(M)} (1-s)^{\alpha-2} E_{\alpha,\alpha-1}(M(1-s)^\alpha)$$

$$+ (t-s)^{\alpha-1} E_{\alpha,\alpha}(M(t-s)^\alpha).$$

Note that

$$E_{\alpha,\alpha-1}(M(1-s)^\alpha) = \sum_{k=0}^{\infty} \frac{M^k(1-s)^{\alpha k}}{\Gamma(\alpha k + \alpha - 1)} \geq (\alpha-1)\sum_{k=0}^{\infty} \frac{M^k(1-s)^{\alpha k}}{\Gamma(\alpha k + \alpha)} = (\alpha-1)E_{\alpha,\alpha}(M(1-s)^\alpha), \quad (43)$$

we have

$$G(0,0) \leq \frac{(1-E_{\alpha,1}(M)) + (\alpha-1)E_{\alpha,2}(M)}{(\alpha-1)F(M)} E_{\alpha,\alpha-1}(M) \leq 0, \quad (44)$$

$$\begin{aligned}
G(1,s) &= \frac{(1-E_{\alpha,1}(M))E_{\alpha,1}(M) + \frac{1}{\alpha}E_{\alpha,\alpha}(M)E_{\alpha,2}(M)}{F(M)}(1-s)^{\alpha-1}E_{\alpha,\alpha}(M(1-s)^\alpha) \\
&\quad + \frac{E_{\alpha,2}(M)E_{\alpha,1}(M) + (1-E_{\alpha,1}(M))E_{\alpha,2}(M)}{F(M)}(1-s)^{\alpha-2}E_{\alpha,\alpha-1}(M(1-s)^\alpha) \\
&\quad + (1-s)^{\alpha-1}E_{\alpha,\alpha}(M(1-s)^\alpha) \\
&\geq \frac{(1-E_{\alpha,1}(M))(1-s) + (\alpha-1)E_{\alpha,2}(M)}{F(M)}(1-s)^{\alpha-2}E_{\alpha,\alpha}(M(1-s)^\alpha).
\end{aligned} \quad (45)$$

Therefore, $G(1,s) \geq 0$ for $s \geq 1 - \frac{(\alpha-1)E_{\alpha,2}(M)}{E_{\alpha,1}(M)-1}$. Thus, we can determine that $G(t,s)$ change sign on $(0,1) \times (0,1)$.

In the following, we denote $G^+(t,s) = \max\{G(t,s), 0\}, t,s \in [0,1]$ as the positive parts of G, and denote $G^-(t,s) = \max\{-G(t,s), 0\}, t,s \in [0,1]$ as the negative parts of G, where G is Green's function of the BVPs (5) and (6).

Theorem 1. *Let* (28) *hold. Assume that g satisfies*
(A1) $\min\{\int_0^1 G^-(t,s)g(s)ds \mid t \in (0,1)\} > 0$;
(A2) There exists $\varepsilon > 0$, *such that*

$$\int_0^1 (G^+(t,s) - (1+\varepsilon)G^-(t,s))g(s)ds > 0, \quad t \in [0,1].$$

Hence, there exists a constant $\lambda_0 > 0$, *for* $\lambda \in (0, \lambda_0)$, *and the BVPs* (5)–(6) *have a positive solution.*

Proof. Let $K > 0$ and define $h : \mathbb{R} \to \mathbb{R}$ by

$$h(u) = \begin{cases} f(0), & u \leq 0, \\ f(u), & 0 < u \leq K, \\ f(K), & K < u. \end{cases} \quad (46)$$

Then, $|h(u)| \leq N = \max_{0 \leq u \leq K} f(u)$ is bounded. Through Lemma 3, the problem (29) and (30) has a solution $u_\lambda \in \mathbb{X}$.

Let $\varkappa > 0$. Then, by the continuity of h, we can deduce that there exists a $\sigma \in (0, K)$, and

$$h(0) - h(0)\varkappa < h(u) < h(0) + h(0)\varkappa, \quad |u| < \sigma. \quad (47)$$

From (39),

$$\begin{aligned}
|u_\lambda(t)| &\leq |\lambda| \int_0^1 |G(t,s)| g(s) |h(u_\lambda(s))| ds \\
&\leq |\lambda| \cdot \frac{(2E_{\alpha,1}(M)-1)(E_{\alpha,1}(M)-1+E_{\alpha,2}(M))}{(\alpha-1)F(M)} \|g\| E_{\alpha,\alpha}(M) N,
\end{aligned} \quad (48)$$

it follows that there exists

$$\lambda_0 = \frac{(\alpha-1)F(M)\sigma}{(2E_{\alpha,1}(M)-1)(E_{\alpha,1}(M)-1+E_{\alpha,2}(M))\|g\|E_{\alpha,\alpha}(M)N} > 0 \qquad (49)$$

such that for $\lambda \in (0, \lambda_0)$, we have $\|u_\lambda\| \leq \sigma$, and

$$\begin{aligned}
u_\lambda(t) &= \lambda \int_0^1 G(t,s)g(s)h(u_\lambda(s))ds \\
&= \lambda \int_0^1 (G^+(t,s) - G^-(t,s))g(s)h(u_\lambda(s))ds \\
&> \lambda \int_0^1 G^+(t,s)g(s)(h(0) - h(0)\varkappa)ds - \lambda \int_0^1 G^-(t,s)g(s)(h(0) + h(0)\varkappa)ds \\
&= \lambda h(0)(1-\varkappa) \int_0^1 (G^+(t,s)g(s) - \tfrac{1+\varkappa}{1-\varkappa}G^-(t,s)g(s))ds \qquad (50) \\
&= \lambda h(0)(1-\varkappa) \int_0^1 (G^+(t,s)g(s) - (1+\varepsilon)G^-(t,s)g(s))ds \\
&\quad + \lambda h(0)(1-\varkappa) \int_0^1 ((1+\varepsilon)G^-(t,s)g(s) - \tfrac{1+\varkappa}{1-\varkappa}G^-(t,s)g(s))ds \\
&> \lambda h(0)(1-\varkappa) \int_0^1 G^-(t,s)g(s)ds \left((1+\varepsilon) - \tfrac{1+\varkappa}{1-\varkappa}\right) > 0.
\end{aligned}$$

Consequently, $0 < u_\lambda \leq K$, for $t \in [0,1]$. Therefore, the BVPs (5) and (6) have a positive solution. □

Denote

$$\beta(t) = \int_0^1 G(t,s)g(s)ds, \quad \beta_1(t) = \int_0^1 G(t,s)g(s)\beta(s)ds, t \in [0,1]. \qquad (51)$$

Theorem 2. *Let* (28) *and* (A1) *hold. Furthermore, assume f is bounded and f is C^2 in some neighborhood of 0, and:*
(A3) There exits $t_0 \in [0,1]$ such that $\beta(t_0) = 0$.
(A4) $\beta_1(t_0)f'(0) < 0$.
Then, the BVPs (5) and (6) have no positive solutions for $\lambda \to 0^+$.

Proof. As f is bounded, the BVPs (5) and (6) have a solution $u_\lambda(t)$ via Lemma 3. Let $u_\lambda(t) = \lambda \varrho(t)$. Then, $\varrho(t)$ satisfies

$$(^C D_{0+}^\alpha \varrho)(t) - M\varrho(t) - g(t)f(\lambda\varrho(t)) = 0, \quad t \in (0,1), \qquad (52)$$

$$\varrho(0) = \varrho(1), \quad \varrho'(0) = \varrho'(1), \qquad (53)$$

and $\varrho(t) = \int_0^1 G(t,s)g(s)f(\lambda\varrho(s))ds$. Through the Lebesgue dominated convergence theorem, it implies that

$$\varrho(t) \to f(0)\beta(t), \quad \lambda \to 0^+. \qquad (54)$$

First, we consider that there exists a constant $t^* \in [0,1]$, and $\beta(t^*) < 0$. Thus, $u_\lambda(t^*) = \lambda \varrho(t^*) < 0$, $\lambda \to 0^+$.

Next, we consider $\beta(t) \geq 0$, $t \in [0,1]$. Since (A3), (A4) and f are continuous in 0, we have

$$\begin{aligned}\varrho(t_0) &= \int_0^1 G(t_0,s)g(s)f(\lambda\varrho(s))ds \\ &= \int_0^1 G(t_0,s)g(s)\left(f(0) + \lambda f'(0)\varrho(s) + \frac{\lambda^2 f''(\xi)}{2}\varrho^2(s)\right)ds \\ &= f(0)\beta(t_0) + \lambda f'(0)\int_0^1 G(t_0,s)g(s)\varrho(s)ds + \frac{\lambda^2 f''(\xi)}{2}\int_0^1 G(t_0,s)g(s)\varrho^2(s)ds \\ &= \lambda f'(0)\int_0^1 G(t_0,s)g(s)\varrho(s)ds + \frac{\lambda^2 f''(\xi)}{2}\int_0^1 G(t_0,s)g(s)\varrho^2(s)ds, \quad \xi > 0,\end{aligned} \quad (55)$$

and it implies that

$$\frac{\varrho(t_0)}{\lambda} \to f'(0)\int_0^1 G(t_0,s)g(s)f(0)\beta(s)ds = f(0)f'(0)\beta_1(t_0) < 0, \text{ for } \lambda \to 0^+. \quad (56)$$

Thus, $u_\lambda(t_0) = \lambda\varrho(t_0) < 0$, $\lambda \to 0^+$.

Therefore, the BVPs (5) and (6) have no positive solutions for $\lambda \to 0^+$. □

4. Examples

Example 1. *Consider*

$$(^CD_{0+}^{1.5}u)(t) - 2u(t) - \lambda(\sin u(t) + 1) = 0, \quad t \in (0,1), \quad (57)$$

$$u(0) = u(1), \quad u'(0) = u'(1), \quad (58)$$

with λ as a parameter, $M = 2$, $\alpha = 1.5$, $g(t) = 1$ and $f(u(t)) = \sin u(t) + 1$. Then, g and f are continuous functions and $g(t) > 0, t \in [0,1], f(0) = 1 > 0$.

Through computing, we have

$$E_{1.5,1}(2) = 3.3487, \quad E_{1.5,2}(2) = 1.7997, \quad E_{1.5,1.5}(2) = 2.5483, \quad (59)$$

$$F(2) = (1 - E_{1.5,1}(2))^2 - \frac{2}{3}E_{1.5,1.5}(2)E_{1.5,2}(2) = 2.4589 > 0, \quad (60)$$

and

$$E_{1.5,1}(2) > E_{1.5,2}(2) + 1, \quad E_{1.5,1}(2) > \frac{2}{3}E_{1.5,1.5}(2) + 1. \quad (61)$$

Then, (28) and (A1) are satisfied, and

$$G(t,s) = \begin{cases} \frac{(-2.3487)E_{1.5,1}(2t^{1.5}) + \frac{2t}{3}\times 2.5483 E_{1.5,2}(2t^{1.5})}{2.4589}(1-s)^{0.5}E_{1.5,1.5}(2(1-s)^{1.5}) \\ \quad + \frac{1.7997 E_{1.5,1}(2t^{1.5}) + t(-2.3487)E_{1.5,2}(2t^{1.5})}{2.4589}(1-s)^{-0.5}E_{1.5,0.5}(2(1-s)^{1.5}) \\ \quad + (t-s)^{0.5}E_{1.5,1.5}(2(t-s)^{1.5}), \hfill s \leq t, \\ \frac{(-2.3487)E_{1.5,1}(2t^{1.5}) + \frac{2t}{3}\times 2.5483 E_{1.5,2}(2t^{1.5})}{2.4589}(1-s)^{0.5}E_{1.5,1.5}(2(1-s)^{1.5}) \\ \quad + \frac{1.7997 E_{1.5,1}(2t^{1.5}) + t(-2.3487)E_{1.5,2}(2t^{1.5})}{2.4589}(1-s)^{-0.5}E_{1.5,0.5}(2(1-s)^{1.5}), \quad t < s. \end{cases} \quad (62)$$

Let

$$\beta(t) = \int_0^1 G(t,s)ds = 0.743 E_{1.5,1}(2t^{1.5}) - 1.624t E_{1.5,2}(2t^{1.5}) + t^{1.5} E_{1.5,2.5}(2t^{1.5}), \quad t \in [0,1]. \tag{63}$$

From Figure 1, we can obtain $\beta(t) > 0$. It implies that there exists $\varepsilon > 0$, and (A2) holds. Thus, all conditions of Theorem 1 are satisfied.

Let $K = \frac{\pi}{2} > 0$. From Theorem 1, we have

$$h(u) = \begin{cases} 1, & u \leq 0, \\ \sin u + 1, & 0 < u \leq \frac{\pi}{2}, \\ 2, & \frac{\pi}{2} < u. \end{cases}$$

Then, $|h(u)| \leq N = 2$. Let $\varkappa = 0.01$. Through (47), we can choose $\sigma = 0.005$. Thus, there exists a constant $\lambda_0 = 5.1 \times 10^{-5}$ defined by (49), and the BVPs (57) and (58) have a positive solution for $\lambda \in (0, \lambda_0)$.

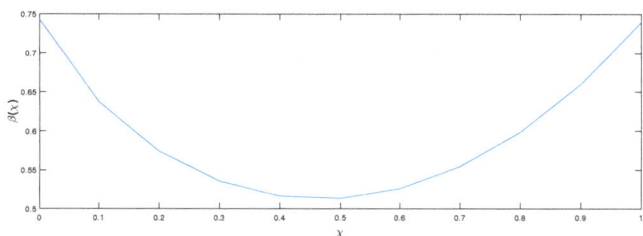

Figure 1. Image of $\beta(t)$ in Example 4.1.

Example 2. *Consider*

$$(^C D_{0+}^{1.5} u)(t) - 5u(t) - \lambda f(u(t)) = 0, \quad t \in (0,1), \tag{64}$$

$$u(0) = u(1), \quad u'(0) = u'(1), \tag{65}$$

with λ as a parameter, $M = 5$, $\alpha = 1.5$, $g(t) = 1$, $f : [0, \infty) \to \mathbb{R}$ is a continuous function and $f(0) > 0$.

By computing, we have

$$E_{1.5,1}(5) = 12.4573, \quad E_{1.5,2}(5) = 4.1355, \quad E_{1.5,1.5}(5) = 7.2468, \tag{66}$$

$$F(5) = (1 - E_{1.5,1}(5))^2 - \frac{2}{3} E_{1.5,1.5}(5) E_{1.5,2}(5) = 111.2903 > 0, \tag{67}$$

and

$$E_{1.5,1}(5) > E_{1.5,2}(5) + 1, \quad E_{1.5,1}(5) > \frac{2}{3} E_{1.5,1.5}(5) + 1. \tag{68}$$

Then, (28) and (A1) are satisfied, and

$$G(t,s) = \begin{cases} \dfrac{(-11.4573)E_{1.5,1}(5t^{1.5}) + \frac{2t}{3} \times 7.2468 E_{1.5,2}(5t^{1.5})}{111.2903}(1-s)^{0.5}E_{1.5,1.5}(5(1-s)^{1.5}) \\ + \dfrac{4.1355 E_{1.5,1}(5t^{1.5}) + t(-11.4573)E_{1.5,2}(5t^{1.5})}{111.2903}(1-s)^{-0.5}E_{1.5,0.5}(5(1-s)^{1.5}) \\ +(t-s)^{0.5}E_{1.5,1.5}(5(t-s)^{1.5}), \qquad\qquad\qquad\qquad\qquad s \leq t, \\ \dfrac{(-11.4573)E_{1.5,1}(5t^{1.5}) + \frac{2t}{3} \times 7.2468 E_{1.5,2}(5t^{1.5})}{111.2903}(1-s)^{0.5}E_{1.5,1.5}(5(1-s)^{1.5}) \\ + \dfrac{4.1355 E_{1.5,1}(5t^{1.5}) + t(-11.4573)E_{1.5,2}(5t^{1.5})}{111.2903}(1-s)^{-0.5}E_{1.5,0.5}(5(1-s)^{1.5}), \quad t < s. \end{cases} \tag{69}$$

From Theorem 2, it results in

$$\beta(t) = \int_0^1 G(t,s)ds = 0.0338 E_{1.5,1}(5t^{1.5}) - 0.6462t E_{1.5,2}(5t^{1.5}) + t^{1.5} E_{1.5,2.5}(5t^{1.5}), \quad t \in [0,1]. \tag{70}$$

It is easy to achieve $\beta(0) = 0.0338$ and $\beta(0.1) = -0.0052$. As $\beta(t)$ is continuous with respect to t, we can conclude that there exists $t_0 \in (0, 0.1) \subseteq [0, 1]$, such that $\beta(t_0) = 0$. Via MATLAb, we know that $t_0 = 0.082333631804161$. Thus, (A3) is satisfied. Figure 2 is the visual representation of $\beta(t)$. In fact, there is another $t_0 = 0.884554959489226 \in [0, 1]$, such that $\beta(t_0) = 0$.

Since

$$\beta_1(t_0) = \int_0^1 G(t_0, s)\beta(s)ds, \tag{71}$$

we take $f(u) = -\sin u + 1$ if $\beta_1(t_0) > 0$, and take $f(u) = \sin u + 1$ if $\beta_1(t_0) < 0$. Then f is bounded and f is C^2 in some neighborhood of 0. Hence, (A4) is satisfied.

Thus, all conditions of Theorem 2 are satisfied. Consequently, the BVPs (64) and (65) have no positive solutions for $\lambda \to 0^+$.

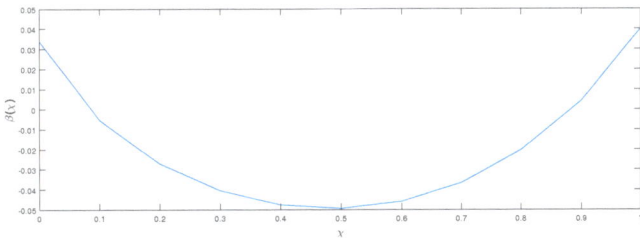

Figure 2. Image of $\beta(t)$ in Example 4.2.

5. Conclusions

In this paper, the existence and nonexistence of the positive solutions of periodic boundary conditions for FDEs are studied. The most remarkable feature of the paper is that the main results are obtained under the conditions that the nonlinearity f and the Green's function are sign-changing. Some sufficient conditions are established to ensure the existence of positive solutions for small values of λ. The paper also provides some sufficient conditions to determine ranges of λ for which no positive solution exists. At the foundation of this paper, one can consider the positive solutions for FDEs involving a p-Laplacian operator, and can also conduct further research on eigenvalue problems of FDEs.

Author Contributions: Conceptualization, R.Y. and Y.Z.; methodology, R.Y.; validation, R.Y. and Y.Z.; formal analysis, R.Y. and Y.Z.; investigation, R.Y. and Y.Z.; writing—original draft preparation, R.Y.; writing—review and editing, Y.Z.; funding acquisition, R.Y. and Y.Z. All authors have read and agreed to the published version of the manuscript.

Funding: This research was funded by National Natural Science Foundation of China (12201199, 61703180), the Natural Science Foundation of the Department of Education of Hunan Province (2022JJ40021), the Educational Department of Hunan Province of China (21B0722), and Science and Technology Program of University of Jinan (1008399).

Institutional Review Board Statement: Not applicable.

Informed Consent Statement: Not applicable.

Data Availability Statement: Not applicable.

Conflicts of Interest: The authors declare no conflict of interest.

References

1. Oldham, K.B.; Spanier, J. *The Fractional Calculus: Theory and Applications of Differentiation and Integration to Arbitrary Order*; Academic Press: New York, NY, USA, 1974.
2. Kilbas, A.A.; Srivastava, H.M.; Trujillo, J.J. *Theory and Applications of Fractional Differential Equations*; Elsevier: Amsterdam, The Netherlands, 2006.
3. Podlubny, I. *Fractional Differential Equations*; Acad Press: San Diego, CA, USA, 1999.
4. Liu, T. Porosity Reconstruction Based on Biot Elastic Model of Porous Media by Homotopy Perturbation Method. *Chaos Solitons Fractals* **2022**, *158*, 112007. [CrossRef]
5. Liu, T.; Xia, K.; Zheng, Y.; Yang, Y.; Qiu, R.; Qi, Y.; Liu, C. A Homotopy Method for the Constrained Inverse Problem in the Multiphase Porous Media Flow. *Processes* **2022**, *10*, 1143. [CrossRef]
6. Zhang, C.; Sun, S. Sturm-Picone Comparison Theorem of a Kind of Conformable Fractional Differential Equations on Time Scales. *J. Appl. Math. Comput.* **2017**, *55*, 191–203. [CrossRef]
7. Feng, L.; Sun, Y.; Han, Z. Philos-Type Oscillation Criteria for Impulsive Fractional Differential Equations. *J. Appl. Math. Comput.* **2020**, *62*, 361–376. [CrossRef]
8. Yan, R.; Ma, Q.; Ding, X. Existence Results for Coupled Nonlinear Fractional Differential Equations with Coupled Strip and Infinite Point Boundary Conditions. *Fixed Point Theory* **2021**, *22*, 913–932. [CrossRef]
9. Almaghamsi, L.; Alruwaily, Y.; Karthikeyan, K.; El-hady, E.-S. On Coupled System of Langevin Fractional Problems with Different Orders of μ-Caputo Fractional Derivatives. *Fractal Fract.* **2023**, *7*, 337. [CrossRef]
10. Al-Khateeb, A.; Zureigat, H.; Abuasbeh, K.; Fadhal, E. Leray—Schauder Alternative for the Existence of Solutions of a Modified Coupled System of Caputo Fractional Differential Equations with Two Point's Integral Boundary Conditions. *Symmetry* **2023**, *15*, 863. [CrossRef]
11. Zhao, Y. On the Existence for a Class of Periodic Boundary Value Problems of Nonlinear Fractional Hybrid Differential Equations. *Appl. Math. Lett.* **2021**, *121*, 107368. [CrossRef]
12. Arab, M.; Awadalla, M.; Manigandan, M.; Abuasbeh, K.; Mahmudov, N.I.; Nandha Gopal, T. On the Existence Results for a Mixed Hybrid Fractional Differential Equations of Sequential Type. *Fractal Fract.* **2023**, *7*, 229. [CrossRef]
13. Khan, H.; Alzabut, J.; Baleanu, D.; Alobaidi, G.; Rehman, M. Existence of solutions and a numerical scheme for a generalized hybrid class of n-coupled modified ABC-fractional differential equations with an application. *AIMS Math.* **2023**, *8*, 6609–6625. [CrossRef]
14. Wattanakejorn, V.; Karthikeyan, P.; Poornima, S.; Karthikeyan, K.; Sitthiwirattham, T. Existence Solutions for Implicit Fractional Relaxation Differential Equations with Impulsive Delay Boundary Conditions. *Axioms* **2022**, *11*, 611. [CrossRef]
15. Telli, B.; Souid, M.S.; Alzabut, J.; Khan, H. Existence and Uniqueness Theorems for a Variable-Order Fractional Differential Equation with Delay. *Axioms* **2023**, *12*, 339. [CrossRef]
16. Zhang, W.; Ni, J. New Multiple Positive Solutions for Hadamard-Type Fractional Differential Equations with Nonlocal Conditions on an Infinite Interval. *Appl. Math. Lett.* **2021**, *118*, 107165. [CrossRef]
17. Liu, T.; Ouyang, D.; Guo, L.; Qiu, R.; Qi, Y.; Xie, W.; Ma, Q.; Liu, C. Combination of Multigrid with Constraint Data for Inverse Problem of Nonlinear Diffusion Equation. *Mathematics* **2023**, *11*, 2887. [CrossRef]
18. Liu, T. Parameter Estimation with the Multigrid-Homotopy Method for a Nonlinear Diffusion Equation. *J. Comput. Appl. Math.* **2022**, *413*, 114393. [CrossRef]
19. Liu, T.; Ding, Z.; Yu, J.; Zhang, W. Parameter Estimation for Nonlinear Diffusion Problems by the Constrained Homotopy Method. *Mathematics* **2023**, *11*, 2642. [CrossRef]
20. Yue, Y.; Tian, Y.; Bai, Z. Infinitely Many Nonnegative Solutions for a Fractional Differential Inclusion with Oscillatory Potential. *Appl. Math. Lett.* **2019**, *88*, 64–72. [CrossRef]

21. Xu, M.; Sun, S. Positivity for Integral Boundary Value Problems of Fractional Differential Equations with Two Nonlinear Terms. *J. Appl. Math. Comput.* **2019**, *59*, 271–283. [CrossRef]
22. Wang, Y.; Wang, H. Triple Positive Solutions for Fractional Differential Equation Boundary Value Problems at Resonanc. *Appl. Math. Lett.* **2020**, *106*, 106376. [CrossRef]
23. Wang, N.; Zhang, J. Existence and Nonexistence of Positive Solutions for a Class of Caputo Fractional Differential Equation. *Sci. Asia* **2021**, *47*, 117–125. [CrossRef]
24. Tudorache, A.; Luca, R. Positive Solutions of a Singular Fractional Boundary Value Problem with r-Laplacian Operators. *Fractal Fract.* **2022**, *6*, 18. [CrossRef]
25. Tudorache, A.; Luca, R. Positive Solutions for a System of Fractional Boundary Value Problems with r-Laplacian Operators, Uncoupled Nonlocal Conditions and Positive Parameters. *Axioms* **2022**, *11*, 164. [CrossRef]
26. Bai, Z.; Lu, H. Positive Solutions for Boundary Value Problem of Nonlinear Fractional Differential Equation. *J. Math. Anal. Appl.* **2005**, *311*, 495–505. [CrossRef]
27. Li, S.; Zhang, Z.; Jiang, W. Multiple Positive Solutions for Four-Point Boundary Value Problem of Fractional Delay Differential Equations with p-Laplacian Operator. *Appl. Numer. Math.* **2021**, *165*, 348–356. [CrossRef]
28. Zhang, Y.; Sun, J.; Zhao, J. Positive Solutions for a Fourth-Order Three-Point BVP with Sign-Changing Green's Function. *Electron. J. Qual. Theory Differ. Equ.* **2018**, *5*, 1–11.
29. Ma, R. Nonlinear Periodic Boundary Value Problems with Sign-Changing Green's Funciton. *Nonlinear Anal.* **2011**, *74*, 1714–1720. [CrossRef]
30. Su, X. Positive Solutions to Singular Boundary Value Problems for Fractional Functional Differential Equations with Changing Sign Nonlinearity. *Comput. Math. Appl.* **2012**, *64*, 3425–3435. [CrossRef]
31. Hai, D. Existence of Positive Solutions for Periodic Boundary Value Problem with Sign-Changing Green's Function. *Positivity* **2018**, *22*, 1269–1279. [CrossRef]
32. Elsanosi, M. Positive Solutions of Nonlinear Neumann Boundary Value Problems with Sign-Changing Green's Function. *Kyungpook Math. J.* **2019**, *59*, 65–71.
33. Dimi33trov, N. Existence Results for a Class of Third Order Equations with Sign-Changing Green's Function. *AIP Conf. Proc.* **2021**, *2333*, 080002.
34. Li, H.; Gao, C.; Dimitrov, N. Existence of Positive Solutions of Discrete Third-Order Three-Point BVP with Sign-Changing Green's Function. *Open Math.* **2022**, *20*, 1229–1245. [CrossRef]

Disclaimer/Publisher's Note: The statements, opinions and data contained in all publications are solely those of the individual author(s) and contributor(s) and not of MDPI and/or the editor(s). MDPI and/or the editor(s) disclaim responsibility for any injury to people or property resulting from any ideas, methods, instructions or products referred to in the content.

Article

An Efficient Convolutional Neural Network with Supervised Contrastive Learning for Multi-Target DOA Estimation in Low SNR

Yingchun Li [1], Zhengjie Zhou [1], Cheng Chen [2,*], Peng Wu [3] and Zhiquan Zhou [1]

[1] School of Information Science and Engineering, Harbin Institute of Technology, Weihai 264209, China; lyc@hit.edu.cn (Y.L.); 2200201031@stu.hit.edu.cn (Z.Z.); zzq@hitwh.edu.cn (Z.Z.)
[2] School of Marine Science and Technology, Northwestern Polytechnical University, Xi'an 710072, China
[3] Institute of Big Data Science and Industry, Shanxi University, Taiyuan 030006, China; pengwu@sxu.edu.cn
* Correspondence: chen.cheng@nwpu.edu.cn

Abstract: In this paper, a modified high-efficiency Convolutional Neural Network (CNN) with a novel Supervised Contrastive Learning (SCL) approach is introduced to estimate direction-of-arrival (DOA) of multiple targets in low signal-to-noise ratio (SNR) regimes with uniform linear arrays (ULA). The model is trained using an on-grid setting, and thus the problem is modeled as a multi-label classification task. Simulation results demonstrate the robustness of the proposed approach in scenarios with low SNR and a small number of snapshots. Notably, the method exhibits strong capability in detecting the number of sources while estimating their DOAs. Furthermore, compared to traditional CNN methods, our refined efficient CNN significantly reduces the number of parameters by a factor of sixteen while still achieving comparable results. The effectiveness of the proposed method is analyzed through the visualization of latent space and through the advanced theory of feature learning.

Keywords: array signal processing; convolution neural network; direction-of-arrival estimation; feature learning; supervised contrastive learning

MSC: 68T07; 94A12; 62R07

Citation: Li, Y.; Zhou, Z.; Chen, C.; Wu, P.; Zhou, Z. An Efficient Convolutional Neural Network with Supervised Contrastive Learning for Multi-Target DOA Estimation in Low SNR. *Axioms* **2023**, *12*, 862. https://doi.org/10.3390/axioms12090862

Academic Editor: Emil Saucan

Received: 16 July 2023
Revised: 23 August 2023
Accepted: 2 September 2023
Published: 7 September 2023

Copyright: © 2023 by the authors. Licensee MDPI, Basel, Switzerland. This article is an open access article distributed under the terms and conditions of the Creative Commons Attribution (CC BY) license (https:// creativecommons.org/licenses/by/ 4.0/).

1. Introduction

Precise direction-of-arrival (DOA) estimation using an antenna or sensor array is critical in various applications, such as microphone, sonar, source localization, and radar. Numerous algorithms have been invented to tackle the DOA estimation problem, and among them, the subspace-based estimation algorithms are well known for their capacity to give a high-resolution estimation. These include MUSIC (Multiple SIgnal Classification), ESPRIT (Estimation of Signal Parameters via Rotational Invariance Techniques), Root-MUSIC (R-MUSIC) [1–3], homotopy method [4,5], multigrid method [6,7], and multigrid-homotopy method [8]. However, in low signal-to-noise ratio (SNR) environments, they suffer from significant biases. To address this issue, deep learning methods have been employed.

Deep learning (DL) methods have recently emerged as promising approaches for direction-of-arrival (DOA) estimation, offering significant advantages over traditional subspace and sparse methods [9,10]. For DOA estimation of multitarget in harsh environments, multi-layer perceptron (MLP) method focuses on the robustness to array imperfections [11]; however, the model is trained at each individual SNR and fixed on a two-source target. The deep Convolutional Neural Networks (CNN) have achieved superior on-grid accuracy in low SNR regimes where the number of sources is unknown, but obtained a relatively large fully connected layer size and increased the number of parameters [12]. The authors in [13] leverage the eigenvalues from Full-row Toeplitz Matrices Reconstruction (FTMR) to enumerate the number of sources, but the error rate is still around 10% at −10 dB. Another approach proposed in [14] is a grid-less method that exploits the Toeplitz property and does not suffer from grid mismatch, but its performance is not sufficient in limited source numeration.

This paper proposes the CNN with Supervised Contrastive Learning (CNN-SCL) for multi-target DOA estimation in low SNR regimes, which is combined with Supervised Contrastive Learning (SCL) for pretraining. SCL is an extension of contrastive learning [15] in supervised task, which encourages the clustering of similar examples in the latent space while promoting the separation of different samples [16]. In this work, SCL is introduced to improve the performance of the model in detecting the number of sources and their DOAs, while also enabling the use of fewer parameters compared to prior work [12]. We make both our demo page and source-code publicly available in https://github.com/Meur3ault/Contrastive-Learning-for-Low-SNR-DOA on 12 September 2023.

2. Signal Model and Data Setting

This study focuses on the following scenario: K far-field and narrowband signals $s(t)$ impinge on an array of antennas from direction angle $\theta = [\theta_1, \theta_2, \theta_3, \cdots \theta_k]$ with L antennas placed uniformly linear in spacing of d. Signals received at the l th sensor is given by:

$$y_l(t) = \sum_{k=1}^{K} s_k(t) e^{-j\frac{2\pi}{\lambda}(l-1)d\sin\theta_k} + n_l(t) \quad (1)$$

where $1 \leq l \leq L$ and $n_l(t)$ is the additive white noise at l th sensors. They can be conveniently expressed in the following matrix form:

$$\begin{aligned} \boldsymbol{y}(t) &= [y_1(t), y_2(t), \ldots, y_L(t)]^T \\ &= [\boldsymbol{a}(\theta_1), \boldsymbol{a}(\theta_2), \ldots, \boldsymbol{a}(\theta_K)]\boldsymbol{s}(t) + \boldsymbol{n}(t) \\ &= \boldsymbol{A}\boldsymbol{s}(t) + \boldsymbol{n}(t) \end{aligned} \quad (2)$$

and where $s(t), y(t), n(t)$ are the transmit signal vector, received signal vector, and noise vector, respectively. Moreover, $a(\theta)$, denotes a steering vector represented as:

$$\boldsymbol{a}(\theta_k) = \begin{bmatrix} e^{-j\frac{2\pi}{\lambda} \cdot 0 \cdot d\sin\theta_k} \\ e^{-j\frac{2\pi}{\lambda} \cdot 1 \cdot d\sin\theta_k} \\ \vdots \\ e^{-j\frac{2\pi}{\lambda} \cdot (L-1) \cdot d\sin\theta_k} \end{bmatrix} = \begin{bmatrix} e^{-j\omega_0\tau_{1i}} \\ e^{-j\omega_0\tau_{2i}} \\ \vdots \\ e^{-j\omega_0\tau_{Li}} \end{bmatrix} \quad (3)$$

that represents the phases of i th transmit signal in L sensors. The w_0 is angular frequency of transmit signal and τ_{li} is the delay of i th signal at l th sensor or antenna. The matrix A or $A(\theta)$ is $L \times K$ array manifold matrix with steering vectors in columns. The ideal array covariance matrix or spatial covariance is given by:

$$\boldsymbol{R}_y = \mathrm{E}\left[\boldsymbol{y}(t)\boldsymbol{y}^H(t)\right] = A(\theta)R_s A^H(\theta) + \sigma^2 \boldsymbol{I}_L \quad (4)$$

where $\mathrm{E}[\bullet]$ and $(\bullet)^H$ denote the expectation and conjugate transpose. In addition, noises are regarded as circularly-symmetric Gaussian white noises with the same variance independent of each other, while noise covariance matrix $\sigma^2 I_L$ is with diagonal elements only. The $R_s = \mathrm{E}\left[s(t)s^H(t)\right]$ represents signal covariance matrix with zero means. R_y is the array received signal covariance matrix or spatial covariance matrix, which is complex and Hermitian. In practice, the ideal matrix is unknown and usually substituted by its T-snapshots unbiased estimation $\widetilde{\boldsymbol{R}}_y = \frac{1}{T}\sum_{t=1}^{T} \boldsymbol{y}(t)\boldsymbol{y}^H(t)$. Here the model is trained with both sample $\widetilde{\boldsymbol{R}}_y$ and ideal R_y. The input data X (generated by R_y) and $\widetilde{X}$ (generated by $\widetilde{\boldsymbol{R}}_y$) in proposed model CNN-SCL are $L \times L \times 3$ matrices, containing the real part, imaginary part, and phase of the spatial covariance matrices, i.e., $\mathbf{X}_{:,:,1} = \mathrm{Re}\{\mathbf{R}_y\}$, $\mathbf{X}_{:,:,2} = \mathrm{Im}\{\mathbf{R}_y\}$, and $\mathbf{X}_{:,:,3} = \angle\{\mathbf{R}_y\}$. During both the pretraining and training phases, the generated data $\mathbf{X}_{(i)}$ is obtained by selecting the discretized angles across the range $\{-60°, \ldots, -1°, 0°, 1°, \ldots, 60°\}$ with 121 grids. The label set H contains the i th label $\mathbf{H}_{(i)}$ for data $\mathbf{X}_{(i)}$, which is sum one-hot 121×1 vector of multiple or single discretized angles with respect to $\mathbf{X}_{(i)}$, e.g., the data $\mathbf{X}_{(i)}$ generated by $\{-60°, -59°, 60°\}$ angles corresponds to 121×1 vector $\mathbf{H}_{(i)} = [1,1,0,\ldots,1]^T$. Thus, the data set is $\mathcal{D} = \left\{\left(\mathbf{X}_{(1)}, \mathbf{H}_{(1)}\right), \left(\mathbf{X}_{(2)}, \mathbf{H}_{(2)}\right), \ldots, \left(\mathbf{X}_{(N)}, \mathbf{H}_{(N)}\right)\right\}$ of size N. In this paper, the inter-element distance d is set to half the wavelength ($d = \lambda/2$) and the number of array elements L is 16.

3. The Proposed Model

The layout of our proposed model is depicted in Figure 1, in which the backbone is modified upon the conventional convolutional structure [17]. The model comprises two distinct components: a feature extractor, denoted as f, consisting of four convolutional layers, and a classifier, denoted as g, consisting of six fully connected (FC) layers. The first four FC layers of the classifier have their weights shared to enhance generalization and reduce the number of parameters [18]. The proposed model is trained in two stages, namely pretraining and training. The total number of learnable parameters in our model is 1,740,457, which is significantly less than the 28.2 million in the current CNN model [12].

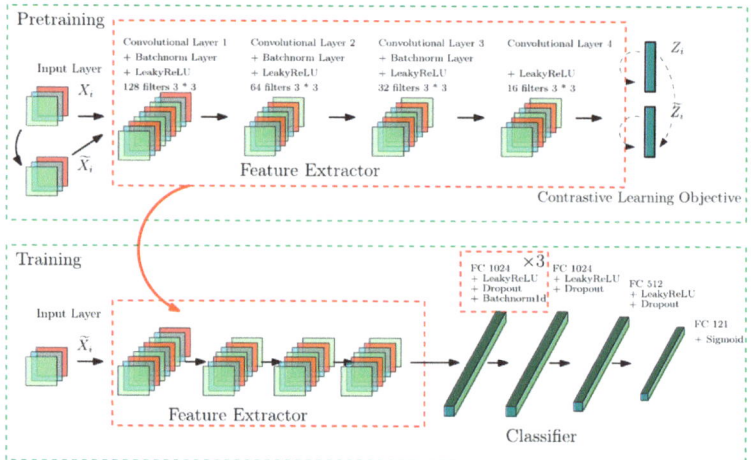

Figure 1. The SCL-based architecture, including pretraining and training. Dropout probability is set to 0.2 and the stride of all convolution filters is 1. The LeakyReLU applies 0.01 negative slope. The first four fully connected layers of Classifier share the same weights. After the pretraining stage, the pretrained feature extractor will be trained with an initialized classifier. The numbers of neurons of fully connected layers are labeled above.

3.1. Pretraining Stage

In the pretraining phase, where SCL is applied, we built up a data set including single-source data in both ideal data X and sampled $\tilde{X}$ of T snapshot. As data augmentation increases the amount of training data to avoid overfitting, the sampled version $\tilde{X}$ are considered as the augmentation of X, i.e., X are generated directly from Equation (4), while $\tilde{X}$ is unbiasedestimationversion. The purpose of data augmentation is to impose consistency regularization, which encourages the model to produce the same classification even when inputs are perturbed [19]. The inclusion of uncertainty in $\tilde{X}$ makes it a suitable option for this purpose. After inputs are fed into the feature extractor f, the features $Z = f(X)$ and $\tilde{Z} = f(\tilde{X})$ are generated in latent space. To achieved better robustness and stability in harsh environments, the supervised contrastive loss is introduced [16], namely supervised contrastive learning objective, denoted by:

$$\mathcal{L}^{sup} = -\sum_{i \in I} \log \left\{ \frac{1}{|P(i)|} \sum_{p \in P(i)} \frac{exp\left(Z_{(i)} \cdot Z_{(p)}/\tau\right)}{\sum_{a \in A(i)} exp\left(Z_{(i)} \cdot Z_{(a)}/\tau\right)} \right\} \quad (5)$$

where $i \in I \equiv \{1 \dots 2N\}$ is the index of an arbitrary sample in data set combined $\tilde{X}$ and X, $A(i) \equiv I \setminus i$, and $\tau \in \mathbb{R}+$ is a scalar temperature parameter. $P(i) = \left\{ p \in A(i) : H_{(p)} = H_{(i)} \right\}$ is the set of indices of all other samples that are same class with i th sample (and thus in equation (5), the $\tilde{Z}$ and Z are indiscriminately denoted as Z cause indexes already involve both). $|P(i)|$ is its cardinality. The supervised contrastive loss encourages the clustering of similar examples in the latent space while also promoting the separation of different samples 16. In pretraining, all the data are single-source and so are the labels, which are one-hot among $\{-60°, \dots, -1°, 0°, 1°, \dots, 60°\}$. Pretraining can be regarded as a supervised contrastive learning process involving 121 classes. The size of the output feature is 32 × 32. For convenience, we dispatched $Z_{(i)}$ or $\tilde{Z}_{(i)}$ into length 32 with 32 views in contrastive training [20].

To generate data, consider K = 1 and generate on-grid data and label in low SNRs among $\{-15, -10, -5, 0\}$ dB. The number of angle pairs of ideal X is $\binom{121}{1} \times 4 = 484$ so as $\tilde{X}$, leading to a double size of data set to $D_0 = 484 \times 2$, where $\tilde{X}$ is the unbiased estimation of X with 100 snapshots. To increase the diversity of data pairs in each randomly split batch, we generated the data set D_0 ten times, resulting in a final data set size of $D = 484 \times 2 \times 10 = 9680$. The data set was randomly split into a validation set (10%) and a training set (90%) with a batch size of 130. The feature extractor was trained for 100 epochs using Adam optimization [21] with an initial learning rate of 0.001, β1 = 0.9, and β2 = 0.999. To achieve convergence, the learning rate was decayed by a factor of $1/\sqrt{2}$ every 10 epochs, and the model was saved when the validation loss reached its minimum. The loss curve is shown in Figure 2a, with a minimum loss of 5.5927.

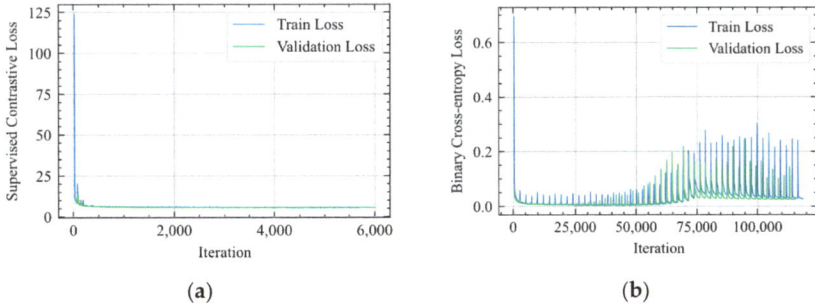

Figure 2. (a) Pretraining loss curve; (b) Training loss curve.

3.2. Training Stage

In the training phase after pretraining, the feature extractor would be trained with initialized classifier together. The final layer in classifier is sigmoid to retain the value in [0, 1] through 121 × 1 output vector $\hat{H}_{(i)}$:

$$\hat{H}_{(i)} = g\left(f\left(\tilde{X}_{(i)}\right)\right) = \begin{pmatrix} \hat{p}_{-60} \\ \vdots \\ \hat{p}_{60} \end{pmatrix} \tag{6}$$

The value $\hat{p}_i$ indicates the probability spectrum of incident signals with on-grid angles. The sigmoid function allows for the prediction of multiple sources and enables the model to handle data beyond that of a single source, thereby input $\tilde{X}$ differs from the pretraining stage. In the training stage, the $\tilde{X}$ are sampled version inputs, as with those in pretraining. Instead of a single source, $\tilde{X}$ here were generated from multiple sources. Finally, the loss L^T for training is:

$$L^T = \frac{1}{N}\sum_{i=1}^{N} L\left(\hat{H}_{(i)}; H_{(i)}\right) \tag{7}$$

while L is the binary cross-entropy loss:

$$L\left(\hat{H}_{(i)}; H_{(i)}\right) = -\frac{1}{121}\sum_{n=1}^{121}\left[H_{(i)}(n)\log\left(\hat{H}_{(i)}(n)\right) + \left(1 - H_{(i)}(n)\right)\log\left(1 - \hat{H}_{(i)}(n)\right)\right] \tag{8}$$

For the input in the training phase, data were generated from varying numbers of source K at low SNRs among −15 dB, −10 dB, −5 dB, and 0 dB using the combinations of K source(s) pairs among 121 on-grid angle pair(s), where K_{max} = 3 and K_{min} = 1, with 1000 snapshots. To cover all the possible incident scenarios and alleviate the problem of unbalanced dataset, the training dataset was composed of 1,212,420 examples, which included $\sum_{k=1}^{K_{max}=3}\binom{121}{k} \times 4 = 1,181,444$ samples (in 4 SNR setting) and $\binom{121}{1} \times 4 \times 64 = 30,976$ random single-source examples. The validation set consisted of 100,000 independent examples with random angles and number of sources. The proposed feature extractor and classifier were trained for 50 epochs using the same optimizer and learning schedule as mentioned before. The model was saved when the validation loss reached its minimum. The loss curve is shown in Figure 2b, with a minimum loss of 0.00556.

4. Simulation Results

4.1. Unknown Number of Sources

In this section, the tests were performed on an uncertain number of sources, a common scenario encountered in real life application of DOA algorithm. Inspired by CFAR (Constant false alarm rate) [22], we first set up threshold p_0 to filter the noises, and then searched the peaks K in the resulting probability spectrum to obtain the predicted angles. However, the mismatch of predicted target numbers will render the RMSE loss metric futile. To address this issue, the Hausdorff distance d_H was introduced in [12], which measures distance between two sets without equal cardinality. It is denoted by:

$$d_H(\mathcal{A}, \mathcal{B}) = max\{d(\mathcal{A}, \mathcal{B}), d(\mathcal{B}, \mathcal{A})\} \tag{9}$$

$$d(\mathcal{A}, \mathcal{B}) = sup\{d(\alpha, \mathcal{B}) \mid \alpha \in \mathcal{A}\} \tag{10}$$

$$d(\alpha, \mathcal{B}) = inf\{|\alpha - \beta|| \beta \in \mathcal{B}\} \tag{11}$$

when the cardinalities are same, it behaves like max absolute error in penalizing deviation, but when the cardinalities are different, it penalizes elements that significantly deviate from overlapping distribution between sets $\mathcal{A}$ and $\mathcal{B}$. For example, if $\mathcal{A} = \{20°, 30°, 60°\}$ and $\mathcal{B} = \{20°, 30°\}$, then $d_{\mathbf{H}}(\mathcal{A}, \mathcal{B}) = 30°$. Similarly, if $\mathcal{A} = \{20°, 30°, 30.5°\}$, then $d_{\mathbf{H}}(\mathcal{A}, \mathcal{B}) = 0.5°$.

The tests were performed using fixed off-grid angles ranging from source number $K = 1$ to $K = 3$. For each K, 10,000 test samples were independently generated with 1000 snapshots to form test sets at 0 dB, -10 dB, and -15 dB, respectively. The angles of first signal, second, and third were $-3.74°$, $11.11°$, and $2.12°$, respectively. The predicted K and their DOAs are obtained by filtering with a threshold p_0 and identifying peaks on probability spectrum output $\hat{H}_{(i)}$ in Equation (6). The results are reported in Table 1, which evaluates the performance of CNN-SCL with mean and max Hausdorff distance. When the SNR is 0 dB, the model firmly predicts $\{-4°, 11°, 2°\}$, resulting in the mean and max Hausdorff distance being fixed on $0.26°$. At -10 dB, the errors are slightly increased but still small, considering the low SNR, while the state-of-the-art CNN approaches obtains high max $d_{\mathbf{H}}$ of $10.8°$ in similar situation [12]. In the -15 dB SNR scenario, the maximum value of the Hausdorff distance increases significantly, and it varies with the number of sources. To avoid falsely identifying a zero target, the threshold value for the one-source scenario is set to 0.2 instead of 0.4, as the latter would result in a 0.53% probability of predicting zero targets. Additionally, Figure 3 indicates the confusion matrix (probability) of source predicted results with respect to 0 dB and -10 dB SNR. When predicting source number in low SNR environments, the model achieves this with only a 0.07% error rate in two-sources scenarios $\{-3.74°, 11.11°\}$ in -10 dB SNR, indicating that our approach achieves high accuracy low SNR environments. In contrast to our CNN-SCL approach, the AIC method has proven to be ineffective in low SNRs [23]. Moreover, the only-CNN-based method retains an error rate of 22.47% for three-source scenario with a similar separation of angles at -10 dB SNR [12]. Compared to the current learning-based spectrum reconstruction method outlined in [13], our approach demonstrates superior accuracy, reducing the error rate significantly. However, our method does have its limitations. First, it is heavily data-driven, which substantially increases the volume of data required. This means hugely increasing the amount of required data. For instance, to predict four targets, we need to add extra $\binom{121}{4}$ samples to the dataset, and $\binom{121}{5}$ for five targets. Furthermore, as the array's element count grows, the matrix size of every data point grows at a quadratic rate. In contrast, learning-based spectrum methods can more seamlessly adapt to various target counts and array sizes.

Table 1. Unknown target estimation in 0 dB, -10 dB, and -15 dB.

Number of Sources K [1]	Threshold p_0	Mean $d_{\mathbf{H}}$ (Degree)	Max $d_{\mathbf{H}}$ (Degree)
SNR = 0 dB			
1	0.4	0.2600	0.2600
2	0.4	0.2600	0.2600
3	0.4	0.2600	0.2600
SNR = -10 dB			
1	0.4	0.2659	0.7400
2	0.4	0.2789	1.2600
3	0.4	0.3052	1.1200

Table 1. *Cont.*

Number of Sources K [1]	Threshold p_0	Mean d_H (Degree)	Max d_H (Degree)
	SNR = −15 dB		
1	0.2	0.4062	23.74
2	0.4	0.4737	15.11
3	0.4	0.7463	10.11

[1] We further tested the false alarm rate of zero target on standard white noise with the same snapshots, 10,000 samples, and Threshold p_0 = 0.4. Under zero-target conditions, there is only a 0.09% chance of mistakenly counting it as one target signal source while 99.91% counting correct.

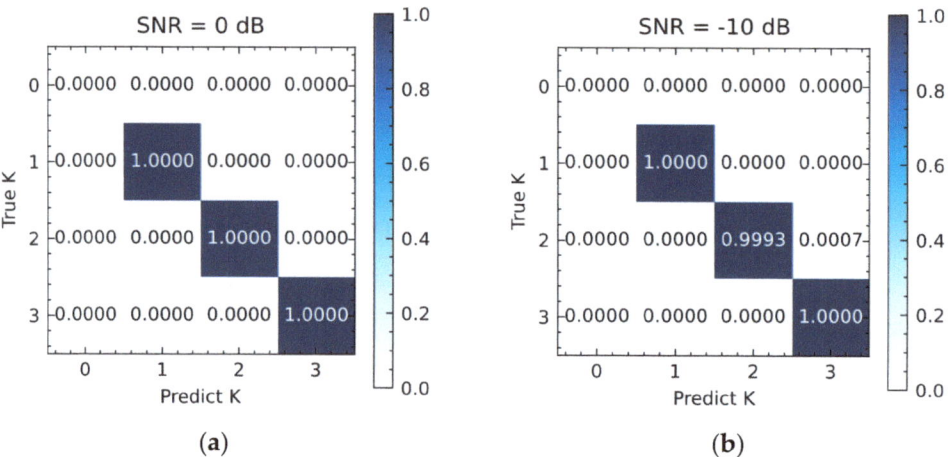

Figure 3. (**a**) Confusion matrix in 0 dB; (**b**) Confusion matrix in −10 dB.

4.2. Known Number of Sources

In the given sources number setting, the experiments were conducted on two-source scenarios with varying SNRs and snapshots. In this case, the output selection approach is modified to choose the two highest values in the probability spectrum without prior filtering. The loss metric used is the RMSE. The performance of the proposed approach is evaluated against existing classical and state-of-the-art methods, and the Cramér–Rao lower bound (CRLB) [24] is provided as benchmark. Additionally, to examine the influence of SCL in proposed approach, the framework without SCL pretraining was evaluated and denoted as CNN-SCL w/o. All the on-grid approaches were set with resolution for one degree of every integer on [−60°, 60°].

4.2.1. RMSE under Varying SNRs

The objective of this experiment is to estimate the DOAs of two sources at different SNRs while keeping the snapshots fixed at 1000. Each data point was tested with 1000 samples. The directions are 10.11° and 12.7°, respectively. The results are shown on Figure 4a. The proposed model exhibits relatively good performance when compared with the CNN in low-SNR regime, with RMSE values of 1.9910°, 0.6253°, and 0.5885° for −20 dB, −15 dB, and −10 dB, respectively. In the high-SNR regime, on-grid methods suffer from grid mismatch and exhibit high RMSE values, while grid-less methods, such as ESPRIT and R-MUSIC, approach the CRLB.

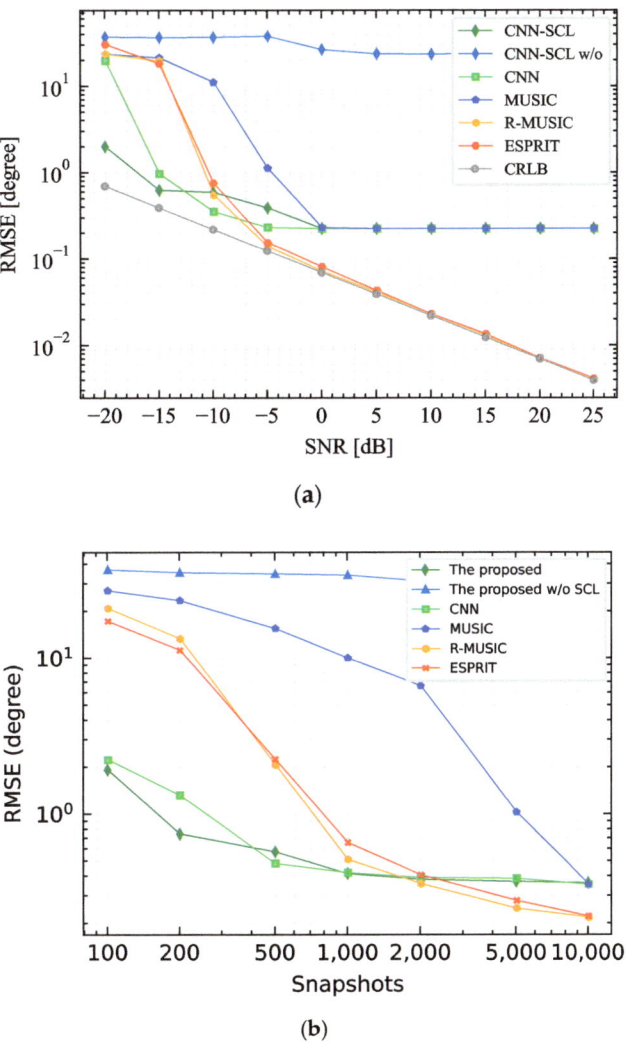

Figure 4. (**a**) Two-target RMSE loss versus SNRs; (**b**) Two-target RMSE loss versus Snapshots.

4.2.2. RMSE versus Varying Snapshots

In this experiment, tests were conducted with two sources at −10 dB SNR while the snapshots ranged from 100 to 10,000. Each datapoint was tested with 1000 samples, with the directions being 9.58° and 12.82°, respectively. Figure 4b illustrates the results. The proposed model achieved superior accuracy at 100 and 200 snapshots, with error of 1.922° and 0.7451°, respectively.

5. Analysis

5.1. Latent Space Visualization

In both experiments conducted with varying SNRs and Snapshots, the framework CNN-SCL w/o without SCL pretraining was found to be difficult to converge. The pretraining was identified as the key factor causing this difference. To investigate the impact of pretraining, t-SNE [25] was employed to visualize the features distribution in latent space

$Z = f(X)$ during both the pretraining stage and training stage by mapping distribution into low-dimensional space while retaining relative distance between data points as much as possible. The values and colors represent the distributions and DOAs of input matrices X. Figure 5a depicts the messy distribution of data processed by the feature extractor without pretraining, whereas the distribution of different classes of angles is well separated by the SCL-pretrained feature extractor, as Figure 5b illustrates. Furthermore, after the training stage with classifier, SCL-pretrained feature extractor separates the features more clearly, forming gradual and continuous distribution, as shown in Figure 5c. As the model only utilizes nearly one-sixteenth of parameters compared with CNN [12], the direct training is hard to fit the data. However, the SCL pretraining provides the feature extractor with a good starting point, as shown in Figure 5b, which enables the training step to proceed more smoothly. This results in the stripe pattern being stretched, as shown in Figure 5c, thus leading to a clear and robust decision boundary. The SCL pretraining enhances parameter efficiency, performance, and generalization in low-SNR DOA estimation. In Figure 6, we visualize the distribution of DOA data after processing through the CNN extractor under various SNR conditions. The findings indicate that the SCL-CNN extracts DOA information based on an amplitude-phase pattern. As illustrated in Figure 6a, when the angle approaches 0, implying minimal phase difference between the array elements, the distribution tends to be closer to the inner side of the center. In Figure 6b, we differentiated data points based on varying SNR levels. It was observed that features extracted from DOA data with lower SNR tend to be located closer to the center. This observation implicitly corroborates the assertions made in the paper [26], suggesting that the information extraction from CNN follows the pattern of pseudospectrum construction in the MUSIC method, where features are extracted based on amplitude and phase and then arranged in ascending order.

5.2. Feature Learning for Analysis

From the theoretical perspective, the recent advancement [27–29] of neural network approximation also provides some intuition for explaining the shift of distribution in Figure 5. In paper [27], Allen-Zhu and Li (2020) demonstrated a novel theoretical framework that characterized the feature learning process of neural networks, which is adopted in paper [28], where Cao et al. (2022) leveraged that framework to analyze the behavior of neural networks under various SNR. Furthermore, in paper [29], Chen Y et al. (2023) go further in analyzing the learning processing of model between spurious and invariant features. The convolutional neural network model analyzed by papers [28,29] is only comprised of two layers at any width, and the deeper neural networks still need further study and investigation. However, as the deeper networks are always more powerful than shallow neural networks in practice, and because they need fewer parameters or units to achieve the same effect as shallow networks [30], we assume that our network can easily fulfill the equivalent conditions that paper [28,29] requests. Thus, the lemmas shall be reasonable to be applied in explaining the effect of pretrain in Figure 5 intuitively.

We consider the simplified model and data set for analysis, which is adopted from papers [28,29]. The analysis focuses on how to suppress the spurious feature and learn the invariant feature in order to achieve Out-of-Distribution (OOD) generalization, namely generalization to other distributions other than the training data set. The spurious features are always correlated with the invariant feature but with contribute negligible information for prediction or estimation. In contrast to the spurious feature, the invariant feature points out the characteristics that are informative and stable inside data. Considering the form of DOA estimation data and matrices are similar to a picture with multiple channels, it is plausible to assume the existence of spurious features.

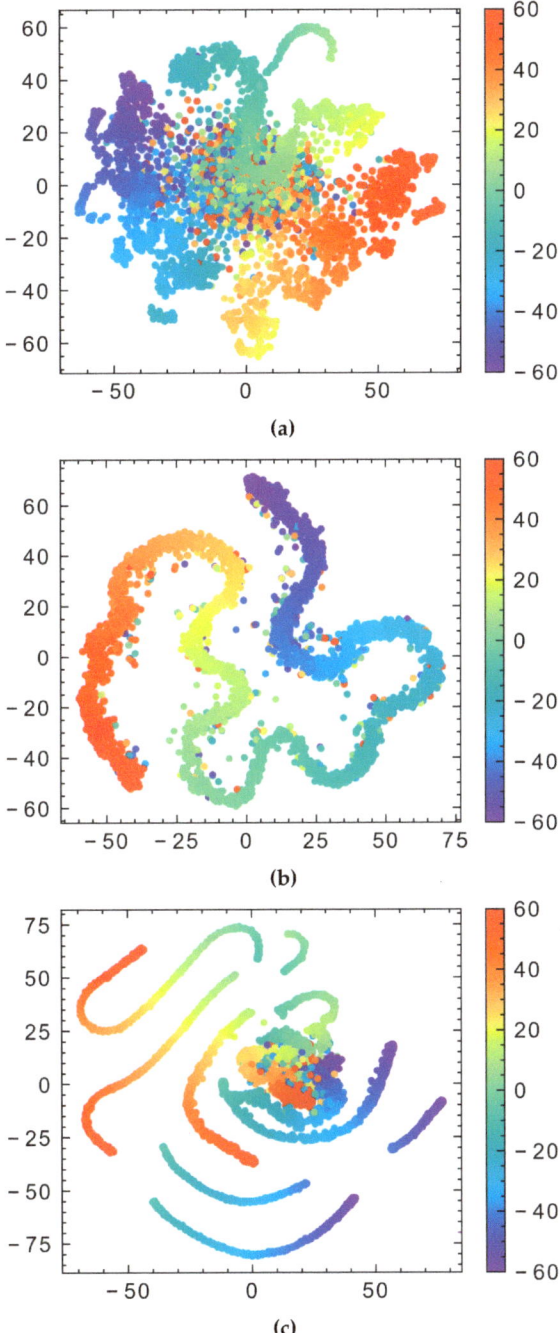

Figure 5. Distributions of output feature from feature extractors with respect to angles at −10 dB, 100 snapshots. (**a**) without SCL pretraining, directly trained with classifier; (**b**) with SCL pretraining only; (**c**) with SCL-pretrained and then further trained with classifier.

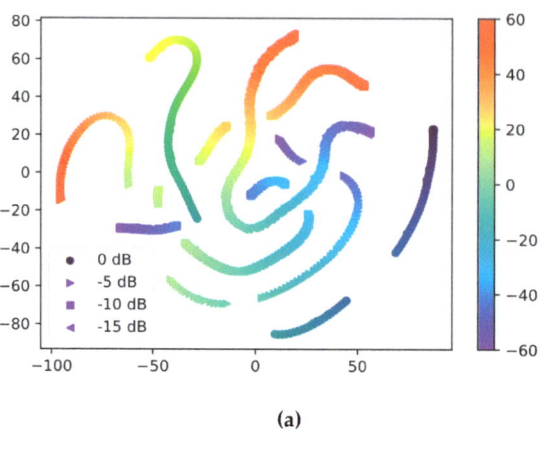

(a)

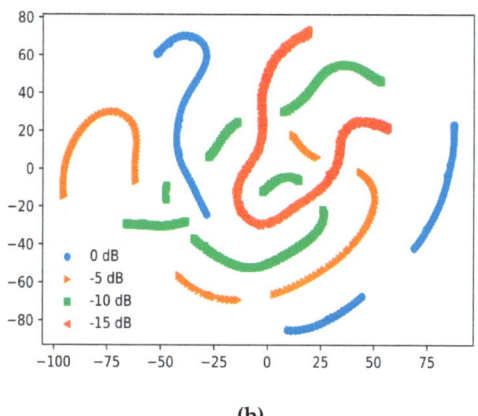

(b)

Figure 6. Distributions of output feature from feature extractors with respect to angles at 0 dB, −5 dB, −10 dB and −15 dB, 1000 snapshots. (**a**) with SCL-pretrained and then further trained with classifier, DOA distribution; (**b**) with SCL-pretrained and then further trained with classifier, SNR distribution.

5.2.1. Preliminary and Ideal Model

Suppose the data set for the ideal model is $\mathcal{D} = \{\mathbf{x}_i, y_i\}_{i=1}^n$, where n is the number of samples, d is the dimension $\mathbf{x} \in \mathbb{R}^{2d}$, and $y \in \{-1, 1\}$. The input data instances $(\mathbf{x}_i, y_i)$ conform to the following distribution:

1. The label y is generated as a Rademacher random variable.
2. Given y, each input $\mathbf{x} = \{\mathbf{x}_1, \mathbf{x}_2\}$ include a feature patch $\mathbf{x}_1$ and a noise patch $\mathbf{x}_2$, that are sampled as:
$$\mathbf{x}_1 = y \cdot Rad(\alpha) \cdot \mathbf{v}_1 + y \cdot Rad(\beta) \cdot \mathbf{v}_2 \quad \mathbf{x}_2 = \xi \quad (12)$$

where $Rad(x)$ presenting the random variable taking value 1 with probability 1-x and −1 with probability x. $\mathbf{v}_1 = [1, 0, 0, \ldots 0]^\top$ and α is usually constant, representing the invariant feature; $\mathbf{v}_2 = [0, 1, 0, \ldots 0]^\top$ and β is usually uncertain with different data, representing the spurious feature with unreliable information.

3. The noise vector conforms to the Gaussian distribution $\mathcal{N}\left(0, \sigma_p^2 \cdot \left(\mathbf{I}_d - \mathbf{v}_1 \mathbf{v}_1^\top - \mathbf{v}_2 \mathbf{v}_2^\top\right)\right)$, indicating a noise orthogonal with both spurious and invariant features.

An ideal two-layer CNN model is trained to classify the label with sigmoid and cross-entropy loss function, the network can be written as $f(\mathbf{W}, \mathbf{x}) = F_{+1}(\mathbf{W}_{+1}, \mathbf{x}) - F_{-1}(\mathbf{W}_{-1}, \mathbf{x})$, with:

$$F_j(\mathbf{W}_j, \mathbf{x}) = \frac{1}{m} \sum_{r=1}^{m} \left[\sigma\left(\mathbf{w}_{j,r}^\top \mathbf{x}_1\right) + \sigma\left(\mathbf{w}_{j,r}^\top \mathbf{x}_2\right) \right] \quad (13)$$

where $\sigma(x)$ is the activation function.

5.2.2. Theorem and Intuition

Lemma 1 (Cao et al. [28]; Chen et al. [29]). *Let $w_{j,r}(t)$ for $j \in \{+1, -1\}$ and $r \in \{1, 2, 3, \ldots m\}$ be the convolution filters of the CNN at t-th iteration of gradient descent. Then there exists unique coefficients $\gamma_{j,r,1}(t), \gamma_{j,r,2}(t) \geq 0$ and $\rho_{j,r,i}(t)$ s.t.:*

$$\mathbf{w}_{j,r}(t) = \mathbf{w}_{j,r}(0) + j \cdot \gamma_{j,r,1}(t) \cdot \mathbf{v}_1 + j \cdot \gamma_{j,r,2}(t) \cdot \mathbf{v}_2 + \sum \rho_{j,r,i}(t) \cdot \| \boldsymbol{\xi}_i \|_2^{-2} \cdot \boldsymbol{\xi}_i \quad (14)$$

Lemma 1 is the basis for following lemmas. It reveals the behavior of neural networks when updated. The weights are the time-varying linear combination of initialized weights $\mathbf{w}_{j,r}(0)$, invariant signal $\mathbf{v}_1$, spurious signal $\mathbf{v}_2$, and noise $\boldsymbol{\xi}_i$. As $\mathbf{w}_{j,r}(0) \approx 0$ and the rest of the components are orthogonal to each other, $\gamma_{j,r,1} \approx \langle \mathbf{w}_{j,r}, \mathbf{v}_1 \rangle$ and $\gamma_{j,r,2} \approx \langle \mathbf{w}_{j,r}, \mathbf{v}_2 \rangle$ learning progress of invariant feature and spurious feature.

Lemma 2 (Chen et al. [29]). *For two samples $x_1^e, x_1^{e'}$. With invariant risk minimization regularization $c(t)$, define $\lambda_0 = \lambda_{min}(H^\infty)$, where $H^\infty_{e,e'} \triangleq \frac{1}{2mn_e n_{e'}} \sum_{i=1}^{n_e} x_{1,i}^{e\top} \sum_{i'=1}^{n_{e'}} x_{1,i'}^{e'}$. Suppose that dimension $d = \Omega(\log(m/\delta))$, network width $m = \Omega(1/\delta)$, regularization factor $\lambda \geq 1/\sigma_0$, noise variance $\sigma_p = O(d^{-2})$, weight initial scale $\sigma_0 = O\left(\min\left\{\frac{\lambda_0^2 m^2}{\log(1/\epsilon)}, \frac{\lambda_0 m}{\sqrt{d \log(1/\epsilon)}}\right\}\right)$, then with probability at least $1 - \delta$, after training iteration $T = \Omega\left(\frac{\log(1/\epsilon)}{\eta \lambda \lambda_0}\right)$, we have:*

$$\| \mathbf{c}(T) \|_2 \leq \epsilon, \gamma_{j,r,1}(T) = o_d(1), \gamma_{j,r,2}(T) = o_d(1) \quad (15)$$

The theorem demonstrates that heavy invariant risk minimization (IRM) regularization hinders the learning process for both spurious and invariant features. The loss stays at constant at the same time. IRM aims to find the invariant feature under whatever possible feature distribution [31]. We observe that the strong weights-share regularization [18] of our CNN-SCL model in the first four FC layers play similar roles as IRM, which not only rise the generalization of the model but the difficulty of training, keeping the training and testing loss as relatively large constant in Figure 4 term *CNN-SCL w/o*.

Lemma 3 (Chen et al. [29]). *Suppose spurious correlations are stronger than invariant correlations $\alpha > \beta$, and $\gamma_{j,r}^{inv}(t_1) = \gamma_{j,r}^{inv}(t_1 - 1)$ and $\gamma_{j,r}^{spu}(t_1) = \gamma_{j,r}^{spu}(t_1 - 1)$ at the end of pretraining iteration t_1. Suppose that $\delta > 0$ and $n > C\log(1/\delta)$, with C being a positive constant, then with a high probability at least $1 - \delta$, we have regularization loss approaches zero and $\gamma_{j,r}^{inv}(t_1 + 1) > \gamma_{j,r}^{inv}(t_1)$ while $\gamma_{j,r}^{spu}(t_1 + 1) < \gamma_{j,r}^{spu}(t_1)$.*

This lemma indicates that the learning processing can start learning process with the strong and enough pretraining, even under heavy regularization. And in the training stage after pretraining stage, the learned invariant feature would be empowered, while the spurious feature would be suppressed. Thus, we can observe the *CNN-SCL* with pretraining perform better than *CNN-SCL w/o* in Figure 4.

In Figure 5a–c, the manifestation of the pattern further validates the effect that Lemma 2 and Lemma 3 point out. In Figure 5a, as Lemma 2 reveals, *CNN-SCL w/o* incurs heavy regularization, performs worst feature distribution, and learns almost nothing.

In Figure 5b, as Lemma 3 suggests, supervised contrastive learning is a very powerful pretraining method to help the model overcome regularization and start learning both spurious and invariant features, so the pattern begins to separate and order. Finally, as Lemma 3 indicates, Figure 5c illustrates that with enough training after pretraining, the invariant features have been learned and the spurious features were suppressed, from which a clear and robust feature distribution forms.

6. Conclusions

In this paper, we introduced a new framework called CNN-SCL for on-grid multi-target DOA estimation in low SNRs and limited snapshots. The proposed method is based on contrastive learning, which aims to separate different features with a regular pattern. The experimental results demonstrate the robustness and generalization capability of our proposed method, outperforming other methods in harsh environments for both number of source classifications and DOA estimations. The analysis confirms the necessity of SCL pretraining in both visualization and theory. Additionally, our approach achieves comparable performance with state-of-the-art methods while number of parameters significantly decreases near 94%. Our future work will focus on exploring the potential of contrastive learning to further reduce the parameters for DOA estimation with deep learning.

Author Contributions: Conceptualization, C.C. and Y.L.; methodology, Z.Z. (Zhengjie Zhou); software, Z.Z. (Zhiquan Zhou) and P.W.; validation, Y.L., C.C. and Z.Z. (Zhiquan Zhou); formal analysis, Z.Z. (Zhengjie Zhou); investigation, Z.Z. (Zhengjie Zhou); resources, Z.Z. (Zhengjie Zhou); data curation, Z.Z. (Zhengjie Zhou); writing—original draft preparation, Z.Z. (Zhengjie Zhou); writing—review and editing, Y.L. and C.C.; visualization, Z.Z. (Zhengjie Zhou); supervision, Y.L.; project administration, Y.L.; funding acquisition, Y.L. All authors have read and agreed to the published version of the manuscript.

Funding: This research was funded by the National Natural Science Foundation of China, grant number [62001143]; the National Natural Science Foundation of Shandong Province, grant number [ZR2020QF006, ZR201910220437]; the Major Scientific and technological innovation project of Shandong Province, grant number [2021ZLGX05, 2022ZLGX04].

Data Availability Statement: Data that support the finding of this study are available from the first author upon reasonable request (rua.zhou@gmail.com).

Conflicts of Interest: The authors declare that they have no known competing financial interests or personal relationships that could have appeared to influence the work reported in this paper.

References

1. Schmidt, R. Multiple emitter location and signal parameter estimation. *IEEE Trans. Antennas Propag.* **1986**, *34*, 276–280. [CrossRef]
2. Roy, R.; Kailath, T. ESPRIT-estimation of signal parameters via rotational invariance techniques. *IEEE Trans. Acoust. Speech Signal Process.* **1989**, *37*, 984–995. [CrossRef]
3. Rao, B.D.; Hari, K.V.S. Performance analysis of root-MUSIC. *IEEE Trans. Acoust. Speech Signal Process.* **1989**, *37*, 1939–1949. [CrossRef]
4. Liu, T. Porosity reconstruction based on Biot elastic model of porous media by homotopy perturbation method. *Chaos Solitons Fractals* **2022**, *158*, 112007. [CrossRef]
5. Liu, T.; Ding, Z.; Yu, J.; Zhang, W. Parameter Estimation for Nonlinear Diffusion Problems by the Constrained Homotopy Method. *Mathematics* **2023**, *11*, 2642. [CrossRef]
6. Liu, T.; Yu, J.; Zheng, Y.; Liu, C.; Yang, Y.; Qi, Y. A nonlinear multigrid method for the parameter identification problem of partial differential equations with constraints. *Mathematics* **2022**, *10*, 2938. [CrossRef]
7. Liu, T.; Ouyang, D.; Guo, L.; Qiu, R.; Qi, Y.; Xie, W.; Ma, Q.; Liu, C. Combination of Multigrid with Constraint Data for Inverse Problem of Nonlinear Diffusion Equation. *Mathematics* **2023**, *11*, 2887. [CrossRef]
8. Liu, T. Parameter estimation with the multigrid-homotopy method for a nonlinear diffusion equation. *J. Comput. Appl. Math.* **2022**, *413*, 114393. [CrossRef]
9. Kumchaiseemak, N.; Chatnuntawech, I.; Teerapittayanon, S.; Kotchapansompote, P.; Kaewlee, T.; Piriyajitakonkij, M.; Wilaiprasitporn, T.; Suwajanakorn, S. Toward Ant-Sized Moving Object Localization Using Deep Learning in FMCW Radar: A Pilot Study. *IEEE Trans. Geosci. Remote Sens.* **2022**, *60*, 1–10. [CrossRef]

10. Kase, Y.; Nishimura, T.; Ohgane, T.; Ogawa, Y.; Kitayama, D.; Kishiyama, Y. DoA estimation of two targets with deep learning. In Proceedings of the 2018 15th Workshop on Positioning, Navigation and Communications (WPNC), Bremen, Germany, 25–26 October 2018; pp. 1–5.
11. Liu, Z.M.; Zhang, C.; Philip, S.Y. Direction-of-arrival estimation based on deep neural networks with robustness to array imperfections. *IEEE Trans. Antennas Propag.* **2018**, *66*, 7315–7327. [CrossRef]
12. Papageorgiou, G.K.; Sellathurai, M.; Eldar, Y.C. Deep networks for direction-of-arrival estimation in low SNR. *IEEE Trans. Signal Process.* **2021**, *69*, 3714–3729. [CrossRef]
13. Lee, K. Deep learning-aided coherent direction-of-arrival estimation with the FTMR algorithm. *IEEE Trans. Signal Process.* **2022**, *70*, 1118–1130.
14. Wu, X.; Yang, X.; Jia, X.; Tian, F. A gridless DOA estimation method based on convolutional neural network with Toeplitz prior. *IEEE Signal Process. Lett.* **2022**, *29*, 1247–1251. [CrossRef]
15. Oord, A.; Li, Y.; Vinyals, O. Representation learning with contrastive predictive coding. *arXiv* **2018**, arXiv:1807.03748.
16. Khosla, P.; Teterwak, P.; Wang, C.; Sarna, A.; Tian, Y.; Isola, P.; Maschinot, A.; Liu, C.; Krishnan, D. Supervised contrastive learning. *Adv. Neural Inf. Process. Syst.* **2020**, *33*, 18661–18673.
17. Gu, J.; Wang, Z.; Kuen, J.; Ma, L.; Shahroudy, A.; Shuai, B.; Liu, T.; Wang, X.; Wang, G.; Cai, J.; et al. Recent advances in convolutional neural networks. *Pattern Recognit.* **2018**, *77*, 354–377. [CrossRef]
18. Nowlan, S.J.; Hinton, G.E. Simplifying neural networks by soft weight-sharing. *Neural Comput.* **1992**, *4*, 473–493. [CrossRef]
19. Cubuk, E.D.; Zoph, B.; Mane, D.; Vasudevan, V.; Le, Q.V. Autoaugment: Learning augmentation policies from data. *arXiv* **2018**, arXiv:1805.09501.
20. Hassani, K.; Khasahmadi, A.H. Contrastive multi-view representation learning on graphs. In Proceedings of the International Conference on Machine Learning, Virtual Event, 13–18 July 2020; pp. 4116–4126.
21. Kingma, D.P.; Ba, J. Adam: A method for stochastic optimization. *arXiv* **2014**, arXiv:1412.6980.
22. Nitzberg, R. Constant-false-alarm-rate signal processors for several types of interference. *IEEE Trans. Aerosp. Electron. Syst.* **1972**, 27–34. [CrossRef]
23. Wong, K.M.; Zhang, Q.T.; Reilly, J.P.; Yip, P.C. On information theoretic criteria for determining the number of signals in high resolution array processing. *IEEE Trans. Acoust. Speech Signal Process.* **1990**, *38*, 1959–1971. [CrossRef]
24. Stoica, P.; Nehorai, A. Performance study of conditional and unconditional direction-of-arrival estimation. *IEEE Trans. Acoust. Speech Signal Process.* **1990**, *38*, 1783–1795. [CrossRef]
25. Van der Maaten, L.; Hinton, G. Visualizing data using t-SNE. *J. Mach. Learn. Res.* **2008**, *9*.
26. Adavanne, S.; Politis, A.; Virtanen, T. Direction of arrival estimation for multiple sound sources using convolutional recurrent neural network. In Proceedings of the 2018 26th European Signal Processing Conference (EUSIPCO), Rome, Italy, 3–7 September 2018; IEEE: Piscataway, NJ, USA, 2018; pp. 1462–1466.
27. Allen-Zhu, Z.; Li, Y. Towards understanding ensemble, knowledge distillation and self-distillation in deep learning. *arXiv* **2020**, arXiv:2012.09816.
28. Cao, Y.; Chen, Z.; Belkin, M.; Gu, Q. Benign overfitting in two-layer convolutional neural networks. *Adv. Neural Inf. Process. Syst.* **2022**, *35*, 25237–25250.
29. Chen, Y.; Huang, W.; Zhou, K.; Bian, Y.; Han, B.; Cheng, J. Towards Understanding Feature Learning in Out-of-Distribution Generalization. *arXiv* **2023**, arXiv:2304.11327.
30. Liang, S.; Srikant, R. Why deep neural networks for function approximation? *arXiv* **2016**, arXiv:1610.04161.
31. Arjovsky, M.; Bottou, L.; Gulrajani, I.; Lopez-Paz, D. Invariant risk minimization. *arXiv* **2019**, arXiv:1907.02893.

Disclaimer/Publisher's Note: The statements, opinions and data contained in all publications are solely those of the individual author(s) and contributor(s) and not of MDPI and/or the editor(s). MDPI and/or the editor(s) disclaim responsibility for any injury to people or property resulting from any ideas, methods, instructions or products referred to in the content.

Article

Sinc Collocation Method to Simulate the Fractional Partial Integro-Differential Equation with a Weakly Singular Kernel

Mingzhu Li, Lijuan Chen * and Yongtao Zhou

School of Science, Qingdao University of Technology, Qingdao 266525, China; limingzhu19820120@126.com (M.L.); zhouyongtao@qut.edu.cn (Y.Z.)
* Correspondence: chenljcool@163.com

Abstract: In this article, we develop an efficient numerical scheme for dealing with fractional partial integro-differential equations (FPIEs) with a weakly singular kernel. The weight and shift Grünwald difference (WSGD) operator is adopted to approximate a time fractional derivative and the Sinc collocation method is applied for discretizing the spatial derivative. The exponential convergence of our proposed method is demonstrated in detail. Finally, numerical evidence is employed to verify the theoretical results and confirm the expected convergence rate.

Keywords: Sinc collocation method; WSGD operator; fractional partial integro-differential equation; convergence

MSC: 65M06; 65M12; 65M15

Citation: Li, M.; Chen, L.; Zhou, Y. Sinc Collocation Method to Simulate the Fractional Partial Integro-Differential Equation with a Weakly Singular Kernel. *Axioms* **2023**, *12*, 898. https://doi.org/10.3390/axioms12090898

Academic Editor: Chris Goodrich

Received: 1 August 2023
Revised: 11 September 2023
Accepted: 14 September 2023
Published: 21 September 2023

Copyright: © 2023 by the authors. Licensee MDPI, Basel, Switzerland. This article is an open access article distributed under the terms and conditions of the Creative Commons Attribution (CC BY) license (https://creativecommons.org/licenses/by/4.0/).

1. Introduction

In recent years, fractional calculus has played an increasingly important role in various fields and has attracted much interest from scholars due to its extensive applications in modeling many complex problems [1–8]. The fractional integro-differential equation is one of the most active fields in fractional calculus [9–15], which can be seen as the extension of classical integral equations by replacing integer-order derivatives with fractional derivatives. Consequently, there is a growing need to explore solution techniques to study these equations. Although there are some ways to get exact solutions of these equations, the exact solutions of these equations are very difficult to find in most cases. For this reason, there has been much research on the effective numerical methods of fractional integral differential equations (FIDEs). Here, we list only a few of them. In [16,17], the homotopy analysis method is used to find the approximate solution of FIDEs. In [18], the spectral Jacobi-collocation method is presented by Ma et al. to solve the solution of general linear FIDEs. In [19], the compact finite difference scheme is constructed to approximate the solution of FIDEs with a weakly singular kernel. In [20], the alternating direction implicit difference scheme combined with a fractional trapezoidal rule is developed to solve two dimensional FIDEs. In [21], the Legendre wavelet collocation method based on the Gauss–Jacobi quadrature is introduced to solve the fractional delay-type integro-differential equations. In [22], the collocation method combined with fractional Genocchi functions is used for the solution of variable-order FIDEs. In [23], the meshless method based on the Laplace transform is constructed for approximating the solution of the two-dimensional multi-term FIDEs. In [24], the finite element method is proposed to solve the two-dimensional weakly singular FIDEs. In [25], the spectral Galerkin method based on Legendre polynomials is presented to solve the one and two-dimensional fourth-order FIDEs. In [26], the Adomian decomposition method and homotopy perturbation method are given to approximate the solution of the time FPIEs. Liu et al. [27–31] used the multigrid method and homotopy method to solve practical problems in the fractional flow formulation of the two-phase porous media flow equations and Biot elastic models.

In this article, we consider the fractional partial integro-differential equations (FPIEs) with a weakly singular kernel as follows:

$$_0D_t^\alpha v(x,t) = \frac{\partial^2 v(x,t)}{\partial x^2} + \int_0^t (t-s)^{-1/2} \frac{\partial^2 v(x,t)}{\partial x^2} ds + f(x,t), \quad x \in [a,b], \; t \in [0,T], \quad (1)$$

with the initial condition:
$$v(x,0) = 0, \quad x \in [a,b], \quad (2)$$

and boundary conditions
$$v(a,t) = v(b,t) = 0, \quad t \in [0,T], \quad (3)$$

where $0 < \alpha < 1$ and $f(x,t)$ is smooth enough. The time fractional derivative $_0D_t^\alpha v(x,t)$ is defined in Riemann–Liouville sense as

$$_0D_t^\alpha v(x,t) = \frac{1}{\Gamma(1-\alpha)} \frac{d}{dt} \int_0^t \frac{v(x,s)^\alpha}{(t-s)} ds,$$

where $\Gamma(\cdot)$ is the Gamma function.

The partial integro-differential equation of integer order has proven to describe some phenomena such as viscoelasticity, population dynamics and heat conduction in materials with memory [32–34]. Over the past three decades, various numerical methods based on the Sinc approximation have been presented, which have the advantages of a very fast convergence of exponential order and handling singularities effectively. The Sinc method proposed by Frank Stenger [35–37] has been increasingly applied to solve a variety of linear and nonlinear models that arise in scientific and engineering applications such as two-point boundary value problems [38], the Blasius equation [39], oceanographic problems with boundary layers [40], fourth-order partial integro-differential equation [41], the Volterra integro-differential equation [42,43], optimal control, heat distribution and astrophysics equations. According to the definition, it can be seen that fractional derivatives and integrals always deal with weak singularities. Therefore, in the past few years, the Sinc method has been widely extended to get the numerical solution of the fractional differential equations [44–47]. The main objective of this work is to provide a new attempt to develop a numerical solution via the use of the Sinc collocation method to solve the fractional partial integro-differential equation with a weakly singular kernel.

The remainder of this article is organized as follows. In Section 2, we introduce some basic formulation and theoretic results of Sinc functions which are required for our subsequent development. In Section 3, we propose a time discrete scheme based on the weight and shift Grünwald difference operator and a space discrete scheme by applying a collocation scheme based on the Sinc functions. In Section 4, the convergence analysis of our scheme is proved and in the meantime the exponential convergence is obtained. Some numerical results are described in Section 5 to illustrate the performance of our method. Finally, we give our conclusion in Section 6.

2. Definitions and Preliminaries

In this section, we describe some main notations and definitions of the Sinc function and review some known results that will be used in the following sections. The reader interested in learning more about the detailed properties of the Sinc function can investigate [35].

The Sinc function is basically defined on the whole real line $-\infty < x < \infty$ by

$$\text{Sinc}(x) = \begin{cases} \frac{\sin(\pi x)}{\pi x}, & x \neq 0, \\ 1, & x = 0. \end{cases}$$

For any mesh size $h > 0$ and $k = 0, \pm 1, \pm 2, \ldots$, the Sinc basis functions with evenly spaced nodes given on $\mathbb{R}$ by

$$S(k,h)(x) = \text{Sinc}\left(\frac{y - kh}{h}\right).$$

Let $f(x)$ be a function defined on the real line, then for $h > 0$ the series

$$C(f,h)(x) = \sum_{k=-\infty}^{\infty} f(kh) S(k,h)(x),$$

is called the Whittaker cardinal expansion of f, whenever this series converges. The properties of Whittaker cardinal expansions which are derived on the infinite strip Q_s of the complex plane have been described and proved in detail in the literature [36].

$$Q_s = \left\{w = t + is : |s| < d \leq \frac{\pi}{2}\right\}.$$

In order to construct approximations on the interval (a, b), we consider the conformal map

$$\phi(z) = \log\left(\frac{z-a}{b-z}\right),$$

which carries the eye-shaped domain of complex plan

$$Q_E = \left\{z = x + iy : \left|\arg\left(\frac{z-a}{b-z}\right)\right| < d \leq \frac{\pi}{2}\right\},$$

onto the infinite strip domain of complex plan Q_s.

Let ψ be the inverse map of $w = \phi(z)$, and we define the range of ϕ^{-1} on $\mathbb{R}$ as

$$(a,b) = \{\psi(u) = \phi^{-1}(u) \in Q_E : -\infty < u < \infty\}.$$

For the uniform grid $\{jh\}_{j=-\infty}^{\infty}$ on $\mathbb{R}$, the Sinc points which correspond to these nodes are denoted by

$$x_j = \psi(jh) = \frac{a + be^{jh}}{1 + e^{jh}}, \quad j = 0, \pm 1, \pm 2, \ldots. \tag{4}$$

The basis functions on (a, b) for $z \in Q_E$ are taken to be the composite translated Sinc functions as

$$S_k(z) = S(k,h) \circ \phi(z) = \text{Sinc}\left(\frac{\phi(z) - kh}{h}\right), \quad k = 0, \pm 1, \pm 2, \ldots. \tag{5}$$

Definition 1. Let $B(Q_E)$ be the class of functions F which are analytic in Q_E and satisfy

$$\int_{\psi(t+\Sigma)} |F(z)| dz \to 0, \quad \text{as } t \to \pm\infty,$$

where $\Sigma = \left\{i\eta : |\eta| < d \leq \frac{\pi}{2}\right\}$ and satisfy

$$N(f) = \int_{\partial Q_E} |F(z) dz| < \infty.$$

where ∂Q_E represents the boundary of Q_E.

Lemma 1 ([37]). *If $F(x), \phi'(x) \in B(Q_E)$ and $h > 0$. Let ϕ be a one-to-one comformal map. For all $x \in (a, b)$*

$$\left|F(x) - \sum_{j=-N}^{N} F(x_j) S_j(x)\right| \leq \frac{2N(f\phi')}{\pi d} e^{-\pi d/h}. \tag{6}$$

Moreover, if $|F(x)| \leq ce^{-\beta|\phi(x)|}$, $x \in (a,b)$, for some positive constants c, l, N and β, and if the selection $h = \sqrt{\pi d / \beta N}$, then

$$\sup_{x \in (0,1)} \left| F(x) - \left(\frac{d}{dx}\right)^l \sum_{j=-N}^{N} f(x_j) S_j(x) \right| \leq C_1 N^{(l+1)/2} e^{-\sqrt{\pi d \beta N}}, \tag{7}$$

where C_1 depends only on F, d and β.

Lemma 1 shows the Sinc interpolation on $B(Q_E)$ is exponentially convergent. We also need the derivative of the complex Sinc function to be evaluated at the nodes. So we introduce the lemma as follows:

Lemma 2 ([48]). *For the step size h and the Sinc points x_j determined by (4), suppose that ϕ is the conformal one-to-one mapping of the simply connected domain Q_E onto Q_d, then we have*

$$\delta_{kj}^{(0)} = \left[S(k,h) \circ \phi(x) \right]\Big|_{x=x_j} = \begin{cases} 1, & j = k, \\ 0, & j \neq k, \end{cases} \tag{8}$$

$$\delta_{kj}^{(1)} = h \frac{d}{d\phi} \left[S(k,h) \circ \phi(x) \right]\Big|_{x=x_j} = \begin{cases} 0, & j = k, \\ \frac{(-1)^{j-k}}{j-k}, & j \neq k, \end{cases} \tag{9}$$

$$\delta_{kj}^{(2)} = h^2 \frac{d^2}{d\phi^2} \left[S(k,h) \circ \phi(x) \right]\Big|_{x=x_j} = \begin{cases} \frac{-\pi^2}{3}, & j = k, \\ \frac{-2(-1)^{j-k}}{(j-k)^2}, & j \neq k. \end{cases} \tag{10}$$

To facilitate the representation of discrete systems, we give the definition of the following matrix as follows:

$$I^{(l)} = [\delta_{kj}^{(l)}], \quad l = 0, 1, 2, \tag{11}$$

where $\delta_{kj}^{(l)}$ is the (k,j) the element of the matrix $I^{(l)}$. The matrix $I^{(0)}$, $I^{(1)}$ and $I^{(2)}$ represents the identity matrix, the skew symmetric Toeplitz matrix and the symmetric Toeplitz matrix, respectively.

3. Derivation of the Numerical Scheme

3.1. The Time Semi-Discretization

For positive integer number N, let $\tau = \frac{T}{N}$ be the time mesh size, $t_n = n\tau$, $n = 0, 1, \cdots, N$, be the mesh points. Denote $v^n = v(x, t_n)$ and $f^n = f(x, t_n)$. Firstly, in order to apply the WSGD operator to discrete the time fractionl derivatives, the approximation order must be used. Therefore, we review the following lemma.

Lemma 3 ([49]). *Suppose that $\varphi(t) \in L_1(\mathbb{R})$ and $\varphi(t) \in C^{\alpha+1}(\mathbb{R})$, and define the shift Grünwald difference operator by*

$$A_{\tau,p}^{\alpha} \varphi(t) = \frac{1}{\tau^{\alpha}} \sum_{k=0}^{\infty} g_k^{(\alpha)} \varphi(t - (k-p)\tau), \tag{12}$$

where p is an integer and the sequences $g_k^{(\alpha)}$ are the coefficients of the power series expansion of the function $(1-z)^{\alpha}$, i.e, $g_0^{(\alpha)} = 1, g_k^{(\alpha)} = (-1)^k \binom{\alpha}{k}, k = 1, 2, \cdots$. Then

$$A_{\tau,p}^{\alpha} \varphi(t) = {}_{-\infty}D_t^{\alpha} \varphi(t) + O(\tau), \tag{13}$$

uniformly for $t \in \mathbb{R}$ as $\tau \to 0$.

Lemma 4 ([50]). *Let $\varphi(t) \in L_1(\mathbb{R})$, $_{-\infty}D_t^{\alpha+2}\varphi(t)$ and its Fourier transform belong to $L_1(\mathbb{R})$. Define the weighted and shifted Grünwald difference operator by*

$$D_{\tau,p,q}^{\alpha}\varphi(t) = \frac{2q-\alpha}{2(q-p)}A_{\tau,p}^{\alpha}\varphi(t) + \frac{2p-\alpha}{2(p-q)}A_{\tau,q}^{\alpha}\varphi(t), \tag{14}$$

where p and q are integers and $p \neq q$. Then,

$$D_{\tau,p,q}^{\alpha}\varphi(t) = {}_{-\infty}D_t^{\alpha}\varphi(t) + O(\tau^2),$$

uniformly for $t \in \mathbb{R}$ as $\tau \to 0$.

Let p and q be equal to 0 and 1 in Lemma 4, we can get

$$\begin{aligned}{}_0D_t^{\alpha}v(x_i,t_n) &= \tau^{-\alpha}\left(\frac{2+\alpha}{2}\sum_{k=0}^{n}g_k^{(\alpha)}v_i^{n-k} - \frac{\alpha}{2}\sum_{k=0}^{n-1}g_k^{(\alpha)}v_i^{n-1-k}\right) + O(\tau^2) \\ &= \tau^{-\alpha}\sum_{k=0}^{n}\lambda_k v_i^{n-k} + R_{n+1,1},\end{aligned} \tag{15}$$

where $R_{n+1,1} = O(\tau^2)$, $\lambda_0 = \frac{2+\alpha}{2}g_0^{(\alpha)}$, $\lambda_k = \frac{2+\alpha}{2}g_k^{(\alpha)} - \frac{1-\alpha}{2}g_{k-1}^{(\alpha)}$, $k \geq 1$.

By using unusual quadrature approximation, the integral term of (1) can be approximated as follows:

$$\begin{aligned}&\int_0^{t_{n+1}}(t_{n+1}-s)^{-1/2}\frac{\partial^2 v(x,s)}{\partial x^2}ds \\ &= \sum_{l=0}^{n}\int_{t_l}^{t_{l+1}}(t_{n+1}-s)^{-1/2}\frac{\partial^2 v(x,s)}{\partial x^2}ds \\ &\approx \sum_{l=0}^{n}\int_{t_l}^{t_{l+1}}(t_{n+1}-s)^{-1/2}\left(\frac{t_{l+1}-s}{\tau}v_{xx}^l(x) + \frac{s-t_l}{\tau}v_{xx}^{l+1}(x)\right)ds \\ &\approx \frac{1}{\tau}\sum_{l=0}^{n}\left(A_{n,l}v_{xx}^l(x) + B_{n,l}v_{xx}^{l+1}(x)\right) + R_{n+1,2},\end{aligned} \tag{16}$$

where

$$R_{n+1,2} = O(\triangle t^{3/2}),$$

$$A_{n,l} = \int_{t_l}^{t_{l+1}}(t_{n+1}-s)^{-1/2}(t_{l+1}-s)ds, \tag{17}$$

$$B_{n,l} = \int_{t_l}^{t_{l+1}}(t_{n+1}-s)^{-1/2}(s-t_l)ds,$$

Substituting (15) and (16) into (1), we have

$$\begin{aligned}&\lambda_0 v^{n+1}(x) - \left(\tau^{\alpha} + \tau^{\alpha-1}B_{n,n}\right)v_{xx}^{n+1}(x) \\ &= \tau^{\alpha-1}\sum_{l=0}^{n}\rho_{n,l}v_{xx}^l(x) - \sum_{k=0}^{n}\lambda_k v^{n+1-k}(x) + \tau^{\alpha}f^{n+1}(x) + R_{n+1},\end{aligned} \tag{18}$$

where

$$|R_{n+1}| \leq \min\left\{|R_{n+1,1}|, |R_{n+1,2}|\right\},$$

$$\rho_{n,0} = A_{n,0},$$

$$\rho_{n,l} = A_{n,l} + B_{n,l-1}.$$

Omitting the truncation error term R_{n+1} from Equation (18), we get the following semidiscrete scheme of Equation (1):

$$\lambda_0 v^{n+1}(x) - \left(\tau^\alpha + \tau^{\alpha-1} B_{n,n}\right) v^{n+1}_{xx}(x)$$
$$= \tau^{\alpha-1} \sum_{l=0}^{n} \rho_{n,l} v^{l}_{xx}(x) - \sum_{k=0}^{n} \lambda_k v^{n+1-k}(x) + \tau^\alpha f^{n+1}(x), \quad (19)$$

and using the initial and boundary conditions (2), we have

$$v^0(x) = g_0(x),$$
$$v^{n+1}(a) = 0, \quad v^{n+1}(b) = 0.$$

3.2. The Sinc Collocation Method for Spatial Discretization

Now we construct the Sinc collocation method to discrete the semidiscrete scheme (19). The approximation solution $v^n(x)$ of the semidiscrete scheme (19) can be approximated by

$$v^n(x) \approx V^n_m(x) = \sum_{k=-N}^{N} c^n_j S(k,h) \circ \phi(x), \quad m = 2N+1, \quad (20)$$

where c^n_j is the undetermined coefficient in (20).

$$\frac{d^2}{dx^2} V^n_m(x) = \sum_{j=-N}^{N} c^n_j \frac{d^2}{dx^2} [S(j,h) \circ \phi(x)]$$
$$= \sum_{j=-N}^{N} c^n_j [\phi''(x) S^{(1)}_j(x) + (\phi'(x))^2 S^{(2)}_j(x)],$$

where

$$S^{(l)}_j = \frac{d^{(l)}}{d\phi^{(l)}} [S(j,h) \circ \phi(x)], \quad l = 1, 2.$$

It then follows from Lemma 2 that

$$\frac{d^2}{dx^2} V^n_m(x_i) = \sum_{j=-N}^{N} c^n_j \left[\phi''(x_i) \frac{\delta^{(1)}_{ji}}{h} + (\phi'(x_i))^2 \frac{\delta^{(2)}_{ji}}{h^2} \right]. \quad (21)$$

Substituting (20) and (21) into (19), we have

$$\lambda_0 \sum_{j=-N}^{j=N} c^{n+1}_j \delta^{(0)}_{ji} - (\tau^\alpha + \tau^{\alpha-1} B_{n,n}) \sum_{j=-N}^{j=N} c^{n+1}_j \left[\phi''(x) \frac{\delta^{(1)}_{ji}}{h} + (\phi'(x))^2 \frac{\delta^{(2)}_{ji}}{h^2} \right]$$
$$= \tau^{\alpha-1} \sum_{l=0}^{n} \sum_{j=-N}^{j=N} \rho_{n,l} c^{n+1}_j \left[\phi''(x) \frac{\delta^{(1)}_{ji}}{h} + (\phi'(x))^2 \frac{\delta^{(2)}_{ji}}{h^2} \right] \quad (22)$$
$$- \sum_{k=0}^{n} \sum_{j=-N}^{j=N} \lambda_k c^{n+1-k}_j \delta^{(0)}_{ji} + \tau^\alpha f^{n+1}_i.$$

A diagonal matrix of order $2N+1$ is defined as follows

$$D(g(x))_{ij} = \begin{cases} g(x_i), & i = j \\ 0, & i \neq j. \end{cases} \quad (23)$$

Multiplying both sides of the above equation by $\frac{1}{(\phi'(x))^2}$, we get

$$\frac{1}{(\phi'(x_i))^2} c_i^{n+1} - \left(\tau^\alpha + \tau^{\alpha-1} B_{n,n}\right) \sum_{j=-N}^{N} c_j^{n+1} \left[\frac{-\phi''(x_i)}{(\phi'(x_i))^2} \frac{\delta_{ij}^{(1)}}{h} + \frac{\delta_{ij}^{(2)}}{h^2}\right]$$
$$= \tau^{\alpha-1} \sum_{l=0}^{n} \sum_{j=-N}^{N} \rho_{n,l} c_j^l \left[\frac{-\phi''(x_i)}{(\phi'(x_i))^2} \frac{\delta_{ij}^{(1)}}{h} + \frac{\delta_{ij}^{(2)}}{h^2}\right] + \frac{1}{(\phi'(x_i))^2} \sum_{k=0}^{n} c_i^k + \frac{\tau^\alpha}{(\phi'(x_i))^2} f_i^{n+1}. \quad (24)$$

Writing the above equation (24) in matrix form as

$$D\left[\left(\frac{1}{\phi'}\right)^2\right] C^{n+1} - \left(\tau^\alpha + \tau^{\alpha-1} B_{n,n}\right) \left[\frac{1}{h} D\left(\frac{1}{\phi'}\right)' I^{(1)} + \frac{1}{h^2} I^{(2)}\right] C^{n+1}$$
$$= \tau^\alpha D\left[\left(\frac{1}{\phi'}\right)^2\right] F^{n+1} + D\left[\left(\frac{1}{\phi'}\right)^2\right] (C^n + C^{n-1} + \ldots + C^1 + C^0) \quad (25)$$
$$+ \tau^{\alpha-1} \sum_{l=0}^{n} \rho_{n,l} \left[\frac{1}{h} D\left(\frac{1}{\phi'}\right)' I^{(1)} + \frac{1}{h^2} I^{(2)}\right] C^l,$$

or in a compact form as

$$PC^{n+1} = R\left(\tau^\alpha F^{n+1} + \sum_{m=0}^{n} C^m\right) + \tau^{\alpha-1} \sum_{l=0}^{n} \rho_{n,l} Q C^l, \quad (26)$$

where

$$R = D\left[\left(\frac{1}{\phi'}\right)^2\right],$$
$$Q = \frac{1}{h} D\left(\frac{1}{\phi'}\right)' I^{(1)} + \frac{1}{h^2} I^{(2)}, \quad (27)$$
$$C^{n+1} = (c_{-N}^{n+1}, c_{-N+1}^{n+1}, \ldots, c_N^{n+1})^T,$$
$$F^{n+1} = (f_{-N}^{n+1}, f_{-N+1}^{n+1}, \ldots, f_N^{n+1})^T,$$
$$P = R - B_{n,n} Q.$$

If we set

$$G^{n+1} = R\left(\tau^\alpha F^{n+1} + \sum_{m=0}^{n} C^m\right) + \tau^{\alpha-1} \sum_{l=0}^{n} \rho_{n,l} Q C^l,$$

then Equation (26) can be written as follows:

$$PC^{n+1} = G^{n+1}, \quad (28)$$

with the additional initial condition

$$C^0 = (V_0(x_{-N}), V_0(x_{-N+1}), \ldots, V_0(x_N))^T.$$

For each n, Formula (28) is a system of $2N+1$ order linear equations including $2N+1$ equations. By solving this system of linear equations, the coefficients of the numerical solutions (20) can be obtained.

4. Convergence Analysis

In this section, we aim to analyze the convergence of the semidiscrete Equation (19) for the FPIEs (1)–(3).

For the sake of convenience, the semidiscrete Equation (19) can be rewritten as

$$\lambda_0 v^{n+1}(x) - \left(\tau^\alpha + \tau^{\alpha-1} B_{n,n}\right) v_{xx}^{n+1}(x) = g(x), \tag{29}$$

where

$$g(x) = \tau^{\alpha-1} \sum_{l=0}^{n} \rho_{n,l} v_{xx}^l(x) - \sum_{k=0}^{n} \lambda_k v^{n+1-k}(x) + \tau^\alpha f^{n+1}(x).$$

The numerical solution $W_m^{n+1}(x)$ of Equation (29) at the point x_j can be obtained by

$$W_m^{n+1}(x) = \sum_{j=-N}^{N} v^{n+1}(x_j) S_j(x), \tag{30}$$

To obtain the bound of $|V^{n+1}(x) - V_m^{n+1}(x)|$, we can start by estimating the boundary of $|V_m^{n+1}(x) - W_m^{n+1}(x)|$.

Lemma 5 ([51]). *For $x \in \phi^{-1}$ and the matrix P defined by Equation (27), we have*

$$\frac{P + P^*}{2} = H - \frac{B_{n,n}}{h^2} I^{(2)},$$

where P^* is the conjugate transpose of P and

$$H = D\left[\operatorname{Re}\left(\left(\frac{1}{\phi'}\right)^2\right)\right] - \frac{B_{n,n}}{2h}\left\{D\left[\left(\frac{1}{\phi'}\right)'\right]I^{(1)} - I^{(1)} D\left[\left(\overline{\frac{1}{\phi'}}\right)'\right]\right\}.$$

If the eigenvalues of the matrix H are non-negative, then there exists a constant c_0 that doesn't depend on N, such that

$$\|P^{-1}\|_2 \leq \frac{4dN}{\beta\pi B_{n,n}}\left(1 + \frac{C_0}{N}\right),$$

for a sufficiently large N.

Theorem 1. *Suppose $V_m^{n+1}(x)$ is an approximate solution of Equation (19), W_m^{n+1} is an approximate solution of Equation (1). Then, there exists a constant C_4 that doesn't depend on N, such that*

$$\sup_{x \in [a,b]} |V_m^{n+1}(x) - W_m^{n+1}(x)| \leq C_4 N^3 e^{-\sqrt{\pi d \beta N}}.$$

Proof. By Equations (20) and (30) and the Cauchy–Schwarz inequality, we gain

$$\begin{aligned}
|V_m^{n+1}(x) - W_m^{n+1}(x)| &= \left|\sum_{j=-N}^{N} c_j^{n+1} S_j(x) - \sum_{j=-N}^{N} v^{n+1}(x_j) S_j(x)\right| \\
&\leq \left(\sum_{j=-N}^{N} |c_j^{n+1} - v^{n+1}(x_j)|^2\right)^{\frac{1}{2}} \left(\sum_{j=-N}^{N} |S_j(x)|^2\right)^{\frac{1}{2}}.
\end{aligned} \tag{31}$$

Since $\left(\sum_{j=-N}^{N} |S_j(x)|^2\right)^{\frac{1}{2}} \leq C_1$, where C_1 is a constant independent of N, we obtain

$$|V_m^{n+1}(x) - W_m^{n+1}(x)| \leq C_1 \|C^{n+1} - U^{n+1}\|_2, \tag{32}$$

where C^{n+1} is given by (27) and denoting the vector V^{n+1} by

$$U^{n+1} = \left(v^{n+1}(x_{-N}), v^{n+1}(x_{-N+1}), \cdots, v^{n+1}(x_N)\right)^{\mathrm{T}}.$$

Based on (19) and (28), we have

$$\|C^{n+1} - U^{n+1}\|_2 = \|P^{-1}(PC^{n+1} - PU^{n+1})\|_2 \leq \|P^{-1}\|_2 \|PU^{n+1} - G^{n+1}\|_2. \quad (33)$$

For simplicity, we denote

$$r_k = \left(PU^{n+1} - G^{n+1}\right)_k, \qquad k = -N, \cdots, N,$$

and using Equation (29), we obtain

$$|r_k| = |g(x_k) - g_m(x_k)|$$
$$= \left| v^{n+1}(x_k) - \left(\tau^\alpha + \tau^{\alpha-1} B_{n,n}\right) \frac{d^2}{dx^2} v^{n+1}(x_k) - V_m^{n+1}(x_k) + \left(\tau^\alpha + \tau^{\alpha-1} B_{n,n}\right) \frac{d^2}{dx^2} V_m^{n+1}(x_k) \right| \quad (34)$$
$$\leq |v^{n+1}(x_k) - V_m^{n+1}(x_k)| + B_{n,n} \left| \frac{d^2}{dx^2} v^{n+1}(x_k) - \frac{d^2}{dx^2} V_m^{n+1}(x_k) \right|.$$

Now, using Theorem 1, we have

$$\|r_k\| \leq C_2 N^{\frac{1}{2}} e^{-\sqrt{\pi d \beta N}} + B_{n,n} C_3 N^{\frac{3}{2}} e^{-\sqrt{\pi d \beta N}}$$
$$\leq e^{-\sqrt{\pi d \beta N}} \left(C_2 N^{\frac{3}{2}} + B_{n,n} C_3 N^{\frac{3}{2}}\right) \quad (35)$$
$$= K N^{\frac{3}{2}} e^{-\sqrt{\pi d \beta N}},$$

where C_2 and C_3 are constants independent of N and $K = C_2 + B_{n,n} C_3$.

$$\|PU^{n+1} - G^{n+1}\|_2 \leq \sqrt{2N+1} \|PU^{n+1} - G^{n+1}\|_\infty,$$

and using inequality (35), we get

$$\|PU^{n+1} - G^{n+1}\|_2 \leq \sqrt{2} K N^2 e^{-\sqrt{\pi d \beta N}}. \quad (36)$$

Now, substituting (36) into (33), we have

$$\|C^{n+1} - U^{n+1}\|_2 \leq \frac{4\sqrt{2} dK(1 + C_0)}{\alpha \pi B_{n,n}} N^3 e^{-\sqrt{\pi d \beta N}}. \quad (37)$$

Based on (32) and (37), we get

$$\sup_{x \in [a,b]} |V_m^{n+1}(x) - W_m^{n+1}(x)| \leq C_4 N^3 e^{-\sqrt{\pi d \beta N}}, \quad (38)$$

where $C_4 = \dfrac{4\sqrt{2} dK(1 + C_0)}{\alpha \pi B_{n,n}}$. □

Theorem 2. *Suppose $V^{n+1}(x)$ be the analytical solution of (29), $V_m^{n+1}(x)$ be its Sinc approximation defined by (20). Then, there exists a constant C_7 that doesn't depend on N, such that*

$$\sup_{x \in [a,b]} |V^{n+1}(x) - V_m^{n+1}(x)| \leq C_7 N^3 e^{-\sqrt{\pi d \beta N}}.$$

Proof. Using the triangular inequality, we get

$$|V^{n+1}(x) - V_m^{n+1}(x)| \leq |V^{n+1}(x) - W_m^{n+1}(x)| + |W_m^{n+1}(x) - V_m^{n+1}(x)|. \quad (39)$$

Using Theorem 1, we can get

$$|V^{n+1}(x) - W_m^{n+1}(x)| \leq C_5 N^3 e^{-\sqrt{\pi d \beta N}}. \tag{40}$$

where C_5 is a constant independent of N. Based on Theorem 2, there exists a constant C_6 that does not depend on N such that

$$|W_m^{n+1}(x) - V_m^{n+1}(x)| \leq C_6 N^3 e^{-\sqrt{\pi d \beta N}}, \tag{41}$$

Finally, we conclude

$$\sup_{x \in [a,b]} |V^{n+1}(x) - V_m^{n+1}(x)| \leq C_7 N^3 e^{-\sqrt{\pi d \beta N}}, \tag{42}$$

where $C_7 = \max\{C_5, C_6\}$. □

5. Numerical Results

In this section, some numerical calculations are performed to demonstrate the validity and accuracy of our method. In numerical examples, we set parameters $d = \frac{\pi}{2}$ and $\beta = 1$ and then $h = \frac{\pi}{\sqrt{2N}}$. All numerical computations are carried out using Matlab 7.14 running on a Lenovo PC (Lenovo, Quarry Bay, Hong Kong) with a 1.6 GHz Intel Core i5-4200 CPU (Intel Corporation, Santa Clara, CA, USA) and 4 GB RAM installed.

To illustrate the accuracy of our method, the error analysis is calculated according to the maximum norm errors, defined as:

$$e_\infty(h, \tau) = \max_{0 \leq n \leq N} \|V^n - v^n\|_\infty.$$

Furthermore, the temporal convergence order can be expressed by

$$rate_1 = \log_2 \left(\frac{e_\infty(h, 2\tau)}{e_\infty(h, \tau)} \right).$$

Example 1. *We consider Equations (1)–(3) with the analytical solution*

$$v(x, t) = t^2 x(x - 1),$$

where $0 < x < 1$, $0 < t < 1$ and

$$f(x, t) = \frac{2}{\Gamma(3 - \alpha)} x(x - 1) t^{2-\alpha} - 2t^2 - \frac{4\Gamma(1/2)}{\Gamma(7/2)} t^{\frac{5}{2}}.$$

Table 1 represents the maximum norm errors and the temporal convergence order for $N = 32$ and $\alpha = 0.1, 0.3, 0.5, 0.7$ with different values of time step size. Table 2 shows a comparative study for the presented method and the method in [19]. It can be observed from the table that the numerical results are better than the method in [19]. The maximum norm errors for $\alpha = 0.8$ and $\tau = \frac{1}{1000}$ with different values of N are plotted in Figure 1. At the same time, it is clear from the figure that the presented scheme converges at an exponential rate as N increases. From these diagrams, it can be seen that the results are in excellent agreement with the theoretical analysis.

Table 1. The maximum norm errors and temporal convergence orders with $N = 32$.

α	τ	$e_\infty(h,\tau)$	$Rate_1$
0.1	1/10	2.71422×10^{-4}	*
	1/20	6.89322×10^{-5}	1.97729
	1/40	1.74371×10^{-5}	1.98507
	1/80	4.40355×10^{-6}	1.98542
0.3	1/10	2.71798×10^{-4}	*
	1/20	6.90718×10^{-5}	1.97637
	1/40	1.74383×10^{-5}	1.98584
	1/80	4.41692×10^{-6}	1.98115
0.5	1/10	2.78117×10^{-4}	*
	1/20	7.06728×10^{-5}	1.97647
	1/40	1.78836×10^{-5}	1.98252
	1/80	4.51750×10^{-6}	1.98504
0.7	1/10	2.90936×10^{-4}	*
	1/20	7.37990×10^{-5}	1.97903
	1/40	1.86602×10^{-5}	1.98365
	1/80	4.71342×10^{-6}	1.98512

The asterisk (*) symbol indicates that the temporal convergence order cannot be calculated.

Table 2. Comparison of the maximum norm errors and temporal convergence orders with $N = 100$.

α	τ	$e_\infty(h,\tau)$	$Rate_1$	$e_\infty(h,\tau)$ [19]	$Rate_1$ [19]
0.6	1/10	2.7821×10^{-4}	*	2.4541×10^{-4}	*
	1/20	7.0565×10^{-5}	1.9791	9.4738×10^{-5}	1.3732
	1/40	1.7991×10^{-5}	1.9717	3.8919×10^{-5}	1.2835
	1/80	4.5933×10^{-6}	1.9696	1.6656×10^{-5}	1.2244
	1/160	1.1502×10^{-6}	1.9976	7.3463×10^{-6}	1.1810
	1/320	2.8781×10^{-7}	1.9987	3.3191×10^{-6}	1.1462

The asterisk (*) symbol indicates that the temporal convergence order cannot be calculated.

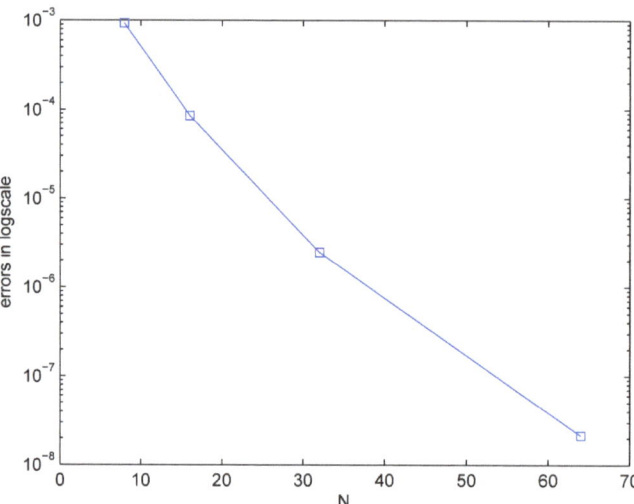

Figure 1. The maximum norm errors with $\alpha = 0.8$ and $\tau = \frac{1}{1000}$.

Example 2. *We consider Equations (1)–(3) with the analytical solution*

$$v(x,t) = t\sin(\pi x),$$

where $0 < x < pi, 0 < t < 1$ and

$$f(x,t) = \sin(\pi x)\left(\frac{1}{\Gamma(2-\alpha)}t^{1-\alpha} + \pi^2 t + \frac{4}{3}\pi^2 t^{\frac{3}{2}}\right).$$

Table 3 represents the maximum norm errors and the temporal convergence order for $N = 128$ and $\alpha = 0.2, 0.4, 0.6, 0.8$ with different values of time step size. The maximum norm errors for $\alpha = 0.4$ and $\tau = \frac{1}{512}$ with different values of N are plotted in Figure 2. The figure also shows that our presented scheme converges at an exponential rate as N increases. Figure 3 depicts the graph of the numerical solution and the exact solution with $\alpha = 0.5, \tau = \frac{1}{512}$ and $N = 64$. These figures confirm that the proposed method solution is in good agreement with the exact solution.

Table 3. The maximum norm errors and temporal convergence orders with $N = 128$.

α	τ	$e_\infty(h, \tau)$	$Rate_1$
0.2	1/10	1.4168×10^{-6}	*
	1/20	3.5892×10^{-7}	1.9809
	1/40	9.0501×10^{-8}	1.9877
	1/80	2.2729×10^{-8}	1.9934
0.4	1/10	6.0618×10^{-6}	*
	1/20	1.5345×10^{-6}	1.9819
	1/40	3.8691×10^{-7}	1.9877
	1/80	9.7218×10^{-8}	1.9918
0.6	1/10	2.1210×10^{-5}	*
	1/20	5.3633×10^{-6}	1.9836
	1/40	1.3508×10^{-6}	1.9894
	1/80	3.3889×10^{-7}	1.9949
0.8	1/10	6.8883×10^{-5}	*
	1/20	1.7426×10^{-5}	1.9829
	1/40	4.3913×10^{-6}	1.9885
	1/80	1.1017×10^{-6}	1.9949

The asterisk (∗) symbol indicates that the temporal convergence order cannot be calculated.

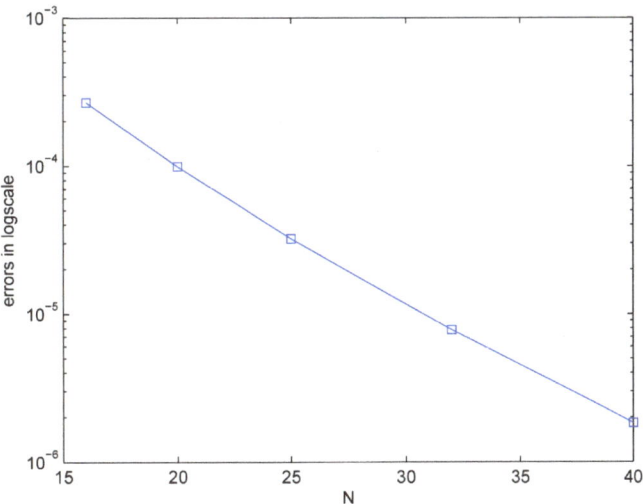

Figure 2. The maximum norm errors with $\alpha = 0.4$ and $\tau = \frac{1}{512}$.

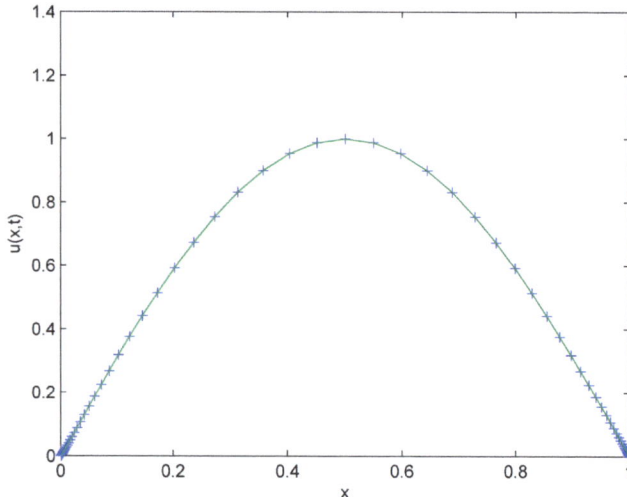

Figure 3. Numerical solution and analytical solution with $\alpha = 0.5$, $\tau = \frac{1}{512}$ and $N = 64$.

6. Conclusions

In the present article, we have presented and analyzed an efficient numerical algorithm for solving FPIEs with a weakly singular kernel. In this technique, the WSGD operator is applied for discretization of the time fractional derivative and the Sinc collocation method is used for discretization of the space derivative. Convergence analysis of our scheme is theoretically proven, and it is shown that the numerical solution converges to the exact solution at the exponential rate in space. Numerical experiments were provided to verify the theoretical results. In the future, we intend to extend the method for solving the higher space dimension equation, which is straightforward, in view of the potential applications.

Author Contributions: Conceptualization, M.L. and L.C.; methodology, M.L. and L.C.; validation, L.C. and Y.Z.; writing—original draft preparation, M.L. and Y.Z.; writing—review and editing, M.L. and Y.Z.; funding acquisition, M.L. and L.C. All authors have read and agreed to the published version of the manuscript.

Funding: This research was supported by the Natural Science Foundation of Shandong Province under Grant ZR2022MA063 and the National Natural Science Foundation of China under Grant 12101037.

Data Availability Statement: Not applicable.

Conflicts of Interest: The authors declare no conflict of interest.

References

1. Hilfer, R. *Applications of Fractional Calculus in Physics*; World Scientific: Singapore, 2000.
2. Podlubny, I. *Fractional Differential Equations*; Academic Press: San Diego, CA, USA, 1999.
3. Povstenko, Y. *Fractional Thermoelasticity*; Springer: New York, NY, USA, 2015.
4. Cheng, X.; Duan, J.; Li, D. A novel compact ADI scheme for two-dimensional Riesz space fractional nonlinear reaction-diffusion equations. *Appl. Math. Comput.* **2019**, *346*, 452–464. [CrossRef]
5. Yousuf, M.; Furati, K. M.; Khaliq, AQM. High-order time-stepping methods for two-dimensional Riesz fractional nonlinear reaction-diffusion equations. *Comput. Math. Appl.* **2020**, *80*, 204–226. [CrossRef]
6. Yousuf, M. A second-order efficient L-stable numerical method for space fractional reaction-diffusion equations. *Int. J. Comput. Math* **2018**, *95*, 1408–1422. [CrossRef]
7. El-Danaf, T.S.; Hadhoud, A.R. Parametric spline functions for the solution of the one time fractional Burgers' equation. *Appl. Math. Model.* **2012**, *36*, 4557–4564. [CrossRef]
8. El-Danaf, T.S.; Hadhoud, A.R. Computational method for solving space fractional Fisher's nonlinear equation. *Math. Methods Appl. Sci.* **2014**, *37*, 657–662. [CrossRef]

9. Panda, R.; Dash, M. Fractional generalized splines and signal processing. *Signal Process.* **2006**, *86*, 2340–2350. [CrossRef]
10. Torvik, P.J.; Bagley, R.L. On the appearance of the fractional derivative in the behavior of real materials. *J. Appl. Mech.* **1984**, *51*, 294–298. [CrossRef]
11. Giona, M.; Cerbelli, S.; Roman, H.E. Fractional diffusion equation and relaxation in complex viscoelastic material. *Phys. A* **1992**, *191*, 449–453. [CrossRef]
12. Jiang, X.; Xu, M.; Qi, H. The fractional diffusion model with an absorption term and modified Fick's law for non-local transport processes. *Nonlinear Anal.* **2010**, *11*, 262–269. [CrossRef]
13. Monami, S.; Odibat, Z. Analytical approach to linear fractional partial differential equations arising in fluid mechanics. *Phys. Lett. A* **2006**, *355*, 271–279.
14. He, J.H. Some applications of nonlinear fractional differential equations and their approximations. *Bull. Sci. Technol.* **1999**, *15*, 86–90.
15. Chow, T. Fractional dynamics of interfaces between soft-nanoparticles and rough substrates. *Phys. Lett.* **2005**, *342*, 148–155. [CrossRef]
16. Yildirim, A.; Sezer, S.A.; Kaplan. Y. Numerical methods for fourth-order fractional integro-differential equations. *Z. Naturforsch. A* **2011**, *65*, 1027–1032. [CrossRef]
17. Abbasbandy, S.; Hashemi, M.S.; Hashim, I. On convergence of homotopy analysis method and its application to fractional integro-differetnial equations. *Quaest. Math.* **2013**, *36*, 93–105. [CrossRef]
18. Ma, X.; Huang, C. Spectral collocation method for linear fractional integro-differetnial equations. *Appl. Math. Model.* **2014**, *38*, 1434–1448. [CrossRef]
19. Mohebbi, A. Compact finite difference shceme for the solution of a time fractional partial integro-differential equation with a weakly singular kernel. *Math. Methods Appl. Sci.* **2017**, *40*, 7627–7639. [CrossRef]
20. Qiao, L.; Xu, D.; Wang, Z. An ADI difference scheme based on fractional trapezoidal rule for fractional integro-differential equation with a weakly singular kernel. *Appl. Math. Comput.* **2019**, *354*, 103–114. [CrossRef]
21. Nemati, S.; Lima, P.M.; Sedaghat, S. Legendre wavelet collocation method combined with the Gauss-Jacobi quadrature for solving fractional delay-type integro-differential equations. *Appl. Numer. Math.* **2020**, *149*, 99–112. [CrossRef]
22. Dehestani, H.; Ordokhani, Y.; Razzaghi, M. Pseudo-operational matrix method for the solution of variable-order fractional partial integro-differential equation. *Eng. Comput.* **2021**, *37*, 1791–1806. [CrossRef]
23. Kamran, K.; Shah, Z.; Kumam, P.; Alreshidi, N.A. A meshless method based on the Laplace transform for the 2D multi-term time fractional partial integro-differential equation. *Mathematics* **2020**, *8*, 1972. [CrossRef]
24. Dehghan, M.; Abbaszadeh, M. Error estimate of finite element/finite difference technique for solution of two-dimensional weakly singular integro-partial differential equation with space and time fractional derivative. *Appl. Numer. Math.* **2019**, *356*, 314–328. [CrossRef]
25. Fakhar-Izadi, F. Fully spectral-Galerkin method for the one and two dimensional fourth order time factional partial integro-differential equaitons with a weakly singular kernel. *J. Numer. Methods Partial Differ. Equ.* **2022**, *38*, 160–176. [CrossRef]
26. Panda, A.; Santra, S.; Mohapatra, J. Adomian decomposition and homotopy perturbation method for the solution of time fractional partial integro-differential equations. *J. Appl. Math. Comput.* **2022**, *68*, 2065–2082. [CrossRef]
27. Liu, T.; Ouyang, D.; Guo, L.; Qiu, R.; Qi, Y.; Xie, W.; Ma, Q.; Liu, C. Combination of multigrid with constraint data for inverse problem of nonlinear diffusion equation. *Mathematics* **2023**, *11*, 2887. [CrossRef]
28. Liu, T. Parameter estimation with the multigrid-homotopy method for a nonlinear diffusion equation. *J. Comput. Appl. Math.* **2022**, *413*, 114393. [CrossRef]
29. Liu, T. Porosity reconstruction based on Biot elastic model of porous media by homotopy perturbation method. *Chaos Solitons Fractals* **2022**, *158*, 112007. [CrossRef]
30. Liu, T.; Ding, Z.; Yu, J.; Zhang, W. Parameter estimation for nonlinear diffusion problems by the constrained homotopy method. *Mathematics* **2023**, *11*, 2642. [CrossRef]
31. Liu, T.; Xia, K.; Zheng, Y.; Yang, Y.; Qiu, R.; Qi, Y.; Liu, C. A homotopy method for the constrained inverse problem in the multiphase porous media flow. *Processes* **2022**, *10*, 1143. [CrossRef]
32. Tuan, V.K. Fractional partial integro-differential equation in wiener spaces. *Fract. Calc. Appl. Anal.* **2020**, *23*, 1300–1328. [CrossRef]
33. Zhu, B.; Han, B.Y. Existence and uniqueness of mild solutions for fractional partial integro-differential equations. *Mediterr. J. Math.* **2020**, *17*, 113. [CrossRef]
34. Maji. S.; Natesan. S. Analytical and numerical solution techniques for a class of time-fractional integro-partial differential equations. *Numer. Algorithms* **2023**, *94*, 229–256. [CrossRef]
35. Stenger, B.F. Numerical methods based on the Whittaker cardinal or Sinc functions. *SIAM Rev.* **1981**, *23*, 165–224. [CrossRef]
36. Stenger, B.F. Sinc Methods for Quadrature and Differential Equations. *SIAM Rev.* **1993**, *35*, 682–683. [CrossRef]
37. Stenger, B.F. *Numerical Methods Based on Sinc and Analytic Functions*; Springer: New York, NY, USA, 1993.
38. Rashidinia, J.; Nabati, M.; Barati, A. Sinc-Galerkin method for solving nonlinear weakly singular two point boundary value problems. *Int. J. Comput. Math.* **2017**, *94*, 79–94. [CrossRef]
39. Parand, K.; Dehghan, M.; Pirkhedri, A. Sinc-collocation method for solving the Blasius equation. *Phys. Lett. A* **2009**, *373*, 4060–4065. [CrossRef]

40. Winter, D.F.; Bowers. K.; Lund. J. Wind-driven currents in a sea with a variable Eddy viscosity calculated via a Sinc–Galerkin technique. *Int. J. Numer. Methods Fluids* **2000**, *33*, 1041–1073. [CrossRef]
41. Qiu, W.; Xu, D.; Guo, J. The Crank-Nicolson-type Sinc-Galerkin method for the fourth-order partial integro-differential equation with a weakly singular kernel. *Appl. Numer. Math.* **2021**, *159*, 239–258. [CrossRef]
42. Okayama, K. Theoretical analysis of a Sinc-Nyström method for Volterra integro-differential equations and its improvement. *Appl. Math. Comput.* **2018**, *324*, 1–15. [CrossRef]
43. AI-Khaled, K.; Darweesh, A.; Yousef, M.H. Covergence of numerical scheme for the solution of partial integro-differential equations used in heat transfer. *J. Appl. Math. Comput.* **2019**, *61*, 657–675. [CrossRef]
44. Nagy, A.M. Numerical solution of time fractional nonlinear Klein–Gordon equation using Sinc-Chebyshev collocation method. *Appl. Math. Comput.* **2017**, *310*, 139–148. [CrossRef]
45. Saadatmandi, A.; Dehghan, M.; Azizi, M. The Sinc-Legendre collocation method for a class of fractional convection-diffusion equations with variable coefficients. *Commun. Nonlinear Sci. Numer. Simul.* **2012**, *17*, 4125–4136. [CrossRef]
46. Pirkhedri, A.; Javadi, H.H.S. Solving the time-fractional diffusion equation via Sinc-Haar collocation method. *Appl. Math. Comput.* **2015**, *257*, 317–326. [CrossRef]
47. Chen, L.; Li, M.; Xu, Q. Sinc-Galerkin method for solving the time fractional convection–diffusion equation with variable coefficients. *Adv. Differ. Equ.* **2020**, *2020*, 504. [CrossRef]
48. Lund, J.; Bowers, K. *Sinc Method for Quadrature and Differential Equations*; SIAM: Philadelphia, PA, USA, 1992.
49. Meerschaert, M.M.; Tadjeran, C. Finite difference approxiamtions for fractional advection dispersion flow equations. *J. Comput. Appl. Math.* **2004**, *172*, 65–77. [CrossRef]
50. Tian, W.Y.; Zhou, H.; Deng, W.H. A class of second order difference approximations for solving space fractional diffusion equations. *Math. Comput.* **2015**, *84*, 1703–1727. [CrossRef]
51. Fahim, A.; Araghi, M.A.F.; Rashidinia, J.; Jalalvand, M. Numerical solution of Volterra paritial integro-differential equations based on Sinc-collocation method. *Adv. Differ. Equ.* **2017**, *2017*, 362. [CrossRef]

Disclaimer/Publisher's Note: The statements, opinions and data contained in all publications are solely those of the individual author(s) and contributor(s) and not of MDPI and/or the editor(s). MDPI and/or the editor(s) disclaim responsibility for any injury to people or property resulting from any ideas, methods, instructions or products referred to in the content.

Article

Asymptotical Stability Criteria for Exact Solutions and Numerical Solutions of Nonlinear Impulsive Neutral Delay Differential Equations

Gui-Lai Zhang *, Zhi-Wei Wang, Yang Sun and Tao Liu

College of Sciences, Northeastern University, Shenyang 110819, China; 2172045@stu.neu.edu.cn (Z.-W.W.); 2101906@stu.neu.edu.cn (Y.S.); liutao@neuq.edu.cn (T.L.)
* Correspondence: zhangguilai@neuq.edu.cn

Abstract: In this paper, the idea of two transformations is first proposed and applied. Some new different sufficient conditions for the asymptotical stability of the exact solutions of nonlinear impulsive neutral delay differential equations (INDDEs) are obtained. A new numerical scheme for INDDEs is also constructed based on the idea. The numerical methods that can preserve the stability and asymptotical stability of the exact solutions are provided. Two numerical examples are provided to demonstrate the theoretical results.

Keywords: Runge–Kutta method; BN_f-stable; implicit Euler method; Lobatto IIIC method

MSC: 65L03; 65L05; 65L20

Citation: Zhang, G.-L.; Wang, Z.-W.; Sun, Y.; Liu, T. Asymptotical Stability Criteria for Exact Solutions and Numerical Solutions of Nonlinear Impulsive Neutral Delay Differential Equations. *Axioms* **2023**, *12*, 988. https://doi.org/10.3390/axioms12100988

Academic Editor: Clemente Cesarano

Received: 30 August 2023
Revised: 11 October 2023
Accepted: 13 October 2023
Published: 18 October 2023

Copyright: © 2023 by the authors. Licensee MDPI, Basel, Switzerland. This article is an open access article distributed under the terms and conditions of the Creative Commons Attribution (CC BY) license (https:// creativecommons.org/licenses/by/ 4.0/).

1. Introduction

There is extensive use of impulsive differential equations in economics, engineering, biology, medicine, etc. In recent years, the theory of INDDEs has been the object of active research. Some scholars have investigated the existence, uniqueness, and continuous dependence of INDDEs (see [1,2]) and the oscillation of the first-order, second-order, and even-order of INDDEs (see [3–5]). In [6], the thermoelasticity of type III for Cosserat media has been studied. In [7], the asymptotic properties of the solutions of nonlinear, non-instantaneous impulsive differential equations has been studied. In [8], the Legendre spectral-collocation method is applied to delay the differential and stochastic delay differential equation. In [9], the convergence and superconvergence of collocation methods for one class of impulsive delay differential equations have been studied, respectively.

However, there are not many studies on the stability of INDDEs. In [10], the asymptotic behavior of some special nonlinear INDDEs were considered by establishing proper Lyapunov functions and certain analysis techniques. In [11], some results ensuring the global exponential stability of impulsive functional equations of neutral type were derived via impulsive delay inequality and certain analysis techniques that are very popular in the application of the dynamical analysis of neural networks. In [3], the authors developed the Razumikhin method for impulsive functional differential equations of neutral type and established some Razumikhin theorems. Recently, we found that there are errors in [12] (Stability of zero solution of linear INDDE with constant coefficients is studied, but zero is not the solution of the linear INDDE in [12]). All the above studies focus on the asymptotic stability of zero solutions, but in this paper we will study the stability of the exact solutions (not necessarily zero solutions) of INDDEs.

Usually, as is well known, it is difficult, sometime maybe impossible, to acquire the explicit solutions for INDDEs, so it is necessary to investigate the numerical methods for INDDEs. Numerical stability refers to the degree to which small perturbations of input data affect the output results of the algorithm when solving numerical problems using an algorithm. A numerically stable algorithm can produce accurate results that are not affected by input perturbations, while a numerically unstable algorithm may produce unpredictable results. Hence, it is necessary to investigate the asymptotical stability of numerical methods for INDDEs.

The stability of the exact solutions and the numerical solutions for NDDEs without impulsive perturbations has also been extensively studied (see [13–27]). There are many classic results found in the literature [14,21,22,28]. Recently, some new and important related developments have emerged. In papers [17–20], Guang-Da Hu and Taketomo Mitsui et al. studied the asymptotical stability of the exact solutions and the numerical solutions of linear NDDEs in real space and complex space, respectively. In [27], Wang and Li studied the stability and asymptotic stability of θ-methods for nonlinear NDDEs with constant delay and with proportional delay. In [15], Enright and Hayashi established sufficient conditions for order of convergence results regarding continuous Runge–Kutta methods for NDDEs with state dependent delays. Zhang, Song, and Liu have studied the asymptotic stability of linear impulsive delay differential equations (IDDEs) (see [29]); the exponential stability of linear IDDEs (see [30]); and the stability and asymptotical stability of nonlinear IDDEs (see [31]. Based on their ideas, the problems of IDDEs are transformed into the problems of delay differential equations without impulsive perturbations. In this paper, this idea is applied to INDDEs for the first time, and to the best of our knowledge no article has previously been written regarding the stability of numerical methods for INDDEs.

The goal of this paper is to provide new different asymptotical stability criteria for exact solutions and numerical solutions of a class of nonlinear impulsive neutral differential equations (INDDEs). We will adopt the idea of two transformations to achieve our goal; the problems of the stability and asymptotical stability of INDDEs are first transformed into the problems of NDDEs without impulsive perturbations, and then transformed into the problems of ordinary differential equations with a forcing term. The organization of this paper is as follows. In Section 2, we first transform the problems of the stability and asymptotical stability of INDDEs into the problems of NDDEs without impulsive perturbations, and we then further transform them into the problems of ordinary different equations with a forcing term. On this basis, two general forms of criteria for the stability and asymptotical of INDDEs are established. Furthermore, when different transforms are chosen, different criterion for the stability and asymptotical stability can be obtained. For brevity, three different transforms are provided to achieve some specific different criteria for stability and asymptotical stability. In Section 3, based on the ideas in Section 2, we will derive the numerical methods of INDDEs, which can preserve the stability and asymptotical stability of the nonlinear INDDEs if corresponding continuous Runge–Kutta methods are BN_f-stable. In Section 4, one linear numerical example and one nonlinear numerical example are chosen to demonstrate the theoretical results.

2. Asymptotical Stability of the Exact Solutions

Firstly, the relationships between INDDEs and NDDEs are constructed in Section 2.1. Based on this idea, the general sufficient conditions for the asymptotical stability of the exact solutions of INDDEs are established in Section 2.2. Finally, the different special relationships between INDDEs and NDDEs are studied, and different sufficient conditions for the asymptotical stability of INDDEs are obtained in Section 2.3.

In this article, we will study the following nonlinear INDDEs:

$$\begin{cases} \frac{d}{dt}(x(t) - G(t, x(t-\tau))) = F(t, x(t), x(t-\tau)), & t \geq 0,\ t \neq k\tau, \\ x(t) = \lambda x(t^-), & t = k\tau, \\ x(t) = \psi(t), & t \in [-\tau, 0), \end{cases} \quad (1)$$

and the same equation with another initial function:

$$\begin{cases} \frac{d}{dt}(\tilde{x}(t) - G(t, \tilde{x}(t-\tau))) = F(t, \tilde{x}(t), \tilde{x}(t-\tau)), & t \geq 0, \ t \neq k\tau, \\ \tilde{x}(t) = \lambda \tilde{x}(t^-), & t = k\tau, \\ \tilde{x}(t) = \tilde{\psi}(t), & t \in [-\tau, 0), \end{cases} \quad (2)$$

where $\tau > 0$, $\lambda \neq 0$, $\lambda \neq 1$, $k \in \mathbb{N} = \{0, 1, 2, \cdots\}$, ψ and $\tilde{\psi}$ are continuous functions on $[-\tau, 0)$, and $\lim_{t \to 0^-} \psi(t)$ and $\lim_{t \to 0^-} \tilde{\psi}(t)$ exist. The right-hand derivative of $x(t)$ is written as $x'(t)$. Assume that $\langle \cdot, \cdot \rangle$ is a given inner product on $\mathbb{C}^d$ and $\|\cdot\|$ is the induced norm. Assume that the function $F : [0, \infty) \times \mathbb{C}^d \times \mathbb{C}^d \to \mathbb{C}^d$ is continuous in t and fulfills the following conditions: for arbitrary $x, x_1, x_2, y_1, y_2 \in \mathbb{C}^d$ and arbitrary $t \in [0, +\infty)$, there are real value functions X, Y from $[0, +\infty)$ to $\mathbb{R}$, such that

$$Y(t) \geq \sup_{y_1 \neq y_2, x} \frac{\Re(\langle H(t, y_1, x) - H(t, y_2, x), y_1 - y_2 \rangle)}{\|y_1 - y_2\|^2} \quad (3)$$

$$X(t) \geq \sup_{y, x_1 \neq x_2} \frac{\|H(t, y, x_1) - H(t, y, x_2)\|}{\|x_1 - x_2\|}, \quad (4)$$

where $H(t, y, x) = F(t, y + G(t, x), x)$, which is the same as that in [14]. Assume that the function $G : [0, \infty) \times \mathbb{C}^d \to \mathbb{C}^d$ is continuous in t and fulfills the following conditions: for arbitrary $x, x_1, x_2, \in \mathbb{C}^d$ and arbitrary $t \in [0, +\infty)$, a real value function Z from $[0, +\infty)$ to $\mathbb{R}$ satisfies

$$Z(t) \geq \sup_{x_1 \neq x_2} \frac{\|G(t, x_1) - G(t, x_2)\|}{\|x_1 - x_2\|}. \quad (5)$$

2.1. Relationships between INDDEs and NDDEs

In order to establish the relationships between INDDEs and NDDEs, setting the scalar function $\alpha : [-\tau, \infty) \to \mathbb{C}$ satisfies the following:

(1) for any $t \in [0, \infty)$, $\alpha(t) = \alpha(t - \tau)$;
(2) $\alpha(t)$ is infinitely smooth on $[0, \tau)$;
(3) $\alpha(0) = 1$ and $\alpha(0^-) = \lambda$;
(4) $\inf_{t \in [0,\tau)} |\alpha(t)| \geq m > 0$.

Theorem 1. *If $x(t)$ is the solution of INDDE (1), $y(t) = \alpha(t)x(t)$ for $t \in [-\tau, +\infty)$, then $y(t)$ is the solution of the following NDDE:*

$$\begin{cases} \frac{d}{dt}(y(t) - I(t, y(t-\tau))) = J(t, y(t), y(t-\tau)), & t \geq 0, \\ y(t) = \Psi(t), & t \in [-\tau, 0], \end{cases} \quad (6)$$

where

$$I(t, x) = \alpha(t) G\left(t, \frac{x}{\alpha(t)}\right)$$

$$J(t, y, z) = \frac{\alpha'(t) y}{\alpha(t)} - \alpha'(t) G\left(t, \frac{z}{\alpha(t)}\right) + \alpha(t) F\left(t, \frac{y}{\alpha(t)}, \frac{z}{\alpha(t)}\right)$$

and

$$\Psi(t) = \begin{cases} \alpha(t) \psi(t), & t \in [-\tau, 0), \\ \alpha(0^-) \psi(0^-), & t = 0. \end{cases}$$

In reverse, assuming $y(t)$ is the solution of NDDE (6), $x(t) = \frac{y(t)}{\alpha(t)}$ for $t \in [-\tau, +\infty)$, then $x(t)$ is the solution of INDDE (1).

Proof. (i) On $[k\tau, (k+1)\tau], k = -1, 0, 1, \cdots, \alpha(t)$ and $x(t)$ are continuous, which implies that $y(t)$ is continuous. We can obtain that

$$\begin{aligned} y(k\tau) &= y(k\tau^+) = \alpha(k\tau^+)x(k\tau^+) \\ &= \alpha(k\tau)\lambda x(k\tau^-) = \alpha(0)\lambda x(k\tau^-) \\ &= \lambda x(k\tau^-) \end{aligned}$$

and

$$y(k\tau^-) = \alpha(k\tau^-)x(k\tau^-) = \lambda x(k\tau^-),$$

implying $y(k\tau) = y(k\tau^+) = y(k\tau^-), k \in \mathbb{N}$. Consequently, $y(t)$ is continuous on $[-\tau, \infty)$. For $t \in [k\tau, (k+1)\tau), k \in \mathbb{N}$, we obtain

$$\begin{aligned} \frac{d}{dt}[y(t) - I(t, y(t-\tau))] &= \frac{d}{dt}[y(t) - \alpha(t)G(t, \frac{y(t-\tau)}{\alpha(t)})] \\ &= \frac{d}{dt}[\alpha(t)x(t) - \alpha(t)G(t, x(t-\tau))] \\ &= \alpha'(t)x(t) - \alpha'(t)G(t, x(t-\tau)) + \alpha(t)\frac{d}{dt}[x(t) - G(t, x(t-\tau))] \\ &= \alpha'(t)x(t) - \alpha'(t)G(t, x(t-\tau)) + \alpha(t)F(t, x(t), x(t-\tau)) \\ &= \frac{\alpha'(t)y(t)}{\alpha(t)} - \alpha'(t)G(t, \frac{y(t-\tau)}{\alpha(t)}) + \alpha(t)F(t, \frac{y(t)}{\alpha(t)}, \frac{y(t-\tau)}{\alpha(t)}) \\ &= J(t, y(t), y(t-\tau)) \end{aligned}$$

(ii) Let $y(t)$ be the solution of (6). For $t \in [k\tau, (k+1)\tau), k \in \mathbb{N}$,

$$\begin{aligned} \frac{d}{dt}[x(t) - G(t, x(t-\tau))] &= \frac{d}{dt}[\frac{y(t)}{\alpha(t)} - G(t, \frac{y(t-\tau)}{\alpha(t)})] \\ &= \frac{y'(t)}{\alpha(t)} - \frac{\alpha'(t)y(t)}{\alpha^2(t)} - [\frac{1}{\alpha(t)}\frac{d}{dt}(\alpha(t)G(t, \frac{y(t-\tau)}{\alpha(t)})) - \frac{\alpha'(t)}{\alpha(t)}G(t, \frac{y(t-\tau)}{\alpha(t)})] \\ &= \frac{1}{\alpha(t)}\frac{d}{dt}[y(t) - I(t, y(t-\tau))] - \frac{\alpha'(t)y(t)}{\alpha^2(t)} + \frac{\alpha'(t)}{\alpha(t)}G(t, \frac{y(t-\tau)}{\alpha(t)})] \\ &= \frac{J(t, y(t), y(t-\tau))}{\alpha(t)} - \frac{\alpha'(t)y(t)}{\alpha^2(t)} + \frac{\alpha'(t)}{\alpha(t)}G(t, \frac{y(t-\tau)}{\alpha(t)})] \\ &= F(t, \frac{y(t)}{\alpha(t)}, \frac{y(t-\tau)}{\alpha(t)}) = F(t, \frac{y(t)}{\alpha(t)}, \frac{y(t-\tau)}{\alpha(t-\tau)}) \\ &= F(t, x(t), x(t-\tau)). \end{aligned}$$

We can easily see that

$$x(k\tau) = \frac{y(k\tau)}{\alpha(k\tau)} = \frac{y(k\tau)}{\alpha(0)} = y(k\tau)$$

and

$$x(k\tau^-) = \lim_{t \to k\tau^-} \frac{y(t)}{\alpha(t)} = \frac{y(k\tau)}{\alpha(k\tau^-)} = \frac{y(k\tau)}{\alpha(\tau^-)} = \frac{y(k\tau)}{\lambda},$$

implying that $x(k\tau) = \lambda x(k\tau^-), k \in \mathbb{N}$. Apparently, we obtain $x(t) = \frac{y(t)}{\alpha(t)} = \psi(t), t \in [-\tau, 0)$. Therefore, $x(t)$ is the solution of INDDE (1). □

Since in Theorem 1, $\alpha(t)$ and $\frac{1}{\alpha(t)}$ are bounded for all $t \in \mathbb{R}$, we can obtain the following result.

Remark 1. *The exact solution $x(t)$ of INDDE (1) is stable if and only if the exact solution $y(t)$ of NDDE (6) is stable when $y(t) = \alpha(t)x(t)$ for $t \in [-\tau, +\infty)$. Moreover, the exact solution*

$x(t)$ of INDDE (1) is asymptotically stable if and only if the exact solution $y(t)$ of NDDE (6) is asymptotically stable when $y(t) = \alpha(t)x(t)$ for $t \in [-\tau, +\infty)$.

2.2. Asymptotical Stability of INDDEs

According to Theorem 1, assuming $\tilde{y}(t) = \alpha(t)\tilde{x}(t)$, $t \geq -\tau$, then $\tilde{x}(t)$ is the solution of (2) if and only if $\tilde{y}(t)$ is the solution of the following equation:

$$\begin{cases} \frac{d}{dt}(\tilde{y}(t) - I(t, \tilde{y}(t-\tau))) = J(t, \tilde{y}(t), \tilde{y}(t-\tau)), & t \geq 0, \\ \tilde{y}(t) = \tilde{\Psi}(t), & t \in [-\tau, 0], \end{cases} \quad (7)$$

where

$$\tilde{\Psi}(t) = \begin{cases} \alpha(t)\tilde{\varphi}(t), & t \in [-\tau, 0), \\ \alpha(0^-)\tilde{\varphi}(0^-), & t = 0. \end{cases}$$

Let

$$P(t) = y(t) - I(t, y(t-\tau)), \quad \tilde{P}(t) = \tilde{y}(t) - I(t, \tilde{y}(t-\tau)),$$

$$Q(t, y, z) = J(t, y + I(t, z), z).$$

Then the NDDE (6) can be expressed as the following ordinary differential equations with forcing term:

$$\begin{cases} P'(t) = Q(t, P(t), y(t-\tau)), & t \geq 0, \\ P(0) = \Psi(0) - I(0, \Psi(-\tau)), \end{cases} \quad (8)$$

coupled with the algebraic recursion

$$y(t) = \begin{cases} \Psi(t), & t \in [-\tau, 0), \\ P(t) + I(t, y(t-\tau)), & t \geq 0. \end{cases}$$

Analogously, the NDDE (7) can also be expressed in the following form:

$$\begin{cases} \tilde{P}'(t) = Q(t, \tilde{P}(t), \tilde{y}(t-\tau)), & t \geq 0, \\ \tilde{P}(0) = \tilde{\Psi}(0) - I(0, \tilde{\Psi}(-\tau)), \end{cases} \quad (9)$$

coupled with the algebraic recursion

$$\tilde{y}(t) = \begin{cases} \tilde{\Psi}(t), & t \in [-\tau, 0), \\ \tilde{P}(t) + I(t, \tilde{y}(t-\tau)), & t \geq 0. \end{cases}$$

Theorem 2. *Assume IDDEs (1) and (2) satisfy (3)–(5). If $Y(t) \leq 0$, there exists a bounded function $r(t)$, integrable in any bounded interval, such that $r(t) \leq 0$, $r(0) < 0$,*

$$\omega X(t) = r(t)\left(\Re(\frac{\alpha'(t)}{\alpha(t)}) + \frac{Y(t)}{\omega^2}\right) \quad (10)$$

and a non-negative constant $\rho \leq 1$, such that

$$\sup_{0 \leq x \leq t} |r(x)| + \omega Z(t) \leq \rho, \quad t \geq 0, \quad (11)$$

then the solution of IDDEs (1) and (2) are bounded stable; that is

$$\|x(t) - \tilde{x}(t)\| \leq \max\{\omega \sup_{t \in [-\tau, 0)} \|\varphi(t) - \tilde{\varphi}(t)\|, \frac{|\lambda| \|\varphi(0^-) - \tilde{\varphi}(0^-)\|}{-mr(0)}\}, \quad t \geq 0.$$

Moreover, if $\rho < 1$ and

$$\Re(\frac{\alpha'(t)}{\alpha(t)}) + \frac{Y(t)}{\omega^2} \leq Y_0 < 0, \quad t \geq 0, \tag{12}$$

then IDDEs (1) and (2) are asymptotically stable; that is

$$\lim_{t \to \infty} \|x(t) - \tilde{x}(t)\| = 0.$$

Proof. We will apply inequalities (3)–(5) to prove that the function $Q : [0, \infty) \times \mathbb{C}^d \times \mathbb{C}^d \to \mathbb{C}^d$ is continuous in t and satisfies the following conditions: for arbitrary $y, y_1, y_2, x_1, x_2 \in \mathbb{C}^d$, and $\forall t \in [0, +\infty)$,

$$\sup_{y_1 \neq y_2, x} \frac{\Re(\langle Q(t, y_1, x) - Q(t, y_2, x), y_1 - y_2 \rangle)}{\|y_1 - y_2\|^2} \leq \Re(\frac{\alpha'(t)}{\alpha(t)}) + \omega^2 Y(t), \tag{13}$$

$$\sup_{y, x_1 \neq x_2} \frac{\|Q(t, y, x_1) - Q(t, y, x_2)\|}{\|x_1 - x_2\|} \leq \omega X(t), \tag{14}$$

$$\sup_{x_1 \neq x_2} \frac{\|G(t, x_1) - G(t, x_2)\|}{\|x_1 - x_2\|} \leq \omega Z(t). \tag{15}$$

First, the inequality (13) can be proven as follows:

$$\Re \langle Q(t, y_1, x) - Q(t, y_2, x), y_1 - y_2, \rangle$$
$$= \Re \langle J(t, y_1 + I(t, x), x) - J(t, y_2 + I(t, x), x), y_1 - y_2, \rangle$$
$$= \Re \langle \frac{\alpha'(t)}{\alpha(t)}(y_1 + I(t, x)) - \alpha'(t)G(t, \frac{x}{\alpha(t)}) + \alpha(t)F(t, \frac{1}{\alpha(t)}(y_1 + I(t, x)), \frac{x}{\alpha(t)})$$
$$- [\frac{\alpha'(t)}{\alpha(t)}(y_2 + I(t, x)) - \alpha'(t)G(t, \frac{x}{\alpha(t)}) + \alpha(t)F(t, \frac{1}{\alpha(t)}(y_2 + I(t, x)), \frac{x}{\alpha(t)})],$$
$$y_1 - y_2 \rangle$$
$$= \Re \langle \frac{\alpha'(t)}{\alpha(t)}(y_1 - y_2) + \alpha(t)[F(t, \frac{1}{\alpha(t)}(y_1 + I(t, x)), \frac{x}{\alpha(t)})$$
$$- \alpha(t)F(t, \frac{1}{\alpha(t)}(y_2 + I(t, x)), \frac{x}{\alpha(t)})], y_1 - y_2 \rangle$$
$$= \Re(\frac{\alpha'(t)}{\alpha(t)})\|y_1 - y_2\|^2 + \Re(\alpha(t)\langle F(t, \frac{y_1}{\alpha(t)} + G(t, \frac{x}{\alpha(t)}), \frac{x}{\alpha(t)})$$
$$- F(t, \frac{y_2}{\alpha(t)} + G(t, \frac{x}{\alpha(t)}), \frac{x}{\alpha(t)})), y_1 - y_2 \rangle)$$
$$= \Re(\frac{\alpha'(t)}{\alpha(t)})\|y_1 - y_2\|^2 + |\alpha(t)|^2 \Re(\langle H(t, \frac{y_1}{\alpha(t)}, \frac{x}{\alpha(t)}) - H(t, \frac{y_2}{\alpha(t)}, \frac{x}{\alpha(t)}), \frac{y_1}{\alpha(t)} - \frac{y_2}{\alpha(t)} \rangle)$$
$$\leq \Re(\frac{\alpha'(t)}{\alpha(t)})\|y_1 - y_2\|^2 + |\alpha(t)|^2 Y(t)\|\frac{y_1}{\alpha(t)} - \frac{y_2}{\alpha(t)}\|^2$$

which implies that, if $Y(t) \leq 0$,

$$\Re \langle Q(t, y_1, x) - Q(t, y_2, x), y_1 - y_2, \rangle \leq [\Re(\frac{\alpha'(t)}{\alpha(t)}) + \frac{Y(t)}{\omega^2}]\|y_1 - y_2\|^2 \tag{16}$$

and if $Y(t) \leq \hat{Y}$ and $\hat{Y} > 0$,

$$\Re \langle Q(t, y_1, x) - Q(t, y_2, x), y_1 - y_2, \rangle \leq [\Re(\frac{\alpha'(t)}{\alpha(t)}) + \omega^2 \hat{Y}]\|y_1 - y_2\|^2 \tag{17}$$

Next, we will prove the inequality (14) as follows:

$$\|Q(t,y,x_1) - Q(t,y,x_2)\|$$
$$= \|J(t,y+I(t,x_1),x_1) - J(t,y+I(t,x_2),x_2)\|$$
$$= \|\frac{\alpha'(t)}{\alpha(t)}(y+I(t,x_1)) - \alpha'(t)G(t,\frac{x_1}{\alpha(t)}) + \alpha(t)F(t,\frac{1}{\alpha(t)}(y+I(t,x_1)),\frac{x_1}{\alpha(t)})$$
$$- [\frac{\alpha'(t)}{\alpha(t)}(y+I(t,x_2)) - \alpha'(t)G(t,\frac{x_2}{\alpha(t)}) + \alpha(t)F(t,\frac{1}{\alpha(t)}(y+I(t,x_2)),\frac{x_2}{\alpha(t)})]\|$$
$$= \omega\|H(t,\frac{y}{\alpha(t)},\frac{x_1}{\alpha(t)}) - H(t,\frac{y}{\alpha(t)},\frac{x_2}{\alpha(t)})\|$$
$$\leq \omega X(t)\|x_1 - x_2\|$$

Finally, the inequality (15) can be proven as follows:

$$\|I(t,x_1) - I(t,x_2)\|$$
$$= \|\alpha(t)G(t,\frac{x_1}{\alpha(t)}) - \alpha(t)G(t,\frac{x_2}{\alpha(t)})\|$$
$$\leq (\sup_{t\geq 0}|\alpha(t)|)\|G(t,\frac{x_1}{\alpha(t)}) - G(t,\frac{x_2}{\alpha(t)})\|$$
$$\leq Z(t)(\sup_{t\geq 0}|\alpha(t)|)\|\frac{x_1}{\alpha(t)} - \frac{x_2}{\alpha(t)}\|$$
$$\leq \omega Z(t)\|x_1 - x_2\|.$$

By [14] (Theorem 9.4.1) or [24] (Theorem 3.1, Theorem 4.2), we can obtain that

$$\|y(t) - \tilde{y}(t)\| \leq \max\{\sup_{t\in[-\tau,0)}\|\Psi(t) - \tilde{\Psi}(t)\|, \frac{\|\Psi(0) - \tilde{\Psi}(0)\|}{-r(0)}\}, \quad t \geq 0$$

and

$$\lim_{t\to\infty}\|y(t) - \tilde{y}(t)\| = 0.$$

Because $x(t) = \frac{y(t)}{\alpha(t)}$, $t \geq -\tau$, we know the theorem holds. □

Theorem 3. *Assume IDDEs (1) and (2) satisfy (3)–(5). If $Y(t) \leq \hat{Y}$, $\hat{Y} > 0$, there exists a bounded function $\bar{r}(t)$, integrable in any bounded interval, such that $\bar{r}(t) \leq 0$, $\bar{r}(0) < 0$,*

$$\omega X(t) = \bar{r}(t)\left(\Re(\frac{\alpha'(t)}{\alpha(t)}) + \omega^2\hat{Y}\right) \tag{18}$$

and a non-negative constant $\bar{\rho} \leq 1$, such that

$$\sup_{0\leq x\leq t}|r(x)| + \omega Z(t) \leq \bar{\rho}, \quad t \geq 0, \tag{19}$$

then the solution of IDDEs (1) and (2) are bounded stable; that is

$$\|x(t) - \tilde{x}(t)\| \leq \max\{\omega \sup_{t\in[-\tau,0)}\|\varphi(t) - \tilde{\varphi}(t)\|, \frac{|\lambda|\|\varphi(0^-) - \tilde{\varphi}(0^-)\|}{-m\bar{r}(0)}\}, \quad t \geq 0.$$

Moreover, if $\bar{\rho} < 1$ and

$$\Re(\frac{\alpha'(t)}{\alpha(t)}) + \omega^2\hat{Y} \leq \bar{Y}_0 < 0, \quad t \geq 0, \tag{20}$$

then IDDEs (1) and (2) are asymptotically stable; that is

$$\lim_{t\to\infty}\|x(t)-\tilde{x}(t)\|=0.$$

2.3. Special Cases

When different functions of $\alpha(t)$ are chosen, different sufficient conditions for the bounded stability and asymptotical stability of the exact solutions of (1) and (2) can be obtained. For brevity, we only consider three of them.

Special Case I. Set $\alpha_1(t) = \lambda^{\{\frac{t}{\tau}\}}$, $t \in [-\tau, \infty)$, where $\{\frac{t}{\tau}\} = \frac{t}{\tau} - \lfloor\frac{t}{\tau}\rfloor$, $\lfloor\frac{t}{\tau}\rfloor$ denotes the floor function. The following theorem can be seen as a special case of Theorem 2 when $\alpha(t) = \alpha_1(t)$.

Theorem 4. *Let $x(t)$ be the solution of (1). If $z_1(t) = \lambda^{\{\frac{t}{\tau}\}} x(t)$, $t \in [-\tau, \infty)$, then $z_1(t)$ is the solution of*

$$\begin{cases} \frac{d}{dt}[z_1(t) - I_1(t, z_1(t-\tau))] = J_1(t, z_1(t), z_1(t-\tau)), & t \geq 0, \\ z_1(t) = \Psi_1(t), & t \in [-\tau, 0], \end{cases} \quad (21)$$

where

$$I_1(t, x)) = \lambda^{\{\frac{t}{\tau}\}} G(t, \lambda^{-\{\frac{t}{\tau}\}} x)$$

$$J_1(t, y, x) = (\frac{\ln \lambda}{\tau}) y - \lambda^{\{\frac{t}{\tau}\}} (\frac{\ln \lambda}{\tau}) G(t, \lambda^{-\{\frac{t}{\tau}\}} x) + \lambda^{\{\frac{t}{\tau}\}} F(t, \lambda^{-\{\frac{t}{\tau}\}} y, \lambda^{-\{\frac{t}{\tau}\}} x)$$

$$\Psi_1(t) = \begin{cases} \lambda^{\frac{t}{\tau}+1} \psi(t), & t \in [-\tau, 0), \\ \lambda \psi(0^-), & t = 0. \end{cases}$$

Conversely, $x(t)$ is the solution of (1) if $z_1(t)$ is the solution of (21) and $x(t) = \lambda^{-\{\frac{t}{\tau}\}} z_1(t)$, $t \in [-\tau, \infty)$.

Theorem 5. *Assume IDDEs (1) and (2) satisfy inequalities (3)–(5). If $Y(t) \leq 0$, there exists a bounded function $r_1(t)$, integrable in any bounded interval, such that $r_1(t) \leq 0$ and $r_1(0) < 0$,*

$$\omega_1 X(t) = r_1(t) \left(\frac{\ln |\lambda|}{\tau} + \frac{Y(t)}{\omega_1^2} \right)$$

and a non-negative constant $\rho_1 \leq 1$, such that

$$\sup_{0 \leq x \leq t} |r_1(x)| + \omega_1 Z(t) \leq \rho_1, \ t \geq 0,$$

then the solutions of IDDEs (1) and (2) are bounded stable,

$$\|x(t) - \tilde{x}(t)\| \leq \max\{\omega_1 \sup_{t \in [-\tau, 0)} \|\varphi(t) - \tilde{\varphi}(t)\|, \frac{|\lambda| \|\varphi(0^-) - \tilde{\varphi}(0^-)\|}{-m_1 r_1(0)}\}, \ t \geq 0.$$

where $\omega_1 = \max\{|\lambda|, \frac{1}{|\lambda|}\}$, $m_1 = \min\{1, |\lambda|\}$. Moreover, if $\rho_1 < 1$ and

$$\frac{\ln |\lambda|}{\tau} + \frac{Y(t)}{\omega_1^2} \leq Y_1 < 0, \ t \geq 0,$$

then IDDEs (1) and (2) are asymptotically stable.

Theorem 6. *Assume IDDEs (1) and (2) satisfy inequalities (3)–(5). If $Y(t) \leq \hat{Y}$, $\hat{Y} > 0$, there exists a bounded function $\bar{r}_1(t)$, integrable in any bounded interval, such that $\bar{r}_1(t) \leq 0$, $\bar{r}_1(0) < 0$,*

$$\omega_1 X(t) = \bar{r}_1(t)\left(\frac{\ln|\lambda|}{\tau} + \omega_1^2 \hat{Y}\right)$$

and a non-negative constant $\bar{\rho}_1 \leq 1$, such that

$$\sup_{0 \leq x \leq t} |r(x)| + \omega_1 Z(t) \leq \bar{\rho}_1, \ t \geq 0,$$

then the solutions of IDDEs (1) and (2) are bounded,

$$\|x(t) - \tilde{x}(t)\| \leq \max\{\omega_1 \sup_{t\in[-\tau,0)} \|\varphi(t) - \tilde{\varphi}(t)\|, \frac{|\lambda|\|\varphi(0^-) - \tilde{\varphi}(0^-)\|}{-m_1 \bar{r}_1(0)}\}, \ t \geq 0.$$

Moreover, if $\bar{\rho}_1 < 1$ and

$$\frac{\ln|\lambda|}{\tau} + \omega_1^2 \hat{Y} \leq \tilde{Y}_1 < 0, \ t \geq 0,$$

then IDDEs (1) and (2) are asymptotically stable.

Special Case II. Let $\alpha_2(t) = 1 + (\lambda - 1)\{\frac{t}{\tau}\}$, $t \in [-\tau, \infty)$, $\lambda > 0$, $\lambda \neq 1$. The following theorem can be seen as a special case of Theorem 2 when $\alpha(t) = \alpha_2(t)$.

Theorem 7. *Assume that $x(t)$ is the solution of (1) and $z_2(t) = [1 + (\lambda - 1)\{\frac{t}{\tau}\}]x(t)$, $t \in [-\tau, \infty)$. Then $z_2(t)$ is the solution of*

$$\begin{cases} \frac{d}{dt}[z_2(t) - I_2(t, z_2(t - \tau))] = J_2(t, z_2(t), z_2(t - \tau)), & t \geq 0, \\ z_2(t) = \Psi_2(t), & t \in [-\tau, 0], \end{cases} \quad (22)$$

where

$$I_2(t, x)) = \alpha_2(t) G(t, \frac{x}{\alpha_2(t)}) = \left(1 + (\lambda - 1)\{\frac{t}{\tau}\}\right) G(t, \frac{x}{(1 + (\lambda - 1)\{\frac{t}{\tau}\})})$$

$$J_2(t, y, x) = \frac{(\lambda - 1)y}{\tau \alpha_2(t)} - \frac{\lambda - 1}{\tau} G(t, \frac{x}{\alpha_2(t)}) + \alpha_2(t) F(t, \frac{y}{\alpha_2(t)}, \frac{x}{\alpha_2(t)})$$

$$\Psi_2(t) = \begin{cases} [1 + (\lambda - 1)(\frac{t}{\tau} + 1)]\psi(t), & t \in [-\tau, 0), \\ \lambda \psi(0^-), & t = 0. \end{cases}$$

Conversely, $x(t)$ is the solution of (1) if $z_2(t)$ is the solution of (22) and $x(t) = \frac{z_2(t)}{1+(\lambda-1)\{\frac{t}{\tau}\}}$, $t \in [-\tau, \infty)$.

Theorem 8. *Assume that $\lambda \in \mathbb{R}$, $\lambda > 0$, $\lambda \neq 1$, IDDEs (1) and (2) satisfy (3)–(5). If $Y(t) \leq 0$, there exists a bounded function $r_2(t)$, integrable in any bounded interval, such that $r_2(t) \leq 0$, $r_2(0) < 0$,*

$$\omega_2 X(t) = r(t)\left(\frac{\lambda - 1}{\tau + (\lambda - 1)\tau\{\frac{t}{\tau}\}} + \frac{Y(t)}{\omega_2^2}\right)$$

and a non-negative constant $\rho_2 \leq 1$, such that

$$\sup_{0 \leq x \leq t} |r_2(x)| + \omega_2 Z(t) \leq \rho_2, \ t \geq 0,$$

then the exact solutions of IDDEs (1) and (2) are bounded stable as follows:

$$\|x(t) - \tilde{x}(t)\| \leq \max\{\omega_2 \sup_{t \in [-\tau,0)} \|\varphi(t) - \tilde{\varphi}(t)\|, \frac{\lambda \|\varphi(0^-) - \tilde{\varphi}(0^-)\|}{-m_2 r_2(0)}\}, \ t \geq 0,$$

where $\omega_2 = \max\{\lambda, \frac{1}{\lambda}\}$, $m_2 = \min\{1, \lambda\}$. Moreover, if $\rho_2 < 1$ and there is a negative constant Y_2 such that

$$\frac{\lambda - 1}{\tau + (\lambda - 1)\tau\{\frac{t}{\tau}\}} + \frac{Y(t)}{\omega_2^2} \leq Y_2 < 0, \ t \geq 0,$$

then IDDEs (1) and (2) are asymptotically stable.

Theorem 9. *Assume that IDDEs (1) and (2) satisfy (3)–(5), $\lambda > 0$ and $\lambda \neq 1$. If $Y(t) \leq \hat{Y}$, $\hat{Y} > 0$, there exists a bounded function $\bar{r}_2(t)$, integrable in any bounded interval, such that $\bar{r}_2(t) \leq 0$, $\bar{r}_2(0) < 0$,*

$$\omega_2 X(t) = r(t)\left(\frac{\lambda - 1}{\tau + (\lambda - 1)\tau\{\frac{t}{\tau}\}} + \omega_2^2 \hat{Y}\right)$$

and a non-negative constant $\bar{\rho}_2 \leq 1$, such that

$$\sup_{0 \leq x \leq t} |r(x)| + \omega_2 Z(t) \leq \bar{\rho}_2, \ t \geq 0,$$

then the exact solutions of IDDEs (1) and (2) are bounded stable as follows:

$$\|x(t) - \tilde{x}(t)\| \leq \max\{\omega_2 \sup_{t \in [-\tau,0)} \|\varphi(t) - \tilde{\varphi}(t)\|, \frac{\lambda \|\varphi(0^-) - \tilde{\varphi}(0^-)\|}{-m_2 \bar{r}_2(0)}\}, \ t \geq 0.$$

Moreover, if $\bar{\rho}_2 < 1$ and there is a negative constant $\bar{Y}_2$, such that

$$\frac{\lambda - 1}{\tau + (\lambda - 1)\tau\{\frac{t}{\tau}\}} + \omega_2^2 \hat{Y} \leq \bar{Y}_2 < 0, \ t \geq 0,$$

then IDDEs (1) and (2) are asymptotically stable.

Because $\frac{\lambda-1}{\tau+(\lambda-1)\tau\{\frac{t}{\tau}\}} \leq \frac{\lambda-1}{\tau}$ for all $\lambda > 0$, $\forall t \in \mathbb{R}$, by Theorems 8 and 9, we can obtain the following two results.

Corollary 1. *Assume that IDDEs (1) and (2) satisfy (3)–(5), $\lambda \neq 1$ and $\lambda > 0$. If $Y(t) \leq 0$, there exists a bounded function $\tilde{r}_2(t)$, integrable in any bounded interval, such that $\tilde{r}_2(t) \leq 0$, $\tilde{r}_2(0) < 0$,*

$$\omega_2 X(t) = \tilde{r}_2(t)\left(\frac{\lambda - 1}{\tau} + \frac{Y(t)}{\omega_2^2}\right)$$

and a non-negative constant $\tilde{\rho}_2 \leq 1$, such that

$$\sup_{0 \leq x \leq t} |\tilde{r}_2(x)| + \omega_2 Z(t) \leq \tilde{\rho}_2, \ t \geq 0,$$

then the exact solutions of IDDEs (1) and (2) are bounded stable as follows:

$$\|x(t) - \tilde{x}(t)\| \leq \max\{\omega_2 \sup_{t \in [-\tau,0)} \|\varphi(t) - \tilde{\varphi}(t)\|, \frac{\lambda \|\varphi(0^-) - \tilde{\varphi}(0^-)\|}{-m_2 \tilde{r}_2(0)}\}, \ t \geq 0.$$

Moreover, if $\tilde{\rho}_2 < 1$ and there is a positive constant Y_2, such that

$$\frac{\lambda - 1}{\tau} + \frac{Y(t)}{\omega_2^2} \leq Y_2 < 0, \quad t \geq 0,$$

then IDDEs (1) and (2) are asymptotically stable.

Corollary 2. *Assume that IDDEs (1) and (2) satisfy (3)–(5) and $\lambda > 0$, $\lambda \neq 1$. If there exists a bounded function $\check{r}_2(t)$, integrable in any bounded interval, such that $\check{r}_2(t) \leq 0, \check{r}_2(0) < 0$,*

$$\omega_2 X(t) = \check{r}_2(t)\left(\frac{\lambda - 1}{\tau} + \omega_2^2 \hat{Y}\right)$$

and a non-negative constant $\check{\rho}_2 \leq 1$, such that

$$\sup_{0 \leq x \leq t} |r(x)| + \omega_2 Z(t) \leq \check{\rho}_2, \quad t \geq 0,$$

then the exact solutions of IDDEs (1) and (2) are bounded stable as follows:

$$\|x(t) - \tilde{x}(t)\| \leq \max\{\omega_2 \sup_{t \in [-\tau, 0)} \|\varphi(t) - \tilde{\varphi}(t)\|, \frac{\lambda\|\varphi(0^-) - \tilde{\varphi}(0^-)\|}{-m_2 \check{r}_2(0)}\}, \quad t \geq 0.$$

Moreover, if $\check{\rho}_2 < 1$ and $\frac{\lambda-1}{\tau} + \omega_2^2 \hat{Y} < 0$, $t \geq 0$, then IDDEs (1) and (2) are asymptotically stable.

Special Case III. Let $\alpha_3(t) = -\{\frac{t}{\tau}\}^2 + \lambda\{\frac{t}{\tau}\} + 1$, $t \in [-\tau, \infty)$, $\lambda \in \mathbb{R}$, $\lambda > 0$, $\lambda \neq 1$. The following theorem can be seen as a special case of Theorem 2 when $\alpha(t) = \alpha_3(t)$.

Theorem 10. *Let $x(t)$ be the solution of (1) and $z_3(t) = (-\{\frac{t}{\tau}\}^2 + \lambda\{\frac{t}{\tau}\} + 1)x(t)$, $t \in [-\tau, \infty)$. Then $z_3(t)$ is the solution of*

$$\begin{cases} \frac{d}{dt}[z_3(t) - I_3(t, z_3(t-\tau))] = J_3(t, z_3(t), z_3(t-\tau)), & t \geq 0, \\ z_3(t) = \Psi_3(t), & t \in [-\tau, 0], \end{cases} \quad (23)$$

where

$$I_3(t, x)) = (-\{\frac{t}{\tau}\}^2 + \lambda\{\frac{t}{\tau}\} + 1)G(t, \frac{x}{-\{\frac{t}{\tau}\}^2 + \lambda\{\frac{t}{\tau}\} + 1})$$

$$J_3(t, y, x) = \frac{(-2\{\frac{t}{\tau}\} + \lambda)y}{\tau\alpha_3(t)} - \frac{(-2\{\frac{t}{\tau}\} + \lambda)}{\tau}G(t, \frac{x}{\alpha_3(t)}) + \alpha_3(t)F(t, \frac{y}{\alpha_3(t)}, \frac{x}{\alpha_3(t)})$$

$$\Psi_3(t) = \begin{cases} [-(\frac{t}{\tau} + 1)^2 + \lambda(\frac{t}{\tau} + 1) + 1]\psi(t), & t \in [-\tau, 0), \\ \lambda\psi(0^-), & t = 0. \end{cases}$$

Conversely, $x(t)$ is the solution of (1) if $z_3(t)$ is the solution of (23) and $x(t) = \frac{z_3(t)}{-\{\frac{t}{\tau}\}^2+\lambda\{\frac{t}{\tau}\}+1}$, $t \in [-\tau, \infty)$.

Theorem 11. *Assume that $\lambda \in \mathbb{R}$ and $\lambda > 0$, and IDDEs (1) and (2) satisfy inequalities (3)–(5). If $Y(t) \leq 0$, there exists a bounded function $r_3(t)$, integrable in any bounded interval, such that $r_3(t) \leq 0, r_3(0) < 0$,*

$$\omega_3 X(t) = r_3(t)\left(\Re(\frac{-2\{\frac{t}{\tau}\} + \lambda}{-\{\frac{t}{\tau}\}^2\tau + \lambda\tau\{\frac{t}{\tau}\} + \tau}) + \frac{Y(t)}{\omega_3^2}\right)$$

and a non-negative constant $\rho_3 \leq 1$, such that

$$\sup_{0 \leq x \leq t} |r(x)| + \omega_3 Z(t) \leq \rho_3, \ t \geq 0,$$

then the exact solutions of IDDEs (1) and (2) are bounded stable as follows:

$$\|x(t) - \tilde{x}(t)\| \leq \max\{\omega_3 \sup_{t \in [-\tau, 0)} \|\varphi(t) - \tilde{\varphi}(t)\|, \frac{\lambda \|\varphi(0^-) - \tilde{\varphi}(0^-)\|}{-m_3 r_3(0)}\}, \ t \geq 0,$$

where $m_3 = \min\{1, \lambda\}$ and

$$\omega_3 = \begin{cases} \frac{\lambda}{4} + \frac{1}{\lambda}, & 0 < \lambda \leq 1, \\ \frac{\lambda^2}{4} + 1, & 1 < \lambda \leq 2, \\ \lambda, & \lambda > 2. \end{cases}$$

Moreover, if $\rho_3 < 1$ and there is a positive constant Y_3, such that

$$\frac{-2\{\frac{t}{\tau}\} + \lambda}{-\{\frac{t}{\tau}\}^2 \tau + \lambda \tau \{\frac{t}{\tau}\} + \tau} + \frac{Y(t)}{\omega_3^2} \leq Y_3 < 0, \ t \geq 0,$$

then IDDEs (1) and (2) are asymptotically stable.

Because $\frac{-2\{\frac{t}{\tau}\} + \lambda}{-\{\frac{t}{\tau}\}^2 \tau + \lambda \tau \{\frac{t}{\tau}\} + \tau} \leq \frac{\lambda}{\tau}$ for all $\lambda > 0, \forall t \in \mathbb{R}$, by Theorem 11, we can obtain the following corollary.

Corollary 3. *Assume that $\lambda \in \mathbb{R}$ and $\lambda > 0$, and the IDDEs (1) and (2) satisfy inequalities (3)–(5). If $Y(t) \leq 0$, there exists a bounded integrable function $\bar{r}_3(t)$ in any bounded interval, such that $\bar{r}_3(t) \leq 0, \bar{r}_3(0) < 0$,*

$$\omega_3 X(t) = \bar{r}_3(t)(\frac{\lambda}{\tau} + \frac{Y(t)}{\omega_3^2})$$

and a non-negative constant $\bar{\rho}_3 \leq 1$, such that

$$\sup_{0 \leq x \leq t} |\bar{r}_3(x)| + \omega_3 Z(t) \leq \bar{\rho}_3, \ t \geq 0,$$

then the exact solutions of IDDEs (1) and (2) are bounded stable as follows:

$$\|x(t) - \tilde{x}(t)\| \leq \max\{\omega_3 \sup_{t \in [-\tau, 0)} \|\varphi(t) - \tilde{\varphi}(t)\|, \frac{\lambda \|\varphi(0^-) - \tilde{\varphi}(0^-)\|}{-m_3 \bar{r}_3(0)}\}, \ t \geq 0.$$

Moreover, if $\bar{\rho}_3 < 1$ and there is a positive constant $\tilde{Y}_3$, such that

$$\frac{\lambda}{\tau} + \frac{Y(t)}{\omega_3^2} \leq \tilde{Y}_3 < 0, \ t \geq 0,$$

then IDDEs (1) and (2) are asymptotically stable.

3. Numerical Methods for INDDEs

Firstly, based on the idea of transformations, the numerical methods for INDDEs are constructed. Furthermore, it is proven that the constructed numerical methods can preserve the boundary stability and asymptotical stability of the nonlinear INDDEs if corresponding continuous Runge–Kutta methods are BN_f-stable.

The numerical method for nonlinear INDDE (1) can be constructed as the following three steps.

Step 1. The numerical solution of (8) is computed by the following continuous Runge–Kutta method:

$$\begin{cases} \Lambda_{n+1}^i = p_n + h \sum_{j=1}^{s} a_{ij} Q(t_{n+1}^j, \Lambda_{n+1}^j, \eta(t_{n+1}^j - \tau)), \quad i = 1, 2, \cdots, s, \\ \lambda(t_n + \theta h) = p_n + h \sum_{i=1}^{s} b_i(\theta) Q(t_{n+1}^i, \Lambda_{n+1}^i, \eta(t_{n+1}^i - \tau)) \\ p_{n+1} = \lambda(t_{n+1}) = p_n + h \sum_{i=1}^{s} b_i Q(t_{n+1}^i, \Lambda_{n+1}^i, \eta(t_{n+1}^i - \tau)), \end{cases} \quad (24)$$

where the stepsize $h = \frac{\tau}{m}$, m is a positive integer, $t_n = nh$, $t_{n+1}^i = t_n + c_i h$, and $c_i = \sum_{j=1}^{s} a_{ij}$, $n \in \mathbb{N}$, $i = 1, 2, \cdots, s$.

Step 2. The numerical solution of (6) can be computed by

$$\eta(t) = \lambda(t) + G(t, \eta(t - \tau)), \; t \geq 0, \quad (25)$$

where

$$\eta(t) = \Psi(t), \; t \in [-\tau, 0].$$

Step 3. The numerical solution $\mu(t)$ of (1) can be computed by

$$\mu(t) = \frac{\eta(t)}{\alpha(t)}, \; t \geq 0. \quad (26)$$

In the above process, the exact solution $P(t)$ of (8) is approximated by $\lambda(t)$ for all $t \geq 0$ and $P(t_n)$ is approximated by p_n, $n \in \mathbb{N}$; $y(t)$ of (6) is approximated by $\eta(t)$ and $x(t)$ of (1) is approximated by $\mu(t)$ for all $t \geq 0$.

Similarly, the numerical method for nonlinear INDDE (2) can be constructed as follows:

$$\begin{cases} \tilde{\Lambda}_{n+1}^i = \tilde{p}_n + h \sum_{j=1}^{s} a_{ij} Q(t_{n+1}^j, \tilde{\Lambda}_{n+1}^j, \tilde{\eta}(t_{n+1}^j - \tau)), \quad i = 1, 2, \cdots, s, \\ \tilde{\lambda}(t_n + \theta h) = \tilde{p}_n + h \sum_{i=1}^{s} b_i(\theta) Q(t_{n+1}^i, \tilde{\Lambda}_{n+1}^i, \tilde{\eta}(t_{n+1}^i - \tau)), \\ \tilde{p}_{n+1} = \tilde{\lambda}(t_{n+1}) = \tilde{p}_n + h \sum_{i=1}^{s} b_i Q(t_{n+1}^i, \tilde{\Lambda}_{n+1}^i, \tilde{\eta}(t_{n+1}^i - \tau)), \\ \tilde{\eta}(t) = \tilde{\lambda}(t) + G(t, \tilde{\eta}(t - \tau)), \; t \geq 0, \\ \tilde{\mu}(t) = \frac{\tilde{\eta}(t)}{\alpha(t)}, \; t \geq 0, \end{cases} \quad (27)$$

where

$$\tilde{\eta}(t) = \tilde{\Psi}(t), \; t \in [-\tau, 0].$$

Theorem 12. *Assume that IDDEs (1) and (2) satisfy inequalities (3)–(5), and assume the constructed numerical methods (24)–(27) are furnished by BN_f-stable continuous Runge–Kutta methods. If $\Upsilon(t) \leq 0$, there exists a bounded function $r(t)$, integrable in any bounded interval, such that $r(t) \leq 0$, $r(0) < 0$, and (10) and (11) hold, then the numerical solution $\mu(t)$ obtained from (24)–(26) and $\tilde{\mu}(t)$ obtained from (27) are bounded, in the following sense:*

$$\|\mu(t) - \tilde{\mu}(t)\| \leq \max\{\omega \sup_{t \in [-\tau, 0)} \|\varphi(t) - \tilde{\varphi}(t)\|, \frac{|\lambda| \|\varphi(0^-) - \tilde{\varphi}(0^-)\|}{-mr(0)}\}, \; t \geq 0.$$

Moreover, if $\rho < 1$ and (12) hold, then the numerical methods (24)–(27) for IDDEs (1) and (2), furnished by BN_f-stable continuous Runge–Kutta methods, are asymptotically stable; that is

$$\lim_{t \to \infty} \|\mu(t) - \tilde{\mu}(t)\| = 0.$$

Proof. By ref. [14] (Theorem 10.5.1)or ref. [24] (Theorem 6.1), the numerical methods (24) and (25), furnished by BN_f-stable continuous Runge–Kutta methods, are bounded; that is

$$\|\eta(t_n) - \tilde{\eta}(t_n)\| \leq \max\{\|\Phi(0) - \tilde{\Phi}(0)\|, \kappa\}.$$

Moreover, ref. [14] (Theorem 10.5.1) or ref. [24] (Theorem 6.3), under the condition of Theorem 2, the numerical methods (24) and (25) furnished by BN_f-stable continuous Runge–Kutta methods, are also asymptotically stable; that is,

$$\lim_{n \to +\infty} \|\eta(t_n) - \tilde{\eta}(t_n)\| = 0.$$

Because of the relationship (26) between the numerical solutions INDDE and NDDE without impulsive perturbations, the theorem holds. □

Similar to Theorem 12, we can obtain that the constructed numerical methods (24)–(27), furnished by BN_f-stable continuous Runge–Kutta methods, preserve the boundary stability and asymptotical stability of the exact solutions, under the conditions of Theorem 3, as follows.

Theorem 13. *Assume that IDDEs (1) and (2) satisfy inequalities (3)–(5), and assume the constructed numerical methods (24)–(27) are furnished by BN_f-stable continuous Runge–Kutta methods. If $Y(t) \leq \hat{Y}$, $\hat{Y} > 0$, there exists a bounded function $r(t)$ integrable in any bounded interval, such that $\bar{r}(t) \leq 0$, $\bar{r}(0) < 0$, (18) and (19) hold, then the numerical solution $\mu(t)$ obtained from (24)–(26) and $\tilde{\mu}(t)$ obtained from (27) are bounded stable, in the following sense:*

$$\|\mu(t) - \tilde{\mu}(t)\| \leq \max\{\omega \sup_{t \in [-\tau,0)} \|\varphi(t) - \tilde{\varphi}(t)\|, \frac{\lambda \|\varphi(0^-) - \tilde{\varphi}(0^-)\|}{-mr(0)}\}, \ t \geq 0.$$

Moreover, if $\rho < 1$ and (20) hold, then the numerical methods (24)–(27) for IDDEs (1) and (2), furnished by BN_f-stable continuous Runge–Kutta methods, are asymptotically stable.

4. Numerical Experiments

In this section, two numerical examples are chosen to confirm the theoretical results.

Example 1. *Consider the following scalar linear INDDEs with different initial functions:*

$$\begin{cases} x'(t) - cx'(t-\tau) = ax(t) + bx(t-\tau), & t \geq 0, t \neq k\tau, k \in \mathbb{N}, \\ x(k\tau) = \lambda x(k\tau^-), \\ x(t) = \phi(t), & t \in [-\tau, 0), \end{cases} \quad (28)$$

where a, b, c, and λ are real constants and $\phi(t)$ is the continuous differential initial function on $[-\tau, 0)$. Obviously, the inequalities (3)–(5) are satisfied with $X(t) = |ac + b|$, $Y(t) = a$, $Z(t) = |c|$. There are many parameters that meet the conditions of the theorems. Obviously, when

$$a = -5, \ b = \frac{4}{5}, \ c = \frac{1}{5}, \ \lambda = \frac{5}{4}, \ \tau = 1,$$

we have

$$X(t) = |ac + b| = |-5 \times \frac{1}{5} + \frac{4}{5}| = \frac{1}{5}, \ Y(t) = a = -5, \ Z(t) = |c| = \frac{1}{5},$$

and

$$\omega_1 = \max\{\frac{5}{4}, \frac{4}{5}\} = \frac{5}{4}.$$

Obviously, there exists $r_1(t)$ as follows:

$$r_1(t) = \frac{\left(\frac{\ln|\lambda|}{\tau} + \frac{Y(t)}{\omega_1^2}\right)}{\omega_1 X(t)} = \frac{1}{4\left(-\frac{16}{5} + \ln(\frac{5}{4})\right)} < 0,$$

such that the first condition of Theorem 5 holds; that is

$$\omega_1 X(t) = r_1(t)\left(\frac{\ln|\lambda|}{\tau} + \frac{Y(t)}{\omega_1^2}\right).$$

So we can obtain that

$$\sup_{0 \le x \le t} |r_1(x)| + \omega_1 Z(t) = \rho_1 = |\frac{1}{4\left(-\frac{16}{5} + \ln(\frac{5}{4})\right)}| + \frac{5}{4} \times \frac{1}{5} < 1$$

and

$$\frac{\ln|\lambda|}{\tau} + \frac{Y(t)}{\omega_1^2} = -\frac{5}{\frac{25}{16}} + \ln(\frac{5}{4}) = Y_1 < 0.$$

Hence, all the conditions of Theorem 5 hold. By Theorem 5, the exact solution of (28) is asymptotically stable.

Similarly, $\omega_2 = \max\{\frac{5}{4}, \frac{4}{5}\} = \frac{5}{4}$ and there exists $r_2(t)$ as follows:

$$r_2(t) = \frac{\left(\frac{\lambda-1}{\tau} + \frac{Y(t)}{\omega_2^2}\right)}{\omega_2 X(t)} = \frac{1}{4\left(\frac{1}{4} - \frac{16}{5} + \right)} < 0,$$

such that the first condition of Corollary 1 holds; that is

$$\omega_2 X(t) = r_2(t)\left(\frac{\lambda-1}{\tau} + \frac{Y(t)}{\omega_2^2}\right).$$

Therefore, we can obtain that

$$\sup_{0 \le x \le t} |r_2(x)| + \omega_2 Z(t) = \rho_2 = |\frac{1}{4\left(-\frac{16}{5} + \frac{1}{4}\right)}| + \frac{5}{4} \times \frac{1}{5} < 1$$

and

$$\frac{\lambda-1}{\tau} + \frac{Y(t)}{\omega_2^2} = \frac{1}{4} - \frac{5}{\frac{25}{16}} = Y_2 < 0.$$

Hence, all the conditions of Corollary 1 hold. By Corollary 1, we also obtain that the exact solution of (28) is asymptotically stable.

Similarly, $\omega_3 = \frac{\lambda^2}{4} + 1 = \frac{89}{64}$, and there exists $r_3(t)$ as follows:

$$r_3(t) = \frac{\left(\frac{\lambda}{\tau} + \frac{Y(t)}{\omega_3^2}\right)}{\omega_3 X(t)} = \frac{89}{5 \times 64 \times \left(\frac{5}{4} - \frac{5 \times 64^2}{89^2}\right)} < 0,$$

such that the first condition of Corollary 3 holds; that is

$$\omega_3 X(t) = r_3(t)\left(\frac{\lambda}{\tau} + \frac{Y(t)}{\omega_3^2}\right).$$

Therefore, we can obtain that

$$\sup_{0 \le x \le t} |r_3(x)| + \omega_3 Z(t) = \rho_3 = |\frac{89}{5 \times 64 \times \left(\frac{5}{4} - \frac{5 \times 64^2}{89^2}\right)}| + \frac{89}{64} \times \frac{1}{5} < 1$$

and

$$\frac{\lambda}{\tau} + \frac{Y(t)}{\omega_3^2} = \frac{5}{4} - 5 \times \frac{64^2}{89^2} = Y_3 < 0.$$

Hence, all the conditions of Corollary 3 hold. By Corollary 3, we also obtain that the exact solution of (28) is asymptotically stable.

By Theorem 12, we can obtain that the constructed numerical methods (24)–(27) for INDDE (28), furnished by BN_f-stable continuous Runge–Kutta methods, are asymptotically stable. From Figures 1 and 2, we can roughly see the trend that the distances between the two numerical solutions (obtained from the constructed numerical methods (24)–(27) for linear INDDE (28), furnished by implicit Euler method or 2-stage Lobatto IIIC method with two different constant initial function 1 and 0.9) become smaller as the time increases.

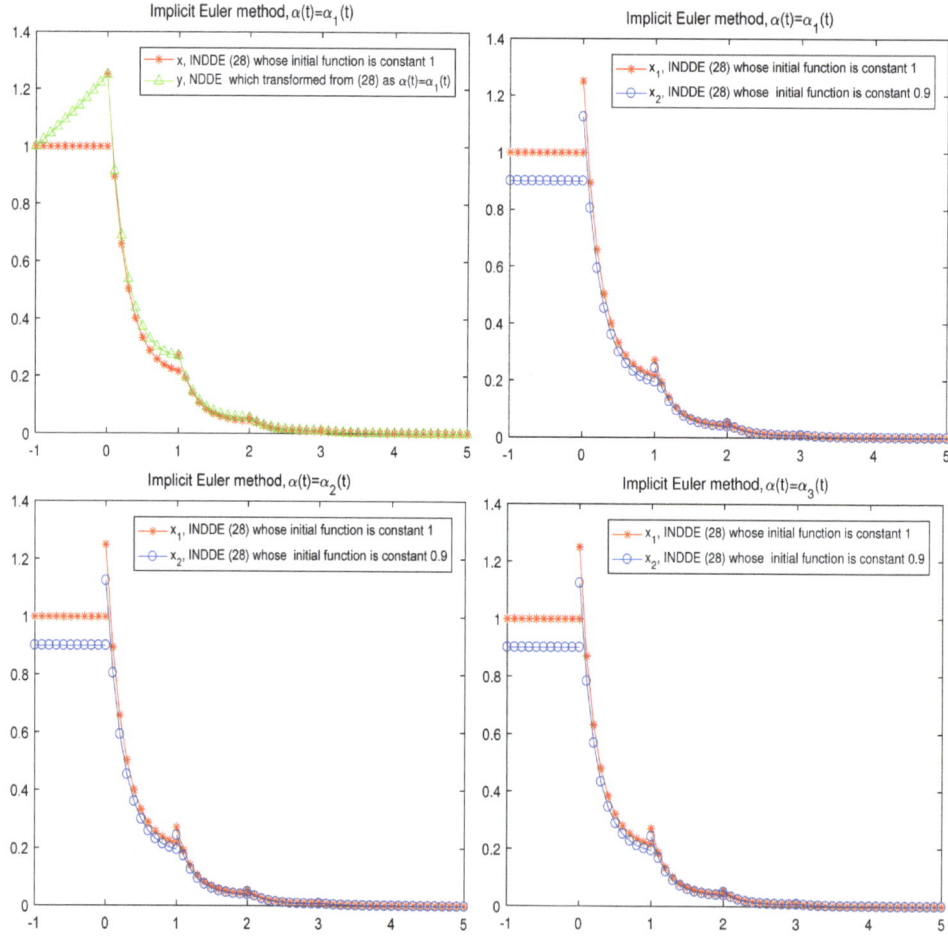

Figure 1. The numerical methods (24)–(27) for (28), furnished by implicit Euler method with the stepsize $h = \frac{1}{10}$.

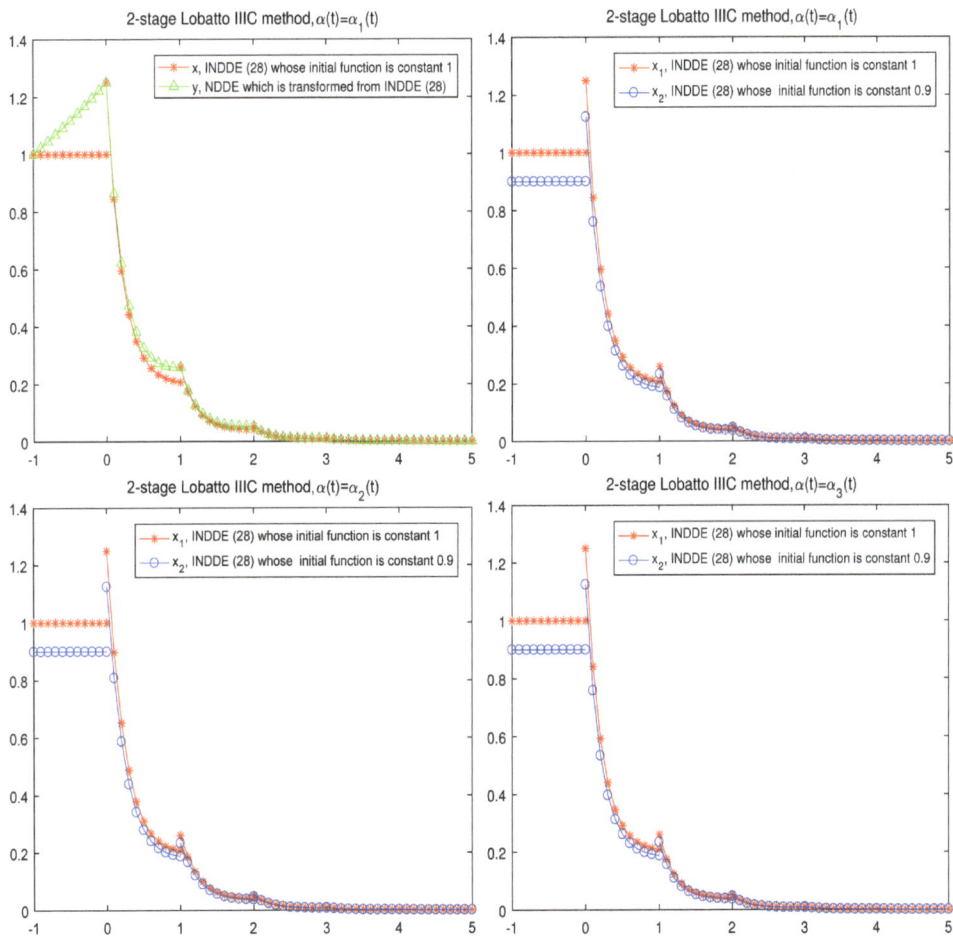

Figure 2. The numerical methods (24)–(27) for (28), furnished by 2-stage Lobatto IIIC method with the stepsize $h = \frac{1}{10}$.

Example 2. *Consider the following scalar nonlinear INDDEs:*

$$\begin{cases} \frac{d}{dt}(x(t) - \nu \cos(x(t-1))) = \beta x(t) + \gamma e^{-t} \sin(x(t-1)), & t \geq 0, t \neq k, k \in \mathbb{N}, \\ x(k) = \lambda x(k^-), \\ x(t) = \phi(t), & t \in [-1, 0), \end{cases} \quad (29)$$

where β, γ, ν, and λ are real constants and $\phi(t)$ is the continuous differential initial functions on $[-1, 0)$. It is easy to verify that the inequalities (3)–(5) are satisfied with $X(t) = |\beta \nu| + |\gamma| e^{-t}$, $Y(t) = \beta$, $Z(t) = |\nu|$. We can see that the one-side Lipschitz coefficient $X(t)$ is non-negative, which is different from the general results of NDDEs without impulsive perturbations. The parameters β, γ, ν, and λ are chosen to satisfy the conditions of Theorem 6:

$$\beta = \frac{1}{10}, \ \gamma = \frac{1}{50}, \ \nu = \frac{1}{5}, \ \lambda = \frac{1}{e},$$

which implies that the exact solution of (29) is stable and asymptotically stable (See Figures 3 and 4). We can see that the one-side Lipschitz coefficient $X(t)$ is non-negative, which is different from NDDEs' (without impulsive perturbations) stability results of Bellen, Zennaro, et al. (See [14] (Theorem 9.4.1) or [24] (Theorem 3.1, Theorem 4.2)).

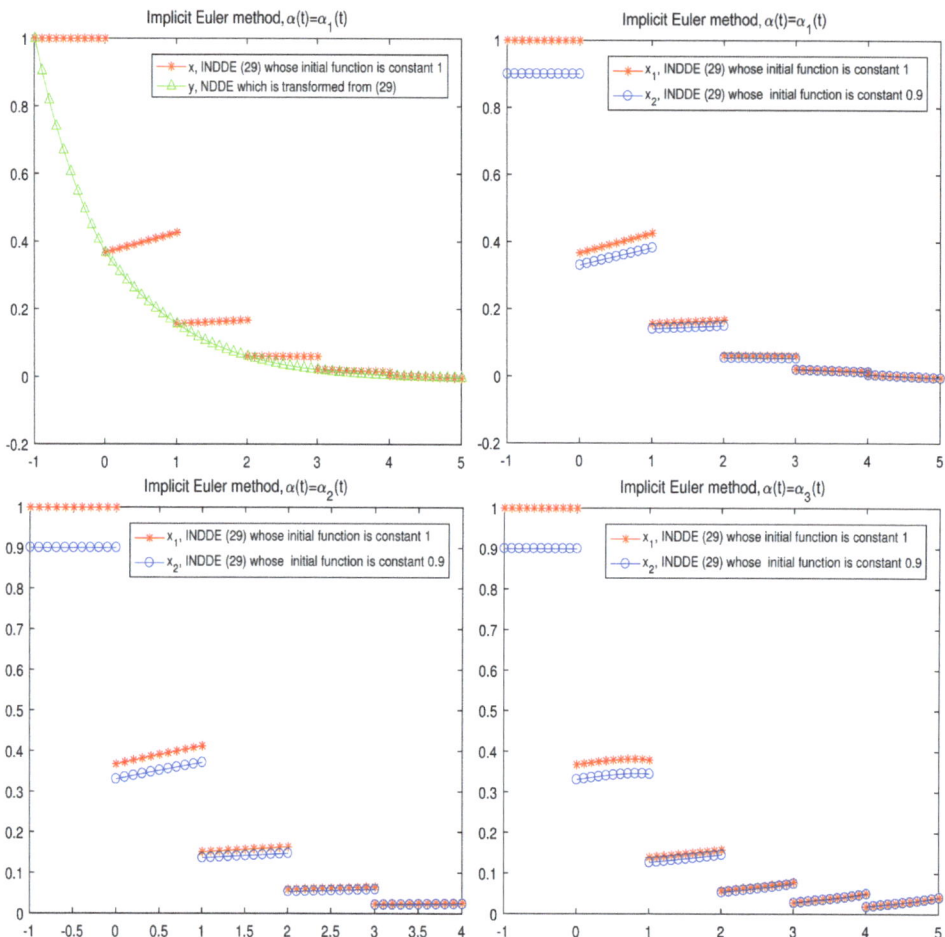

Figure 3. The numerical methods (24)–(27) for (29) furnished by implicit Euler method with the stepsize $h = \frac{1}{10}$.

By Theorem 13, we can obtain that the constructed numerical methods (24)–(27) for nonlinear INDDE (29), furnished by BN_f-stable continuous Runge–Kutta methods, are asymptotically stable. From Figures 3 and 4, we can roughly see the trend that the distances between the two numerical solutions (obtained from the constructed numerical methods (24)–(27) for INDDE (29), furnished by implicit Euler method or 2-stage Lobatto IIIC method with two different constant initial function 1 and 0.9) become smaller as the time increases.

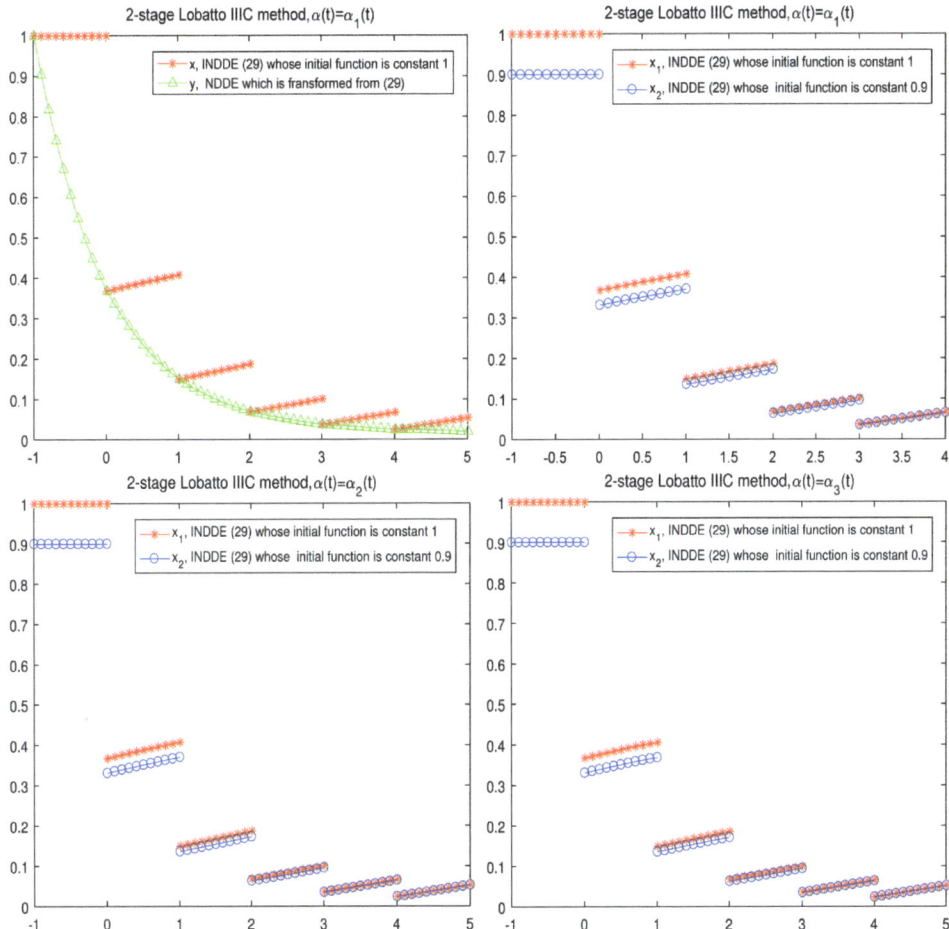

Figure 4. The numerical methods (24)–(27) for (29), furnished by 2-stage Lobatto IIIC method with the stepsize $h = \frac{1}{10}$.

In Tables 1–6, AE denotes the absolute errors between the numerical solutions and the exact solution of INDDEs. Similarly, RE denotes the relative errors between the numerical solutions and the exact solution of INDDEs. As is well known, when the step size is halved, the global errors of the numerical methods of p-order convergence will become approximately the same as the original times. We can see from the tables that the average ratio of the absolute errors (or relative errors) between the numerical solutions obtained from (24)–(26), furnished by implicit Euler method and the exact solution of (28), is close to 2 (the reciprocal of $\frac{1}{2}$) and the average ratio of the absolute errors (or relative errors) between the numerical solutions obtained from (24)–(26), furnished by 2-stage Lobatto IIIC method and the exact solution of (29), is close to 4 (the reciprocal of $\frac{1}{2^2}$) when the step size doubles and three different kinds of the transformations are used. Hence, Tables 1–6 roughly show that the constructed method, furnished by backward Euler method, is convergent of order 1 and by 2-stage Lobatto IIIC method is convergent of order 2 when the different transformations are chosen.

Table 1. The errors between the numerical solutions obtained from (24)–(26) and the exact solution of (28) at $t = 10$, when $\alpha(t) = \alpha_1(t) = \lambda^{\{t\}}, t \geq -1$.

	The Implicit Euler		2-Lobatto IIIC	
m	AE	RE	AE	RE
10	$3.6581941667 \times 10^{-8}$	0.0551236000	$3.3993997914 \times 10^{-9}$	0.0051223952
20	$1.6188740613 \times 10^{-8}$	0.0243940486	$9.5844940891 \times 10^{-10}$	0.0014442422
40	$7.5674842099 \times 10^{-9}$	0.0114030845	$2.5770607279 \times 10^{-10}$	$3.8832512532 \times 10^{-4}$
80	$3.6514998468 \times 10^{-9}$	0.0055022726	$6.7075180094 \times 10^{-11}$	$1.0107242500 \times 10^{-4}$
Ratio	2.1571322845	2.1571322845	3.7026585356	3.7026585356

Table 2. The errors between the numerical solutions obtained from (24)–(26) and the exact solution of (28) at $t = 10$, when $\alpha(t) = \alpha_2(t) = 1 + (\lambda - 1)\{t\}, t \geq -1$.

	The Implicit Euler		2-Lobatto IIIC	
m	AE	RE	AE	RE
10	$3.6469927694 \times 10^{-8}$	0.0549548115	$3.3341478657 \times 10^{-9}$	0.0050240702
20	$1.6145910077 \times 10^{-8}$	0.0243295093	$9.2718600641 \times 10^{-10}$	0.0013971329
40	$7.5491598720 \times 10^{-9}$	0.0113754724	$2.4224957236 \times 10^{-10}$	$3.6503445423 \times 10^{-4}$
80	$3.6430871304 \times 10^{-9}$	0.0054895959	$6.7075212665 \times 10^{-11}$	$8.9455329107 \times 10^{-5}$
Ratio	2.1565761938	2.1565761938	3.8346733002	3.8346733002

Table 3. The errors between the numerical solutions obtained from (24)–(26) and the exact solution of (28) at $t = 10$, when $\alpha(t) = \alpha_3(t) = -\{t\}^2 + \lambda\{t\} + 1, t \geq -1$.

	The Implicit Euler		2-Lobatto IIIC	
m	AE	RE	AE	RE
10	$3.2928273582 \times 10^{-8}$	0.0496180603	$3.5224011714 \times 10^{-9}$	0.0053077402
20	$1.4792658001 \times 10^{-8}$	0.0222903577	$9.9361388805 \times 10^{-10}$	0.0014972299
40	$6.9719562429 \times 10^{-9}$	0.0105057116	$2.6736493834 \times 10^{-10}$	$4.0287961420 \times 10^{-4}$
80	$3.3787413432 \times 10^{-9}$	0.0050912658	$6.9626687974 \times 10^{-11}$	$1.0491717188 \times 10^{-4}$
Ratio	2.1370673472	2.1370673472	3.7004462838	3.7004462838

Table 4. The errors between the numerical solutions obtained from (24)–(26) and the exact solution of (29) at $t = 5$, when $\alpha(t) = \alpha_1(t)$.

	The Implicit Euler		2-Lobatto IIIC	
m	AE	RE	AE	RE
20	0.0022369766	0.2202504769	$5.7299369527 \times 10^{-6}$	$2.3107308782 \times 10^{-4}$
40	0.0011276564	0.1110279231	$1.4405875293 \times 10^{-6}$	$5.8095056092 \times 10^{-5}$
80	$5.6614685412 \times 10^{-4}$	0.0557422526	$3.6113985329 \times 10^{-7}$	$1.4563807896 \times 10^{-5}$
160	$2.8365495107 \times 10^{-4}$	0.0279283826	$9.0363875351 \times 10^{-8}$	$3.6441342859 \times 10^{-6}$
Ratio	1.9904827766	1.9904827766	3.9876695906	3.9876695906

Table 5. The errors between the numerical solutions obtained from (24)–(26) and the exact solution of (29) at $t = 5$, when $\alpha(t) = \alpha_2(t)$.

	The Implicit Euler		2-Lobatto IIIC	
m	AE	RE	AE	RE
20	$1.9815130517 \times 10^{-4}$	0.0195097711	$2.3187856183 \times 10^{-5}$	$9.4091835401 \times 10^{-4}$
40	$1.0076686770 \times 10^{-4}$	0.0099214008	$5.9673597828 \times 10^{-6}$	$2.4210841877 \times 10^{-4}$
80	$5.0814463184 \times 10^{-5}$	0.0050031391	$1.5136126717 \times 10^{-6}$	$6.1405921789 \times 10^{-5}$
160	$2.5515894339 \times 10^{-5}$	0.0025122684	$3.8502245644 \times 10^{-7}$	$1.5462538456 \times 10^{-5}$
Ratio	1.9803170077	1.9803170077	3.9334584227	3.9334584227

Table 6. The errors between the numerical solutions obtained from (24)–(26) and the exact solution of (29) at $t = 5$, when $\alpha(t) = \alpha_3(t)$.

	The Implicit Euler		2-Lobatto IIIC	
m	AE	RE	AE	RE
20	0.0046567801	0.4585012456	$1.5888036813 \times 10^{-4}$	0.0064072219
40	0.0024075383	0.2370434701	$4.2949208184 \times 10^{-5}$	0.0017320271
80	0.0012240906	0.1205225617	$1.1161651179 \times 10^{-5}$	$4.5011964909 \times 10^{-4}$
160	$6.1718429346 \times 10^{-4}$	0.0607672605	$2.8446726005 \times 10^{-6}$	$1.1471806565 \times 10^{-4}$
Ratio	1.9614646923	1.9614646923	3.8236303912	3.8236303912

5. Conclusions and Future Works

In this paper, some new different asymptotical stability criteria are given for the exact solutions of a class of nonlinear INDDEs, based on the following idea: first the problems of the stability and asymptotical stability of INDDEs are transformed into the problems of NDDEs without impulsive perturbations, and then transformed into the problems of ordinary differential equations with a forcing term. Based on the above idea, some new sufficient conditions for the stability and asymptotical stability of the exact solutions of INDDEs are obtained and the numerical methods for INDDEs are constructed. Moreover, the numerical method is asymptotically stable if the corresponding continuous Runge–Kutta methods are BN_f-stable, under these different sufficient conditions.

In the future, we will study the asymptotical stability of more general INDDEs with the following characteristics: the size of the delay in continuous dynamics can be flexible, and there is no magnitude between the delay in continuous flow and impulsive delay. Finally, we propose the discontinuous Galerkin method (see [32]) as a stable and highly efficient alternative for solving INDDEs. Its application to these equations holds substantial potential and could produce promising outcomes.

Author Contributions: Conceptualization, G.-L.Z.; Software, Z.-W.W. and Y.S.; Formal analysis, T.L.; Writing—original draft, Z.-W.W. and Y.S.; Writing—review & editing, G.-L.Z. and T.L. All authors have read and agreed to the published version of the manuscript.

Funding: This research was supported by the National Natural Science Foundation of China (No. 11701074).

Data Availability Statement: The datasets generated during the current study are available from the corresponding author on reasonable request.

Conflicts of Interest: The authors declare no conflict of interest.

References

1. Anguraj, A.; Karthikeyan, K. Existence of solutions for impulsive neutral functional differential equations with nonlocal conditions. *Nonlinear Anal.* **2009**, *70*, 2717–2721. [CrossRef]
2. Cuevas, C.; Hernández, E.; Rabelo, M. The existence of solutions for impulsive neutral functional differential equations. *Comput. Math. Appl.* **2009**, *58*, 744–757. [CrossRef]
3. Li, X.D.; Deng, F.Q. Razumikhin method for impulsive functional differential equations of neutral type. *Chaos Solitons Fractals* **2017**, *101*, 41–49. [CrossRef]
4. Li, T.X.; Rogovchenko, Y.V. Oscillation of second-order neutral differential equations. *Math. Nachr.* **2015**, *288*, 1150–1162. [CrossRef]
5. Li, T.X.; Rogovchenko, Y.V. Oscillation criteria for even-order neutral differential equations. *Appl. Math. Lett.* **2016**, *61*, 35–41. [CrossRef]
6. Marin, M.; Seadawy, A.; Vlase, S.; Chirila, A. On mixed problem in thermoelasticity of type III for Cosserat media. *J. Taibah Univ. Sci.* **2022**, *16*, 1264–1274. [CrossRef]
7. Yang, D.; Wang, J.R.; O'Regan, D. Asymptotic properties of the solutions of nonlinear non-instantaneous impulsive differential equations. *J. Frankl. Inst.* **2017**, *354*, 6978–7011. . [CrossRef]
8. Khan, S.U.; Ali, I. Application of Legendre spectral-collocation method to delay differential and stochastic delay differential equation. *Aip Adv.* **2018**, *8*, 035301. [CrossRef]
9. Wang, Z.W.; Zhang, G.L.; Sun, Y. Convergence of collocation methods for one class of impulsive delay differential equations. *Axioms* **2023**, *12*, 700. [CrossRef]

10. Shen, J.; Liu, Y.; Li, J. Asymptotic behavior of solutions of nonlinear neutral differential equations with impulses. *J. Math. Anal. Appl.* **2007**, *332*, 179–189. [CrossRef]
11. Xu, L.; Xu, D. Exponential stability of nonlinear impulsive neutral integro-differential equations. *Nonlinear Anal.* **2008**, *69*, 2910–2923. [CrossRef]
12. Yeniçerioğlu, A.F. Stability of linear impulsive neutral differential equations with constant coefficients. *J. Math. Anal. Appl.* **2019**, *479*, 2196–2213. [CrossRef]
13. Bellen, A.; Jackiewicz, Z.; Zennaro, M. Stability analysis of one-step methods for neutral delay-differential equations. *Numer. Math.* **1988**, *52*, 605–619. [CrossRef]
14. Bellen, A.; Zennaro, M. *Numerical Methods for Delay Differential Equations*; Oxford University Press: Oxford, UK, 2003.
15. Enright, W.H.; Hayashi, H. Convergence analysis of the solution of retarded and neutral delay differential equations by continuous numerical methods. *SIAM J. Numer. Anal.* **1998**, *35*, 572–585. [CrossRef]
16. Engelborghs, K.; Luzyanina, T.; Hout, K.I.; Roose, D. Collocation methods for the computation of periodic solutions of delay differential equations. *SIAM J. Sci. Comput.* **2001**, *22*, 1593–1609. [CrossRef]
17. Di Hu, G.; Da Hu, G. Some simple stability criterion of neutral delay-differential systems. *Appl. Math. Comput.* **1996**, *80*, 257–271.
18. Da Hu, G.; Di Hu, G. Stability of neutral delay-differential systems: Boundary criterion. *Appl. Math. Comput.* **1997**, *87*, 247–259.
19. Da Hu, G.; Di Hu, G.; Cahlon, B. Algebraic criterion for stability of linear neutral systems with a single delay. *J. Comput. Appl. Math.* **2001**, *135*, 125–133.
20. Da Hu, G.; Mitsui, T. Delay-dependent stability of numerical methods for delay differential systems of neutral type. *BIT Numer. Math.* **2017**, *57*, 731–752.
21. Hale, J.K. *Theory of Functional Differential Equations*; Springer: New York, NY, USA, 1977.
22. Hale, J.K.; Verduyn Lunel, S.M. *Introduction to Functional Differential Equations*; Springer: New York, NY, USA, 1993.
23. Liu, Y.K. Numerical solution of implicit neutral functional differential equations. *SIAM J. Numer. Anal.* **1999**, *36*, 516–528. [CrossRef]
24. Vermiglio, R.; Torelli, L. A stable numerical approach for implicit non-linear neutral delay differential equations. *BIT Numer. Math.* **2003**, *43*, 195–215. [CrossRef]
25. Wang, W.S; Li, S.F. Stability analysis of nonlinear delay differential equations of neutral type. *Math. Numer. Sin.* **2004**, *26*, 303–314.
26. Wang, W.S.; Zhang, Y.; Li, S.F. Stability of continuous Runge-Kutta-type methods for nonlinear neutral delay-differential equations. *Appl. Math. Model.* **2009**, *33*, 3319–3329. [CrossRef]
27. Wang, W.S.; Li, S.F. Stability analysis of θ-methods for nonlinear neutral functional differential equations. *SIAM J. Sci. Comput.* **2008**, *30*, 2181–2205. [CrossRef]
28. Kolmanovskii, V.; Myshkis, A. *Introduction to the Theory and Applications of Functional Differential Equations*; Kluwer Academic Publishers: Dordrecht, Germany, 1999.
29. Zhang, G.L.; Song, M.H.; Liu, M.Z. Asymptotic stability of a class of impulsive delay differential equations. *J. Appl. Math.* **2012**, *2012*, 723893. [CrossRef]
30. Zhang, G.L.; Song, M.H.; Liu, M.Z. Exponential stability of the exact solutions and the numerical solutions for a class of linear impulsive delay differential equations. *J. Comput. Appl. Math.* **2015**, *285*, 32–44. [CrossRef]
31. Zhang, G.L.; Song, M.; Liu, M.Z. Asymptotical stability of the exact solutions and the numerical solutions for a class of impulsive differential equations. *Appl. Math. Comput.* **2015**, *258*, 12–21. [CrossRef]
32. Baccouch, M.; Temimi, H. A high-order space-time ultra-weak discontinuous Galerkin method for the second-order wave equation in one space dimension. *J. Comput. Appl. Math.* **2021**, *389*, 113331. [CrossRef]

Disclaimer/Publisher's Note: The statements, opinions and data contained in all publications are solely those of the individual author(s) and contributor(s) and not of MDPI and/or the editor(s). MDPI and/or the editor(s) disclaim responsibility for any injury to people or property resulting from any ideas, methods, instructions or products referred to in the content.

Article

On a Backward Problem for the Rayleigh–Stokes Equation with a Fractional Derivative

Songshu Liu [1,*], Tao Liu [1] and Qiang Ma [2]

[1] School of Mathematics and Statistics, Northeastern University at Qinhuangdao, Qinhuangdao 066004, China; liutao@neuq.edu.cn

[2] Department of Mathematics, Harbin Institute of Technology at Weihai, Weihai 264209, China; hitmaqiang@hit.edu.cn

* Correspondence: liusongshu@neuq.edu.cn

Abstract: The Rayleigh–Stokes equation with a fractional derivative is widely used in many fields. In this paper, we consider the inverse initial value problem of the Rayleigh–Stokes equation. Since the problem is ill-posed, we adopt the Tikhonov regularization method to solve this problem. In addition, this paper not only analyzes the ill-posedness of the problem but also gives the conditional stability estimate. Finally, the convergence estimates are proved under two regularization parameter selection rules.

Keywords: Rayleigh–Stokes equation with a fractional derivative; backward problem; Tikhonov regularization method; convergence estimate

MSC: 35R25; 35R30

1. Introduction

Fractional derivatives and integrals provide a good tool to describe phenomena with non-locality and memory characteristics. Fractional derivatives and fractional equations are also widely used in many scientific fields such as engineering, physics, finance, and hydrology [1–4]. So far, fractional integrals and derivatives have taken many forms, such as the Riemann–Liouville, Grünwald–Letnikov, Riesz, Caputo, Hadamard, and Caputo–Fabrizio. As a generalized form of integral calculus, fractional calculus has been paid more attention to by scholars because it is more in line with the actual phenomenon and has unique advantages compared with integral calculus. Fractional differential equations have important applications in the fields of fluid mechanics, economics, and control theory. Although fractional differential equation can describe the actual phenomenon more accurately [2,5,6], it is difficult to obtain the analytical solution of a fractional differential equation because of the non-local property of the fractional derivative. Therefore, it is necessary to find an effective numerical method to solve fractional differential equations.

In recent years, the Rayleigh–Stokes equation for a heated generalized second-grade fluid has played an important role in describing the practical problems of non-Newtonian fluid mechanics, which have attracted much attention from many researchers. Many achievements have been made in the study of the direct problems of Rayleigh–Stokes equation. In [7], Fourier coefficients transform and the fractional Laplace transform are used to solve the exact solution of the Rayleigh–Stokes problem. In [8], the exact solution of some oscillatory motions of the generalized Rayleigh–Stokes problem is discussed, and the velocity field and corresponding analytical expressions of infinite plate oscillating flow are given. The vibration caused by the oscillatory pressure gradient is determined by the Fourier sine transform and the Laplace transform. In [9], the authors use the fractional derivative method to solve the Rayleigh–Stokes problem on the boundary. In addition, some scholars have used numerical methods to study the Rayleigh–Stokes problem. In [10],

Citation: Liu, S.; Liu, T.; Ma, Q. On a Backward Problem for the Rayleigh–Stokes Equation with a Fractional Derivative. *Axioms* **2024**, *13*, 30. https://doi.org/10.3390/axioms13010030

Academic Editor: Feliz Manuel Minhós

Received: 15 November 2023
Revised: 28 December 2023
Accepted: 28 December 2023
Published: 30 December 2023

Copyright: © 2023 by the authors. Licensee MDPI, Basel, Switzerland. This article is an open access article distributed under the terms and conditions of the Creative Commons Attribution (CC BY) license (https://creativecommons.org/licenses/by/4.0/).

the authors used implicit and explicit difference numerical methods to obtain numerical solutions of second-order generalized thermal fluid Rayleigh–Stokes problems with fractional derivatives. In [11], an approximate numerical method is proposed for the Rayleigh–Stokes problem of generalized second-order fluids in a bounded domain. In [12], the numerical methods with fourth-order spatial accuracy for Rayleigh–Stokes' first problem is studied. In [13,14], the authors study the numerical solutions of Rayleigh–Stokes problems for generalized second-order thermal fluids with fractional derivatives. The other numerical methods for solving Rayleigh–Stokes problems can be seen in the cited works [15–17].

However, in practical problems, the parameters used in most model equations, such as physical parameters, source terms, initial conditions, and boundary conditions are unknown, and these unknown parameters need to be identified through measurement data. Thus, it leads to the inverse problems of the Rayleigh–Stokes equation for second-grade fluids. According to the current research status, the research on the inverse problem of the Rayleigh–Stokes equation is still limited. In [18], an inverse problem to estimate an unknown order of a Riemann–Liouville fractional derivative for a fractional Stokes' first problem is considered. In [19], the authors use the filter regularization method to analyze the Rayleigh–Stokes inverse problem with Gaussian random noise. In [20], the authors use the filter regularization method to identify the unknown source term of the Rayleigh–Stokes problem with Gaussian random noise and prove the error estimation between the regularized solution and the exact solution. But the regularization parameter is an a priori choice rule, which depends on an unknown priori bound. In [21], the authors provide the existence and regularity of the inverse problem for the nonlinear fractional Rayleigh–Stokes equations. In [22,23], the authors give a Tikhonov regularization method and filter regularization method to identify the source term for the Rayleigh–Stokes problem. In [24], the authors use the trigonometric method in nonparametric regression associated to regularize the instable solution of the initial inverse problem for the nonlinear fractional Rayleigh–Stokes equation with random discrete data. In [25], the authors consider the regularity of the solution for a final value problem for the Rayleigh–Stokes equation.

In the following, we consider the backward problem for the Rayleigh–Stokes equation in a general bounded domain. Let $T > 0$ be a given positive number, and Ω be a bounded domain in $\mathbb{R}^d$. The mathematical problem is given by

$$\begin{cases} \partial_t u(x,t) - (1 + \gamma \partial_t^\alpha) \Delta u(x,t) = 0, & (x,t) \in \Omega \times (0,T), \\ u(x,t) = 0, & x \in \partial\Omega, \ t \in (0,T], \\ u(x,T) = g(x), & x \in \Omega, \end{cases} \quad (1)$$

where $\gamma > 0$ is a constant, u is the velocity distribution. $\partial_t = \partial/\partial t$, and ∂_t^α is the Riemann–Liouville fractional derivative of order $\alpha \in (0,1)$ defined by [1]

$$\partial_t^\alpha u(x,t) = \frac{d}{dt} \int_0^t \omega_{1-\alpha}(t-s) u(x,s) ds, \quad \omega_\alpha = \frac{t^{\alpha-1}}{\Gamma(\alpha)}, \quad 0 < \alpha < 1. \quad (2)$$

The backward problem is to find the initial data $u(x,0) = f(x)$ from the given measured data at the final condition $u(x,T) = g(x)$. In practice, the exact data g are approximated by the noisy observation data g^δ, which are assumed to satisfy

$$\|g^\delta - g\| \leq \delta, \quad (3)$$

where $\|\cdot\|$ denotes the $L^2(\Omega)$-norm, and the constant $\delta > 0$ is a noise level.

In this paper, the Tikhonov regularization method is used to study the backward problem of the Rayleigh–Stokes equation with a fractional derivative. This method has dealt with a number of inverse problems, such as the backward problem [26,27] and the inverse unknown source problem [28–30]. We prove the error estimate between the regularized solution and the exact solution under a priori and a posteriori regularization parameter selection rules. The posteriori regularization parameter selection rules only depend on the measured data and do not depend on the priori bound of the exact solution.

The structure of this paper is as follows. Section 2 introduces some preliminary results. Section 3 gives the ill-posedness of problem (1) and the conditional stability of problem (1). In Section 4, the Tikhonov regularization method is used to deal with the backward problem, and the error estimates between the exact solution and the regularized solution are obtained under a priori and a posteriori regularization parameter choice rules.

2. Preliminary Results

Throughout this article, we use the following definitions.

Definition 1. *Let $\{\lambda_n, \phi_n\}$ be the Dirichlet eigenvalues and corresponding eigenvectors of the Laplacian operator $-\Delta$ in Ω. The family of eigenvalues $\{\lambda_n\}_{n=1}^{\infty}$ satisfies $0 < \lambda_1 \leq \lambda_2 \leq \cdots \leq \lambda_n \leq \cdots$, where $\lambda_n \to \infty$ as $n \to \infty$:*

$$\begin{cases} \Delta \phi_n(x) = -\lambda_n \phi_n(x), & x \in \Omega, \\ \phi_n(x) = 0, & x \in \partial\Omega. \end{cases} \quad (4)$$

Definition 2. *For $k > 0$, we define*

$$H^k(\Omega) := \left\{ f \in L^2(\Omega) \,\Big|\, \sum_{n=1}^{\infty} \lambda_n^{2k} |(f, \phi_n)|^2 < +\infty \right\}, \quad (5)$$

equipped with the norm

$$\|f\|_{H^k(\Omega)} = \left(\sum_{n=1}^{\infty} \lambda_n^{2k} |(f, \phi_n)|^2 \right)^{\frac{1}{2}}, \quad k > 0. \quad (6)$$

In the following, we present the solution of the direct problem of the Rayleigh–Stokes equation

$$\begin{cases} \partial_t u(x,t) - (1 + \gamma \partial_t^{\alpha}) \Delta u(x,t) = 0, & (x,t) \in \Omega \times (0,T), \\ u(x,t) = 0, & x \in \partial\Omega,\ t \in (0,T], \\ u(x,0) = f(x), & x \in \Omega. \end{cases} \quad (7)$$

Indeed, suppose that the direct problem (7) has a solution $u(x,t) \in C([0,T]; L^2(\Omega)) \cap C([0,T]; H^2(\Omega) \cap H_0^1(\Omega))$, and using the Equation (2.21) in [31], we obtain

$$u(x,t) = \sum_{n=1}^{\infty} f_n u_n(t) \phi_n(x). \quad (8)$$

Here, $f_n = (f(x), \phi_n(x))$ is the Fourier coefficient, and the function $u_n(t)$ satisfies

$$u_n(t) = \int_0^{\infty} e^{-st} B_n(s) ds, \quad (9)$$

where

$$B_n(s) = \frac{\gamma}{\pi} \frac{\lambda_n s^{\alpha} \sin \alpha\pi}{(-s + \lambda_n \gamma s^{\alpha} \cos \alpha\pi + \lambda_n)^2 + (\lambda_n \gamma s^{\alpha} \sin \alpha\pi)^2}.$$

According to the condition $u(x,T) = g(x)$, and using (9), we obtain

$$g(x) = \sum_{n=1}^{\infty} f_n u_n(T) \phi_n(x) := Kf(x), \quad (10)$$

or equivalently,

$$g_n = f_n u_n(T), \quad (11)$$

where $g_n = (g(x), \phi_n(x))$ is the Fourier coefficient. Here, the linear operator $K : L^2(\Omega) \to L^2(\Omega)$ is defined by

$$Kf(x) = \sum_{n=1}^{\infty} \left[\int_0^{\infty} e^{-sT} B_n(s) ds \right] (f(x), \phi_n(x)) \phi_n(x) = \int_{\Omega} k(x, \omega) f(\omega) d\omega, \quad (12)$$

where

$$k(x, \omega) = \sum_{n=1}^{\infty} \left[\int_0^{\infty} e^{-sT} B_n(s) ds \right] \phi_n(x) \phi_n(\omega).$$

Then, we can obtain the solution of the backward problem (1) as follows

$$f(x) = \sum_{n=1}^{\infty} \frac{g_n}{u_n(T)} \phi_n(x). \quad (13)$$

3. Ill-Posedness and Conditional Stability Estimate

To analyze the ill-posedness and give the conditional stability estimate of the backward problem, we need to provide the following lemmas.

Lemma 1 ([31]). *The functions $u_n(t), n = 1, 2, \cdots$ have the following properties:*

(a) $u_n(0) = 1, \quad 0 < u_n(t) \leq 1, \quad t \geq 0$;
(b) $u_n(t)$ are completely monotone for $t \geq 0$;
(c) $|\lambda_n u_n(t)| \leq c \min\{t^{-1}, t^{\alpha-1}\}, \quad t > 0$;
(d) $\int_0^T |u_n(t)| dt < \frac{1}{\lambda_n}, \quad T > 0$,

where the constant c does not depend on n and t.

Lemma 2 ([19]). *Let us assume that $\alpha \in (0, 1)$. The following estimate holds for all $t \in [0, T]$*

$$u_n(t) \geq \frac{C(\gamma, \alpha, \lambda_1)}{\lambda_n}, \quad (14)$$

where

$$C(\gamma, \alpha, \lambda_1) = \gamma \sin \alpha \pi \int_0^{+\infty} \frac{e^{-sT} s^{\alpha} ds}{\gamma^2 s^{2\alpha} + \frac{s^2}{\lambda_1^2} + 1}. \quad (15)$$

Now, we will prove that the backward problem is ill-posed. By using the result in Lemma 1, for $t > 0$, we have

$$\frac{1}{u_n(T)} \geq \frac{\lambda_n}{c \min\{T^{-1}, T^{\alpha-1}\}}. \quad (16)$$

Hence, we know that $\frac{1}{u_n(T)}$ is a completely monotonic increasing function with respect to λ_n. Then, the small error in the high-frequency components for $g^{\delta}(x)$ will be amplified by the factor $\frac{1}{u_n(T)}$. So, the initial data $u(x, 0) = f(x)$ from the given measured data $g^{\delta}(x)$ are ill-posed.

In the following, we introduce a conditional stability estimate of the backward problem for the fractional Rayleigh–Stokes Equation (1).

Theorem 1. *Let $f \in H^k(\Omega)$ be such that*

$$\|f\|_{H^k(\Omega)} \leq E, \quad (17)$$

for some $E > 0$. Then, we have the following estimate

$$\|f\|_{L^2(\Omega)} \leq C_1 E^{\frac{1}{k+1}} \|g\|^{\frac{k}{k+1}}, \quad (18)$$

where $C_1 = C^{-\frac{k}{k+1}}(\gamma, \alpha, \lambda_1)$.

Proof. From Formula (13), and applying the Hölder inequality, we know

$$\begin{aligned}
\|f\|_{L^2(\Omega)}^2 &= \sum_{n=1}^{\infty} \left| \frac{(g(x), \phi_n(x))}{u_n(T)} \right|^2 \\
&= \sum_{n=1}^{\infty} \frac{|(g(x), \phi_n(x))|^{\frac{2}{k+1}} |(g(x), \phi_n(x))|^{\frac{2k}{k+1}}}{|u_n(T)|^2} \\
&\leq \left[\sum_{n=1}^{\infty} \frac{|(g(x), \phi_n(x))|^2}{|u_n(T)|^{2k+2}} \right]^{\frac{1}{k+1}} \left[\sum_{n=1}^{\infty} |(g(x), \phi_n(x))|^2 \right]^{\frac{k}{k+1}} \\
&\leq \left[\sum_{n=1}^{\infty} \frac{|(f(x), \phi_n(x))|^2}{|u_n(T)|^{2k}} \right]^{\frac{1}{k+1}} \|g\|_{L^2(\Omega)}^{\frac{2k}{k+1}}.
\end{aligned} \qquad (19)$$

By using Lemma 2, we obtain

$$\sum_{n=1}^{\infty} \frac{|(f(x), \phi_n(x))|^2}{|u_n(T)|^{2k}} \leq \sum_{n=1}^{\infty} \frac{\lambda_n^{2k} |(f(x), \phi_n(x))|^2}{C^{2k}(\gamma, \alpha, \lambda_1)} = \frac{\|f\|_{H^k(\Omega)}^2}{C^{2k}(\gamma, \alpha, \lambda_1)}. \qquad (20)$$

Combining Formulas (19) and (20), we obtain

$$\|f\|_{L^2(\Omega)}^2 \leq \frac{\|f\|_{H^k(\Omega)}^{\frac{2}{k+1}}}{C^{\frac{2k}{k+1}}(\gamma, \alpha, \lambda_1)} \|g\|_{L^2(\Omega)}^{\frac{2k}{k+1}}.$$

Hence, we have

$$\|f\|_{L^2(\Omega)} \leq C_1 E^{\frac{1}{k+1}} \|g\|^{\frac{k}{k+1}},$$

where $C_1 = C^{-\frac{k}{k+1}}(\gamma, \alpha, \lambda_1)$. □

Remark 1. Essentially, Theorem 1 provides the following conditional stability estimate

$$\|f_1 - f_2\|_{L^2(\Omega)} \leq C_1 \|f_1 - f_2\|_{H^k(\Omega)}^{\frac{1}{k+1}} \|Kf_1 - Kf_2\|^{\frac{k}{k+1}}.$$

4. Tikhonov Regularization Method and Convergence Estimates

In this section, we solve the backward problem (1) by using the Tikhonov regularization method, which minimizes the function

$$\|Kf - g\|^2 + \beta^2 \|f\|^2; \qquad (21)$$

here, β is a regularization parameter. By Theorem 2.12 in [32], we know that its minimizer $f_\beta(x)$ satisfies

$$K^* K f_\beta(x) + \beta^2 f_\beta(x) = K^* g(x). \qquad (22)$$

Due to the singular value decomposition for a compact self-adjoint operator, we have

$$f_\beta(x) = \sum_{n=1}^{\infty} \frac{u_n(T)}{\beta^2 + u_n^2(T)} (g, \phi_n) \phi_n. \qquad (23)$$

If the observed data $g^\delta(x)$ are noise-contaminated, we have

$$f_\beta^\delta(x) = \sum_{n=1}^{\infty} \frac{u_n(T)}{\beta^2 + u_n^2(T)} (g^\delta, \phi_n) \phi_n. \qquad (24)$$

4.1. A Priori Choice Rule

We first give two lemmas.

Lemma 3. *Assume condition (3) holds, and we have the following estimate*

$$\|f_\beta^\delta(x) - f_\beta(x)\| \leq \frac{\delta}{2\beta}. \qquad (25)$$

Proof. According to the Formulas (3), (23), and (24), we have

$$\begin{aligned}
\|f_\beta^\delta(x) - f_\beta(x)\|^2 &= \left\| \sum_{n=1}^\infty \frac{u_n(T)}{\beta^2 + u_n^2(T)} (g^\delta, \phi_n)\phi_n - \sum_{n=1}^\infty \frac{u_n(T)}{\beta^2 + u_n^2(T)} (g, \phi_n)\phi_n \right\|^2 \\
&= \left\| \sum_{n=1}^\infty \frac{u_n(T)}{\beta^2 + u_n^2(T)} (g^\delta - g, \phi_n)\phi_n \right\|^2 \\
&= \sum_{n=1}^\infty \left(\frac{u_n(T)}{\beta^2 + u_n^2(T)} \right)^2 (g_n^\delta - g_n)^2 \\
&\leq \delta^2 (\sup_{n \geq 1} A(n))^2,
\end{aligned} \qquad (26)$$

where,

$$A(n) = \frac{|u_n(T)|}{\beta^2 + u_n^2(T)} \leq \frac{1}{2\beta}.$$

Thus, we obtain

$$\|f_\beta^\delta(x) - f_\beta(x)\| \leq \frac{\delta}{2\beta}. \qquad (27)$$

The proof of Lemma 3 is complete. □

Lemma 4. *Assume that the condition (17) holds; then, we have*

$$\|f(x) - f_\beta(x)\| = \begin{cases} \beta E \frac{\lambda_1^{1-k}}{2C(\gamma,\alpha,\lambda_1)}, & 0 < k < 1, \\ \beta^k E \sqrt{(\frac{1}{2C(\gamma,\alpha,\lambda_1)})^2 + 1}, & k \geq 1. \end{cases} \qquad (28)$$

Proof. From Formulas (13) and (23), we know

$$\begin{aligned}
\|f(x) - f_\beta(x)\|^2 &= \sum_{n=1}^\infty \left(\frac{1}{u_n(T)} - \frac{u_n(T)}{\beta^2 + u_n^2(T)} \right)^2 g_n^2 \\
&= \sum_{n=1}^\infty \left(\frac{\beta^2}{(\beta^2 + u_n^2(T))u_n(T)} \right)^2 g_n^2 \\
&= \sum_{n=1}^\infty \left(\frac{\beta^2 \lambda_n^k \lambda_n^{-k}}{(\beta^2 + u_n^2(T))u_n(T)} \right)^2 g_n^2 \\
&\leq (\sup_{n \geq 1} B(n))^2 \sum_{n=1}^\infty \frac{\lambda_n^{2k} g_n^2}{u_n^2(T)} \\
&= (\sup_{n \geq 1} B(n))^2 \|f\|_{H^k(\Omega)}^2.
\end{aligned} \qquad (29)$$

Here,

$$B(n) = \frac{\beta^2 \lambda_n^{-k}}{\beta^2 + u_n^2(T)}. \qquad (30)$$

Now, by using Lemma 2, we estimate $B(n)$,

$$B(n) \leq \frac{\beta^2 \lambda_n^{-k}}{2\beta u_n(T)} = \frac{\beta \lambda_n^{-k}}{2 u_n(T)} \leq \frac{\beta \lambda_n^{1-k}}{2C(\gamma, \alpha, \lambda_1)}. \qquad (31)$$

We divide this into the two following cases:
Case 1: If $k \geq 1$, we know

$$\lambda_n^{1-k} = \frac{1}{\lambda_n^{k-1}} \leq \frac{1}{\lambda_1^{k-1}} = \lambda_1^{1-k}. \qquad (32)$$

Combining (29), (31), and (32), we obtain

$$\|f(x)-f_\beta(x)\| \leq \frac{\beta\lambda_1^{1-k}}{2C(\gamma,\alpha,\lambda_1)}\|f\|_{H^k(\Omega)} \leq \beta E \frac{\lambda_1^{1-k}}{2C(\gamma,\alpha,\lambda_1)}. \tag{33}$$

Case 2: If $0 < k < 1$, we choose any $\eta \in (0,1)$ and rewrite $\mathbb{N} = \mathcal{A}_1 \cup \mathcal{A}_2$, where

$$\mathcal{A}_1 = \{n \in \mathbb{N}, \lambda_n^{1-k} \leq \beta^{-\eta}\}, \quad \mathcal{A}_2 = \{n \in \mathbb{N}, \lambda_n^{1-k} > \beta^{-\eta}\}. \tag{34}$$

From Formula (31), we have

$$
\begin{aligned}
\|f(x)-f_\beta(x)\|^2 &\leq \sup_{n\in\mathcal{A}_1}\left(\frac{\beta\lambda_n^{1-k}}{2C(\gamma,\alpha,\lambda_1)}\right)^2 \sum_{n\in\mathcal{A}_1}\lambda_n^{2k}(f(x),\phi_n(x))^2 \\
&\quad + \sup_{n\in\mathcal{A}_2}\left(\frac{\beta^2 \lambda_n^{-k}}{\beta^2 + u_n^2(T)}\right)^2 \sum_{n\in\mathcal{A}_2}\lambda_n^{2k}(f(x),\phi_n(x))^2 \\
&\leq \left(\frac{1}{2C(\gamma,\alpha,\lambda_1)}\right)^2 \beta^{2-2\eta}\|f\|_{H^k(\Omega)}^2 + \sup_{n\in\mathcal{A}_2}\lambda_n^{-2k}\|f\|_{H^k(\Omega)}^2 \\
&\leq \left(\frac{1}{2C(\gamma,\alpha,\lambda_1)}\right)^2 \beta^{2-2\eta}\|f\|_{H^k(\Omega)}^2 + \beta^{\frac{2\eta k}{1-k}}\|f\|_{H^k(\Omega)}^2.
\end{aligned}
\tag{35}
$$

Choosing $\eta = 1-k$, and the Formula (17), we obtain

$$
\begin{aligned}
\|f(x)-f_\beta(x)\|^2 &\leq \left(\frac{1}{2C(\gamma,\alpha,\lambda_1)}\right)^2 \beta^{2-2\eta}\|f\|_{H^k(\Omega)}^2 + \beta^{\frac{2\eta k}{1-k}}\|f\|_{H^k(\Omega)}^2 \\
&= \beta^{2k}E^2\left(\left(\frac{1}{2C(\gamma,\alpha,\lambda_1)}\right)^2 + 1\right).
\end{aligned}
\tag{36}
$$

This means

$$\|f(x)-f_\beta(x)\| \leq \beta^k E \sqrt{\left(\frac{1}{2C(\gamma,\alpha,\lambda_1)}\right)^2 + 1}. \tag{37}$$

The proof of Lemma 4 is complete. □

Theorem 2. *Suppose that a priori condition (17) and the noise assumption (3) hold; then,*
(1) If $k \geq 1$, and we choose $\beta = (\frac{\delta}{E})^{\frac{1}{2}}$, we have the convergence estimate

$$\|f_\beta^\delta(x) - f(x)\| \leq \frac{1}{2}\delta^{\frac{1}{2}}E^{\frac{1}{2}}\left(1 + \frac{\lambda_1^{1-k}}{C(\gamma,\alpha,\lambda_1)}\right). \tag{38}$$

(2) If $0 < k < 1$, and we choose $\beta = (\frac{\delta}{E})^{\frac{1}{k+1}}$, we obtain the convergence estimate

$$\|f_\beta^\delta(x) - f(x)\| \leq \delta^{\frac{k}{k+1}}E^{\frac{1}{k+1}}\left(\frac{1}{2} + \sqrt{\left(\frac{1}{2C(\gamma,\alpha,\lambda_1)}\right)^2 + 1}\right). \tag{39}$$

Proof. According to the triangle inequality and Lemmas 3 and 4, we know

$$\|f_\beta^\delta(x) - f(x)\| \leq \|f_\beta^\delta(x) - f_\beta(x)\| + \|f_\beta(x) - f(x)\|.$$

Hence, we can easily obtain the conclusion to Theorem 2. □

4.2. A Posteriori Choice Rule

In this subsection, we derive the convergence estimate by using a posteriori regularization choice rule (namely Morozov's discrepancy principle).

According to Morozov's discrepancy principle [32], we choose the regularization parameter β as the solution of the following equation

$$\|Kf_\beta^\delta(x) - g^\delta(x)\| = \tau\delta, \tag{40}$$

where $\tau > 1$ is a constant.

Lemma 5. *Set $\rho(\beta) = \|Kf_\beta^\delta(x) - g^\delta(x)\|$. Then, the following results hold*

(a) $\rho(\beta)$ is a continuous function;
(b) $\lim_{\beta \to 0} \rho(\beta) = 0$;
(c) $\lim_{\beta \to +\infty} \rho(\beta) = \|g^\delta(x)\|$;
(d) $\rho(\beta)$ is a strictly increasing function over $(0, +\infty)$.

Proof. The proof follows from the straightforward results using the expressions of

$$Kf_\beta^\delta(x) = \sum_{n=1}^{\infty} \frac{u_n^2(T)}{\beta^2 + u_n^2(T)} (g^\delta(x), \phi_n(x)) \phi_n(x), \tag{41}$$

and

$$\rho(\beta) = \|Kf_\beta^\delta(x) - g^\delta(x)\| = \left(\sum_{n=1}^{\infty} \left(\frac{\beta^2}{\beta^2 + u_n^2(T)} \right)^2 (g^\delta(x), \phi_n(x))^2 \right)^{\frac{1}{2}}. \tag{42}$$

□

Remark 2. *According to Lemma 5, we know there exists a unique solution for Equation (40) if $\|g^\delta\| > \tau\delta > 0$.*

Lemma 6. *If β is the solution of Equation (40), we can obtain the following inequality*

$$\frac{1}{\beta} \leq \begin{cases} \left(\frac{C_2}{\tau-1} \right)^{\frac{1}{k+1}} \left(\frac{E}{\delta} \right)^{\frac{1}{k+1}}, & 0 < k < 1, \\ \left(\frac{C_3}{\tau-1} \right)^{\frac{1}{2}} \left(\frac{E}{\delta} \right)^{\frac{1}{2}}, & k \geq 1, \end{cases} \tag{43}$$

where $C_2 = \frac{1}{2} M(k+1)^{\frac{k+1}{2}} (1-k)^{\frac{1-k}{2}} C^{-k-1}(\gamma, \alpha, \lambda_1)$ and $C_3 = \frac{M\lambda_1^{1-k}}{C^2(\gamma, \alpha, \lambda_1)}$ are independent of s.

Proof. From Equation (40), we have

$$\begin{aligned}
\tau\delta &= \left\| \sum_{n=1}^{\infty} \frac{\beta^2}{\beta^2 + u_n^2(T)} (g^\delta(x), \phi_n(x)) \phi_n(x) \right\| \\
&\leq \left\| \sum_{n=1}^{\infty} \frac{\beta^2}{\beta^2 + u_n^2(T)} (g^\delta(x) - g(x), \phi_n(x)) \phi_n(x) \right\| \\
&\quad + \left\| \sum_{n=1}^{\infty} \frac{\beta^2}{\beta^2 + u_n^2(T)} (g(x), \phi_n(x)) \phi_n(x) \right\| \\
&\leq \delta + \left\| \sum_{n=1}^{\infty} \frac{\beta^2}{\beta^2 + u_n^2(T)} (g(x), \phi_n(x)) \phi_n(x) \right\|.
\end{aligned} \tag{44}$$

Then, we obtain

$$(\tau - 1)\delta \leq \left\| \sum_{n=1}^{\infty} \frac{\beta^2}{\beta^2 + u_n^2(T)} (g(x), \phi_n(x)) \phi_n(x) \right\|. \tag{45}$$

Using the a priori bound condition of $f(x)$, we obtain

$$\left\| \sum_{n=1}^{\infty} \frac{\beta^2}{\beta^2 + u_n^2(T)} (g(x), \phi_n(x)) \phi_n(x) \right\|$$

$$\leq \left\| \sum_{n=1}^{\infty} \frac{\beta^2 u_n(T) \lambda_n^{-k}}{\beta^2 + u_n^2(T)} \frac{\lambda_n^k (g(x), \phi_n(x)) \phi_n(x)}{u_n(T)} \right\|$$

$$\leq \sup_{n \geq 1} \frac{\beta^2 u_n(T) \lambda_n^{-k}}{\beta^2 + u_n^2(T)} \left[\sum_{n=1}^{\infty} \frac{\lambda_n^{2k} g_n^2(x)}{u_n^2(T)} \right]^{\frac{1}{2}}$$

$$= \sup_{n \geq 1} \frac{\beta^2 u_n(T) \lambda_n^{-k}}{\beta^2 + u_n^2(T)} \|f\|_{H^k(\Omega)}, \qquad (46)$$

where

$$H(n) = \frac{\beta^2 u_n(T) \lambda_n^{-k}}{\beta^2 + u_n^2(T)}. \qquad (47)$$

Due to Lemma 2 and Formula (16), we obtain

$$H(n) = \frac{\beta^2 u_n(T) \lambda_n^{-k}}{\beta^2 + u_n^2(T)} \leq \frac{\beta^2 \frac{c \min\{T^{-1}, T^{\alpha-1}\}}{\lambda_n} \lambda_n^{-k}}{\beta^2 + (\frac{C(\gamma, \alpha, \lambda_1)}{\lambda_n})^2} = \frac{\beta^2 c \min\{T^{-1}, T^{\alpha-1}\} \lambda_n^{1-k}}{\beta^2 \lambda_n^2 + C^2(\gamma, \alpha, \lambda_1)}. \qquad (48)$$

Let $s = \lambda_n, M = c \min\{T^{-1}, T^{\alpha-1}\}$; then, we set

$$G(s) = \frac{\beta^2 M s^{1-k}}{\beta^2 s^2 + C^2(\gamma, \alpha, \lambda_1)}. \qquad (49)$$

We divide this into the two following cases:

Case 1: If $0 < k < 1$, then we have $\lim_{s \to 0} G(s) = \lim_{s \to \infty} G(s) = 0$; thus, we know

$$G(s) \leq \sup_{s \in (0, +\infty)} G(s) \leq G(s_0),$$

where $s_0 \in (0, +\infty)$ such that $G'(s_0) = 0$. It is easy to prove that $s_0 = \sqrt{\frac{1-k}{k+1}} \frac{C(\gamma, \alpha, \lambda_1)}{\beta} > 0$; thus, we have

$$G(s) \leq G(s_0) = \frac{1}{2} M (k+1)^{\frac{k+1}{2}} (1-k)^{\frac{1-k}{2}} C^{-k-1}(\gamma, \alpha, \lambda_1) \beta^{k+1} := C_2 \beta^{k+1}. \qquad (50)$$

Case 2: If $k \geq 1$, then we have

$$G(s) \leq \frac{\beta^2 M s^{1-k}}{C^2(\gamma, \alpha, \lambda_1)} \leq \frac{\beta^2 M \lambda_1^{1-k}}{C^2(\gamma, \alpha, \lambda_1)} := C_3 \beta^2. \qquad (51)$$

Combining Formulas (45) and (50) with (51), we obtain

$$(\tau - 1) \delta \leq \begin{cases} C_2 \beta^{k+1} E, & 0 < k < 1, \\ C_3 \beta^2 E, & k \geq 1. \end{cases} \qquad (52)$$

This yields

$$\frac{1}{\beta} \leq \begin{cases} (\frac{C_2}{\tau-1})^{\frac{1}{k+1}} (\frac{E}{\delta})^{\frac{1}{k+1}}, & 0 < k < 1, \\ (\frac{C_3}{\tau-1})^{\frac{1}{2}} (\frac{E}{\delta})^{\frac{1}{2}}, & k \geq 1. \end{cases}$$

Thus, the proof of Lemma 6 is complete. □

Theorem 3. *Suppose a priori condition (17) and the noise assumption (3) hold, and we take the solution of Equation (40) as the regularization parameter; then,*

(1) If $k \geq 1$, we obtain the following convergence estimate

$$\|f_\beta^\delta(x) - f(x)\| \leq C_1(\tau+1)^{\frac{k}{k+1}} \delta^{\frac{k}{k+1}} E^{\frac{1}{k+1}} + \frac{1}{2}\left(\frac{C_3}{\tau-1}\right)^{\frac{1}{2}} \delta^{\frac{1}{2}} E^{\frac{1}{2}}. \qquad (53)$$

(2) If $0 < k < 1$, we obtain the following convergence estimate

$$\|f_\beta^\delta(x) - f(x)\| \leq \left[C_1(\tau+1)^{\frac{k}{k+1}} + \frac{1}{2}\left(\frac{C_2}{\tau-1}\right)^{\frac{1}{k+1}}\right] \delta^{\frac{k}{k+1}} E^{\frac{1}{k+1}}, \qquad (54)$$

where $C_1 = C^{-\frac{k}{k+1}}(\gamma, \alpha, \lambda_1)$, $C_2 = \frac{1}{2}M(k+1)^{\frac{k+1}{2}}(1-k)^{\frac{1-k}{2}} C^{-k-1}(\gamma, \alpha, \lambda_1)$ *and* $C_3 = \frac{M\lambda_1^{1-k}}{C^2(\gamma, \alpha, \lambda_1)}$ *are independent of s.*

Proof. Due to the triangle inequality, we have

$$\|f_\beta^\delta(x) - f(x)\| \leq \|f_\beta^\delta(x) - f_\beta(x)\| + \|f_\beta(x) - f(x)\|. \qquad (55)$$

Firstly, we give an estimate for the second term on the right side of Formula (55),

$$\begin{aligned} Kf_\beta(x) - Kf(x) &= \sum_{n=1}^{\infty} \frac{-\beta^2}{\beta^2 + u_n^2(T)}(g(x), \phi_n(x)) \phi_n(x) \\ &= \sum_{n=1}^{\infty} \frac{-\beta^2}{\beta^2 + u_n^2(T)}(g(x) - g^\delta(x), \phi_n(x)) \phi_n(x) \\ &+ \sum_{n=1}^{\infty} \frac{-\beta^2}{\beta^2 + u_n^2(T)}(g^\delta(x), \phi_n(x)) \phi_n(x). \end{aligned} \qquad (56)$$

Combining Formulas (3) and (40), we obtain

$$\|Kf_\beta(x) - Kf(x)\| \leq \delta + \tau\delta = (\tau+1)\delta. \qquad (57)$$

In addition, by applying a priori bound condition of $f(x)$, we obtain

$$\begin{aligned} \|f_\beta(x) - f(x)\|_{H^k(\Omega)}^2 &= \sum_{n=1}^{\infty} \left(\frac{\beta^2}{\beta^2 + u_n^2(T)}\right)^2 \frac{\lambda_n^{2k}|(g(x), \phi_n(x))|^2}{u_n^2(T)} \\ &\leq \sum_{n=1}^{\infty} \frac{\lambda_n^{2k}|(g(x), \phi_n(x))|^2}{u_n^2(T)} = \|f\|_{H^k(\Omega)}^2 \leq E^2. \end{aligned} \qquad (58)$$

By Theorem 1 and Formula (57), we have

$$\|f_\beta(x) - f(x)\| \leq C_1(\tau+1)^{\frac{k}{k+1}} \delta^{\frac{k}{k+1}} E^{\frac{1}{k+1}}. \qquad (59)$$

Now, we give an estimate for the first term on the right side of Formula (55); similar to Formula (25), we have

$$\|f_\beta^\delta(x) - f_\beta(x)\| \leq \frac{\delta}{2\beta}. \qquad (60)$$

Substituting Formula (43) into Formula (60), we obtain

$$\|f_\beta^\delta(x) - f_\beta(x)\| \leq \begin{cases} \frac{1}{2}\left(\frac{C_2}{\tau-1}\right)^{\frac{1}{k+1}} \delta^{\frac{k}{k+1}} E^{\frac{1}{k+1}}, & 0 < k < 1, \\ \frac{1}{2}\left(\frac{C_3}{\tau-1}\right)^{\frac{1}{2}} \delta^{\frac{1}{2}} E^{\frac{1}{2}}, & k \geq 1. \end{cases} \qquad (61)$$

Combining Formula (59) with Formula (61), we conclude

$$\|f_\beta^\delta(x) - f(x)\| \leq \begin{cases} [C_1(\tau+1)^{\frac{k}{k+1}} + \frac{1}{2}\left(\frac{C_2}{\tau-1}\right)^{\frac{1}{k+1}}] \delta^{\frac{k}{k+1}} E^{\frac{1}{k+1}}, & 0 < k < 1, \\ C_1(\tau+1)^{\frac{k}{k+1}} \delta^{\frac{k}{k+1}} E^{\frac{1}{k+1}} + \frac{1}{2}\left(\frac{C_3}{\tau-1}\right)^{\frac{1}{2}} \delta^{\frac{1}{2}} E^{\frac{1}{2}}, & k \geq 1. \end{cases} \qquad (62)$$

The proof of Theorem 3 is complete. □

5. Conclusions

This paper studies the inverse problem of the Rayleigh–Stokes equation and adopts the Tikhonov regularization method to solve this inverse problem. Based on the conditional stability results, the corresponding convergence estimates are obtained under a priori and a posteriori regularization parameter choice rules, respectively. However, this paper provides a theoretical proof. In future, the validity and stability of the proposed method will be verified numerically. Moreover, we are currently considering the one parameter inversion problem, and next we will consider multi-parameter inversion problems.

Author Contributions: Conceptualization, S.L.; methodology, S.L.; validation, S.L.; formal analysis, T.L.; writing—original draft preparation, S.L. and Q.M.; funding acquisition, S.L. All authors have read and agreed to the published version of the manuscript.

Funding: This work is supported by the Research project of higher school science and technology in Hebei province (QN2021305).

Data Availability Statement: There is no dataset related to this manuscript.

Conflicts of Interest: The authors declare no conflict of interest.

References

1. Podlubny, I. *Fractional Diffusion Equation*; Academic Press: New York, NY, USA, 1999.
2. Podlubny, I. Geometric and physical interpretation of fractional integration and fractional differential differentiation. *Fract. Calc. Appl. Anal.* **2002**, *5*, 367–386.
3. Oldham, K.B.; Spanier, J. *The Fractional Calculus*; Academic Press: New York, NY, USA, 1974.
4. Miller, K.S.; Ross, B. *An Introduction to the Fractional Calculus and Fractional Differential Equations*; John Wiley: New York, NY, USA, 1993.
5. Machado, J.T. A probabilistic interpretation of the fractional-order differentiation. *J. Fract. Calc. Appl. Anal.* **2003**, *6*, 73–80.
6. Hilfer, R. *Application of Fractional Calculus in Physics*; World Scientific: Singapore, 2000.
7. Shen, F.; Tan, W.; Zhao, Y.; Masuoka, T. The Rayleigh-Stokes problem for a heated generalized second grade fluid with fractional derivative model. *Nonliear Anal. Real World Appl.* **2006**, *7*, 1072–1080. [CrossRef]
8. Khan, M.; Anjum, A.; Qi, H.T.; Fetecau, C. On exact solutions for some oscillating motions of a generalized Oldroyd-B fluid. *Z. Angew. Math. Phys.* **2010**, *61*, 133–145. [CrossRef]
9. Khan, M. The Rayleigh-Stokes problem for an edge in a viscoelastic fluid with a fractional derivative model. *Nonlinear-Anal.-Real World Appl.* **2009**, *10*, 3190–3195. [CrossRef]
10. Chen, C.M.; Liu, F.; Burrage, K.; Chen, Y. Numerical methods of the variable-order Rayleigh-Stokes problem for a heated generalized second grade fluid with fractional derivative. *IMA J. Appl. Math.* **2013**, *78*, 924–944. [CrossRef]
11. Zhuang, P.H.; Liu, Q.X. Numerical method of Rayleigh-Stokes problem for heated generalized second grade fluid with fractional derivative. *Appl. Math. Mech. Engl. Ed.* **2009**, *30*, 1533–1546. [CrossRef]
12. Chen, C.M.; Liu, F.; Turner, I.; Anh, V. Numerical methods with fourth-order spatial accuracy for variable-order nonlinear Stokes' first problem for a heated generalized second grade fluid. *Comput. Math. Appl.* **2011**, *62*, 971–986. [CrossRef]
13. Wu, C.H. Numerical solution for Stokes' first problem for a heated generalized second grade fluid with fractional derivative. *Appl. Numer. Math.* **2009**, *59*, 2571–2583. [CrossRef]
14. Mohebbi, A.; Abbaszadeh, M.; Dehghan, M. Compact finite diffeence scheme and RBF meshless approach for solving 2D Rayleigh-Stokes problem for a heated generalized second grade fluid with fractional derivatives. *Comput. Methods Appl. Mech. Eng.* **2013**, *264*, 163–177. [CrossRef]
15. Dehghan, M.; Abbaszadeh, M. A finite element method for the numerical solution of Rayleigh-Stokes problem for a heated generalized second grade fluid with fractional derivates. *Eng. Comput.* **2017**, *33*, 587–605. [CrossRef]
16. Zaky, A.M. An improved tau method for the multi-dimensional fractional Rayleigh-Stokes problem for a heated generalized second grade fluid. *Comput. Math. Appl.* **2018**, *75*, 2243–2258. [CrossRef]
17. Guan, Z.; Wang, X.D.; Ouyang, J. An improved finite difference/finite element method for the fractional Rayleigh-Stokes problem with a nonlinear source term. *J. Appl. Math. Comput.* **2021**, *65*, 451–579. [CrossRef]
18. Yu, B.; Jiang, X.Y.; Qi, H.T. An inverse problem to estimate an unknown order of a Riemann-Liouville fractional derivative for a fractional Stokes' first problem for a heated generalized second grade fluid. *Acta Mech. Sin.* **2015**, *31*, 153–161. [CrossRef]
19. Nguyen, H.L.; Nguyen, H.T.; Mokhtar, K.; Dang, X.T.D. Identifying initial condition of the Rayleigh-Stokes problem with random noise. *Math. Methods Appl. Sci.* **2019**, *42*, 1561–1571. [CrossRef]
20. Nguyen, A.T.; Luu, V.C.H.; Nguyen, H.L.; Nguyen, H.T.; Nguyen, V.T. Identification of source term for the Rayleigh-Stokes problem with Gaussian random noise. *Math. Methods Appl. Sci.* **2018**, *41*, 5593–5601. [CrossRef]

21. Bao, N.T.; Hoang, L.N.; Van, A.V.; Nguyen, H.T.; Zhou, Y. Existence and regularity of inverse problem for the nonlinear fractional Rayleigh-Stokes equations. *Math. Methods Appl. Sci.* **2021**, *44*, 2532–2558.
22. Binh, T.T.; Nashine, H.K.; Long, L.D.; Luc, N.H.; Nguyen, C. Identification of source term for the ill-posed Rayleigh-Stokes problem by Tikhonov regularization method. *Adv. Differ. Equations* **2019**, *2019*, 331. [CrossRef]
23. Liu, S.S. Filter regularization method for inverse source problem of the Rayleigh-Stokes equation. *Taiwan. J. Math.* **2023**, *27*, 847–861. [CrossRef]
24. Tuan, N.H.; Zhou, Y.; Thach, T.N.; Can, N.H. Initial inverse problem for the nonlinear fractional Rayleigh-Stokes equation with discrete data. *Commun. Nonlinear Sci. Numer. Simul.* **2019**, *78*, 104873. [CrossRef]
25. Nguyen, H.L.; Nguyen, H.T.; Zhou, Y. Regularity of the solution for a final value problem for the Rayleigh-Stokes equation. *Math. Methods Appl. Sci.* **2019**, *42*, 3481–3495. [CrossRef]
26. Tuan, N.H.; Long, L.D.; Tatar, S. Tikhonov regularization method for a backward problem for the inhomogeous time-fractional diffusion equation. *Appl. Anal.* **2018**, *97*, 842–863. [CrossRef]
27. Wang, J.G.; Wei, T.; Zhou, Y.B. Tikhonov regularization method for a backward problem for the time-fractional diffusion equation. *Appl. Math. Model.* **2013**, *37*, 8518–8532. [CrossRef]
28. Yang, F.; Zhang, P.; Li, X.X.; Ma, X.Y. Tikhonov regularization method for identifying the space-dependent source for time-fractional diffusion equation on a columnar symmetric domain. *Adv. Differ. Equ.* **2020**, *128*, 2020. [CrossRef]
29. Li, J.; Tong, G.S.; Duan, R.Z.; Qin, S.L. Tikhonov regularization method of an inverse space-dependent source problem for a time-space fractional diffusion equation. *J. Appl. Anal. Comput.* **2021**, *11*, 2387–2401. [CrossRef]
30. Dien, N.M.; Hai, D.N.D.; Viet, T.Q.; Trong, D.D. On Tikhonov's method and optimal error bound for inverse source problem for a time-fractional diffusion equation. *Comput. Math. Appl.* **2020**, *80*, 61–81. [CrossRef]
31. Bazhlekova, E.; Jin, B.T.; Lazarov, R.; Zhou, Z. An analysis of the Rayleigh-Stokes problem for a generalized second-grade fluid. *Numer. Math.* **2015**, *131*, 1–31. [CrossRef]
32. Kirsch, A. *An Introduction to the Mathematical Theory of Inverse Problems*; Springer: Berlin/Heidelberg, Germany, 2011.

Disclaimer/Publisher's Note: The statements, opinions and data contained in all publications are solely those of the individual author(s) and contributor(s) and not of MDPI and/or the editor(s). MDPI and/or the editor(s) disclaim responsibility for any injury to people or property resulting from any ideas, methods, instructions or products referred to in the content.

Article

Solvability Criterion for a System Arising from Monge–Ampère Equations with Two Parameters

Liangyu Wang and Hongyu Li *

College of Mathematics and Systems Science, Shandong University of Science and Technology, Qingdao 266590, China
* Correspondence: skd992179@sdust.edu.cn

Abstract: Monge–Ampère equations have important research significance in many fields such as geometry, convex geometry and mathematical physics. In this paper, under some superlinear and sublinear conditions, the existence of nontrivial solutions for a system arising from Monge–Ampère equations with two parameters is investigated based on the Guo–Krasnosel'skii fixed point theorem. In the end, two examples are given to illustrate our theoretical results.

Keywords: fixed point theorem; Monge–Ampère equations; boundary value problem

MSC: 35J60; 34B15; 47H10

1. Introduction

In this paper, we concentrate on the existence of nontrivial solutions for the boundary value problem:

$$\begin{cases} ((u'(s))^N)' = \lambda N r^{N-1} f(-u(s), -v(s)), & 0 < s < 1, \\ ((v'(s))^N)' = \mu N r^{N-1} g(-u(s), -v(s)), & 0 < s < 1, \\ u'(0) = u(1) = 0, \; v'(0) = v(1) = 0, \end{cases} \quad (1)$$

where $N \geq 1$, $f, g : [0,1] \times [0, +\infty) \times [0, +\infty) \to [0, +\infty)$ are continuous, λ and μ are two positive parameters. Problem (1) emerges when considering the existence of nontrivial solutions for the following Dirichlet problem related to Monge–Ampère equations:

$$\begin{cases} \det(D^2 u) = \lambda f(-u, -v) \text{ in } B, \\ \det(D^2 v) = \mu g(-u, -v) \text{ in } B, \\ u = v = 0 \text{ on } \partial B, \end{cases}$$

where $D^2 u = (\frac{\partial^2 u}{\partial x_i \partial x_j})$ is the Hessian matrix of u, $D^2 v = (\frac{\partial^2 v}{\partial x_i \partial x_j})$ is the Hessian matrix of v, $B = \{x \in R^N : |x| < 1\}$.

Monge–Ampère equations play a crucial role in the exploration of mathematical physics, engineering, biological sciences and other hot application disciplines (see [1]). As is known, Figalli was awarded the Fields Medal in 2018 for his contribution to the Monge–Ampère equation, e.g., see [2]. Caffarelli received the Abel Prize in 2023 for his pioneering contributions to the understanding of the regularity theory of nonlinear partial differential equations, including the Monge–Ampère equation, e.g., see [3]. On the basis of their research, an increasing number of researchers have conducted some investigations associated with Monge–Ampère equations. For example, Mohammed and Mooney studied the singular problems of the Monge–Ampère equation, see [4,5]; Son, Wang, Aranda and Godoy substituted the p-Laplacian operator for the Monge–Ampère operator, thus offering a new conclusion to the corresponding singular problem, which can be found

in [6,7]. Recently, Feng [8] considered the singular problems of p-Monge–Ampère equations. In addition, some scholars have studied the existence of nontrivial radial convex solutions for a single Monge–Ampère equation or systems of such equations, utilizing the theory of topological degree, bifurcation techniques, the upper and lower solutions method, and so on. For further details, see [2–5,8–25] and the references therein.

For example, in [18], Ma and Gao investigated the following boundary value problem:

$$\begin{cases} ((u_1'(t))^n)' = \lambda n t^{n-1} f(-u(t)), \ 0 < t < 1, \\ u'(0) = u(1) = 0. \end{cases} \quad (2)$$

Boundary value Problem (2) arose from the following Monge–Ampère equation:

$$\begin{cases} \det(D^2 u) = \lambda f(-u) \text{ in } B, \\ u = 0 \text{ on } \partial B, \end{cases} \quad (3)$$

where $D^2 u = (\frac{\partial^2 u}{\partial x_i \partial x_j})$ is the Hessian matrix of u, $B = \{x \in R^n : |x| < 1\}$. The global bifurcation technique was applied to ascertain the optimal intervals of parameter λ, thereby further guaranteeing the existence of single or multiple solutions to Problem (2).

In [21], Wang established two solvability criteria for a weakly coupled system:

$$\begin{cases} ((u_1'(t))^N)' = N t^{N-1} f(-u_2(t)), \ 0 < t < 1, \\ ((u_2'(t))^N)' = N t^{N-1} g(-u_1(t)), \ 0 < t < 1, \\ u_1'(0) = u_2'(0) = 0, \ u_1(1) = u_2(1) = 0, \end{cases} \quad (4)$$

where $N \geq 1$. System (4) arose from the following Monge–Ampère equations:

$$\begin{cases} \det(D^2 u_1) = f(-u_2) \text{ in } B, \\ \det(D^2 u_2) = g(-u_1) \text{ in } B, \\ u_1 = u_2 = 0 \text{ on } \partial B, \end{cases}$$

where $B = \{x \in R^N : |x| < 1\}$, and $D^2 u_i$ is the determinant of the Hessian matrix $(\frac{\partial^2 u_i}{\partial x_m \partial x_n})$ of u_i. The existence of convex radial solutions for Problem (4) was established in both the superlinear and sublinear instances, utilizing fixed point theorems within a cone.

In [20], Wang and An discussed the following system of Monge–Ampère equations:

$$\begin{cases} \det(D^2 u_1) = f_1(-u_1, \cdots, -u_n) \text{ in } B, \\ \cdots \\ \det(D^2 u_n) = f_n(-u_1, \cdots, -u_n) \text{ in } B, \\ u(x) = 0 \text{ on } \partial B, \end{cases} \quad (5)$$

where $D^2 u_i = (\frac{\partial^2 u_i}{\partial x_i \partial x_j})$ is the Hessian matrix of u_i, $B = \{x \in R^N : |x| < 1\}$. Obviously, System (5) can readily be changed into the subsequent boundary value problem:

$$\begin{cases} ((u_1'(r))^N)' = N r^{N-1} f_1(-u_1, \cdots, -u_n), \ 0 < r < 1, \\ \cdots \\ ((u_n'(r))^N)' = N r^{N-1} f_n(-u_1, \cdots, -u_n), \ 0 < r < 1, \\ u_i'(0) = u_i(1) = 0, \ i = 1, \cdots, n, \end{cases}$$

where $N \geq 1$. The existence of triple nontrivial radial convex solutions was obtained through the application of the Leggett–Williams fixed point theorem.

In [22], the author studied the following system:

$$\begin{cases} ((u_1'(r))^N)' = \lambda N r^{N-1} f_1(-u_1, \cdots, -u_n), \ 0 < r < 1, \\ \cdots \\ ((u_n'(r))^N)' = \lambda N r^{N-1} f_n(-u_1, \cdots, -u_n), \ 0 < r < 1, \\ u_i'(0) = u_i(1) = 0, \ i = 1, \cdots, n, \end{cases} \quad (6)$$

where $N \geq 1$. System (6) arose from the following system:
$$\begin{cases} \det(D^2 u_1) = \lambda f_1(-u_1, \cdots, -u_n) \text{ in } B, \\ \cdots \\ \det(D^2 u_n) = \lambda f_n(-u_1, \cdots, -u_n) \text{ in } B, \\ u_i = 0 \text{ on } \partial B, i = 1, \cdots, n, \end{cases}$$

where $D^2 u_i = (\frac{\partial^2 u_i}{\partial x_i \partial x_j})$ is the Hessian matrix of u_i, $B = \{x \in R^N : |x| < 1\}$.

Using fixed point theorems and considering sublinear and superlinear conditions, Wang explored the existence of two nontrivial radial solutions for System (6) with a carefully selected parameter.

In [14], Gao and Wang considered the following boundary value problem:
$$\begin{cases} ((u_1'(r))^N)' = \lambda_1 N r^{N-1} f_1(-u_1, -u_2, \cdots, -u_n), \\ ((u_2'(r))^N)' = \lambda_2 N r^{N-1} f_2(-u_1, -u_2, \cdots, -u_n), \\ \cdots \\ ((u_n'(r))^N)' = \lambda_n N r^{N-1} f_n(-u_1, -u_2, \cdots, -u_n), \\ u_i'(0) = u_i(1) = 0, \ i = 1, 2, \cdots, n, \ 0 < r < 1, \end{cases} \quad (7)$$

where $N \geq 1$. System (7) arose from the following system:
$$\begin{cases} \det(D^2 u_1) = \lambda_1 f_1(-u_1, \cdots, -u_n) \text{ in } B, \\ \det(D^2 u_2) = \lambda_2 f_2(-u_1, \cdots, -u_n) \text{ in } B, \\ \cdots \\ \det(D^2 u_n) = \lambda_n f_n(-u_1, \cdots, -u_n) \text{ in } B, \\ u_i = 0 \text{ on } \partial B, i = 1, \cdots, n, \end{cases}$$

where $D^2 u_i = (\frac{\partial^2 u_i}{\partial x_i \partial x_j})$ is the Hessian matrix of u_i, and $B = \{x \in R^N : |x| < 1\}$. By using the method of upper and lower solutions and the fixed point index theory, they established the existence, nonexistence, and multiplicity of convex solutions for Problem (7).

In [12], Feng continued to consider the uniqueness and existence of nontrivial radial convex solutions of System (3). And the author also studied the following system:
$$\begin{cases} \det(D^2 u_1) = \lambda_1 f_1(-u_2) \text{ in } B, \\ \det(D^2 u_2) = \lambda_2 f_2(-u_3) \text{ in } B, \\ \cdots \\ \det(D^2 u_n) = \lambda_n f_n(-u_1) \text{ in } B, \\ u_1 = u_2 \cdots = u_n = 0 \text{ on } \partial B, \end{cases} \quad (8)$$

where $\lambda_i (i = 1, 2, \cdots, n)$ are positive parameters. The author derived novel existence results for nontrivial radial convex solutions of System (8) via employing the eigenvalue theory in a cone and defining composite operators.

In addition, in recent decades, some authors have investigated the existence of nontrivial solutions to other differential equations with parameters. For example, in [26], by employing the Guo–Krasnosel'skii fixed point theorem, Hao et al. considered the existence of positive solutions for a class of nonlinear fractional differential systems, specifically nonlocal boundary value problems with parameters and a p-Laplacian operator. In [27], Yang studied the existence of positive solutions for the Dirichlet boundary value problem of certain nonlinear differential systems using the upper and lower solution method and the fixed point index theory. In [28], Jiang and Zhai investigated a coupled system of nonlinear fourth-order equations based on the Guo–Krasnosel'skii fixed point theorem and Green's functions.

Inspired by literatures [12,14,20–22,26–28], we consider Problem (1). In this paper, under some different combinations of superlinearity and sublinearity of the nonlinear terms, we use the Guo–Krasnosel'skii fixed point theorem to investigate the existence results of System (1) and establish some existence results of nontrivial solutions based on various different values values of λ and μ. Here, we extend the study in literature [21], and the main results differ from those in literatures [12,14,21].

2. Preliminaries

In this section, we list some basic preliminaries to be used in Section 3. For further background knowledge of cone, we refer readers to papers [21,29] for more details.

Lemma 1 (see [29]). *Let E be a Banach space, and $P \subset E$ be a cone. Assume that Ω_1 and Ω_2 are bounded open sets in E, $\theta \in \Omega_1, \overline{\Omega}_1 \subset \Omega_2$; operator $A : P \cap (\overline{\Omega}_2 \backslash \Omega_1) \to P$ is completely continuous. If the following conditions are satisfied,*

$$(i) \|Ax\| \leq \|x\|, \forall x \in P \cap \partial\Omega_1, \|Ax\| \geq \|x\|, \forall x \in P \cap \partial\Omega_2, or$$
$$(ii) \|Ax\| \geq \|x\|, \forall x \in P \cap \partial\Omega_1, \|Ax\| \leq \|x\|, \forall x \in P \cap \partial\Omega_2,$$

then operator A has at least one fixed point in $P \cap (\overline{\Omega}_2 \backslash \Omega_1)$.

In order to solve System (1), we offer a simple transformation, $x(s) = -u(s), y(s) = -v(s)$, in System (1); then, System (1) can be changed to the following system:

$$\begin{cases} ((-x'(s))^N)' = \lambda N s^{N-1} f(x(s), y(s)), & 0 < s < 1, \\ ((-y'(s))^N)' = \mu N s^{N-1} g(x(s), y(s)), & 0 < s < 1, \\ x'(0) = x(1) = 0, \ y'(0) = y(1) = 0. \end{cases} \quad (9)$$

In the following, we treat the existence of positive solutions of System (9).

We let $E = C[0,1] \times C[0,1]$ with norm $\|(x,y)\|_E = \|x\| + \|y\|$, where $\|x\| = \max_{s \in [0,1]} |x(s)|$ and $\|y\| = \max_{s \in [0,1]} |y(s)|$.

We define

$$P = \{(x,y) \in E : x(s) \geq 0, y(s) \geq 0, \forall s \in [0,1], \min_{s \in [\frac{1}{4}, \frac{3}{4}]} (x(s) + y(s)) \geq \frac{1}{4} \|(x,y)\|_E\}.$$

Then, P is a cone of E.

According to literature [21], now, we denote operators A_1, A_2 and A by

$$A_1(x,y)(s) = \int_s^1 \left(\int_0^u \lambda N \tau^{N-1} f(x(\tau), y(\tau)) d\tau \right)^{\frac{1}{N}} du, \ s \in [0,1],$$

$$A_2(x,y)(s) = \int_s^1 \left(\int_0^u \mu N \tau^{N-1} g(x(\tau), y(\tau)) d\tau \right)^{\frac{1}{N}} du, \ s \in [0,1].$$

and $A(x,y) = (A_1(x,y), A_2(x,y)), (x,y) \in E$. Thus, it is easy to see that the fixed points of operator A correspond to solutions of System (9).

Similar to the proof of Lemma 2.3 in literature [21], we can easily obtain the lemma as follows.

Lemma 2. $A : P \to P$ *is completely continuous.*

3. Main Results

We denote

$$f_0 = \limsup_{x+y \to 0^+} \frac{f(x,y)}{(x+y)^N}, \quad g_0 = \limsup_{x+y \to 0^+} \frac{g(x,y)}{(x+y)^N},$$

$$f_\infty = \liminf_{x+y\to\infty} \frac{f(x,y)}{(x+y)^N}, \quad g_\infty = \liminf_{x+y\to\infty} \frac{g(x,y)}{(x+y)^N},$$

$$\widehat{f}_0 = \liminf_{x+y\to 0^+} \frac{f(x,y)}{(x+y)^N}, \quad \widehat{g}_0 = \liminf_{x+y\to 0^+} \frac{g(x,y)}{(x+y)^N},$$

$$\widehat{f}_\infty = \limsup_{x+y\to\infty} \frac{f(x,y)}{(x+y)^N}, \quad \widehat{g}_\infty = \limsup_{x+y\to\infty} \frac{g(x,y)}{(x+y)^N}.$$

$$F = \int_0^1 \left(\int_0^u N\tau^{N-1} d\tau\right)^{\frac{1}{N}} du, \quad G = \int_{\frac{1}{4}}^{\frac{3}{4}} \left(\int_{\frac{1}{4}}^u N\tau^{N-1} d\tau\right)^{\frac{1}{N}} du.$$

For $f_0, g_0, f_\infty, g_\infty \in (0, \infty)$, we define the symbols below:

$$M_1 = \frac{2^N}{G^N f_\infty}, \quad M_2 = \frac{1}{2^N F^N f_0},$$

$$M_3 = \frac{2^N}{G^N g_\infty}, \quad M_4 = \frac{1}{2^N F^N g_0}.$$

Theorem 1. *(1) Assume that $f_0, g_0, f_\infty, g_\infty \in (0, \infty)$, $M_1 < M_2$, $M_3 < M_4$; then, for $\lambda \in (M_1, M_2)$ and $\mu \in (M_3, M_4)$, System (9) has at least one positive solution.*

(2) Assume that $f_0 = 0, g_0, f_\infty, g_\infty \in (0, \infty), M_3 < M_4$; then, for $\lambda \in (M_1, \infty)$ and $\mu \in (M_3, M_4)$, System (9) has at least one positive solution.

(3) Assume that $f_0, f_\infty, g_\infty \in (0, \infty), g_0 = 0, M_1 < M_2$; then, for $\lambda \in (M_1, M_2)$ and $\mu \in (M_3, \infty)$, System (9) has at least one positive solution.

(4) Assume that $f_0 = g_0 = 0, f_\infty, g_\infty \in (0, \infty)$; then, for $\lambda \in (M_1, \infty)$ and $\mu \in (M_3, \infty)$, System (9) has at least one positive solution.

(5) Assume that $f_0, g_0 \in (0, \infty), f_\infty = \infty$ or $f_0, g_0 \in (0, \infty), g_\infty = \infty$; then, for $\lambda \in (0, M_2)$ and $\mu \in (0, M_4)$, System (9) has at least one positive solution.

(6) Assume that $f_0 = 0, g_0 \in (0, \infty), g_\infty = \infty$ or $f_0 = 0, g_0 \in (0, \infty), f_\infty = \infty$; then, for $\lambda \in (0, \infty)$ and $\mu \in (0, M_4)$, System (9) has at least one positive solution.

(7) Assume that $f_0 \in (0, \infty), g_0 = 0, g_\infty = \infty$ or $f_0 \in (0, \infty), g_0 = 0, f_\infty = \infty$; then, for $\lambda \in (0, M_2)$ and $\mu \in (0, \infty)$, System (9) has at least one positive solution.

(8) Assume that $f_0 = g_0 = 0, g_\infty = \infty$ or $f_0 = g_0 = 0, f_\infty = \infty$; then, for $\lambda \in (0, \infty)$ and $\mu \in (0, \infty)$, System (9) has at least one positive solution.

Proof. Due to the similarity in the proofs of the above cases, we demonstrate Case (1) and Case (6).

(1) For each $\lambda \in (M_1, M_2)$ and $\mu \in (M_3, M_4)$, there exists $\varepsilon > 0$ such that

$$\frac{2^N}{G^N(f_\infty - \varepsilon)} \leq \lambda \leq \frac{1}{2^N F^N(f_0 + \varepsilon)},$$

$$\frac{2^N}{G^N(g_\infty - \varepsilon)} \leq \mu \leq \frac{1}{2^N F^N(g_0 + \varepsilon)}.$$

It follows from the definitions of f_0 and g_0 that there exists $r_1 > 0$ such that

$$f(x,y) < (f_0 + \varepsilon)(x+y)^N, \ 0 \leq x + y \leq r_1,$$

$$g(x,y) < (g_0 + \varepsilon)(x+y)^N, \ 0 \leq x + y \leq r_1.$$

Further, we choose the set $\Omega_1 = \{(x,y) \in E : \|(x,y)\|_E < r_1\}$; then, for any $(x,y) \in P \cap \partial\Omega_1$, we obtain

$$0 \leq x(s) + y(s) \leq \|x\| + \|y\| = \|(x,y)\|_E = r_1, \ \forall s \in [0,1],$$

by simple calculation, we have

$$\begin{aligned}
A_1(x,y)(s) &= \int_s^1 \left(\int_0^u \lambda N\tau^{N-1} f(x(\tau),y(\tau)) d\tau\right)^{\frac{1}{N}} du \\
&\leq \int_0^1 \left(\int_0^u \lambda N\tau^{N-1} f(x(\tau),y(\tau)) d\tau\right)^{\frac{1}{N}} du \\
&\leq \int_0^1 \left(\int_0^u \lambda N\tau^{N-1} (f_0+\varepsilon)(x(\tau)+y(\tau))^N d\tau\right)^{\frac{1}{N}} du \\
&\leq (f_0+\varepsilon)^{\frac{1}{N}} \int_0^1 \left(\int_0^u \lambda N\tau^{N-1} (\|x\|+\|y\|)^N d\tau\right)^{\frac{1}{N}} du \\
&= (f_0+\varepsilon)^{\frac{1}{N}} \lambda^{\frac{1}{N}} \int_0^1 \left(\int_0^u N\tau^{N-1} d\tau\right)^{\frac{1}{N}} du \cdot \|(x,y)\|_E \\
&\leq \frac{\|(x,y)\|_E}{2}.
\end{aligned}$$

Next, we show that

$$\|A_1(x,y)\| \leq \frac{1}{2}\|(x,y)\|_E, \ \forall (x,y) \in P \cap \partial\Omega_1. \tag{10}$$

By applying the same method, we deduce

$$\begin{aligned}
A_2(x,y)(s) &= \int_s^1 \left(\int_0^u \mu N\tau^{N-1} g(x(\tau),y(\tau)) d\tau\right)^{\frac{1}{N}} du \\
&\leq \int_0^1 \left(\int_0^u \mu N\tau^{N-1} g(x(\tau),y(\tau)) d\tau\right)^{\frac{1}{N}} du \\
&\leq \int_0^1 \left(\int_0^u \mu N\tau^{N-1} (g_0+\varepsilon)(x(\tau)+y(\tau))^N d\tau\right)^{\frac{1}{N}} du \\
&\leq (g_0+\varepsilon)^{\frac{1}{N}} \int_0^1 \left(\int_0^u \mu N\tau^{N-1} (\|x\|+\|y\|)^N d\tau\right)^{\frac{1}{N}} du \\
&= (g_0+\varepsilon)^{\frac{1}{N}} \mu^{\frac{1}{N}} \int_0^1 \left(\int_0^u N\tau^{N-1} d\tau\right)^{\frac{1}{N}} du \cdot \|(x,y)\|_E \\
&\leq \frac{\|(x,y)\|_E}{2}.
\end{aligned}$$

Next, we show that

$$\|A_2(x,y)\| \leq \frac{1}{2}\|(x,y)\|_E, \ \forall (x,y) \in P \cap \partial\Omega_1. \tag{11}$$

Thus, by (10) and (11), we have

$$\|A(x,y)\|_E = \|A_1(x,y)\| + \|A_2(x,y)\| \leq \|(x,y)\|_E, \ \forall (x,y) \in P \cap \partial\Omega_1. \tag{12}$$

On the other hand, considering the definitions of f_∞ and g_∞, it is easy to see that there exists $\bar{r}_2 > 0$ such that

$$f(x,y) \geq (f_\infty - \varepsilon)(x+y)^N, \ x+y \geq \bar{r}_2,$$

$$g(x,y) \geq (g_\infty - \varepsilon)(x+y)^N, \ x+y \geq \bar{r}_2.$$

Further, we choose $r_2 = \max\{2r_1, 4\bar{r}_2\}$ and denote $\Omega_2 = \{(x,y) \in E : \|(x,y)\|_E < r_2\}$; then, for any $(x,y) \in P \cap \partial\Omega_2$, we obtain

$$\min_{s \in [\frac{1}{4},\frac{3}{4}]} (x(s)+y(s)) \geq \frac{1}{4}\|(x,y)\|_E = \frac{1}{4}r_2 \geq \bar{r}_2,$$

in the following, we deduce

$$A_1(x,y)(\tfrac{1}{4}) = \int_{\tfrac{1}{4}}^{1}(\int_{0}^{u}\lambda N\tau^{N-1}f(x(\tau),y(\tau))d\tau)^{\tfrac{1}{N}}du$$

$$\geq \int_{\tfrac{1}{4}}^{\tfrac{3}{4}}(\int_{\tfrac{1}{4}}^{u}\lambda N\tau^{N-1}f(x(\tau),y(\tau))d\tau)^{\tfrac{1}{N}}du$$

$$\geq \int_{\tfrac{1}{4}}^{\tfrac{3}{4}}(\int_{\tfrac{1}{4}}^{u}\lambda N\tau^{N-1}(f_\infty-\varepsilon)(x(\tau)+y(\tau))^N d\tau)^{\tfrac{1}{N}}du$$

$$\geq (f_\infty-\varepsilon)^{\tfrac{1}{N}}\int_{\tfrac{1}{4}}^{\tfrac{3}{4}}(\int_{\tfrac{1}{4}}^{u}\lambda N\tau^{N-1}(\tfrac{1}{4}\|(x,y)\|_E)^N d\tau)^{\tfrac{1}{N}}du$$

$$= \tfrac{1}{4}(f_\infty-\varepsilon)^{\tfrac{1}{N}}\lambda^{\tfrac{1}{N}}\int_{\tfrac{1}{4}}^{\tfrac{3}{4}}(\int_{\tfrac{1}{4}}^{u}N\tau^{N-1}d\tau)^{\tfrac{1}{N}}du \cdot \|(x,y)\|_E$$

$$\geq \tfrac{\|(x,y)\|_E}{2}.$$

Now, we know that

$$\|A_1(x,y)\| \geq \tfrac{1}{2}\|(x,y)\|_E, \quad \forall (x,y) \in P \cap \partial\Omega_2. \tag{13}$$

In a similar manner, for any $(x,y) \in P \cap \partial\Omega_2$, we obtain

$$A_2(x,y)(\tfrac{1}{4}) = \int_{\tfrac{1}{4}}^{1}(\int_{0}^{u}\mu N\tau^{N-1}g(x(\tau),y(\tau))d\tau)^{\tfrac{1}{N}}du$$

$$\geq \int_{\tfrac{1}{4}}^{\tfrac{3}{4}}(\int_{\tfrac{1}{4}}^{u}\mu N\tau^{N-1}g(x(\tau),y(\tau))d\tau)^{\tfrac{1}{N}}du$$

$$\geq \int_{\tfrac{1}{4}}^{\tfrac{3}{4}}(\int_{\tfrac{1}{4}}^{u}\mu N\tau^{N-1}(g_\infty-\varepsilon)(x(\tau)+y(\tau))^N d\tau)^{\tfrac{1}{N}}du$$

$$\geq (g_\infty-\varepsilon)^{\tfrac{1}{N}}\int_{\tfrac{1}{4}}^{\tfrac{3}{4}}(\int_{\tfrac{1}{4}}^{u}\mu N\tau^{N-1}(\tfrac{1}{4}\|(x,y)\|_E)^N d\tau)^{\tfrac{1}{N}}du$$

$$= \tfrac{1}{4}(g_\infty-\varepsilon)^{\tfrac{1}{N}}\mu^{\tfrac{1}{N}}\int_{\tfrac{1}{4}}^{\tfrac{3}{4}}(\int_{\tfrac{1}{4}}^{u}N\tau^{N-1}d\tau)^{\tfrac{1}{N}}du \cdot \|(x,y)\|_E$$

$$\geq \tfrac{\|(x,y)\|_E}{2}.$$

Now, we know that

$$\|A_2(x,y)\| \geq \tfrac{1}{2}\|(x,y)\|_E, \quad \forall (x,y) \in P \cap \partial\Omega_2. \tag{14}$$

Consequently, by means of (13) and (14), we show that

$$\|A(x,y)\|_E = \|A_1(x,y)\| + \|A_2(x,y)\| \geq \|(x,y)\|_E, \quad \forall (x,y) \in P \cap \partial\Omega_2. \tag{15}$$

Obviously, it follows from (12), (15) and Lemma 1 that A has at least one fixed point $(x,y) \in P \cap (\overline{\Omega}_2 \setminus \Omega_1)$ such that $r_1 \leq \|(x,y)\|_E \leq r_2$. Thus, System (9) has at least one positive solution. The proof of Case (1) is completed.

(6) We assume $f_0 = 0, g_0 \in (0,\infty), g_\infty = \infty$; then, for each $\lambda \in (0,\infty)$ and $\mu \in (0, M_4)$, there exists $\varepsilon > 0$ such that

$$0 < \lambda < \tfrac{1}{2^N F^N \varepsilon}, \quad \tfrac{4^N \varepsilon}{G^N} < \mu < \tfrac{1}{2^N F^N(g_0+\varepsilon)}.$$

Notice that the definitions of f_0 and g_0, and there exists $r_3 > 0$ such that

$$f(x,y) < \varepsilon(x+y)^N, \ 0 \le x+y \le r_3,$$

$$g(x,y) < (g_0+\varepsilon)(x+y)^N, \ 0 \le x+y \le r_3.$$

Further, we choose the set $\Omega_3 = \{(x,y) \in E : \|(x,y)\|_E < r_3\}$; then, for any $(x,y) \in P \cap \partial\Omega_3$, we have

$$\begin{aligned}
A_1(x,y)(s) &= \int_s^1 (\int_0^u \lambda N\tau^{N-1} f(x(\tau),y(\tau)) d\tau)^{\frac{1}{N}} du \\
&\le \int_0^1 (\int_0^u \lambda N\tau^{N-1} f(x(\tau),y(\tau)) d\tau)^{\frac{1}{N}} du \\
&\le \int_0^1 (\int_0^u \lambda N\tau^{N-1} \varepsilon(x(\tau)+y(\tau))^N d\tau)^{\frac{1}{N}} du \\
&\le \varepsilon^{\frac{1}{N}} \int_0^1 (\int_0^u \lambda N\tau^{N-1} (\|x\|+\|y\|)^N d\tau)^{\frac{1}{N}} du \\
&= \varepsilon^{\frac{1}{N}} \lambda^{\frac{1}{N}} \int_0^1 (\int_0^u N\tau^{N-1} d\tau)^{\frac{1}{N}} du \cdot \|(x,y)\|_E \\
&< \frac{\|(x,y)\|_E}{2}.
\end{aligned} \tag{16}$$

Therefore,

$$\|A_1(x,y)\| \le \frac{1}{2}\|(x,y)\|_E, \ \forall (x,y) \in P \cap \partial\Omega_3.$$

Similarly, we have

$$\|A_2(x,y)\| \le \frac{1}{2}\|(x,y)\|_E, \ \forall (x,y) \in P \cap \partial\Omega_3;$$

clearly,

$$\|A(x,y)\|_E \le \|(x,y)\|_E, \ \forall (x,y) \in P \cap \partial\Omega_3. \tag{17}$$

On the other hand, since $g_\infty = \infty$, we know that there exists $\bar{r}_4 > 0$ such that

$$g(x,y) \ge \frac{1}{\varepsilon}(x+y)^N, \ x,y \ge 0, \ x+y \ge \bar{r}_4.$$

Further, we choose $r_4 = \max\{2r_3, 4\bar{r}_4\}$ and denote $\Omega_4 = \{(x,y) \in E : \|(x,y)\|_E < r_4\}$; then, for any $(x,y) \in P \cap \partial\Omega_4$, we have $\min_{s \in [\frac{1}{4},\frac{3}{4}]}(x(s)+y(s)) \ge \frac{1}{4}\|(x,y)\|_E = \frac{1}{4}r_4 \ge \bar{r}_4$. Now, we deduce that

$$\begin{aligned}
A_2(x,y)(\frac{1}{4}) &= \int_{\frac{1}{4}}^1 (\int_0^u \mu N\tau^{N-1} g(x(\tau),y(\tau)) d\tau)^{\frac{1}{N}} du \\
&\ge \int_{\frac{1}{4}}^{\frac{3}{4}} (\int_{\frac{1}{4}}^u \mu N\tau^{N-1} g(x(\tau),y(\tau)) d\tau)^{\frac{1}{N}} du \\
&\ge \int_{\frac{1}{4}}^{\frac{3}{4}} (\int_{\frac{1}{4}}^u \mu N\tau^{N-1} \frac{1}{\varepsilon}(x(\tau)+y(\tau))^N d\tau)^{\frac{1}{N}} du \\
&\ge (\frac{1}{\varepsilon})^{\frac{1}{N}} \int_{\frac{1}{4}}^{\frac{3}{4}} (\int_{\frac{1}{4}}^u \mu N\tau^{N-1} (\frac{1}{4}\|(x,y)\|_E)^N d\tau)^{\frac{1}{N}} du \\
&= \frac{1}{4}(\frac{1}{\varepsilon})^{\frac{1}{N}} \mu^{\frac{1}{N}} \int_{\frac{1}{4}}^{\frac{3}{4}} (\int_{\frac{1}{4}}^u N\tau^{N-1} d\tau)^{\frac{1}{N}} du \cdot \|(x,y)\|_E \\
&> \|(x,y)\|_E.
\end{aligned}$$

Then, it is easy to see that

$$\|A(x,y)\|_E \geq \|A_2(x,y)\| \geq \|(x,y)\|_E, \quad (x,y) \in P \cap \partial\Omega_4. \tag{18}$$

Hence, it follows from (17), (18) and Lemma 1 that A has at least one fixed point $(x,y) \in P \cap (\overline{\Omega}_4 \setminus \Omega_3)$ such that $r_3 \leq \|(x,y)\|_E \leq r_4$, namely (x,y) is a positive solution for System (9), so the proof is completed. □

For $\widehat{f}_0, \widehat{g}_0, \widehat{f}_\infty, \widehat{g}_\infty \in (0, \infty)$, we define the symbols below:

$$Q_1 = \frac{2^N}{G^N \widehat{f}_0}, \quad Q_2 = \frac{1}{2^N F^N \widehat{f}_\infty},$$

$$Q_3 = \frac{2^N}{G^N \widehat{g}_0}, \quad Q_4 = \frac{1}{2^N F^N \widehat{g}_\infty}.$$

Theorem 2. *(1) Assume that $\widehat{f}_0, \widehat{g}_0, \widehat{f}_\infty, \widehat{g}_\infty \in (0, \infty), Q_1 < Q_2, Q_3 < Q_4$; then, for $\lambda \in (Q_1, Q_2)$ and $\mu \in (Q_3, Q_4)$, System (9) has at least one positive solution.*
(2) Assume that $\widehat{f}_0, \widehat{g}_0, \widehat{f}_\infty \in (0, \infty), \widehat{g}_\infty = 0$, and $Q_1 < Q_2$; then, for each $\lambda \in (Q_1, Q_2)$ and $\mu \in (Q_3, \infty)$, System (9) has at least one positive solution.
(3) Assume that $\widehat{f}_0, \widehat{g}_0, \widehat{g}_\infty \in (0, \infty), \widehat{f}_\infty = 0$, and $Q_3 < Q_4$; then, for each $\lambda \in (Q_1, \infty)$ and $\mu \in (Q_3, Q_4)$, System (9) has at least one positive solution.
(4) Assume that $\widehat{f}_0, \widehat{g}_0 \in (0, \infty), \widehat{f}_\infty = \widehat{g}_\infty = 0$; then, for each $\lambda \in (Q_1, \infty)$ and $\mu \in (Q_3, \infty)$, System (9) has at least one positive solution.
(5) Assume that $\widehat{f}_\infty, \widehat{g}_\infty \in (0, \infty), \widehat{f}_0 = \infty$ or $\widehat{f}_\infty, \widehat{g}_\infty \in (0, \infty), \widehat{g}_0 = \infty$; then, for each $\lambda \in (0, Q_2)$ and $\mu \in (0, Q_4)$, System (9) has at least one positive solution.
(6) Assume that $\widehat{f}_0 = \infty, \widehat{f}_\infty \in (0, \infty), \widehat{g}_\infty = 0$ or $\widehat{f}_\infty \in (0, \infty), \widehat{g}_\infty = 0, \widehat{g}_0 = \infty$; then, for each $\lambda \in (0, Q_2)$ and $\mu \in (0, \infty)$, System (9) has at least one positive solution.
(7) Assume that $\widehat{f}_0 = \infty, \widehat{g}_\infty \in (0, \infty), \widehat{f}_\infty = 0$ or $\widehat{g}_\infty \in (0, \infty), \widehat{g}_0 = \infty, \widehat{f}_\infty = 0$; then, for each $\lambda \in (0, \infty)$ and $\mu \in (0, Q_4)$, System (9) has at least one positive solution.
(8) Assume that $\widehat{f}_\infty = \widehat{g}_\infty = 0, \widehat{f}_0 = \infty$ or $\widehat{f}_\infty = \widehat{g}_\infty = 0, \widehat{g}_0 = \infty$; then, for each $\lambda \in (0, \infty)$ and $\mu \in (0, \infty)$, System (9) has at least one positive solution.

Proof. Due to the similarity in the proofs of the above cases, we demonstrate Case (1) and Case (6).

(1) For each $\lambda \in (Q_1, Q_2)$ and $\mu \in (Q_3, Q_4)$, there exists $\varepsilon > 0$ such that

$$\frac{2^N}{G^N(\widehat{f}_0 - \varepsilon)} \leq \lambda \leq \frac{1}{2^N F^N(\widehat{f}_\infty + \varepsilon)},$$

$$\frac{2^N}{G^N(\widehat{g}_0 - \varepsilon)} \leq \mu \leq \frac{1}{2^N F^N(\widehat{g}_\infty + \varepsilon)}.$$

It follows from the definitions of $\widehat{f}_0$ and $\widehat{g}_0$ that there exists $r_1 > 0$ such that

$$f(x,y) \geq (\widehat{f}_0 - \varepsilon)(x+y)^N, \quad x, y \geq 0, x+y \leq r_1,$$

$$g(x,y) \geq (\widehat{g}_0 - \varepsilon)(x+y)^N, \quad x, y \geq 0, x+y \leq r_1.$$

Further, we define the set $\Omega_1 = \{(x,y) \in E : \|(x,y)\|_E < r_1\}$; then, for any $(x,y) \in P \cap \partial\Omega_1$, we obtain

$$A_1(x,y)(\frac{1}{4}) = \int_{\frac{1}{4}}^{1}(\int_{0}^{u}\lambda N\tau^{N-1}f(x(\tau),y(\tau))d\tau)^{\frac{1}{N}}du$$

$$\geq \int_{\frac{1}{4}}^{\frac{3}{4}}(\int_{\frac{1}{4}}^{u}\lambda N\tau^{N-1}f(x(\tau),y(\tau))d\tau)^{\frac{1}{N}}du$$

$$\geq \int_{\frac{1}{4}}^{\frac{3}{4}}(\int_{\frac{1}{4}}^{u}\lambda N\tau^{N-1}(\widehat{f_0}-\varepsilon)(x(\tau)+y(\tau))^N d\tau)^{\frac{1}{N}}du$$

$$\geq (\widehat{f_0}-\varepsilon)^{\frac{1}{N}}\int_{\frac{1}{4}}^{\frac{3}{4}}(\int_{\frac{1}{4}}^{u}\lambda N\tau^{N-1}(\frac{1}{4}\|(x,y)\|_E)^N d\tau)^{\frac{1}{N}}du$$

$$= \frac{1}{4}(\widehat{f_0}-\varepsilon)^{\frac{1}{N}}\lambda^{\frac{1}{N}}\int_{\frac{1}{4}}^{\frac{3}{4}}(\int_{\frac{1}{4}}^{u}N\tau^{N-1}d\tau)^{\frac{1}{N}}du \cdot \|(x,y)\|_E$$

$$\geq \frac{\|(x,y)\|_E}{2}.$$

Next, we show that

$$\|A_1(x,y)\| \geq \frac{1}{2}\|(x,y)\|_E, \ \forall (x,y) \in P \cap \partial\Omega_1. \tag{19}$$

In a similar manner, for any $(x,y) \in P \cap \partial\Omega_1$, we deduce

$$A_2(x,y)(\frac{1}{4}) = \int_{\frac{1}{4}}^{1}(\int_{0}^{u}\mu N\tau^{N-1}g(x(\tau),y(\tau))d\tau)^{\frac{1}{N}}du$$

$$\geq \int_{\frac{1}{4}}^{\frac{3}{4}}(\int_{\frac{1}{4}}^{u}\mu N\tau^{N-1}g(x(\tau),y(\tau))d\tau)^{\frac{1}{N}}du$$

$$\geq \int_{\frac{1}{4}}^{\frac{3}{4}}(\int_{\frac{1}{4}}^{u}\mu N\tau^{N-1}(\widehat{g_0}-\varepsilon)(x(\tau)+y(\tau))^N d\tau)^{\frac{1}{N}}du$$

$$\geq (\widehat{g_0}-\varepsilon)^{\frac{1}{N}}\int_{\frac{1}{4}}^{\frac{3}{4}}(\int_{\frac{1}{4}}^{u}\mu N\tau^{N-1}(\frac{1}{4}\|(x,y)\|_E)^N d\tau)^{\frac{1}{N}}du$$

$$= \frac{1}{4}(\widehat{g_0}-\varepsilon)^{\frac{1}{N}}\mu^{\frac{1}{N}}\int_{\frac{1}{4}}^{\frac{3}{4}}(\int_{\frac{1}{4}}^{u}N\tau^{N-1}d\tau)^{\frac{1}{N}}du \cdot \|(x,y)\|_E$$

$$\geq \frac{\|(x,y)\|_E}{2}.$$

Next, we show that

$$\|A_2(x,y)\| \geq \frac{1}{2}\|(x,y)\|_E, \ \forall (x,y) \in P \cap \partial\Omega_1. \tag{20}$$

Thus, from (19) and (20) we deduce

$$\|A(x,y)\|_E = \|A_1(x,y)\| + \|A_2(x,y)\| \geq \|(x,y)\|_E, \ \forall (x,y) \in P \cap \partial\Omega_1. \tag{21}$$

We let $f^*(u) = \max\limits_{0 \leq x+y \leq u} f(x,y)$, $g^*(u) = \max\limits_{0 \leq x+y \leq u} g(x,y)$; then, we have

$$f(x,y) \leq f^*(u), \ x,y \geq 0, \ x+y \leq u,$$

$$g(x,y) \leq g^*(u), \ x,y \geq 0, \ x+y \leq u.$$

Similar to the proof of [26], we have

$$\limsup_{u \to +\infty}\frac{f^*(u)}{u^N} \leq \widehat{f}_\infty, \ \limsup_{u \to +\infty}\frac{g^*(u)}{u^N} \leq \widehat{g}_\infty.$$

According to the above inequality, there exists $\bar{r}_2 > 0$ such that

$$\frac{f^*(u)}{u^N} \leq \limsup_{u \to +\infty} \frac{f^*(u)}{u^N} + \varepsilon \leq \widehat{f}_\infty + \varepsilon, \ u \geq \bar{r}_2,$$

$$\frac{g^*(u)}{u^N} \leq \limsup_{u \to +\infty} \frac{g^*(u)}{u^N} + \varepsilon \leq \widehat{g}_\infty + \varepsilon, \ u \geq \bar{r}_2;$$

consequently, we have

$$f^*(u) \leq (\widehat{f}_\infty + \varepsilon)u^N, \ g^*(u) \leq (\widehat{g}_\infty + \varepsilon)u^N, \ u \geq \bar{r}_2.$$

Further, we define $r_2 = \max\{2r_1, \bar{r}_2\}$ and denote $\Omega_2 = \{(x,y) \in E : \|(x,y)\|_E < r_2\}$; then, for any $(x,y) \in P \cap \partial \Omega_2$, we obtain

$$f(x(s) + y(s)) \leq f^*(\|(x,y)\|_E), \ g(x(s) + y(s)) \leq g^*(\|(x,y)\|_E),$$

by simple calculation, we have

$$A_1(x,y)(s) \leq \int_0^1 \left(\int_0^u \lambda N \tau^{N-1} f^*(\|(x,y)\|_E) d\tau \right)^{\frac{1}{N}} du$$

$$\leq \int_0^1 \left(\int_0^u \lambda N \tau^{N-1} (\widehat{f}_\infty + \varepsilon)(\|(x,y)\|_E)^N d\tau \right)^{\frac{1}{N}} du$$

$$= (\widehat{f}_\infty + \varepsilon)^{\frac{1}{N}} \lambda^{\frac{1}{N}} \int_0^1 \left(\int_0^u N \tau^{N-1} d\tau \right)^{\frac{1}{N}} du \cdot \|(x,y)\|_E$$

$$\leq \frac{\|(x,y)\|_E}{2}.$$

Now, we know that

$$\|A_1(x,y)\| \leq \frac{1}{2}\|(x,y)\|_E, \ \forall (x,y) \in P \cap \partial \Omega_2. \tag{22}$$

In a similar manner, for any $(x,y) \in P \cap \partial \Omega_2$, we have

$$A_2(x,y)(s) \leq \int_0^1 \left(\int_0^u \mu N \tau^{N-1} g^*(\|(x,y)\|_E) d\tau \right)^{\frac{1}{N}} du$$

$$\leq \int_0^1 \left(\int_0^u \mu N \tau^{N-1} (\widehat{g}_\infty + \varepsilon)(\|(x,y)\|_E)^N d\tau \right)^{\frac{1}{N}} du$$

$$= (\widehat{g}_\infty + \varepsilon)^{\frac{1}{N}} \mu^{\frac{1}{N}} \int_0^1 \left(\int_0^u N \tau^{N-1} d\tau \right)^{\frac{1}{N}} du \cdot \|(x,y)\|_E$$

$$\leq \frac{\|(x,y)\|_E}{2}.$$

Now, we know that

$$\|A_2(x,y)\| \leq \frac{1}{2}\|(x,y)\|_E, \ \forall (x,y) \in P \cap \partial \Omega_2. \tag{23}$$

Clearly, by means of (22) and (23), we deduce that

$$\|A(x,y)\|_E = \|A_1(x,y)\| + \|A_2(x,y)\| \leq \|(x,y)\|_E, \ \forall (x,y) \in P \cap \partial \Omega_2. \tag{24}$$

Consequently, by using (21), (24) and Lemma 1, we conclude that A has at least one fixed point $(x,y) \in P \cap (\overline{\Omega}_2 \setminus \Omega_1)$ such that $r_1 \leq \|(x,y)\| \leq r_2$.

(6) We assume $\widehat{f}_0 = \infty, \widehat{f}_\infty \in (0,\infty), \widehat{g}_\infty = 0$; then, for any $\lambda \in (0, Q_2)$ and $\mu \in (0,\infty)$, there exists $\varepsilon > 0$ such that

$$\frac{4^N \varepsilon}{G^N} < \lambda < \frac{1}{2^N F^N(\widehat{f}_\infty + \varepsilon)}, \quad 0 < \mu < \frac{1}{2^N F^N \varepsilon}.$$

Since $\widehat{f}_0 = \infty$, there exists $r_3 > 0$ such that

$$f(x,y) \geq \frac{1}{\varepsilon}(x+y)^N, \ x, y \geq 0, \ 0 \leq x+y \leq r_3.$$

Further, we define the set $\Omega_3 = \{(x,y) \in E : \|(x,y)\|_E < r_3\}$; then, for any $(x,y) \in P \cap \partial\Omega_3$, we have

$$\begin{aligned} A_1(x,y)(\tfrac{1}{4}) &\geq \int_{\frac{1}{4}}^{\frac{3}{4}} (\int_{\frac{1}{4}}^{u} \lambda N \tau^{N-1} f(x(\tau), y(\tau)) d\tau)^{\frac{1}{N}} du \\ &\geq \int_{\frac{1}{4}}^{\frac{3}{4}} (\int_{\frac{1}{4}}^{u} \lambda N \tau^{N-1} \frac{1}{\varepsilon}(x(\tau)+y(\tau))^N d\tau)^{\frac{1}{N}} du \\ &\geq (\frac{1}{\varepsilon})^{\frac{1}{N}} \int_{\frac{1}{4}}^{\frac{3}{4}} (\int_{\frac{1}{4}}^{u} \lambda N \tau^{N-1} (\frac{1}{4}\|(x,y)\|_E)^N d\tau)^{\frac{1}{N}} du \\ &= \frac{1}{4}(\frac{1}{\varepsilon})^{\frac{1}{N}} \lambda^{\frac{1}{N}} \int_{\frac{1}{4}}^{\frac{3}{4}} (\int_{\frac{1}{4}}^{u} N \tau^{N-1} d\tau)^{\frac{1}{N}} du \cdot \|(x,y)\|_E \\ &\geq \|(x,y)\|_E. \end{aligned}$$

Obviously,

$$\|A(x,y)\|_E \geq \|A_1(x,y)\| \geq \|(x,y)\|_E, \ \forall (x,y) \in P \cap \partial\Omega_3. \tag{25}$$

We let $f^*(u) = \max\limits_{0 \leq x+y \leq u} f(x,y)$, $g^*(u) = \max\limits_{0 \leq x+y \leq u} g(x,y)$. Similar to the proof of [26], we have

$$\limsup_{u \to +\infty} \frac{f^*(u)}{u^N} \leq \widehat{f}_\infty, \ \limsup_{u \to +\infty} \frac{g^*(u)}{u^N} = 0.$$

Moreover, for above $\varepsilon > 0$, it is easy to see that there exists $\bar{r}_4 > 0$ such that

$$\frac{f^*(u)}{u^N} \leq \limsup_{u \to +\infty} \frac{f^*(u)}{u^N} + \varepsilon \leq \widehat{f}_\infty + \varepsilon, \ u \geq \bar{r}_4,$$

$$\frac{g^*(u)}{u^N} \leq \limsup_{u \to +\infty} \frac{g^*(u)}{u^N} + \varepsilon = \varepsilon, \ u \geq \bar{r}_4;$$

consequently, we obtain

$$f^*(u) \leq (\widehat{f}_\infty + \varepsilon)u^N, \ g^*(u) \leq \varepsilon u^N, \ u \geq \bar{r}_4.$$

Further, we define $r_4 = \max\{2r_3, \bar{r}_4\}$ and denote $\Omega_4 = \{(x,y) \in E : \|(x,y)\|_E < r_4\}$; then, for any $(x,y) \in P \cap \partial\Omega_4$, we have

$$f(x(s)+y(s)) \leq f^*(\|(x,y)\|_E), \ g(x(s)+y(s)) \leq g^*(\|(x,y)\|_E),$$

Now, we deduce that

$$A_1(x,y)(s) \leq \int_0^1 (\int_0^u \lambda N\tau^{N-1} f^*(\|(x,y)\|_E) d\tau)^{\frac{1}{N}} du$$
$$\leq \int_0^1 (\int_0^u \lambda N\tau^{N-1} (\widehat{f}_\infty + \varepsilon)(\|(x,y)\|_E)^N d\tau)^{\frac{1}{N}} du$$
$$= (\widehat{f}_\infty + \varepsilon)^{\frac{1}{N}} \lambda^{\frac{1}{N}} \int_0^1 (\int_0^u N\tau^{N-1} d\tau)^{\frac{1}{N}} du \cdot \|(x,y)\|_E$$
$$\leq \frac{\|(x,y)\|_E}{2}.$$

Therefore,

$$\|A_1(x,y)\| \leq \frac{1}{2}\|(x,y)\|_E, \quad \forall (x,y) \in P \cap \partial\Omega_4. \tag{26}$$

Likewise, for any $(x,y) \in P \cap \partial\Omega_4$, we have

$$A_2(x,y)(s) \leq \int_0^1 (\int_0^u \mu N\tau^{N-1} g^*(\|(x,y)\|_E) d\tau)^{\frac{1}{N}} du$$
$$\leq \int_0^1 (\int_0^u \mu N\tau^{N-1} \varepsilon(\|(x,y)\|_E)^N d\tau)^{\frac{1}{N}} du$$
$$= \varepsilon^{\frac{1}{N}} \mu^{\frac{1}{N}} \int_0^1 (\int_0^u N\tau^{N-1} d\tau)^{\frac{1}{N}} du \cdot \|(x,y)\|_E$$
$$\leq \frac{\|(x,y)\|_E}{2}.$$

That is,

$$\|A_2(x,y)\| \leq \frac{1}{2}\|(x,y)\|_E, \quad \forall (x,y) \in P \cap \partial\Omega_4. \tag{27}$$

Obviously, from (26) and (27), we deduce

$$\|A(x,y)\|_E = \|A_1(x,y)\| + \|A_2(x,y)\| \leq \|(x,y)\|_E, \quad \forall (x,y) \in P \cap \partial\Omega_4. \tag{28}$$

Hence, by using (25), (28) and Lemma 1, we conclude that A has at least one fixed point $(x,y) \in P \cap (\overline{\Omega}_4 \setminus \Omega_3)$ such that $r_3 \leq \|(x,y)\|_E \leq r_4$, namely (x,y) is a positive solution for System (9). □

4. Applications

Example 1. *We consider the following boundary value problem:*

$$\begin{cases} ((-x'(s))^3)' = 3\lambda s^2 f(x(s), y(s)), & 0 < s < 1, \\ ((-y'(s))^3)' = 3\mu s^2 g(x(s), y(s)), & 0 < s < 1, \\ x'(0) = x(1) = 0, \ y'(0) = y(1) = 0, \end{cases} \tag{29}$$

We take $f(x,y) = (x+y)^{N+2}$, $g(x,y) = (x+y)^N + (x+y)^N e^{x+y}$, where $N = 3$. By simple calculation, we obtain $M_4 \approx 0.0625$, and

$$f_0 = \limsup_{x+y \to 0^+} \frac{f(x,y)}{(x+y)^N} = \limsup_{x+y \to 0^+} (x+y)^2 = 0,$$

$$g_0 = \limsup_{x+y \to 0^+} \frac{g(x,y)}{(x+y)^N} = \limsup_{x+y \to 0^+} (1 + e^{x+y}) = 2,$$

$$f_\infty = \liminf_{x+y \to \infty} \frac{f(x,y)}{(x+y)^N} = \liminf_{x+y \to \infty} (x+y)^2 = \infty.$$

Then, for each $\lambda \in (0,\infty)$ and $\mu \in (0,0.0625)$, by Theorem 1 (6), we determine that System (29) has at least one positive solution.

Example 2. We consider the following boundary value problem:

$$\begin{cases} ((-x'(s))^3)' = 3\lambda s^2 f(x(s), y(s)), & 0 < s < 1, \\ ((-y'(s))^3)' = 3\mu s^2 g(x(s), y(s)), & 0 < s < 1, \\ x'(0) = x(1) = 0, \ y'(0) = y(1) = 0, \end{cases} \quad (30)$$

We take $f(x,y) = \frac{(x+y)^N}{\tan(x+y)^N}$, $g(x,y) = \frac{1}{x+y}$, where $N = 3$. By simple calculation, we obtain $Q_2 \approx 0.1962$, and

$$\widehat{f}_0 = \liminf_{x+y \to 0^+} \frac{f(x,y)}{(x+y)^N} = \liminf_{x+y \to 0^+} \frac{1}{\arctan(x+y)^N} = \infty,$$

$$\widehat{g}_\infty = \limsup_{x+y \to \infty} \frac{g(x,y)}{(x+y)^N} = \limsup_{x+y \to \infty} \frac{1}{(x+y)^{N+1}} = 0,$$

$$\widehat{f}_\infty = \limsup_{x+y \to \infty} \frac{f(x,y)}{(x+y)^N} = \limsup_{x+y \to \infty} \frac{1}{\arctan(x+y)^N} = \frac{2}{\pi}.$$

Then, for each $\lambda \in (0, 0.1962)$ and $\mu \in (0, \infty)$, by Theorem 2 (6), we determine that System (30) has at least one positive solution.

5. Conclusions

The system of Monge–Ampère equations is significant in various fields of study, including geometry, mathematical physics, materials science, and others. In this paper, by considering some combinations of superlinearity and sublinearlity of functions f and g, we use the Guo–Krasnosel'skii fixed point theorem to study the existence of nontrivial solutions for a system of Monge–Ampère equations with two parameters and establish diverse existence outcomes for nontrivial solutions based on various values of λ and μ which enrich the theories for the system of Monge–Ampère equations. The research in this paper is different from reference [21]. When $\lambda = \mu = 1$ in System (1), System (1) can be reduced to System (4) of reference [21]; then, it can be simply seen that System (4) is a special case of this paper, so this paper can be said to be a generalization of reference [21].

Author Contributions: Conceptualization, L.W. and H.L.; methodology, H.L.; validation, L.W. and H.L.; writing—original draft preparation, L.W.; writing—review and editing, H.L. All authors have read and agreed to the published version of the manuscript.

Funding: The project is supported by the National Natural Science Foundation of China (11801322) and Shandong Natural Science Foundation (ZR2021MA064).

Data Availability Statement: Data are contained within the article.

Acknowledgments: The authors would like to thank reviewers for their valuable comments, which help to enrich the content of this paper.

Conflicts of Interest: The authors declare no conflicts of interest.

References

1. Gilbarg, D.; Trudinger, N.S. *Elliptic Partial Differential Equations of Second Order*; Springer: Berlin/Heidelberg, Germany, 2001.
2. Figalli, A. *The Monge-Ampère Equation and Its Applications*; European Mathematical Society: Helsinki, Finland, 2017.
3. Caffarelli, L.A. Interior $W^{2,p}$ estimates for solutions of the Monge-Ampère equation. *Ann. Math.* **1990**, *131*, 135–150. [CrossRef]
4. Mohammed, A. Singular boundary value problems for the Monge-Ampère equation. *Nonlinear Anal-Theor.* **2009**, *70*, 457–464. [CrossRef]
5. Mooney, C. Partial regularity for singular solutions to the Monge-Ampère equation. *Commun. Pure Appl. Math.* **2015**, *68*, 1066–1084. [CrossRef]

6. Aranda, C.; Godoy, T. Existence and multiplicity of positive solutions for a singular problem associated to the *p*-laplacian operator. *Electron. J. Differ. Eq.* **2004**, *2004*, 281–286.
7. Son, B.; Wang, P. Analysis of positive radial solutions for singular superlinear *p*-Laplacian systems on the exterior of a ball. *Nonlinear Anal.* **2020**, *192*, 111657. [CrossRef]
8. Feng, M. Eigenvalue problems for singular *p*-Monge-Ampère equations. *J. Math. Anal. Appl.* **2023**, *528*, 127538. [CrossRef]
9. Bruno, F.; Nicolai, K.; Sergio, P. Nontrivial solutions for Monge-Ampère type operators in convex domains. *Manuscripta Math.* **1993**, *79*, 13–26. [CrossRef]
10. Delanoë, P. Radially symmetric boundary value problems for real and complex elliptic Monge-Ampère equations. *J. Differ. Equ.* **1985**, *58*, 318–344. [CrossRef]
11. Feng, M. A class of singular coupled systems of superlinear Monge-Ampère equations. *Acta Math. Appl. Sin. Engl. Ser.* **2022**, *38*, 925–942. [CrossRef]
12. Feng, M. Convex solutions of Monge-Ampère equations and systems: Existence, uniqueness and asymptotic behavior. *Adv. Nonlinear Anal.* **2020**, *10*, 371–399. [CrossRef]
13. Froese Hamfeldt, B. A strong comparison principle for the generalized Dirichlet problem for Monge-Ampère. *arXiv* **2023**, arXiv:2306.01532v1.
14. Gao, M.; Wang, F. Existence of convex solutions for systems of Monge-Ampère equations. *Bound. Value Probl.* **2015**, *2015*, 88–92. [CrossRef]
15. Hu, S.; Wang, H. Convex solutions of boundary value problem arising from Monge-Ampère equations. *Discret. Contin. Dyn. Syst.* **2006**, *16*, 705–720. [CrossRef]
16. Kutev, N.D. Nontrivial solutions for the equations of Monge-Ampère type. *J. Math. Anal.* **1988**, *132*, 424–433. [CrossRef]
17. Li, Y.; Lu, S. Existence and nonexistence to exterior Dirichlet problem for Monge-Ampère equation. *Calc. Var. Partial Differ. Equ.* **2018**, *57*, 161. [CrossRef]
18. Ma, R.; Gao, H. Positive convex solutions of boundary value problems arising from Monge-Ampère equations. *Appl. Math. Comput.* **2015**, *259*, 390–402. [CrossRef]
19. Tso, K. On a real Monge-Ampère functional. *Invent. Math.* **1990**, *101*, 425–448. [CrossRef]
20. Wang, F.; An, Y. Triple nontrivial radial convex solutions of systems of Monge-Ampère equations. *Appl. Math. Lett.* **2012**, *25*, 88–92. [CrossRef]
21. Wang, H. Convex solutions of systems arising from Monge-Ampère equations. *Electron. J. Qual. Theory Differ. Equ.* **2009**, *2009*, 1–8.
22. Wang, H. Convex solutions of systems of Monge-Ampère equations. *arXiv* **2010**, arXiv:1007.3013v2.
23. Zhang, X.; Du, Y. Sharp conditions for the existence of boundary blow-up solutions to the Monge-Ampère equation. *Calc. Var. Partial Differ. Equ.* **2018**, *57*, 30. [CrossRef]
24. Zhang, X.; Feng, M. Blow-up solutions to the Monge-Ampère equation with a gradient term: Sharp conditions for the existence and asymptotic estimates. *Calc. Var. Partial Differ. Equ.* **2022**, *61*, 208. [CrossRef]
25. Zhang, X.; Feng, M. Boundary blow-up solutions to the Monge-Ampère equation: Sharp conditions and asymptotic behavior. *Adv. Nonlinear Anal.* **2020**, *9*, 729–744. [CrossRef]
26. Hao, X.; Wang, H.; Liu, L.; Cui, Y. Positive solutions for a system of nonlinear fractional nonlocal boundary value problems with parameters and *p*-Laplacian operator. *Bound. Value Probl.* **2017**, *2017*, 182. [CrossRef]
27. Yang, X. Existence of positive solutions for 2m-order nonlinear differential systems. *Nonlinear Anal-Theor.* **2005**, *61*, 77–95. [CrossRef]
28. Jiang, R.; Zhai, C. Positive solutions for a system of fourth-order differential equations with integral boundary conditions and two parameters. *Nonlinear Anal-Model.* **2018**, *23*, 401–422. [CrossRef]
29. Guo, D.; Lakshmikantham, V. *Nonlinear Problems in Abstract Cones*; Academic Press: San Diego, CA, USA, 2014.

Disclaimer/Publisher's Note: The statements, opinions and data contained in all publications are solely those of the individual author(s) and contributor(s) and not of MDPI and/or the editor(s). MDPI and/or the editor(s) disclaim responsibility for any injury to people or property resulting from any ideas, methods, instructions or products referred to in the content.

Article

New Simplified High-Order Schemes for Solving SDEs with Markovian Switching Driven by Pure Jumps

Yang Li *, Yingmei Xu, Qianhai Xu and Yu Zhang

College of Science, University of Shanghai for Science and Technology, Shanghai 200093, China; 212122286@st.usst.edu.cn (Y.X.); 222122151@st.usst.edu.cn (Q.X.); 222122200@st.usst.edu.cn (Y.Z.)
* Correspondence: yangli@usst.edu.cn

Abstract: New high-order weak schemes are proposed and simplified to solve stochastic differential equations with Markovian switching driven by pure jumps (PJ-SDEwMs). Using Malliavin calculus theory, it is rigorously proven that the new numerical schemes can achieve a high-order convergence rate. Some numerical experiments are provided to show the efficiency and accuracy.

Keywords: numerical scheme; pure jumps; Markovian switching; Malliavin calculus

MSC: 65C30; 60H35

Citation: Li, Y.; Xu, Y.; Xu, Q.; Zhang, Y. New Simplified High-Order Schemes for Solving SDEs with Markovian Switching Driven by Pure Jumps. Axioms **2024**, 13, 190. https://doi.org/10.3390/axioms13030190

Academic Editor: Valery Y. Glizer

Received: 25 January 2024
Revised: 7 March 2024
Accepted: 11 March 2024
Published: 13 March 2024

Copyright: © 2024 by the authors. Licensee MDPI, Basel, Switzerland. This article is an open access article distributed under the terms and conditions of the Creative Commons Attribution (CC BY) license (https:// creativecommons.org/licenses/by/ 4.0/).

1. Introduction

Let $(\Omega, \mathscr{F}, \{\mathscr{F}_t\}_{t\geq 0}, P)$ be a complete probability space with a filtration $\{\mathscr{F}_t\}_{t\geq 0}$ generated by a Poisson process. In this paper, we mainly study the second-order weak schemes of the following Equations (PJ-SDEwMs) on the probability space $(\Omega, \mathscr{F}, \{\mathscr{F}_t\}_{t\geq 0}, P)$:

$$X_t = X_0 + \int_0^t a(s, X_s, r_s)ds + \int_0^t \int_{\mathcal{E}} b(s, X_s, r_s, e)\tilde{N}(de, ds) \tag{1}$$

with initial value $X_0 \in \mathbb{R}^d$, where r_s is Markov chain, $\tilde{N}(de, ds)$ is a compensated Poisson measure, and $\mathcal{E} = \mathbb{R}^d \setminus \{0\}$ is equipped with its Borel field E. The drift coefficient is denoted by $a : [0, T] \times \mathbb{R}^d \times \mathbb{S} \to \mathbb{R}^d$, and the jump diffusion coefficient is represented by $b : [0, T] \times \mathbb{R}^d \times \mathbb{S} \times \mathcal{E} \to \mathbb{R}^d$.

Recently, the study of SDEs with Markovian switching driven by pure jumps has attracted increasing interest. PJ-SDEwMs can be seen as a generalization of the SDEs with jump. It is also possible to think of it as a generalization of SDEs with Markovian switching, of course. It is not only used in finance but also has a wide range of applications in control systems, bio-mathematics, chemistry and mechanics (see [1–3]). The authors [4] study mode coupling in a multimode step-index microstructured polymer optical fibers for potential sensing and communication applications. Ji and Chizeck [5] focused on the control problem for systems with continuous-time Markovian jump parameters. Mao [6] discussed the exponential stability for general nonlinear SDEwMs. Similar to SDEs with jump, it is difficult to obtain an explicit solution for SDEwMs. Therefore, we need effective schemes which are accurate and computationally convenient to approximate the true solutions. Yuan and Mao [7] discovered the convergence of the Euler–Maruyama scheme, which is used to obtain the stationary distribution of SDEwMs in [8]. Mao and Yuan [9] gave the systematic presentation of the theory of SDEs with Markovian switching. Then, the existence and uniqueness of solutions for neutral SDEwMs were proven in [10] under non-Lipschitz conditions, and Euler approximate solutions were provided for solving SDEwMs. Common numerical schemes for solving SDEs with jumps or SDEwMs include Euler–Maruyama scheme [7,9,11,12], Milstein scheme [13,14], and jump-adapted scheme [15,16]. The authors of [17] studied the balanced implicit numerical methods for solving SDEs driven by Poisson jumps. Zhou and Mamon [18] expanded three short-rate models, integrating the switching of economic regimes via a discrete-time finite-state Markov chain.

A high-order model incorporating drift and volatility modulation by a discrete-time weak Markov chain is introduced in [19]. Yang, Yin and Li [20] utilized stochastic approximation techniques to analyze the stability of numerical solutions for jump diffusions with Markovian switching. Furthermore, the authors [21] study the convergence of SDEs differential equations containing delay and Markovian switching, and an Euler scheme for solving SDEwMs under non-Lipschitz conditions is given in [22]. Given the application requirements in finance and related fields, there is an increasing interest in studying high-order numerical schemes for solving SDEs. For instance, Fan [23] developed a strong approximation order 1.5 scheme for solutions of SDEwMs. Liu and Li [24] proved the convergence of the weak stochastic Taylor scheme with an appropriate order. In [25], a new weak scheme for solving SDEwMs driven by Brownian motion was proposed and achieved the convergence rate of second-order. Additionally, the numerical results of several weak schemes are presented, with a focus on the second-order weak stochastic Taylor scheme and the extrapolation of the Euler scheme. We refer to the high-order numerical methods of solving SDEs in [24–27] to propose novel numerical schemes of pure jump SDEs, which can achieve a weak second-order convergence rate.

The primary contributions of this paper can be succinctly highlighted as follows:

- For PJ-SDEwMs with mark-dependent jump coefficient $b = b(t, X_t, r_t, e)$, we first propose Scheme 1 using Wagner–Platen expansion. However, Scheme 1 contains multiple stochastic integrals, which are not easily computed. Thus, to avoid the use of some double integrals, we propose another new Scheme 2, by employing the trapezoidal rule to approximate the following multiple stochastic integrals

$$\int_{t_n}^{t_{n+1}} \int_{t_n}^{t} \int_{\mathcal{E}} L_e^1 a(s, X_s, r_s) \tilde{N}(de, ds) \, dt \quad \text{and} \quad \int_{t_n}^{t_{n+1}} \int_{\mathcal{E}} \int_{t_n}^{t} L^0 b(s, X_s, r_s, e) ds \, \tilde{N}(de, dt).$$

Furthermore, we can use the definition of compound Poisson process to compute

$$\int_{t_n}^{t_{n+1}} \int_{\mathcal{E}} \int_{t_n}^{t} \int_{\mathcal{E}} L_{e_1} b(s, X_s, r_s, e_2) \tilde{N}(de_1, ds) \tilde{N}(de_2, dt),$$

which has no high-accuracy based on the truncation approximation.

- Especially, for PJ-SDEwMs with mark-independent jump coefficient $b = b(t, X_t, r_t)$, we propose Scheme 3 by using the trapezoidal rule and duality formula, which does not involve multiple stochastic integrals. Moreover, Scheme 3 is not a special case of Scheme 2. Using Malliavin calculus theory, it is strictly proven that Scheme 3 has a local weak order-3.0 convergence rate. The greatest state difference and the upper bound of the state value are connected to the convergence rate.

- The convergence and stability results of Schemes 2 and 3 are validated through numerical experiments, which are also compared with the Euler scheme to verify its effectiveness and accuracy. Scheme 3 is simpler and faster than Scheme 2 in the case of mark-independent PJ-SDEwMs.

The following is a list of some notations to be used later: In Section 2, we give the introduction of fundamental concepts, encompassing the Markov Chain, Itô-Taylor expansion, and Malliavin stochastic calculus which include duality formula and chain rule. Section 3 presents our novel weak second-order numerical schemes, accompanied by a rigorous proof establishing their local weak convergence order of 3.0. In Section 4, we give the practical application of our proposed new schemes, where we present some numerical examples to validate the effectiveness and accuracy of them. The paper concludes with Section 5, providing a succinct summary of our work.

The following notations are listed for future reference:

- $C_b^{l,k}$ is the set of continuously differential functions $\psi : [0,T] \times \mathbb{R}^q \to \mathbb{R}^q$ with uniformly bounded partial derivatives $\partial_t^{l_1}\psi$ and $\partial_x^{k_1}\psi$ for $1 \le l_1 \le l$ and $1 \le k_1 \le k$. The notation C_b^k is similarly defined.
- $C_p(\mathbb{R}^d, \mathbb{R})$ is the set of functions which have at most polynomial growth.
- C is a generic constant depending only on the upper bounds of derivatives of a, b, g and the largest state difference.

2. Preliminaries and Notation

2.1. Markov Chain

On the probability space $(\Omega, \mathscr{F}, \{\mathscr{F}_t\}_{t\ge 0}, P)$, we assume that $\{r_t, t \ge 0\}$ is a right-continuous Markov chain and takes values in a finite state space $\mathbb{S} = \{1, 2, \ldots, M\}$ with generator $Q = (q_{ij})_{M\times M}$

$$P(r_{t+\delta} = j \mid r_t = i) = \begin{cases} q_{ij}\delta + o(\delta), & \text{if } i \ne j \\ 1 + q_{ii}\delta + o(\delta), & \text{if } i = j \end{cases} \quad (2)$$

where $\delta > 0$, $q_{ij} \ge 0$ and, for $i \ne j$, $q_{ii} = -\sum_{i\ne j} q_{ij}$. Let $\mathcal{E} = \mathbb{R}\setminus\{0\}$ be the mark set equipped with its Borel field $\mathcal{B}(\mathcal{E})$. Now, on $\mathcal{E} \times [0,T]$, we consider a given intensity measure of the form $\lambda(de) := \gamma(e)de$ with kernel function $\gamma(e) \ge 0$ for all $e \in \mathcal{E}$ and $\lambda(de) := 0$ for $e \notin \mathcal{E}$, and suppose that the total intensity $\lambda_{\mathcal{E}} := \int_{\mathcal{E}} \gamma(e)de < \infty$. Moreover, $dr_t = \int_{\mathcal{E}} h(r_{t-}, e) N(de, dt)$ with $h(i,e) = j - i$ for $e \in \Delta_{ij}$ and $h(i,e) = 0$ for $e \notin \Delta_{ij}$, which the intervals Δ_{ij} have length q_{ij}, that is

$$\begin{aligned}
\Delta_{12} &= [0, q_{12}), \quad \Delta_{13} = [q_{12}, q_{12}+q_{13}), \quad \ldots, \quad \Delta_{1M} = \left[\sum_{j=2}^{M-1} q_{1j}, \sum_{j=2}^{M} q_{1j}\right), \\
\Delta_{21} &= \left[\sum_{j=2}^{M} q_{1j}, \sum_{j=2}^{M} q_{1j} + q_{21}\right), \quad \Delta_{23} = \left[\sum_{j=2}^{M} q_{1j} + q_{21}, \sum_{j=2}^{M} q_{1j} + q_{21} + q_{23}\right), \ldots, \\
\Delta_{2M} &= \left[\sum_{j=2}^{M} q_{1j} + \sum_{\substack{j=1\\j\ne 2}}^{M-1} q_{2j}, \sum_{j=2}^{M} q_{1j} + \sum_{\substack{j=1\\j\ne 2}}^{M} q_{2j}\right), \ldots,
\end{aligned} \quad (3)$$

and so on (see [9]).

2.2. Wagner–Platen expansion

First, we give Itô's isometry for jump martingale and multi-dimensional Itô formula for PJ-SDEwMs (see [9,27]).

Lemma 1 (Itô's isometry for jump martingale, see [27]). *If $u(s,e)$ is $\mathscr{F}_s$-adapted stochastic process, then*

$$\mathbb{E}\left[\left(\int_0^T \int_{\mathcal{E}} u(s,e)\tilde{N}(de,ds)\right)^2\right] = \mathbb{E}\left[\int_0^T \int_{\mathcal{E}} u^2(s,e)\lambda(de)ds\right]. \quad (4)$$

Lemma 2 (Itô formula, see [9]). *If $V \in C^{1,2,2}([0,T] \times \mathbb{R}^d \times \mathbb{N}; \mathbb{R})$, for any $t \ge 0$, we have*

$$U(s, X_s, r_s) = U(0, X_0, r_0) + \int_0^s L^0 U(t, X_t, r_t) dt + \int_0^s \int_{\mathcal{E}} L_e^1 U(t, X_t, r_t) \tilde{N}(de, dt), \quad (5)$$

with the operators

$$L_e^1 U(t, X_t, r_t) = U(t, X_t, i_0 + h(r_t, e)) - U(t, X_t, r_t),$$

$$L^0 U(t, X_t, j) = \frac{\partial}{\partial t} U(t, X_t, j) + \sum_{i=1}^{d} \frac{\partial}{\partial x_k} U(t, X_t, j) a_k(t, x, j) + \frac{1}{2} \text{trace}\left(b(t, X_t, j)^\top \frac{\partial^2}{\partial x^2} U(t, X_t, j) b(t, X_t, j)\right) + \sum_{k\in S} U(t, X_t, j) q_{jk}$$

with $i_0 = r_0$ and
$$\frac{\partial^2}{\partial x^2} U(t, X_t, j) = \left(\frac{\partial^2}{\partial x_m \partial x_n} U(t, X_t, j)\right)_{d \times d}.$$

A higher order of PJ-SDEwMs can be obtained via the Wagner–Platen expansion. However, there are a few more definitions and notations that must be introduced before we can discuss the order of approximation. When $j_i \in \{0, 1\}$ for $i \in \{1, 2, ..., l\}$, we designate a row vector $\alpha = (j_1, j_2, ..., j_l)$ as a multi-index of length $l : l(\alpha) \in \mathbb{N}^+$. Then, the set of all multi-indices α is denoted by

$$\mathcal{M} = \{(j_1, j_2, ..., j_l) : j_i \in \{0, 1\}, i \in \{0, 1, ..., l\} \text{ for } l = 1, 2, ...\} \cup \{v\}.$$

where v is the multi-index of length zero ($l(v) = 0$). Assume that $\Gamma_l = \{\alpha \in \mathcal{M} : l(\alpha) \leq l\}$ is the hierarchical set, and $\mathcal{B}(\Gamma_l) = \{\alpha \in \mathcal{M} : l(\alpha) = l + 1\}$ is the corresponding remainder set. Given a multi-index $\alpha \in \mathcal{M}$ with $l(\alpha) > 1$, we write $\alpha-$ and $-\alpha$ for the multi-index obtained by eliminating the last component and the first component of α, respectively. Let us define recursively the Itô coefficient functions $f_{k,\alpha}$ by

$$f_{k,\alpha} = \begin{cases} f_{k,(0)} = a_k, \ g_{k,(i)} = b_k, & l = 1. \\ L^1_e f_{k,-\alpha}, & l > 1. \end{cases} \tag{6}$$

Furthermore, let the multiple Itô integral $I_\alpha[f_{k,\alpha}(\cdot, X., r., e.)]_{\varrho, \tau}$ be defined by

$$I_\alpha[f_{k,\alpha}(\cdot, X., r., e.)]_{\varrho, \tau} = \begin{cases} \int_\varrho^\tau I_{\alpha-}[f_{k,\alpha}(\cdot, X., r., e.)]_{\varrho, s} ds, & l \geq 1, \ j_l = 0, \\ \int_\varrho^\tau \int_\mathcal{E} I_{\alpha-}[f_{k,\alpha}(\cdot, X., r., e.)]_{\varrho, s_l} \tilde{N}(de_l, ds_l), & l \geq 1, \ j_l = 1. \end{cases} \tag{7}$$

For $\alpha = (j_1, j_2, j_3)$ and $\varrho, \tau \in [0, T]$, we assume

$$I^{0_3}_{\lambda_\alpha}[f_{k,\alpha}(\cdot, X., r., e.)]_{\varrho, \tau} := \begin{cases} \int_\varrho^\tau I_{\alpha-}[f_{k,\alpha}(\cdot, X., r., e.)]_{\varrho, s} ds, & l \geq 1, \ j_3 = 0, \\ \int_\varrho^\tau \int_\mathcal{E} I_{\alpha-}[f_{k,\alpha}(\cdot, X., r., e.)]_{\varrho, s_l} \lambda(de) ds, & l \geq 1, \ j_3 = 1. \end{cases} \tag{8}$$

For example if $\alpha = (1, 1, 1)$,

$$I^{0_3}_{\lambda_\alpha}[H(\cdot, X., r., e)]_{\varrho, \tau} := \int_\varrho^\tau \int_\mathcal{E} \int_\varrho^{s_3} \int_\mathcal{E} \int_\varrho^{s_2} \int_\mathcal{E} H(s_1, X_{s_1}, r_{s_1}, e_1) \lambda(de_1) \, ds_1 \, \lambda(de_2) \, ds_2 \, \lambda(de_3) \, ds_3.$$

2.3. Malliavin Stochastic Calculus

Suppose the operator $D_{t,e}$ is the Malliavin derivative of Poisson process at (t, e). A random variable U is Malliavin differentiable if and only if $U \in \mathbb{D}^{l,m}$. Here, the stochastic Sobolev spaces $\mathbb{D}^{l,m}$ consist of all $\mathcal{F}_T$-measurable $U \in L^2(P)$ with the norm

$$\|U\|^2_{l,m} = \mathbb{E}[|U|^m] + \mathbb{E}\left[\left(\int_0^T \int_0^{s_l} \cdots \int_0^{s_2} |D^\alpha_{s_1...s_l, e} U|^2 ds_1 ds_2 \ldots ds_l\right)^m\right], \tag{9}$$

where the Malliavin derivative $D^\alpha_{s_1...s_l, e}$ is defined as

$$D^\alpha_{s_1...s_l, e} = D^{(j_1,...,j_l)}_{s_1...s_l, e} = D^{j_1}_{s_1, e} \cdots D^{j_l}_{s_l, e}$$

with especially $D^0_{s_j, e} = 1$ for $1 \leq j \leq l$.

Lemma 3 (Duality formula, see [28]). *Assume $F \in \mathbb{D}^{1,2}$ and $u(t,e) \in \mathbb{D}^{1,2}$ for $0 \le t \le T$, we obtain the duality formula*

$$\mathbb{E}\left[F \int_0^T \int_{\mathcal{E}} u(t,e)\tilde{N}(de,dt)\right] = \mathbb{E}\left[\int_0^T \int_{\mathcal{E}} u(t,e) D_{t,e} F \lambda(de) dt\right],$$

Lemma 4 (Chain rule, see [28]). *Let $G_1, G_2 \in \mathbb{D}^{1,2}$, then $G_1 G_2 \in \mathbb{D}^{1,2}$ and*

$$D_{t,e}(G_1 G_2) = G_1 D_{t,e} G_2 + G_2 D_{t,e} G_1 + D_{t,e} G_1 D_{t,e} G_2.$$

Let $G \in \mathbb{D}^{1,2}$ and ϕ be a real continuous function on $\mathcal{E}$ and $\phi(G) \in \mathbb{D}^{1,2}$. Then,

$$D_{t,e}\phi(G) = \phi(G + D_{t,e}G) - \phi(G). \tag{10}$$

Lemma 5 (See [28]). *For $t \in [0,T]$ and the stochastic process $u(s,e) \in \mathbb{D}^{1,2}$, we have*

$$D_{t,e} \int_0^T \int_{\mathcal{E}} u(s,e)\tilde{N}(de,ds) = u(t,e) + \int_t^T \int_{\mathcal{E}} D_{t,e} u(s,e)\tilde{N}(de,ds),$$

and

$$D_{t,e} \int_0^T \int_{\mathcal{E}} \int_0^{s_2} \int_{\Delta_{ij}} \tilde{N}(de_1,ds_1)\tilde{N}(de_2,ds_2) = \int_0^t \int_{\Delta_{ij}} \tilde{N}(de_1,ds) + I_{\Delta_{ij}}(e) \int_t^T \int_{\mathcal{E}} \tilde{N}(de_1,ds),$$

where $I_{\Delta_{ij}}(e)$ is the indicator function defined by $I_{\Delta_{ij}}(e) = 1$ for $e \in \Delta_{ij}$ and $I_{\Delta_{ij}}(e) = 0$ for $e \notin \Delta_{ij}$.

3. Main Results

First, we consider a regular time uniform discretization: $0 = t_0 < \cdots < t_{N-1} < t_N = T$ with $\Delta t = t_{n+1} - t_n$ for $n = 0, 1, \ldots, N-1$. For a basic depiction, we consider $r_t^{n,i} := i + \int_{t_n}^t \int_{\mathcal{E}} h\left(r_{s-}^{n,i}, e\right) N(de, ds)$ and $X_{k,t_{n+1}}^{n,i} := X_{k,t_{n+1}}^{t_n, X^{n,i}}$, which is the k-th component of $X_{t_{n+1}}^{t_n, X^{n,i}}$. Using the classical Wagner–Platen expansion, we can derive the following Scheme 1 for solving SDEwMs with mark-dependent jump coefficient.

Scheme 1 (Wagner–Platen expansion). *Given the initial condition $X^{0,i}$. For $0 \le n \le N-1$, we solve $X^{n+1,i}$ with its k-th component $X_k^{n+1,i}$ by*

$$X_k^{n+1,i} = X_k^{n,i} + \sum_{\alpha \in \Gamma_2 \setminus \{v\}} I_\alpha [f_{k,\alpha}(t_n, X^{n,i}, i, e)]_{t_n, t_{n+1}}. \tag{11}$$

From the Wagner–Platen expansion and trapezoidal rule we obtain

$$X_{k,t_{n+1}}^{n,i} = X_k^{n,i} + \int_{t_n}^{t_{n+1}} a_k(t, X_t^{n,i}, r_t^{n,i}) dt + \int_{t_n}^{t_{n+1}} \int_{\mathcal{E}} b_k(t, X_t^{n,i}, r_t^{n,i}, e) \tilde{N}(de, dt) = X_k^{n+1,i} + R_{k,1}^{n,i}, \tag{12}$$

where the truncation error

$$\begin{aligned}R_{k,1}^{n,i} = &\int_{t_n}^{t_{n+1}} \int_{t_n}^{t} \int_{\mathcal{E}} L_e^1 a_k^{n,i} \tilde{N}(de, ds)\, dt - \frac{1}{2}\Delta t \sum_{j \in S} L^{i,j} a_k^{n,i} \int_{t_n}^{t_{n+1}} \int_{\Delta_{ij}} \tilde{N}(de, dt) \\ &+ \int_{t_n}^{t_{n+1}} \int_{\mathcal{E}} \int_{t_n}^{t} L^0 b_{k,e}^{n,i} ds\, \tilde{N}(de, dt) - \frac{1}{2}\Delta t \int_{t_n}^{t_{n+1}} \int_{\mathcal{E}} L^0 b_{k,e}^{n,i} \tilde{N}(de, dt) + \sum_{\alpha \in B(\Gamma_2)} I_\alpha [f_{k,\alpha}(\cdot, X^{n,i}, r_\cdot^{n,i}, e)]_{t_n, t_{n+1}}\end{aligned} \tag{13}$$

with $L^{i,j} a_k^{n,i} = a_k(t_n, X^{n,i}, j) - a_k(t_n, X^{n,i}, i)$. Here, we write $a_k^{n,i}$ for $a_k(t_n, X^{n,i}, i)$ and $b_{k,e}^{n,i}$ for $b_k(t_n, X^{n,i}, i, e)$. Then, by Equation (12), we propose the following second-order new scheme.

Scheme 2. *Given the initial condition $X^{0,i}$. For $0 \le n \le N-1$, we solve $X^{n+1,i}$ with its k-th component $X_k^{n+1,i}$ by*

$$X_k^{n+1,i} = X_k^{n,i} + a_k^{n,i} \Delta t + \int_{t_n}^{t_{n+1}} \int_{\mathcal{E}} b_{k,e}^{n,i} \tilde{N}(de, dt) + \frac{1}{2} L^0 a_k^{n,i} (\Delta t)^2 + \frac{1}{2} \Delta t \sum_{j \in S} L^{i,j} a_k^{n,i} \int_{t_n}^{t_{n+1}} \int_{\Delta_{ij}} \tilde{N}(de, dt)$$
$$+ \frac{1}{2} \Delta t \int_{t_n}^{t_{n+1}} \int_{\mathcal{E}} L^0 b_{k,e}^{n,i} \tilde{N}(de, dt) + \sum_{j \in S} \int_{t_n}^{t_{n+1}} \int_{\mathcal{E}} \int_{t_n}^{t} \int_{\Delta_{ij}} L^{i,j} b_{k,e_2}^{n,i} \tilde{N}(de_1, ds) \tilde{N}(de_2, dt)$$
(14)

with $\Delta t = t_{n+1} - t_n$.

Remark 1. *If the jump coefficient function $b = b(t, X_t, r_t, e)$, we generate the compound Poisson process*

$$\int_{t_n}^{t_{n+1}} \int_{\mathcal{E}} b_{k,e}^{n,i} \tilde{N}(de, dt) = \int_{t_n}^{t_{n+1}} \int_{\mathcal{E}} b(t_n, X^{n,i}, i, e)(N(de, dt) - \lambda(de) dt)$$
$$= \sum_{k=N_{t_n}+1}^{N_{t_{n+1}}} b(t_n, X^{n,i}, i, \zeta_k) - \int_{t_n}^{t_{n+1}} \int_{\mathcal{E}} b(t_n, X^{n,i}, i, e) \lambda(de) dt,$$

and the multiple stochastic integral in Scheme 2 can be computed by

$$\int_{t_n}^{t_{n+1}} \int_{\mathcal{E}} \int_{t_n}^{t} \int_{\Delta_{ij}} \tilde{N}(de_1, ds) \tilde{N}(de_2, dt)$$
$$= \int_{t_n}^{t_{n+1}} \int_{\mathcal{E}} \left(N_t^{\Delta_{ij}} - N_{t_n}^{\Delta_{ij}} - \lambda_{\Delta_{ij}}(t - t_n) \right) \tilde{N}(de_2, dt)$$
$$= \sum_{m=N_{t_n}+1}^{N_{t_{n+1}}} \left(N_{\tau_m}^{\Delta_{ij}} - N_{t_n}^{\Delta_{ij}} - \lambda_{\Delta_{ij}}(\tau_m - t_n) \right) - \int_{t_n}^{t_{n+1}} \int_{\mathcal{E}} \left(N_t^{\Delta_{ij}} - N_{t_n}^{\Delta_{ij}} - \lambda_{\Delta_{ij}}(t - t_n) \right) \lambda(de_2) dt$$
$$= \sum_{m=N_{t_n}+1}^{N_{t_{n+1}}} \left(N_{\tau_m}^{\Delta_{ij}} - N_{t_n}^{\Delta_{ij}} - \lambda_{\Delta_{ij}}(\tau_m - t_n) \right) - \lambda_{\mathcal{E}} \left(\int_{t_n}^{t_{n+1}} N_t^{\Delta_{ij}} dt - N_{t_n}^{\Delta_{ij}} \Delta t - \frac{1}{2} \lambda_{\Delta_{ij}} (\Delta t)^2 \right),$$
(15)

where the pairs (τ_k, ζ_k) of k-th jump time and marks are independent uniformly distributed in the planar region $[0, T] \times \mathcal{E}$, $\tilde{N}_t^{\Delta_{ij}} = \int_0^t \int_{\Delta_{ij}} \tilde{N}(de_1, ds)$, $N_t^{\Delta_{ij}} = \int_0^t \int_{\Delta_{ij}} N(de_1, ds)$ and $\lambda_{\Delta_{ij}} = \int_{\Delta_{ij}} \lambda(de) = \int_{\Delta_{ij}} \gamma(e) de$. For the Lebesgue–Stieltjes stochastic integral $\int_{t_n}^{t_{n+1}} N_t^{\Delta_{ij}} dt$, we can use trapezoidal rule to approximate it, that is

$$\int_{t_n}^{t_{n+1}} N_t^{\Delta_{ij}} dt = \frac{1}{2} (N_{t_n}^{\Delta_{ij}} + N_{t_{n+1}}^{\Delta_{ij}}) \Delta t + R_N^n.$$

In the special case of a mark-independent jump coefficient $b(t, X_t, r_t, e) = b(t, X_t, r_t)$, we use the following discrete-time approximation

$$X_{k,t_{n+1}}^{n,i} = X_k^{n,i} + \int_{t_n}^{t_{n+1}} a_k(t, X_t^{n,i}, r_t^{n,i}) dt + \int_{t_n}^{t_{n+1}} \int_{\mathcal{E}} b_k(t, X_t^{n,i}, r_t^{n,i}) \tilde{N}(de, dt) = X_k^{n+1,i} + R_{k,2}^{n,i} \quad (16)$$

with the truncation error

$$R_{k,2}^{n,i} = \int_{t_n}^{t_{n+1}} \int_{t_n}^{t} \int_{\mathcal{E}} L_e^1 a_k^{n,i} \tilde{N}(de, ds) \, dt - \frac{1}{2\lambda_{\mathcal{E}}} \Delta t \Delta \tilde{N}_n \sum_{j \in S} L^{i,j} a_k^{n,i} \lambda_{\Delta_{ij}}$$
$$+ \int_{t_n}^{t_{n+1}} \int_{\mathcal{E}} \int_{t_n}^{t} L^0 b_k^{n,i} ds \, \tilde{N}(de, dt) - \frac{1}{2} L^0 b_k^{n,i} \Delta t \Delta \tilde{N}_n$$
$$+ \int_{t_n}^{t_{n+1}} \int_{\mathcal{E}} \int_{t_n}^{t} \int_{\mathcal{E}} L_{e_1}^1 b_k^{n,i} \tilde{N}(de_1, ds) \tilde{N}(de_2, dt) - \frac{1}{2\lambda_{\mathcal{E}}} \left((\Delta \tilde{N}_n)^2 - \lambda_{\mathcal{E}} \Delta t - \Delta \tilde{N}_n \right) \sum_{j \in S} L^{i,j} b_k^{n,i} \lambda_{\Delta_{ij}}$$
$$+ \sum_{\alpha \in \mathcal{B}(\Gamma_2)} I_\alpha [f_{k,\alpha}(\cdot, X_\cdot^{n,i}, r_\cdot^{n,i})]_{t_n, t_{n+1}}.$$
(17)

Based on Equation (16), we propose the following simplified scheme for solving mark-independent PJ-SDEwMs.

Scheme 3. *Given the initial condition $X^{0,i}$. For $0 \leq n \leq N-1$, we solve $X^{n+1,i}$ with its k-th component $X_k^{n+1,i}$ by*

$$X_k^{n+1,i} = X_k^{n,i} + a_k^{n,i}\Delta t + b_k^{n,i}\Delta \tilde{N}_n + \frac{1}{2}L^0 a_k^{n,i}(\Delta t)^2 + \frac{1}{2\lambda_\mathcal{E}}\Delta t \Delta \tilde{N}_n \sum_{j \in S} L^{i,j} a_k^{n,i} \lambda_{\Delta_{ij}}$$
$$+ \frac{1}{2}L^0 b_k^{n,i}\Delta t \Delta \tilde{N}_n + \frac{1}{2\lambda_\mathcal{E}}\left((\Delta \tilde{N}_n)^2 - \lambda_\mathcal{E}\Delta t - \Delta \tilde{N}_n\right) \sum_{j \in S} L^{i,j} b_k^{n,i} \lambda_{\Delta_{ij}}, \quad (18)$$

where $\Delta t = t_{n+1} - t_n$, $\Delta \tilde{N}_n = \tilde{N}_{t_{n+1}} - \tilde{N}_{t_n}$ and $\lambda_{\Delta_{ij}} = \int_{\Delta_{ij}} \lambda(de) = \int_{\Delta_{ij}} \gamma(e)de$.

Remark 2. *Here, $\gamma(e)$ is a kernel function, which may be symmetric, i.e., $\gamma(e) = \gamma(-e)$; or non-symmetric, i.e.,*

$$\gamma(e) = \begin{cases} 1, & \text{if } e \in [-c,c] \\ 0, & \text{if } e \notin [-c,c] \end{cases}, \quad c \in \mathbb{R}^+; \quad (19)$$

or singular, i.e.

$$\gamma(e) = \begin{cases} \frac{1}{c^2\sqrt{c|e|}} & \text{for } e \in [-c,c] \\ 0, & \text{for } e \notin [-c,c] \end{cases}, \quad c \in \mathbb{R}^+. \quad (20)$$

Local Weak Convergence Theorems

In this section, using Malliavin stochastic analysis and the Wagner–Platen expansion, we rigorously prove and obtain the local weak order-3.0 convergence of Schemes 1–3.

Theorem 1. *(Local weak convergence) Suppose that $X_{t_{n+1}}^{n,i}$ and $X^{n+1,i}$ ($0 \leq n \leq N-1$) satisfy Equation (12) and Scheme 1, respectively. If the functions $a,b \in C_p(\mathbb{R}^d, \mathbb{R})$, $a, b \in C_b^{2,4}$ and $g \in C_b^2$, then*

$$\left|\mathbb{E}\left[g(X_{t_{n+1}}^{n,i}) - g(X^{n+1,i})|\mathcal{F}_{t_n}\right]\right| \leq C(1 + |X^{n,i}|^m)(\Delta t)^3, \quad (21)$$

where $m \in \mathbb{N}^+$ is a generic constant, which can vary from line to line.

Proof of Theorem 1: Subtracting Equation (18) from Equation (12) yields

$$X_{k,t_{n+1}}^{n,i} - X_k^{n+1,i} = \sum_{\alpha \in \mathcal{B}(\Gamma_2)} I_\alpha[f_{k,\alpha}(\cdot, X_\cdot^{n,i}, r_\cdot^{n,i}, e)]_{t_n, t_{n+1}}. \quad (22)$$

Then, by the mean value formula of integrals and duality formula, we have

$$\mathbb{E}\left[g(X_{t_{n+1}}^{n,i}) - g(X^{n+1,i})|\mathcal{F}_{t_n}\right] = \sum_{k=1}^{d} \mathbb{E}\left[F_k^{n+1,i}(X_{k,t_{n+1}}^{n,i} - X_k^{n+1,i})|\mathcal{F}_{t_n}\right]$$
$$= \sum_{k=1}^{d} \sum_{\alpha \in \mathcal{B}(\Gamma_2)} \mathbb{E}\left[F_k^{n+1,i} I_\alpha[f_{k,\alpha}(\cdot, X_\cdot^{n,i}, r_\cdot^{n,i}, e)]_{t_n, t_{n+1}}|\mathcal{F}_{t_n}\right] \quad (23)$$
$$= \sum_{k=1}^{d} \sum_{\alpha \in \mathcal{B}(\Gamma_2)} I_{\lambda_\alpha}^{0_3}\left[\mathbb{E}\left[D_{s_1 s_2 s_3, e}^{\alpha}\left(F_k^{n+1,i}\right) f_{k,\alpha}(\cdot, X_\cdot^{n,i}, r_\cdot^{n,i}, e)|\mathcal{F}_{t_n}\right]\right]_{t_n, t_{n+1}}$$

with

$$F_k^{n+1,i} = \int_0^1 \frac{\partial}{\partial x_k} g(X^{n+1,i} + \mu(X_{t_{n+1}}^{n,i} - X^{n+1,i}))d\mu. \quad (24)$$

Under the conditions of this theorem, we finally obtain the inequality (21). □

Theorem 2. *Suppose that $X_{t_{n+1}}^{n,i}$ and $X^{n+1,i}$ $(0 \leq n \leq N-1)$ satisfy Equation (12) and Scheme 2, respectively. If the functions $a, b \in C_p(\mathbb{R}^d, \mathbb{R})$, $a, b \in C_b^{2,4}$ and $g \in C_b^2$, then*

$$\left|\mathbb{E}\left[g(X_{t_{n+1}}^{n,i}) - g(X^{n+1,i})|\mathscr{F}_{t_n}\right]\right| \leq C(1 + |X^{n,i}|^m)(\Delta t)^3, \tag{25}$$

where $m \in \mathbb{N}^+$ is a generic constant, which can vary from line to line.

Proof of Theorem 2. Using the multi-dimensional Taylor formula, for ease of proof, we assume

$$I^n = \mathbb{E}\left[g(X_{t_{n+1}}^{n,i}) - g(X^{n+1,i})|\mathscr{F}_{t_n}\right] = I_1^n + I_2^n, \tag{26}$$

where

$$\begin{aligned}
I_1^n &= \mathbb{E}\Big[\sum_{k=1}^d \frac{\partial}{\partial x_k} g(X^{n+1,i})(X_{k,t_{n+1}}^{n,i} - X_k^{n+1,i})\big|\mathscr{F}_{t_n}\Big], \\
I_2^n &= \int_0^1 \int_0^1 \mathbb{E}\Big[\big(\sum_{k=1}^d (X_{k,t_{n+1}}^{n,i} - X_k^{n+1,i})\frac{\partial}{\partial x_k}\big)^2 g(X^{n+1,i} + \mu_1\mu_2(X_{t_{n+1}}^{n,i} - X^{n+1,i}))\big|\mathscr{F}_{t_n}\Big]\mu_1 d\mu_1 d\mu_2.
\end{aligned} \tag{27}$$

Assume $X_{k,t_{n+1}}^{n,i}$ is the k-th component of explicit solution $X_{t_{n+1}}^{n,i}$. Then, it follows from the Itô–Taylor expansion that

$$\begin{aligned}
X_{k,t_{n+1}}^{n,i} &= X_k^{n,i} + \sum_{\alpha \in \Gamma_2 \setminus \{v\}} I_\alpha[f_{k,\alpha}(t_n, X^{n,i}, i, e)]_{t_n, t_{n+1}} + \sum_{\alpha \in \mathcal{B}(\Gamma_2)} I_\alpha[f_{k,\alpha}(\cdot, X_{\cdot}^{n,i}, r_{\cdot}^{n,i}, e)]_{t_n, t_{n+1}} \\
&= X_k^{n,i} + a_k^{n,i}\Delta t + \int_{t_n}^{t_{n+1}} \int_{\mathcal{E}} b_k^{i,e}\tilde{N}(de, dt) + L^0 a_k^{n,i} \int_{t_n}^{t_{n+1}} \int_{t_n}^{s_2} ds_1 ds_2 + \int_{t_n}^{t_{n+1}} \int_{t_n}^{s_2} \int_{\mathcal{E}} L_e^1 a_k^{n,i} \tilde{N}(de, ds_1)\,ds_2 \\
&\quad + \int_{t_n}^{t_{n+1}} \int_{\mathcal{E}} \int_{t_n}^{s_2} L^0 b_k^{i,e} ds_1 \tilde{N}(de, ds_2) + \int_{t_n}^{t_{n+1}} \int_{\mathcal{E}} \int_{t_n}^{s_2} \int_{\mathcal{E}} L_{e_1}^1 b_k^{i,e_2} \tilde{N}(de_1, ds_1)\tilde{N}(de_2, ds_2) \\
&\quad + \sum_{\alpha \in \mathcal{B}(\Gamma_2)} I_\alpha[f_{k,\alpha}(\cdot, X_{\cdot}^{n,i}, r_{\cdot}^{n,i}, e)]_{t_n, t_{n+1}},
\end{aligned} \tag{28}$$

which by the fact $L^0 a_k^{n,i} \int_{t_n}^{t_{n+1}} \int_{t_n}^{s_2} ds_1 ds_2 = \frac{1}{2} L^0 a_k^{n,i} (\Delta t)^2$ yields

$$\begin{aligned}
& X_{k,t_{n+1}}^{n,i} - X_k^{n+1,i} \\
&= \sum_{\alpha \in \mathcal{B}(\Gamma_2)} I_\alpha[f_{k,\alpha}(\cdot, X_{\cdot}^{n,i}, r_{\cdot}^{n,i}, e)]_{t_n, t_{n+1}} + \int_{t_n}^{t_{n+1}} \int_{t_n}^{s_2} \int_{\mathcal{E}} L_e^1 a_k^{n,i} \tilde{N}(de, ds_1)\,ds_2 - \frac{1}{2}\Delta t \sum_{j \in S} L^{i,j} a_k^{n,i} \int_{t_n}^{t_{n+1}} \int_{\Delta_{ij}} \tilde{N}(de, ds) \\
&\quad + \int_{t_n}^{t_{n+1}} \int_{\mathcal{E}} \int_{t_n}^{s_2} L^0 b_k^{i,e} ds_1 \tilde{N}(de, ds_2) - \frac{1}{2}\Delta t \int_{t_n}^{t_{n+1}} \int_{\mathcal{E}} L^0 b_k^{i,e} \tilde{N}(de, ds) \\
&\quad + \int_{t_n}^{t_{n+1}} \int_{\mathcal{E}} \int_{t_n}^{s_2} \int_{\mathcal{E}} L_{e_1}^1 b_k^{i,e_2}\tilde{N}(de_1, ds_1)\tilde{N}(de_2, ds_2) - \sum_{j \in S} \int_{t_n}^{t_{n+1}} \int_{\mathcal{E}} \int_{t_n}^{s_2} \int_{\Delta_{ij}} L^{i,j} b_k^{i,e_2} \tilde{N}(de_1, ds_1)\tilde{N}(de_2, ds_2).
\end{aligned} \tag{29}$$

It follows from the definition of the operator $L_{e_1}^1$ that

$$\begin{aligned}
& \int_{t_n}^{t_{n+1}} \int_{\mathcal{E}} \int_{t_n}^{s_2} \int_{\mathcal{E}} L_{e_1}^1 b_k^{i,e_2} \tilde{N}(de_1, ds_1)\tilde{N}(de_2, ds_2) \\
&= \int_{t_n}^{t_{n+1}} \int_{\mathcal{E}} \int_{t_n}^{s_2} \int_{\mathcal{E}} \big(b_k(t_n, X^{n,i}, i + h(i, e_1), e_2) - b_k(t_n, X^{n,i}, i, e_2)\big) \tilde{N}(de_1, ds_1)\tilde{N}(de_2, ds_2) \\
&= \sum_{j \in S} \int_{t_n}^{t_{n+1}} \int_{\mathcal{E}} \int_{t_n}^{s_2} \int_{\Delta_{ij}} \big(b_k(t_n, X^{n,i}, j, e_2) - b_k(t_n, X^{n,i}, i, e_2)\big) \tilde{N}(de_1, ds_1)\tilde{N}(de_2, ds_2) \\
&= \sum_{j \in S} \int_{t_n}^{t_{n+1}} \int_{\mathcal{E}} \int_{t_n}^{s_2} \int_{\Delta_{ij}} L^{i,j} b_k^{i,e_2} \tilde{N}(de_1, ds_1)\tilde{N}(de_2, ds_2).
\end{aligned} \tag{30}$$

By the duality formula in Lemma 3 and from Equations (29) and (30), we deduce

$$I_1^n = \mathbb{E}\Big[\sum_{k=1}^{d}\frac{\partial}{\partial x_k}g(X^{n+1,i})(X_{k,t_{n+1}}^{n,i} - X_k^{n+1,i})|\mathscr{F}_{t_n}\Big] = \sum_{k=1}^{d}\sum_{l=1}^{3}\zeta_{g,k}^{l}, \quad (31)$$

where

$$\zeta_{g,k}^1 = \mathbb{E}\Big[\frac{\partial}{\partial x_k}g(X^{n+1,i})\Big(\int_{t_n}^{t_{n+1}}\int_{\mathcal{E}}\int_{t_n}^{s_2}L^0 b_k^{i,e}ds_1\,\tilde{N}(de,ds_2) - \frac{1}{2}\Delta t\int_{t_n}^{t_{n+1}}\int_{\mathcal{E}}L^0 b_k^{i,e}\tilde{N}(de,ds)\Big)\Big|\mathscr{F}_{t_n}\Big],$$

$$\zeta_{g,k}^2 = \sum_{j\in S}L^{i,j}a_k^{n,i}\mathbb{E}\Big[\frac{\partial}{\partial x_k}g(X^{n+1,i})\Big(\int_{t_n}^{t_{n+1}}\int_{t_n}^{s_2}\int_{\Delta_{ij}}\tilde{N}(de,ds_1)\,ds_2 - \frac{1}{2}\Delta t\int_{t_n}^{t_{n+1}}\int_{\Delta_{ij}}\tilde{N}(de,ds)\Big)\Big|\mathscr{F}_{t_n}\Big],$$

$$\zeta_{g,k}^3 = \sum_{\alpha\in\mathcal{B}(\Gamma_2)}\mathbb{E}\Big[\frac{\partial}{\partial x_k}g(X^{n+1,i})\,I_\alpha[f_{k,\alpha}(\cdot,X_\cdot^{n,i},r_\cdot^{n,i},e)]_{t_n,t_{n+1}}|\mathscr{F}_{t_n}\Big].$$

By taking Malliavin derivative with respect to $X_k^{n+1,i}$, we obtain

$$\begin{aligned}D_{t,e_2}X_k^{n+1,i} = b_k^{i,e_2} + \frac{1}{2}\Delta t\,\Big(L^0 b_k^{i,e_2} + \sum_{j\in S}L^{i,j}a_k^{n,i}\Big)\\ + \sum_{j\in S}\Big(L^{i,j}b_k^{i,e_2}\int_{t_n}^{t}\int_{\Delta_{ij}}\tilde{N}(de_1,ds) + I_{\Delta_{ij}}(e_2)\int_{t}^{t_{n+1}}\int_{\mathcal{E}}L^{i,j}b_k^{i,e_1}\tilde{N}(de_1,ds)\Big)\end{aligned} \quad (32)$$

for $t_n < t \leq t_{n+1}$ and $e_2 \in \mathcal{E}$. Furthermore, the chain rule (10) gives

$$D_{t,e}\frac{\partial}{\partial x_k}g(X^{n+1,i}) = \frac{\partial}{\partial x_k}g(X^{n+1,i} + D_{t,e}X^{n+1,i}) - \frac{\partial}{\partial x_k}g(X^{n+1,i}). \quad (33)$$

Then, it follows from Taylor formula and Lemma 5 that

$$\begin{aligned}&\frac{\partial}{\partial x_k}g(X^{n+1,i} + D_{t,e_2}X^{n+1,i})\\ =&\frac{\partial}{\partial x_k}g(Y_{i,e_2}^{n+1}) + \sum_{j\in S}\sum_{l=1}^{d}F_{g,l,e_2}^{n+1}\Big(L^{i,j}b_l^{i,e_2}\int_{t_n}^{t}\int_{\Delta_{ij}}\tilde{N}(de_1,ds) + I_{\Delta_{ij}}(e_2)\int_{t}^{t_{n+1}}\int_{\mathcal{E}}L^{i,j}b_l^{i,e_1}\tilde{N}(de_1,ds)\Big),\end{aligned} \quad (34)$$

where $Y_{i,e_2}^{n+1} = X^{n+1,i} + b^{i,e_2} + \frac{1}{2}\Delta t(L^0 b^{i,e_2} + \sum_{j\in S}L^{i,j}a^i)$ and

$$F_{g,l,e_2}^{n+1} = \int_0^1 \frac{\partial^2}{\partial x_k \partial x_l}g\Big(Y_{i,e_2}^{n+1} + \mu(X^{n+1,i} + D_{t,e_2}X^{n+1,i} - Y_{i,e_2}^{n+1})\Big)d\mu.$$

By the duality formula, we have

$$\begin{aligned}\mathbb{E}\Big[F_{g,l,e_2}^{n+1}\int_{t_n}^{s_2}\int_{\Delta_{ij}}\tilde{N}(de_1,ds_1)|\mathscr{F}_{t_n}\Big] &= \int_{t_n}^{s_2}\int_{\Delta_{ij}}\mathbb{E}\big[D_{s_1,e_1}F_{g,l,e_2}^{n+1}|\mathscr{F}_{t_n}\big]\lambda(de_1)\,ds_1,\\ \mathbb{E}\Big[F_{g,l,e_2}^{n+1}\int_{s_2}^{t_{n+1}}\int_{\mathcal{E}}L^{i,j}b_k^{i,e_1}\tilde{N}(de_1,ds_1)|\mathscr{F}_{t_n}\Big] &= \int_{s_2}^{t_{n+1}}\int_{\mathcal{E}}\mathbb{E}\big[D_{s_1,e_1}F_{g,l,e_2}^{n+1}|\mathscr{F}_{t_n}\big]L^{i,j}b_k^{i,e_1}\lambda(de_1)\,ds_1.\end{aligned} \quad (35)$$

Now by Lemma 3, from Equations (33)–(35), we have

$$\begin{aligned}
\zeta_{g,k}^1 &= \int_{t_n}^{t_{n+1}} \int_{\mathcal{E}} \int_{t_n}^{s_2} \mathbb{E}\big[D_{s_2,e}\frac{\partial}{\partial x_k}g(X^{n+1,i})\big|\mathcal{F}_{t_n}\big]L^0 b_k^{i,e} ds_1\,\lambda(de)\,ds_2 \\
&\quad - \frac{1}{2}\Delta t \int_{t_n}^{t_{n+1}} \int_{\mathcal{E}} \mathbb{E}\big[D_{s,e}\frac{\partial}{\partial x_k}g(X^{n+1,i})\big|\mathcal{F}_{t_n}\big]L^0 b_k^{i,e}\,\lambda(de)\,ds \\
&= \int_{t_n}^{t_{n+1}} \int_{\mathcal{E}} \int_{t_n}^{s_2} \mathbb{E}\big[\frac{\partial}{\partial x_k}g(Y_{i,e}^{n+1}) - \frac{\partial}{\partial x_k}g(X^{n+1,i})\big|\mathcal{F}_{t_n}\big]L^0 b_k^{i,e}\,\lambda(de)\,ds_1\,ds_2 \\
&\quad + \sum_{j\in S}\sum_{l=1}^{d} \int_{t_n}^{t_{n+1}} \int_{\mathcal{E}} \int_{t_n}^{s_2} \int_{\Delta_{ij}} \Big(\mathbb{E}\big[D_{s_1,e_1}F_{g,l,e_2}^{n+1}\big|\mathcal{F}_{t_n}\big]L^{i,j}b_l^{i,e_2}L^0 b_k^{i,e_2}(s_2 - t_n)\Big)\lambda(de_1)\,ds_1\,\lambda(de_2)\,ds_2 \\
&\quad + \sum_{j\in S}\sum_{l=1}^{d} \int_{t_n}^{t_{n+1}} \int_{\Delta_{ij}} \int_{s_2}^{t_{n+1}} \int_{\mathcal{E}} \Big(\mathbb{E}\big[D_{s_1,e_1}F_{g,l,e_2}^{n+1}\big|\mathcal{F}_{t_n}\big]L^{i,j}b_l^{i,e_1}L^0 b_k^{i,e_2}(s_2 - t_n)\Big)\lambda(de_1)\,ds_1\,\lambda(de_2)\,ds_2 \\
&\quad - \frac{1}{2}\Delta t \int_{t_n}^{t_{n+1}} \int_{\mathcal{E}} \mathbb{E}\big[\frac{\partial}{\partial x_k}g(Y_{i,e}^{n+1}) - \frac{\partial}{\partial x_k}g(X^{n+1,i})\big|\mathcal{F}_{t_n}\big]L^0 b_k^{i,e}\,\lambda(de)\,ds \\
&\quad - \frac{1}{2}\Delta t \sum_{j\in S}\sum_{l=1}^{d} \int_{t_n}^{t_{n+1}} \int_{\mathcal{E}} \int_{t_n}^{s_2} \int_{\Delta_{ij}} \Big(\mathbb{E}\big[D_{s_1,e_1}F_{g,l,e_2}^{n+1}\big|\mathcal{F}_{t_n}\big]L^{i,j}b_l^{i,e_2}L^0 b_k^{i,e_2}\Big)\lambda(de_1)\,ds_1\,\lambda(de_2)\,ds_2 \\
&\quad - \frac{1}{2}\Delta t \sum_{j\in S}\sum_{l=1}^{d} \int_{t_n}^{t_{n+1}} \int_{\Delta_{ij}} \int_{s_2}^{t_{n+1}} \int_{\mathcal{E}} \Big(\mathbb{E}\big[D_{s_1,e_1}F_{g,l,e_2}^{n+1}\big|\mathcal{F}_{t_n}\big]L^{i,j}b_l^{i,e_1}L^0 b_k^{i,e_2}\Big)\lambda(de_1)\,ds_1\,\lambda(de_2)\,ds_2,
\end{aligned} \quad (36)$$

which by using the fact

$$\int_{t_n}^{t_{n+1}} \int_{\mathcal{E}} \int_{t_n}^{s_2} \mathbb{E}\big[\frac{\partial}{\partial x_k}g(Y_{i,e}^{n+1}) - \frac{\partial}{\partial x_k}g(X^{n+1,i})\big|\mathcal{F}_{t_n}\big]L^0 b_k^{i,e}\,\lambda(de)\,ds_1\,ds_2$$
$$= \frac{1}{2}\Delta t \int_{t_n}^{t_{n+1}} \int_{\mathcal{E}} \mathbb{E}\big[\frac{\partial}{\partial x_k}g(Y_{i,e}^{n+1}) - \frac{\partial}{\partial x_k}g(X^{n+1,i})\big|\mathcal{F}_{t_n}\big]L^0 b_k^{i,e}\,\lambda(de)\,ds$$
$$= \frac{1}{2}(\Delta t)^2 \int_{\mathcal{E}} \mathbb{E}\big[\frac{\partial}{\partial x_k}g(Y_{i,e}^{n+1}) - \frac{\partial}{\partial x_k}g(X^{n+1,i})\big|\mathcal{F}_{t_n}\big]L^0 b_k^{i,e}\,\lambda(de)$$

yields

$$\begin{aligned}
|\zeta_{g,k}^1| &= \Big|\sum_{j\in S}\sum_{l=1}^{d} \int_{t_n}^{t_{n+1}} \int_{\mathcal{E}} \int_{t_n}^{s_2} \int_{\Delta_{ij}} \Big(\mathbb{E}\big[D_{s_1,e_1}F_{g,l,e_2}^{n+1}\big|\mathcal{F}_{t_n}\big]L^{i,j}b_l^{i,e_2}L^0 b_k^{i,e_2}(s_2 - t_n)\Big)\lambda(de_1)\,ds_1\,\lambda(de_2)\,ds_2 \\
&\quad + \sum_{j\in S}\sum_{l=1}^{d} \int_{t_n}^{t_{n+1}} \int_{\Delta_{ij}} \int_{s_2}^{t_{n+1}} \int_{\mathcal{E}} \Big(\mathbb{E}\big[D_{s_1,e_1}F_{g,l,e_2}^{n+1}\big|\mathcal{F}_{t_n}\big]L^{i,j}b_l^{i,e_1}L^0 b_k^{i,e_2}(s_2 - t_n)\Big)\lambda(de_1)\,ds_1\,\lambda(de_2)\,ds_2 \\
&\quad - \frac{1}{2}\Delta t \sum_{j\in S}\sum_{l=1}^{d} \int_{t_n}^{t_{n+1}} \int_{\mathcal{E}} \int_{t_n}^{s_2} \int_{\Delta_{ij}} \Big(\mathbb{E}\big[D_{s_1,e_1}F_{g,l,e_2}^{n+1}\big|\mathcal{F}_{t_n}\big]L^{i,j}b_l^{i,e_2}L^0 b_k^{i,e_2}\Big)\lambda(de_1)\,ds_1\,\lambda(de_2)\,ds_2 \\
&\quad - \frac{1}{2}\Delta t \sum_{j\in S}\sum_{l=1}^{d} \int_{t_n}^{t_{n+1}} \int_{\Delta_{ij}} \int_{s_2}^{t_{n+1}} \int_{\mathcal{E}} \Big(\mathbb{E}\big[D_{s_1,e_1}F_{g,l,e_2}^{n+1}\big|\mathcal{F}_{t_n}\big]L^{i,j}b_l^{i,e_1}L^0 b_k^{i,e_2}\Big)\lambda(de_1)\,ds_1\,\lambda(de_2)\,ds_2\Big| \\
&\leq C(1 + |X^{n,i}|^m)(\Delta t)^3.
\end{aligned} \quad (37)$$

Note that

$$\int_{t_n}^{t_{n+1}} \int_{t_n}^{s_2} \int_{\Delta_{ij}} \mathbb{E}\big[\frac{\partial}{\partial x_k}g(Y_{i,e}^{n+1}) - \frac{\partial}{\partial x_k}g(X^{n+1,i})\big|\mathcal{F}_{t_n}\big]\lambda(de)\,ds_1\,ds_2$$
$$= \frac{1}{2}\Delta t \int_{t_n}^{t_{n+1}} \int_{\Delta_{ij}} \mathbb{E}\big[\frac{\partial}{\partial x_k}g(Y_{i,e}^{n+1}) - \frac{\partial}{\partial x_k}g(X^{n+1,i})\big|\mathcal{F}_{t_n}\big]\lambda(de)\,ds$$
$$= \frac{1}{2}(\Delta t)^2 \int_{\Delta_{ij}} \mathbb{E}\big[\frac{\partial}{\partial x_k}g(Y_{i,e}^{n+1}) - \frac{\partial}{\partial x_k}g(X^{n+1,i})\big|\mathcal{F}_{t_n}\big]\lambda(de),$$

and we deduce from Lemma 3 that

$$\zeta_{g,k}^2 = \sum_{j \in S} L^{i,j} a_k^{n,i} \Big(\int_{t_n}^{t_{n+1}} \int_{t_n}^{s_2} \int_{\Delta_{ij}} \mathbb{E}\big[D_{s_1,e} \frac{\partial}{\partial x_k} g(X^{n+1,i}) | \mathcal{F}_{t_n}\big] \lambda(de) \, ds_1 \, ds_2$$

$$- \frac{1}{2} \Delta t \int_{t_n}^{t_{n+1}} \int_{\Delta_{ij}} \mathbb{E}\big[D_{s,e} \frac{\partial}{\partial x_k} g(X^{n+1,i}) | \mathcal{F}_{t_n}\big] \lambda(de) \, ds \Big)$$

$$= \sum_{j_1 \in S} \sum_{j_2 \in S} \sum_{l=1}^{d} L^{i,j_1} a_k^{n,i} \int_{t_n}^{t_{n+1}} \int_{t_n}^{s_3} \int_{\Delta_{ij_2}} \int_{t_n}^{s_2} \int_{\Delta_{ij_1}} \mathbb{E}\big[D_{s_1,e_1} F_{g,l,e_2}^{n+1} | \mathcal{F}_{t_n}\big] L^{i,j_1} b_l^{i,e_1} \lambda(de_1) \, ds_1 \, \lambda(de_2) \, ds_2 \, ds_3$$

$$+ \sum_{j \in S} \sum_{l=1}^{d} L^{i,j} a_k^{n,i} \int_{t_n}^{t_{n+1}} \int_{t_n}^{s_3} \int_{\Delta_{ij}} \int_{s_2}^{t_{n+1}} \int_{\Delta_{ij}} \mathbb{E}\big[D_{s_1,e_1} F_{g,l,e_2}^{n+1} | \mathcal{F}_{t_n}\big] L^{i,j_1} b_l^{i,e_1} \lambda(de_1) \, ds_1 \, \lambda(de_2) \, ds_3 \quad (38)$$

$$- \frac{1}{2} \Delta t \sum_{j_1 \in S} \sum_{j_2 \in S} \sum_{l=1}^{d} L^{i,j_1} a_k^{n,i} \int_{t_n}^{t_{n+1}} \int_{\Delta_{ij_2}} \int_{t_n}^{s_2} \int_{\Delta_{ij_1}} \mathbb{E}\big[D_{s_1,e_1} F_{g,l,e}^{n+1} | \mathcal{F}_{t_n}\big] L^{i,j_1} b_l^{i,e_1} \lambda(de_1) \, ds_1 \, \lambda(de_2) \, ds_2$$

$$- \frac{1}{2} \Delta t \sum_{j \in S} \sum_{l=1}^{d} L^{i,j} a_k^{n,i} \int_{t_n}^{t_{n+1}} \int_{\Delta_{ij}} \int_{s_2}^{t_{n+1}} \int_{\Delta_{ij}} \mathbb{E}\big[D_{s_1,e_1} F_{g,l,e}^{n+1} | \mathcal{F}_{t_n}\big] L^{i,j} b_l^{i,e_1} \lambda(de_1) \, ds_1 \, \lambda(de_2) \, ds_2,$$

which gives

$$|\zeta_{g,k}^2| \leq C(1 + |X^{n,i}|^m)(\Delta t)^3. \quad (39)$$

Using the duality formula in Lemma 3, we conclude that

$$|\zeta_{g,k}^3| = \Big| \sum_{\alpha \in \mathcal{B}(\Gamma_2)} I_{\lambda_\alpha}^{0_3} \Big[\mathbb{E}\big[D_{s_1 s_2 s_3,e}^\alpha (\frac{\partial}{\partial x_k} g(X^{n+1,i})) f_{k,\alpha}(s_1, X_{s_1}^{n,i}, r_{s_1}^{n,i}, e) | \mathcal{F}_{t_n}\big] \Big]_{t_n, t_{n+1}} \Big| \leq C(1 + |X^{n,i}|^m)(\Delta t)^3. \quad (40)$$

Combining the inequalities (37)–(40), we obtain

$$|I_1^n| = \Big| \mathbb{E}\Big[\sum_{k=1}^{d} \frac{\partial}{\partial x_k} g(X^{n+1,i})(X_{k,t_{n+1}}^{n,i} - X_k^{n+1,i}) | \mathcal{F}_{t_n}\Big] \Big| \leq C(1 + |X^{n,i}|^m)(\Delta t)^3. \quad (41)$$

For $\alpha = (1,1,1)$, applying the Itô isometry Formula (4), we have

$$\mathbb{E}\Big[\Big(\int_{t_n}^{t_{n+1}} \int_{t_n}^{s_3} \int_{t_n}^{s_2} f_{k,\alpha}(s_1, X_{s_1}^{n,i}, r_{s_1}^{n,i}, e_1) d\tilde{N}_{s_1} d\tilde{N}_{s_2} d\tilde{N}_{s_3} \Big)^2 \Big| \mathcal{F}_{t_n} \Big]$$

$$= \mathbb{E}\Big[\int_{t_n}^{t_{n+1}} \int_{\mathcal{E}} \int_{t_n}^{s_3} \int_{\mathcal{E}} \int_{t_n}^{s_2} \int_{\mathcal{E}} \big(f_{k,\alpha}(s_1, X_{s_1}^{n,i}, r_{s_1}^{n,i}, e_1)\big)^2 \lambda(de_1) \, ds_1 \, \lambda(de_2) \, ds_2 \, \lambda(de_3) \, ds_3 \Big| \mathcal{F}_{t_n} \Big] \quad (42)$$

$$= I_{\lambda_\alpha}^{0_3} \Big[\mathbb{E}\big[\big(f_{k,\alpha}(s_1, X_{s_1}^{n,i}, r_{s_1}^{n,i}, e_1)\big)^2 | \mathcal{F}_{t_n}\big] \Big]_{t_n, t_{n+1}}.$$

For $\alpha \neq (1,1,1)$, we obtain

$$\sum_{\substack{\alpha \in \mathcal{B}(\Gamma_2) \\ \alpha \neq (1,1,1)}} \Big| \mathbb{E}\big[I_\alpha \big[f_{k,\alpha}(s_1, X_{s_1}^{n,i}, r_{s_1}^{n,i}, e_1)\big]_{t_n, t_{n+1}} | \mathcal{F}_{t_n}\big] \Big|^2 \leq C(1 + |X^{n,i}|^m)(\Delta t)^3. \quad (43)$$

By the inequalities (42) and (43), we deduce

$$|I_2^n| = \Big| \int_0^1 \int_0^1 \mathbb{E}\Big[\Big(\sum_{k=1}^{d} (X_{k,t_{n+1}}^{n,i} - X_k^{n+1,i}) \frac{\partial}{\partial x_k} \Big)^2 g(X^{n+1,i} + \mu_1 \mu_2 (X_{t_{n+1}}^{n,i} - X^{n+1,i})) | \mathcal{F}_{t_n} \Big] \mu_1 d\mu_1 d\mu_2 \Big| \leq C(1 + |X^{n,i}|^m)(\Delta t)^3. \quad (44)$$

From the inequalities (41) and (44), we finally obtain

$$\big| \mathbb{E}\big[g(X_{t_{n+1}}^{n,i}) - g(X^{n+1,i}) | \mathcal{F}_{t_n}\big] \big| \leq C(1 + |X^{n,i}|^m)(\Delta t)^3.$$

□

Theorem 3. *Assume that $X_{t_{n+1}}^{n,i}$ and $X^{n+1,i}$ ($0 \leq n \leq N-1$), respectively, satisfy Equation (16) and Scheme 3. If the functions $a, b \in C_p(\mathbb{R}^d, \mathbb{R})$, $a, b \in C_b^{2,4}$ and $g \in C_b^2$, then*

$$\left| \mathbb{E}\left[g(X_{t_{n+1}}^{n,i}) - g(X^{n+1,i}) | \mathcal{F}_{t_n} \right] \right| \leq C(1 + |X^{n,i}|^m)(\Delta t)^3, \tag{45}$$

where $m \in \mathbb{N}^+$ is a generic constant, which could change line by line.

Proof of Theorem 3: Using multi-dimensional Taylor formula, to make the proof easier, we have

$$J^n = \mathbb{E}\left[g(X_{t_{n+1}}^{n,i}) - g(X^{n+1,i}) | \mathcal{F}_{t_n} \right] = J_1^n + J_2^n, \tag{46}$$

where

$$\begin{aligned}
J_1^n &= \mathbb{E}\Big[\sum_{k=1}^d \frac{\partial}{\partial x_k} g(X^{n+1,i})(X_{k,t_{n+1}}^{n,i} - X_k^{n+1,i}) \big| \mathcal{F}_{t_n} \Big], \\
J_2^n &= \int_0^1 \int_0^1 \mathbb{E}\Big[\big(\sum_{k=1}^d (X_{k,t_{n+1}}^{n,i} - X_k^{n+1,i}) \frac{\partial}{\partial x_k} \big)^2 g(X^{n+1,i} + \mu_1 \mu_2 (X_{t_{n+1}}^{n,i} - X^{n+1,i})) \big| \mathcal{F}_{t_n} \Big] \mu_1 d\mu_1 d\mu_2.
\end{aligned} \tag{47}$$

Assume $X_{k,t_{n+1}}^{n,i}$ is the k-th component of explicit solution $X_{t_{n+1}}^{n,i}$. Then, from the Itô–Taylor expansion, we can obtain

$$\begin{aligned}
X_{k,t_{n+1}}^{n,i} &= X_k^{n,i} + \sum_{\alpha \in \Gamma_2 \setminus \{v\}} f_{k,\alpha}(t_n, X^{n,i}, i) I_\alpha[1]_{t_n, t_{n+1}} + \sum_{\alpha \in \mathcal{B}(\Gamma_2)} I_\alpha[f_{k,\alpha}(\cdot, X_\cdot^{n,i}, r_\cdot^{n,i})]_{t_n, t_{n+1}} \\
&= X_k^{n,i} + a_k^{n,i} \Delta t + b_k^{n,i} \Delta \tilde{N}_n + L^0 a_k^{n,i} \int_{t_n}^{t_{n+1}} \int_{t_n}^t ds dt + \int_{t_n}^{t_{n+1}} \int_{t_n}^t L_e^1 a_k^{n,i} d\tilde{N}_s dt \\
&\quad + L^0 b_k^{n,i} \int_{t_n}^{t_{n+1}} \int_{t_n}^t ds d\tilde{N}_t + \int_{t_n}^{t_{n+1}} \int_{t_n}^t L_e^1 b_k^{n,i} d\tilde{N}_s d\tilde{N}_t + \sum_{\alpha \in \mathcal{B}(\Gamma_2)} I_\alpha[f_{k,\alpha}(\cdot, X_\cdot^{n,i}, r_\cdot^{n,i})]_{t_n, t_{n+1}},
\end{aligned} \tag{48}$$

which yields

$$\begin{aligned}
X_{k,t_{n+1}}^{n,i} - X_k^{n+1,i} &= \int_{t_n}^{t_{n+1}} \int_{t_n}^t L_e^1 a_k^{n,i} d\tilde{N}_s dt - \frac{1}{2\lambda_\mathcal{E}} \Delta t \Delta \tilde{N}_n \sum_{j \in S} L^{i,j} a_k^{n,i} \lambda_{\Delta_{ij}} \\
&\quad + L^0 b_k^{n,i} \Big[\int_{t_n}^{t_{n+1}} \int_{t_n}^t ds d\tilde{N}_t - \frac{1}{2} \Delta t \Delta \tilde{N}_n \Big] + \int_{t_n}^{t_{n+1}} \int_{t_n}^t L_e^1 b_k^{n,i} d\tilde{N}_s d\tilde{N}_t \\
&\quad - \frac{1}{2\lambda_\mathcal{E}} \sum_{j \in S} L^{i,j} b_k^{n,i} \lambda_{\Delta_{ij}} \big((\Delta \tilde{N}_n)^2 - \lambda_\mathcal{E} \Delta t - \Delta \tilde{N}_n \big) + \sum_{\alpha \in \mathcal{B}(\Gamma_2)} I_\alpha[f_{k,\alpha}(\cdot, X_\cdot^{n,i}, r_\cdot^{n,i})]_{t_n, t_{n+1}}.
\end{aligned} \tag{49}$$

By the duality formula in Lemma 3 and from Equation (49), we deduce

$$J_1^n = \mathbb{E}\Big[\sum_{k=1}^d \frac{\partial}{\partial x_k} g(X^{n+1,i})(X_{k,t_{n+1}}^{n,i} - X_k^{n+1,i}) \big| \mathcal{F}_{t_n} \Big] = \sum_{k=1}^d \sum_{l=1}^4 \epsilon_{g,k}^l, \tag{50}$$

where

$$\begin{aligned}
\epsilon_{g,k}^1 &= L^0 b_k^i \mathbb{E}\Big[\frac{\partial}{\partial x_k} g(X^{n+1,i}) \Big(\int_{t_n}^{t_{n+1}} \int_{t_n}^t ds d\tilde{N}_t - \frac{1}{2} \Delta t \Delta \tilde{N}_n \Big) \Big| \mathcal{F}_{t_n} \Big], \\
\epsilon_{g,k}^2 &= \mathbb{E}\Big[\frac{\partial}{\partial x_k} g(X^{n+1,i}) \Big(\int_{t_n}^{t_{n+1}} \int_{t_n}^s L_e^1 a_k^{n,i} d\tilde{N}_t ds - \frac{1}{2\lambda_\mathcal{E}} \Delta t \Delta \tilde{N}_n \sum_{j \in S} L^{i,j} a_k^{n,i} \lambda_{\Delta_{ij}} \Big) \Big| \mathcal{F}_{t_n} \Big], \\
\epsilon_{g,k}^3 &= \mathbb{E}\Big[\frac{\partial}{\partial x_k} g(X^{n+1,i}) \Big(\int_{t_n}^{t_{n+1}} \int_{t_n}^t L_e^1 b_k^{n,i} d\tilde{N}_s d\tilde{N}_t - \frac{1}{2\lambda_\mathcal{E}} \big((\Delta \tilde{N}_n)^2 - \lambda_\mathcal{E} \Delta t - \Delta \tilde{N}_n \big) \sum_{j \in S} L^{i,j} b_k^{n,i} \lambda_{\Delta_{ij}} \Big) \Big| \mathcal{F}_{t_n} \Big], \\
\epsilon_{g,x_k}^4 &= \sum_{\alpha \in \mathcal{B}(\Gamma_2)} \mathbb{E}\Big[\frac{\partial}{\partial x_k} g(X^{n+1,i}) I_\alpha[f_{k,\alpha}(\cdot, X_\cdot^{n,i}, r_\cdot^{n,i})]_{t_n, t_{n+1}} \big| \mathcal{F}_{t_n} \Big].
\end{aligned}$$

For $t_n < s \leq t \leq t_{n+1}$, by using Malliavin derivative in relation to $X_k^{n+1,i}$, we get

$$D_{t,e}X_k^{n+1,i} = b_k^{n,i} + \frac{1}{2}\Delta t L^0 b_k^{n,i} + \frac{1}{2\lambda_{\mathcal{E}}}\sum_{j \in S}\left(\Delta t L^{i,j}a_k^{n,i} + (2\Delta\tilde{N}_n - 1)L^{i,j}b_k^{n,i}\right)\lambda_{\Delta_{ij}},$$

$$D_{s,e}D_{t,e}X_k^{n+1,i} = \frac{1}{\lambda_{\mathcal{E}}}\sum_{j \in S}L^{i,j}b_k^{n,i}\lambda_{\Delta_{ij}},$$

(51)

which by combining chain rule (10) gives

$$D_{t,e}\frac{\partial}{\partial x_k}g(X^{n+1,i}) = \frac{\partial}{\partial x_k}g(X^{n+1,i} + D_{t,e}X^{n+1,i}) - \frac{\partial}{\partial x_k}g(X^{n+1,i}) := \Phi(t_n, X^n, \Delta t, \Delta\tilde{N}_n),$$

$$D_{s,e}D_{t,e}\frac{\partial}{\partial x_k}g(X^{n+1,i}) = D_{s,e}\Phi(t_n, X^n, \Delta t, \Delta\tilde{N}_n) := \Psi(t_n, X^n, \Delta t, \Delta\tilde{N}_n),$$

where the functions $\Phi(t_n, X^n, \Delta t, \Delta\tilde{N}_n)$ and $\Psi(t_n, X^n, \Delta t, \Delta\tilde{N}_n)$ do not depending only on t and e. Furthermore, from Lemma 3, using the notation $\lambda_{\mathcal{E}} := \int_{\mathcal{E}}\lambda(de) = \int_{\mathcal{E}}\gamma(e)de$, we have

$$\epsilon_{g,k}^1 = L^0 b_k^{n,i}\left(\int_{t_n}^{t_{n+1}}\int_{\mathcal{E}}\int_{t_n}^{t}\mathbb{E}\left[D_{t,e}\frac{\partial}{\partial x_k}g(X^{n+1,i})|\mathcal{F}_{t_n}\right]ds\lambda(de)dt - \frac{1}{2}\Delta t\int_{t_n}^{t_{n+1}}\int_{\mathcal{E}}\mathbb{E}\left[D_{t,e}\frac{\partial}{\partial x_k}g(X^{n+1,i})|\mathcal{F}_{t_n}\right]\lambda(de)dt\right)$$

$$= L^0 b_k^{n,i}\mathbb{E}\left[\Phi(t_n, X^n, \Delta t, \Delta\tilde{N}_n)|\mathcal{F}_{t_n}\right]\left(\int_{t_n}^{t_{n+1}}\int_{t_n}^{t}\int_{\mathcal{E}}\lambda(de)dsdt - \frac{1}{2}\Delta t\int_{t_n}^{t_{n+1}}\int_{\mathcal{E}}\lambda(de)dt\right),$$

(52)

which by using the fact

$$\int_{t_n}^{t_{n+1}}\int_{t_n}^{t}\int_{\mathcal{E}}\lambda(de)dsdt = \frac{1}{2}\Delta t\int_{t_n}^{t_{n+1}}\int_{\mathcal{E}}\lambda(de)dt = \frac{1}{2}(\Delta t)^2\lambda_{\mathcal{E}}$$

gives $\epsilon_{g,x_k}^1 = 0$. Similarly, note that

$$\int_{\mathcal{E}}L_e^1 a_k^{n,i}\lambda(de) = \sum_{j \in S}\int_{\Delta_{ij}}\left(a_k(t_n, X^{n,i}, i + h(i,e)) - a_k(t_n, X^{n,i}, i)\right)\lambda(de)$$

$$= \sum_{j \in S}\int_{\Delta_{ij}}\left(a_k(t_n, X^{n,i}, j) - a_k(t_n, X^{n,i}, i)\right)\lambda(de) = \sum_{j \in S}L^{i,j}a_k^{n,i}\lambda_{\Delta_{ij}},$$

(53)

we deduce

$$\epsilon_{g,k}^2 = \int_{t_n}^{t_{n+1}}\int_{t_n}^{s}\mathbb{E}\left[D_{t,e}\frac{\partial}{\partial x_k}g(X^{n+1,i})|\mathcal{F}_{t_n}\right]\int_{\mathcal{E}}L_e^1 a_k^{n,i}\lambda(de)\,dt\,ds$$

$$- \frac{1}{2\lambda_{\mathcal{E}}}\Delta t\sum_{j \in S}L^{i,j}a_k^{n,i}\lambda_{\Delta_{ij}}\int_{t_n}^{t_{n+1}}\int_{\mathcal{E}}\mathbb{E}\left[D_{t,e}\frac{\partial}{\partial x_k}g(X^{n+1,i})|\mathcal{F}_{t_n}\right]\lambda(de)\,dt$$

$$= \frac{1}{2}(\Delta t)^2\left(\int_{\mathcal{E}}L_e^1 a_k^{n,i}\lambda(de) - \sum_{j \in S}L^{i,j}a_k^{n,i}\lambda_{\Delta_{ij}}\right)\mathbb{E}\left[\Phi(t_n, X^n, \Delta t, \Delta\tilde{N}_n)|\mathcal{F}_{t_n}\right] = 0.$$

(54)

Using Itô's formula, we can obtain $\int_{t_n}^{t_{n+1}}\int_{t_n}^{t}d\tilde{N}_s d\tilde{N}_t = \frac{1}{2}((\Delta\tilde{N}_n)^2 - \lambda_{\mathcal{E}}\Delta t - \Delta\tilde{N}_n)$, note also that

$$\int_{\mathcal{E}}L_e^1 b_k^{n,i}\lambda(de) = \sum_{j \in S}\int_{\Delta_{ij}}\left(b_k(t_n, X^{n,i}, i + h(i,e)) - b_k(t_n, X^{n,i}, i)\right)\lambda(de)$$

$$= \sum_{j \in S}\int_{\Delta_{ij}}\left(b_k(t_n, X^{n,i}, j) - b_k(t_n, X^{n,i}, i)\right)\lambda(de) = \sum_{j \in S}L^{i,j}b_k^{n,i}\lambda_{\Delta_{ij}},$$

(55)

by the duality formula we have

$$\epsilon_{g,k}^3 = \mathbb{E}\Big[\frac{\partial}{\partial x_k}g(X^{n+1,i})\Big(\int_{t_n}^{t_{n+1}}\int_{t_n}^{t}L_e^1 b_k^{n,i}d\tilde{N}_s d\tilde{N}_t - \frac{1}{2\lambda_{\mathcal{E}}}\sum_{j\in S}L^{i,j}b_k^{n,i}\lambda_{\Delta_{ij}}((\Delta\tilde{N}_n)^2 - \lambda_{\mathcal{E}}\Delta t - \Delta\tilde{N}_n)\Big)\Big|\mathcal{F}_{t_n}\Big]$$

$$= \int_{t_n}^{t_{n+1}}\int_{\mathcal{E}}\int_{t_n}^{t}\int_{\mathcal{E}} L_{e_1}^1 b_k^{n,i}\mathbb{E}[D_{s,e_1}D_{t,e_2}\frac{\partial}{\partial x_k}g(X^{n+1,i})|\mathcal{F}_{t_n}]\lambda(de_1)\,ds\,\lambda(de_2)\,dt$$

$$- \frac{1}{2\lambda_{\mathcal{E}}}\Delta t \sum_{j\in S}L^{i,j}b_k^{n,i}\lambda_{\Delta_{ij}}\int_{t_n}^{t_{n+1}}\int_{\mathcal{E}}\int_{t_n}^{t}\int_{\mathcal{E}}\mathbb{E}[D_{s,e_1}D_{t,e_2}\frac{\partial}{\partial x_k}g(X^{n+1,i})|\mathcal{F}_{t_n}]\lambda(de_1)\,ds\,\lambda(de_2)\,dt \quad (56)$$

$$= \frac{1}{2}(\Delta t)^2 \lambda_{\mathcal{E}} \Big(\int_{\mathcal{E}} L_e^1 b_k^{n,i}\lambda(de) - \sum_{j\in S} L^{i,j}b_k^{n,i}\lambda_{\Delta_{ij}}\Big)\mathbb{E}\big[\Psi(t_n, X^n, \Delta t, \Delta\tilde{N}_n)|\mathcal{F}_{t_n}\big] = 0.$$

Applying the duality formula in Lemma 3, we have

$$|\epsilon_{g,k}^4| = \Big|\sum_{\alpha \in \mathcal{B}(\Gamma_2)} I_{\lambda_\alpha}^{03}\Big[\mathbb{E}[D_{s_1 s_2 s_3, e}^\alpha(\frac{\partial}{\partial x_k}g(X^{n+1,i}))f_{k,\alpha}(s_1, X_{s_1}^{n,i}, r_{s_1}^{n,i})|\mathcal{F}_{t_n}]\Big]_{t_n, t_{n+1}}\Big| \leq C(1+|X^{n,i}|^m)(\Delta t)^3. \quad (57)$$

Combining Equation (50), $\epsilon_{g,k}^1 = \epsilon_{g,k}^2 = \epsilon_{g,k}^3 = 0$, and inequality (57), we have

$$|J_1^n| = \Big|\mathbb{E}\Big[\sum_{k=1}^d \frac{\partial}{\partial x_k}g(X^{n+1,i})(X_{k,t_{n+1}}^{n,i} - X_k^{n+1,i})|\mathcal{F}_{t_n}\Big]\Big| \leq C(1+|X^{n,i}|^m)(\Delta t)^3. \quad (58)$$

For $\alpha = (1,1,1)$, by using the Itô isometry Formula (4), we obtain

$$\mathbb{E}\Big[\Big(\int_{t_n}^{t_{n+1}}\int_{t_n}^{s_3}\int_{t_n}^{s_2} f_{k,\alpha}(s_1, X_{s_1}^{n,i}, r_{s_1}^{n,i})d\tilde{N}_{s_1}d\tilde{N}_{s_2}d\tilde{N}_{s_3}\Big)^2\Big|\mathcal{F}_{t_n}\Big]$$

$$= \mathbb{E}\Big[\int_{t_n}^{t_{n+1}}\int_{\mathcal{E}}\int_{t_n}^{s_3}\int_{\mathcal{E}}\int_{t_n}^{s_2}\int_{\mathcal{E}} f_{k,\alpha}^2(s_1, X_{s_1}^{n,i}, r_{s_1}^{n,i})\lambda(de_1)ds_1\lambda(de_2)ds_2\lambda(de_3)ds_3\Big|\mathcal{F}_{t_n}\Big] \quad (59)$$

$$= I_{\lambda_\alpha}^{03}\mathbb{E}[f_{k,\alpha}^2(\cdot, X_\cdot^{n,i}, r_\cdot^{n,i})|\mathcal{F}_{t_n}].$$

For $\alpha \neq (1,1,1)$, we obtain

$$\sum_{\substack{\alpha \in \mathcal{B}(\Gamma_2) \\ \alpha \neq (1,1,1)}} \Big|\mathbb{E}\big[I_\alpha[f_{k,\alpha}(s_1, X_{s_1}^{n,i}, r_{s_1}^{n,i})]\big|\mathcal{F}_{t_n}\big]\Big|^2 \leq C(1+|X^{n,i}|^m)(\Delta t)^3. \quad (60)$$

Combining inequalities (59) and (60), we have

$$J_2^n = \int_0^1\int_0^1 \mathbb{E}\Big[\Big(\sum_{k=1}^d (X_{k,t_{n+1}}^{n,i} - X_k^{n+1,i})\frac{\partial}{\partial x_k}\Big)^2 g(X^{n+1,i} + \mu_1\mu_2(X_{t_{n+1}}^{n,i} - X^{n+1,i}))\Big|\mathcal{F}_{t_n}\Big]\mu_1 d\mu_1 d\mu_2 \leq C(1+|X^{n,i}|^m)(\Delta t)^3. \quad (61)$$

From inequalities (58) and (61), we finally obtain

$$\Big|\mathbb{E}\big[g(X_{t_{n+1}}^{n,i}) - g(X^{n+1,i})|\mathcal{F}_{t_n}\big]\Big| \leq C(1+|X^{n,i}|^m)(\Delta t)^3.$$

□

4. Numerical Experiments

Assume that the state space Markov chain r_t is in $\mathbb{S} = \{1,2,3\}$, and the transition probability matrix is

$$P = \begin{bmatrix} 0.3 & 0.6 & 0.1 \\ 0.2 & 0.7 & 0.1 \\ 0.4 & 0.4 & 0.2 \end{bmatrix}_{3\times 3}.$$

We choose $N_{sp} = 5000$ as the sample size for our numerical experiments, where N_{sp} is the total number of sample pathways. We can measure the average errors of local weak convergence and the errors of global weak convergence as follows:

$$e_{\Delta t}^{\text{global}} := \left| \frac{1}{N_{sp}} \sum_{i=1}^{N_{sp}} \left(\varphi(X_i^N) - \varphi(X_{i,t_N}) \right) \right|, e_{\Delta t}^{\text{local}} := \left| \frac{1}{N_{sp}} \frac{1}{N} \sum_{i=1}^{N_{sp}} \sum_{j=1}^{N} \left(\varphi(X_i^j) - \varphi(X_{i,t_j}) \right) \right|,$$

where $N = T/\Delta t$, Δt are $\frac{1}{8}, \frac{1}{16}, \frac{1}{32}, \frac{1}{64}, \frac{1}{128}$. We let $\varphi(X_i^j) = \sin(X_i^j)$. Let $X^{n,i}$ represent numerical solution and X_{t_n} represent explicit solutions at the time t_n, where $j \in \{1, 2, ..., N\}$.

Now, we give three numerical examples, including mark-dependent PJ-SDEwMs, mark-independent PJ-SDEwMs (Ornstein-Uhlenbeck type) and PJ-SDEwMs (geometrical type).

Example 1. *We consider the following mark-dependent PJ-SDEwMs:*

$$\begin{cases} dX_t = -\mu X_t dt + \int_{\mathcal{E}} g(r_t) \, e \, \tilde{N}(de, dt), \\ X_0 = 0.5, r_0 = 0.5, \end{cases} \quad (62)$$

where μ is a constant and the Markov chain r_t is in $\mathbb{S} = \{1, 2, 3\}$. The group coefficients g are given by $g(1) = 0.35, g(2) = 0.3, g(3) = 0.25$. We use the Itô formula to obtain the explicit solution of Equation (62) which is

$$X_t = X_0 \cdot e^{-\mu t} + e^{-\mu t} \int_0^t \int_{\mathcal{E}} g(r_s) e^{\mu s} e \tilde{N}(de, ds).$$

Assume $T = 1$ and $\mathcal{E} = [0, 1]$, and the pairs (τ_m, ζ_m) $(N_{t_n} + 1 \leq m \leq N_{t_{n+1}})$ are independent uniformly distributed in the square $[0, 1] \times [0, 1]$. Assume the kernel function $\gamma(e) = e$, we have for $\Delta_{ij} = [a_{ij}, a_{ij} + q_{ij}]$

$$\lambda_{\Delta_{ij}} = \int_{\Delta_{ij}} \lambda(de) = \int_{\Delta_{ij}} e\,de = \frac{1}{2} e^2 \Big|_{a_{ij}}^{a_{ij}+q_{ij}} = \frac{1}{2} q_{ij}(2a_{ij} + q_{ij}),$$

$$\int_{t_n}^{t_{n+1}} \int_{\mathcal{E}} e \tilde{N}(de, ds) = \sum_{m=N_{t_n}+1}^{N_{t_{n+1}}} \zeta_m, \quad \int_{\mathcal{E}} \lambda(de) = \int_0^1 \gamma(e) de = \frac{1}{2}.$$

Then, for solving the PJ-SDEwMs (62), we have Scheme 2 with the form

$$X^{n+1,i} = X^{n,i} - \mu X^{n,i} \Delta t + g(i) \int_{t_n}^{t_{n+1}} \int_{\mathcal{E}} e \tilde{N}(de, dt) + \frac{1}{2}(\Delta t)^2 \mu^2 X^{n,i} + \frac{1}{2} \sum_{j \in S} (g(j) - g(i)) q_{ij} \Delta t \int_{t_n}^{t_{n+1}} \int_{\mathcal{E}} e \tilde{N}(de, dt)$$

$$+ \int_{t_n}^{t_{n+1}} \int_{\mathcal{E}} \int_{t_n}^{t} \int_{\mathcal{E}} L_{e_1}^1 g(i) \, e_2 \tilde{N}(de_1, ds) \tilde{N}(de_2, dt),$$

which by the computation of compound Poisson process (see [27]) and the trapezoidal rule gives

$$\int_{t_n}^{t_{n+1}} \int_{\mathcal{E}} \int_{t_n}^{t} \int_{\mathcal{E}} L_{e_1}^1 g(i)\, e_2 \tilde{N}(de_1, ds) \tilde{N}(de_2, dt)$$

$$= \sum_{j \in S}(g(j) - g(i)) \int_{t_n}^{t_{n+1}} \int_{\mathcal{E}} e_2 \left(N_t^{\Delta_{ij}} - N_{t_n}^{\Delta_{ij}} - \lambda_{\Delta_{ij}}(t - t_n) \right) N(de_2, dt)$$

$$- \sum_{j \in S}(g(j) - g(i)) \int_{\mathcal{E}} e_2 \lambda(de_2) \int_{t_n}^{t_{n+1}} \left(N_t^{\Delta_{ij}} - N_{t_n}^{\Delta_{ij}} - \lambda_{\Delta_{ij}}(t - t_n) \right) dt$$

$$= \sum_{j \in S} \sum_{m=N_{t_n}+1}^{N_{t_{n+1}}} (g(j) - g(i))\, \xi_m \left(N_{\tau_m}^{\Delta_{ij}} - N_{t_n}^{\Delta_{ij}} - \lambda_{\Delta_{ij}}(\tau_m - t_n) \right)$$

$$- \frac{1}{6} \sum_{j \in S}(g(j) - g(i)) \Delta t \left(N_{t_{n+1}}^{\Delta_{ij}} - N_{t_n}^{\Delta_{ij}} - \lambda_{\Delta_{ij}} \Delta t + 2 R_N^n \right),$$

where $\int_{\mathcal{E}} e_2 \lambda(de_2) = \int_0^1 e_2^2 de_2 = \frac{1}{3}$, $\int_{t_n}^{t_{n+1}}(t - t_n)dt = \frac{1}{2}(\Delta t)^2$, $\tilde{N}_t^{\Delta_{ij}} = \int_0^t \int_{\Delta_{ij}} \tilde{N}(de, ds)$, $N_t^{\Delta_{ij}} = \int_0^t \int_{\Delta_{ij}} N(de, ds)$,

$$\int_{t_n}^{t_{n+1}} N_t^{\Delta_{ij}} dt = \frac{1}{2}(N_{t_n}^{\Delta_{ij}} + N_{t_{n+1}}^{\Delta_{ij}}) \Delta t + R_N^n.$$

We use CR to represent the rate of convergence over the time step Δt. To evaluate the performance of Scheme 2, we calculate their global errors and average local errors. It is gratifying to find that the global convergence rate (Glo.CR) has order 2.0, while the average local convergence rate (Avg.local CR) has order 3.0. This means that Scheme 2 has excellent convergence properties and shows the great accuracy in numerical calculations (see Table 1). At the same time, we draw trajectories of numerical and analytical solutions in Figure 1. By comparing different state values, it was found that regardless of how the state values change, the simulation efficacy demonstrated by Scheme 2 remains highly favorable.

Table 1. The results of convergence rates and errors for Scheme 2 in Example 1.

N	Global Errors	CR	Avg. Local Errors	CR
8	1.619×10^{-3}		2.296×10^{-4}	
16	4.007×10^{-4}	1.9921	3.001×10^{-5}	2.993
32	8.914×10^{-5}	2.0111	2.967×10^{-6}	3.0846
64	2.107×10^{-5}	2.0237	3.601×10^{-7}	3.1007
128	6.108×10^{-6}	2.1063	5.229×10^{-8}	3.0991

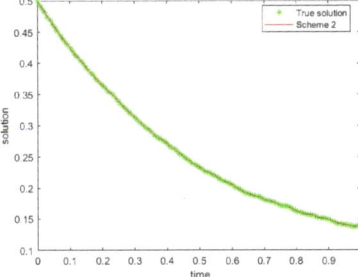
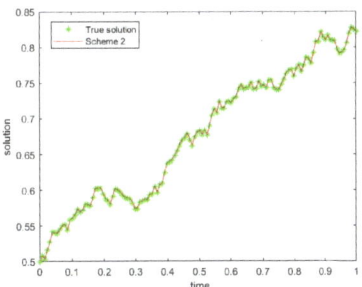

Figure 1. (**Left**) True solution and numerical solution when $g(1) = 0.35, g(2) = 0.3$. (**Right**) True solution and numerical solution when $g(1) = 3.5, g(2) = 3$.

Example 2. *Consider the Ornstein–Uhlenbeck (O-U) PJ-SDEwMs as follows:*

$$\begin{cases} dX_t = -\mu X_t dt + \int_{\mathcal{E}} g(r_t)\tilde{N}(de,dt), \\ X_0 = 0.5, r_0 = 0.5, \end{cases} \quad (63)$$

where μ is a constant and the Markov chain r_t is in $\mathbb{S} = \{1,2\}$, and the group coefficients g are given by $g(1) = 0.3$ and $g(2) = 0.25$. It is evident that Equation (63) possesses an explicit solution:

$$X_t = X_0 \cdot e^{-\mu t} + \int_0^t \int_{\mathcal{E}} e^{-\mu(t-s)} g(r_s)\tilde{N}(de,ds).$$

According to the evaluation results presented in Table 2, a detailed analysis was conducted regarding the performance of Schemes 2 and 3. The evaluation included the calculation of their global error and average local error. Interestingly, both Schemes 2 and 3 demonstrated a second-order convergence rate during the global convergence process, indicating a relatively rapid approach towards the optimal solution. Furthermore, in terms of local convergence performance, both schemes exhibited a higher level of convergence with a third-order average convergence rate. This finding suggests that both Schemes 2 and 3 exhibit favorable performance. In Table 3, we compare the global errors and convergence rate of the Euler scheme, Schemes 2 and 3. It is obvious that Scheme 3 makes it simpler and more convenient for us to calculate in comparison to Scheme 2. Equally gratifying is that Scheme 3 greatly reduces the computing time. Scheme 3 takes 3.597104 seconds, while Scheme 2 takes 10.024912 seconds.

Table 2. The results of convergence rates and errors for Scheme 3 in Example 2.

N	Global Errors	CR	Avg. Local Errors	CR
8	1.723×10^{-3}		2.157×10^{-4}	
16	3.880×10^{-4}	2.1502	2.430×10^{-5}	3.1497
32	9.239×10^{-5}	2.1103	2.887×10^{-6}	3.1114
64	2.255×10^{-5}	2.0835	3.542×10^{-7}	3.0823
128	5.583×10^{-6}	2.0643	4.350×10^{-8}	3.0651

Table 3. The results of global convergence rates and errors for three schemes in Example 2.

N	8	16	32	64	128	CR	Time (s)
Euler Scheme	1.765×10^{-2}	8.645×10^{-3}	4.277×10^{-3}	2.124×10^{-3}	1.060×10^{-3}	1.0139	0.382757
Scheme 2	1.186×10^{-2}	4.874×10^{-4}	3.115×10^{-5}	2.992×10^{-5}	6.502×10^{-6}	2.0992	10.024912
Scheme 3	1.723×10^{-2}	3.889×10^{-4}	9.249×10^{-5}	2.255×10^{-5}	5.587×10^{-6}	2.0646	3.597104

Example 3. *We consider the following PJ-SDEwMs with mark-independent jump coefficient:*

$$\begin{cases} dX_t = X_t \cdot f(r_t)dt + \int_{\mathcal{E}} X_t \cdot g(r_t)\tilde{N}(de,dt), \\ X_0 = 0.5, r_0 = 0.5, \end{cases} \quad (64)$$

where the Markov chain r_t is in $\mathbb{S} = \{1,2\}$, and $\tilde{N}(de,dt)$ represents a compensated Poisson measure in one dimension. Assuming that N_t and r_t are independent, with the group coefficients f and g provided by

$$f(1) = 2, g(1) = 0.3, f(2) = 1.5, g(2) = 0.2.$$

We utilize the Itô formula to derive the explicit solution for Equation (64) as

$$X_t = X_0 \exp\left(\int_0^t f(r_s)ds + \int_0^t \int_{\mathcal{E}} \ln|1 + g(r_s)|\tilde{N}(de,ds)\right).$$

The time $t \in [0, T]$ with $T = 1$ is set in Table 4, and we use Scheme 3 to solve the PJ-SDEwMs (64). Scheme 3 has the second-order global convergence rate (Glo.CR) and the third-order average local convergence rate (Avg.local CR). In Tables 5 and 6, we compare the Euler Scheme with Scheme 3 with different state values. For clearer display, we draw two pictures (errors of the new scheme and CPU times) according to the two tables in Figure 1. In Figure 2 (left), we clearly demonstrate that there are differences in global errors between individual states and transition states. For a more intuitive presentation, Figure 3 (right) illustrates the fluctuation of convergence rates as the number of times changes, showcasing the process of convergence rate variation with the change in state value times (CTSV). These visualizations allow us to gain a clearer understanding of the impact of state changes on convergence rates. The observation enhances our comprehension of the dynamic nature of the system.

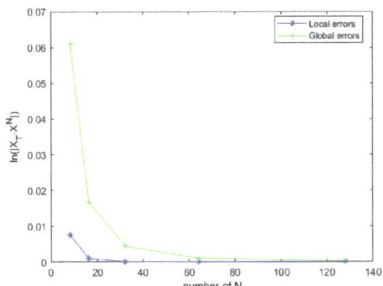 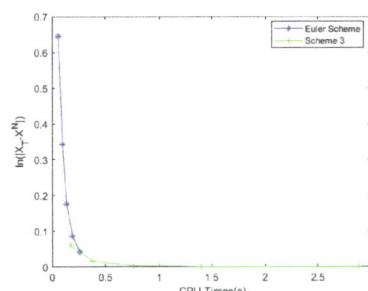

Figure 2. (**Left**) The results of the global errors and the average local errors for Scheme 3 in Example 3. (**Right**) The correlations for global errors and CPU time of all schemes.

Table 4. The results of convergence rates and errors for Scheme 3 in Example 3.

N	Global Errors	CR	Avg. Local Errors	CR
8	6.129×10^{-2}		7.646×10^{-3}	
16	1.558×10^{-2}	1.9764	9.623×10^{-4}	2.9902
32	3.931×10^{-3}	1.9814	1.219×10^{-4}	2.9854
64	1.019×10^{-3}	1.9717	1.518×10^{-5}	2.9909
128	1.944×10^{-4}	2.0535	1.825×10^{-6}	3.0051

Table 5. Global convergence rates of multiple groups of different state values for two schemes with $X_0 = 0.5$.

$[f(1), f(2)]$ $[g(1), g(2)]$	[3, 2.5] [0.35, 0.3]	[3, 2] [0.35, 0.26]	[3, 1.5] [0.35, 0.2]	[3, 1] [0.35, 0.18]	[3, 0.1] [0.35, 0.1]	[3, 0.05] [0.35, 0.02]	[3, 0.01] [0.35, 0.01]
Euler Scheme CR1	0.9187	0.9793	1.0371	1.0837	1.169	1.1682	1.1703
Scheme 3 CR1	1.9163	2.0072	2.0197	2.0328	2.0446	2.0501	2.0418

Table 6. Global convergence rates of multiple groups of different state values in two schemes with $X_0 = 0.5$.

$[f(1), f(2)]$ $[g(1), g(2)]$	[2, 1.5] [0.3, 0.2]	[3.5, 3] [0.4, 0.3]	[5.5, 5] [0.6, 0.5]	[8, 7.5] [1, 0.9]	[12.5, 12] [1.8, 1.7]	[15, 14.5] [2.8, 2.7]	[17.5, 17] [3.5, 3.4]
Euler Scheme CR2	0.9881	0.8845	0.7432	0.5731	0.3326	0.2439	0.1410
Scheme 3 CR2	1.9813	1.9160	1.8405	1.7114	1.4414	1.2898	1.0951

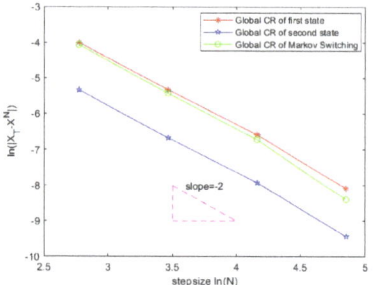 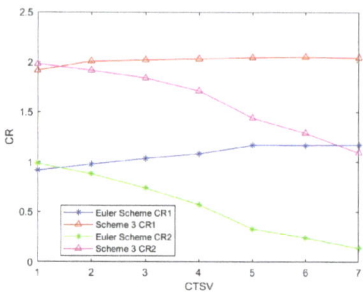

Figure 3. (**Left**) The convergence rates of different states. (**Right**) The correlations for global convergence rates and the variation of state values.

5. Discussion

In this work, we mainly study stochastic differential equations with Markovian switching driven by pure jumps (PJ-SDEwMs) and give three numerical schemes. In general, PJ-SDEwMs contains mark-dependent jump coefficient $b = b(t, X_t, r_t, e)$, which we can solve using Schemes 1 and 2. Compared to the Itô-Taylor expansion scheme (Scheme 1), Scheme 2 is easier to calculate by using the trapezoidal rule to approximate the following multiple stochastic integrals:

$$\int_{t_n}^{t_{n+1}} \int_{t_n}^{t} \int_{\mathcal{E}} L_e^1 a(s, X_s, r_s) \tilde{N}(de, ds) \, dt \quad \text{and} \quad \int_{t_n}^{t_{n+1}} \int_{\mathcal{E}} \int_{t_n}^{t} L^0 b(s, X_s, r_s, e) ds \, \tilde{N}(de, dt).$$

In particular, PJ-SDEwMs contains mark-independent jump coefficient $b = b(t, X_t, r_t)$, we can compute it in Schemes 2 and 3. Because multidimensional random integrals are avoided, Scheme 3 is simpler and more convenient (Example 2 demonstrates this very well). In addition, by using Malliavin calculus theory, we strictly proved that the proposed new schemes have local weak order-3.0 convergence rates. However, through Example 3, we find that as the upper bound of the state values gradually increases, the simulation effect of Scheme 3 is still good, but the convergence rates will gradually decrease.

6. Conclusions

In this paper, we propose three new weak second-order numerical schemes to solve stochastic differential equations with Markovian switching driven by pure jumps. By using the Malliavin stochastic analysis method, the new schemes are strictly analyzed theoretically, and the second-order convergence rate is proven. Finally, the correctness and effectiveness of the second-order schemes are verified by three numerical experiments. In addition, we find that as the upper bound of the state values increases, the global convergence rate of Scheme 3 gradually decreases to the first-order. Besides, the maximum state difference and the variation of Markov chains have a certain impact on the convergence rate.

Author Contributions: Conceptualization, Y.L.; methodology, Y.L.; software, Q.X. and Y.X; validation, Y.L., Y.X., Q.X. and Y.Z.; formal analysis, Y.L. and Y.X; investigation, Y.L., Y.X., Q.X. and Y.Z.; resources, Y.L.; data curation, Y.L., Y.X., Q.X. and Y.Z.; writing—original draft preparation, Y.L. and Y.X.; writing—review and editing, Y.L., Y.X., Q.X. and Y.Z.; visualization, Y.X.; supervision, Y.L.; project administration, Y.L.; funding acquisition, Y.L. All authors have read and agreed to the published version of the manuscript.

Funding: This research received no external funding.

Data Availability Statement: No new data were created or analyzed in this study. Data sharing is not applicable to this article.

Conflicts of Interest: The authors declare no conflict of interest.

References

1. Jang, J. Jump diffusion processes and their applications in insurance and finance. *Math. Econ.* **2007**, *41*, 62–70. [CrossRef]
2. Geman, H. Pure jump Levy processes for asset price modeling. *J. Bank. Financ.* **2002**, *26*, 1297–1316. [CrossRef]
3. He, H.; Qi, W.; Kao, Y. HMM-based adaptive attack-resilient control for Markov jump system and application to an aircraft model. *Appl. Math. Comput.* **2021**, *392*, 125–668.
4. Savović, S.; Li, L.Q.; Savović, I.; Djordjevich, A.; Min, R. Treatment of Mode Coupling in Step-Index Multimode Microstructured Polymer Optical Fibers by the Langevin Equation. *Polymers* **2022**, *14*, 1243.
5. Ji, Y.; Chizeck, H.J. Controllability, stabilizability and continuous-time Markovian jump linear quadratic control. *IEEE Trans. Automat. Control.* **1990**, *35*, 777–788. [CrossRef]
6. Mao, X. Stability of stochastic differential equations with Markovian switching. *Stoch. Process.Their Appl.* **1999**, *79*, 45–67. [CrossRef]
7. Yuan, C.; Mao, X. Convergence of the Euler–Maruyama method for stochastic differential equations with Markovian switching. *Math. Comput. Simul.* **2004**, *64*, 223–235. [CrossRef]
8. Mao, X.; Yuan, C.; Yin, G. Numerical method for stationary distribution of stochastic differential equations with Markovian switching. *J. Comput. Appl. Math.* **2005**, *174*, 1–27. [CrossRef]
9. Mao, X.; Yuan, C. *Stochastic Differential Equations with Markovian Switching*; Imperial College Press: London, UK, 2006.
10. Mao, W.; Mao, X. On the approximations of solutions to neutral SDEs with Markovian switching and jumps under non-Lipschitz conditions. *Appl. Math. Comput.* **2014**, *230*, 104–119. [CrossRef]
11. Li, M.; Huang, C.; Chen, Z. Compensated projected Euler–Maruyama method for stochastic differential equations with superlinear jumps. *Appl. Math. Comput.* **2021**, *393*, 125–760. [CrossRef]
12. Yin, B.; Ma, Z. Convergence of the semi-implicit Euler method for neutral stochastic delay differential equations with phase semi-Markovian switching. *Appl. Math. Model.* **2011**, *35*, 2094–2109. [CrossRef]
13. Ren, Q.; Tian, H. Compensated θ-Milstein methods for stochastic differential equations with Poisson jumps. *Appl. Numer. Math.* **2020**, *150*, 27–37. [CrossRef]
14. Chaman, K.; Tejinder, K. On explicit tamed Milstein-type scheme for stochastic differential equation with Markovian switching. *J. Comput. Appl. Math.* **2020**, *377*, 112917.
15. Kohatsu-Higa, A.; Tankov, P. Jump-adapted discretization schemes for Lévy-driven SDEs. *Stoch. Process. Their Appl.* **2010**, *120*, 2258–2285. [CrossRef]
16. Mikulevicius, R. On the rate of convergence of simple and jump-adapted weak Euler schemes for Lévy driven SDEs. *Math. Naclir.* **2012**, *122*, 2730–2757. [CrossRef]
17. Hu, L.; Gan, S. Convergence and stability of the balanced methods for stochastic differential equations with jumps. *Int. J. Comput. Math.* **2011**, *88*, 2089–2108. [CrossRef]
18. Zhou, N.; Mamon, R. An accessible implementation of interest rate models with Markov-switching. *Expert Syst. Appl.* **2012**, *39*, 4679–4689. [CrossRef]
19. Siu, T.; Ching, W.; Fung, E.; Ng, M.; Li, X. A high-order Markov-switching model for risk measurement. *Comput. Math. Appl.* **2009**, *58*, 1–10. [CrossRef]
20. Yang, Z.; Yin, G.; Li, H. Stability of numerical methods for jump diffusions and Markovian switching jump diffusions. *J. Comput. Appl. Math.* **2015**, *275*, 197–212. [CrossRef]
21. Li, R.H.; Chang, Z. Convergence of numerical solution to stochastic delay differential equation with poisson jump and Markovian switching. *Appl. Math. Comput.* **2007**, *184*, 451–463.
22. Chen, Y.; Xiao, A.; Wang, W. Numerical solutions of SDEs with Markovian switching and jumps under non-Lipschitz conditions. *J. Comput. Appl. Math.* **2019**, *360*, 41–54. [CrossRef]
23. Fan, Z. Convergence of numerical solutions to stochastic differential equations with Markovian switching. *Appl. Math. Comput.* **2017**, *315*, 176–187. [CrossRef]
24. Liu, X.; Li, C. Weak approximations and extrapolations of stochastic differential equations with jumps. *SIAM J. Numer. Anal.* **2000**, *37*, 1747–1767. [CrossRef]
25. Li, Y.; Wang, Y.; Feng, T.; Xin, Y. A High Order Accurate and Effective Scheme for Solving Markovian Switching Stochastic Models. *Mathematics* **2021**, *9*, 588. [CrossRef]
26. Buckwar, E.; Riedler, M.G. Runge–Kutta methods for jump-diffusion differential equations. *J. Comput. Appl. Math.* **2011**, *236*, 1155–1182. [CrossRef]
27. Platen, E.; Bruti-Liberati, N. *Numerical Solutions of Stochastic Differential Equations with Jump in Finance*; Springer: Berlin/Heidelberg, Germany, 2010.
28. Giulia, D. N.; Bernt, Ø.; Frank P. *Malliavin Calculus for Lévy Processes with Applications to Finance*; Springer: Berlin/Heidelberg, Germany, 2008.

Disclaimer/Publisher's Note: The statements, opinions and data contained in all publications are solely those of the individual author(s) and contributor(s) and not of MDPI and/or the editor(s). MDPI and/or the editor(s) disclaim responsibility for any injury to people or property resulting from any ideas, methods, instructions or products referred to in the content.

Article

On the Kantorovich Theory for Nonsingular and Singular Equations

Ioannis K. Argyros [1], Santhosh George [2], Samundra Regmi [3,*] and Michael I. Argyros [4]

[1] Department of Mathematical Sciences, Cameron University, Lawton, OK 73505, USA; iargyros@cameron.edu
[2] Department of Mathematical and Computational Sciences, National Institute of Technology Karnataka, Mangaluru 575 025, India; sgeorge@nitk.edu.in
[3] Department of Mathematics, University of Houston, Houston, TX 77205, USA
[4] Department of Computer Sciences, University of Oklahoma, Norman, OK 73501, USA; michael.i.argyros-1@ou.edu
* Correspondence: sregmi5@uh.edu

Abstract: We develop a new Kantorovich-like convergence analysis of Newton-type methods to solve nonsingular and singular nonlinear equations in Banach spaces. The outer or generalized inverses are exchanged by a finite sum of linear operators making the implementation of these methods easier than in earlier studies. The analysis uses relaxed generalized continuity of the derivatives of operators involved required to control the derivative and on real majorizing sequences. The same approach can also be implemented on other iterative methods with inverses. The examples complement the theory by verifying the convergence conditions and demonstrating the performance of the methods.

Keywords: outer inverse; generalized inverse; Banach space; Newton-type method; convergence; Hilbert space

MSC: 65J15; 65H10; 90C30; 90C53; 49M15

1. Introduction

Let T_1, T_2 denote Banach spaces, and let $\mathcal{B}(T_1, T_2)$ be the space of linear and continuous operators from T_1 to T_2. Newton-type methods (NTMs) [1]

$$x_{n+1} = x_n - E(x_n)^\# Y(x_n), \ n = 0, 1, 2, \ldots \quad (1)$$

have been used to solve the equation

$$DY(x) = 0. \quad (2)$$

Here, the operator $Y : \Omega \subset T_1 \longrightarrow T_2$ is a differentiable operator in the Fréchet sense, $D \in \mathcal{B}(T_2, T_1)$, $E(x_n) \in \mathcal{B}(T_1, T_2)$ approximates $Y'(x_n)$. Moreover, $E(x_n)^\#$ stands for an outer inverse (OI) of $E(x_n)$, i.e., $E(x_n)^\# E(x_n) E(x_n)^\# = E(x_n)^\#$.

A plethora of applications in optimization such as penalization problems, minimax problems, and goal programming are formulated as (2) using Mathematical Modelling [2–15].

Method (2) specializes to the Gauss–Newton method (GNM) for solving nonlinear least squares problems, the generalized NTM for undetermined systems, and an NTM for ill-posed Equations [16–36].

As an example of (1) and (2), let T_1 and T_2 stand for Hilbert spaces. Then, consider the task of finding a local minimum $\tilde{u}$ of

$$\min H(u), \quad (3)$$

where $H(u) = \frac{1}{2}\|Y(u)\|^2$. Then, the GNM is defined by

$$x_{n+1} = x_n - Y'(x_n)^\dagger Y(x_n) \tag{4}$$

to solve

$$Y'(u)^* Y(u) = 0, \tag{5}$$

where $Y'(x_n)^\dagger$ is the Moore–Penrose inverse [5,15,31], and $Y'(u)^*$ is the adjoint of the linear operator $Y'(u)$ (see also the Remark 1).

Ben-Israel [5,17] utilized the conditions

$$\begin{aligned} \|Y(u) - Y(\tilde{u}) - Y'(\tilde{u})(u - \tilde{u})\| &\leq c_1 \|u - \tilde{u}\|, \\ \|(Y'(u)^+ - Y'(\tilde{u})^+) Y(\tilde{u})\| &\leq c_2 \|u - \tilde{u}\| \end{aligned}$$

and

$$c_1 \|Y'(\tilde{u})^+\| + c_2 < 1$$

for all $u, \tilde{u}$ in a neighborhood of $x_0 \in \Omega$. He also used these conditions with $Y'(u)^\#$ [5,17]. These results are not semilocal since they require information about $Y'(\tilde{u})^+$ or $Y'(\tilde{u})^\#$. Moreover, if $Y'(x_0)^{-1} \in \mathcal{B}(T_2, T_1)$, they require conditions not required in the Kantorovich theory [1,16,33,37–41]. Later Deuflhard and Heindl [39], Haussler [29], and Yamamoto [1] gave Kantorovich-type theorems for the GNM like (4) using convergence conditions involving either OI of Moore–Penrose inverses:

$$\|Y'(\tilde{u})^\# (I - Y'(u) Y'(u)^\#) Y(u)\| \leq c(u) \|u - \tilde{u}\|, c(u) \leq \bar{c} < 1, \tag{6}$$

for each $u, \tilde{u} \in \Omega$. This condition is strong and does not hold in concrete examples (see Section 4 in [31]). A Kantorovich-like result with generalized inverses can be found in [42] without (6). However, it was assumed that T_1 and T_2 are finite-dimensional and $T_2 = R(E(x_0))$, where $R(D)$ denotes the range of a linear operator D. Other drawbacks of the earlier works are that only properties of OI are used. That is $BEB = B$ and the projectional properties of EB and BE. However, the stability and perturbation bounds for OI are not given for method (1). However, this was accomplished through the elegant work of Nashed and Chen [31]. This work reduces to the Kantorovich theory for (2) when $E(u)^\#$ is replaced by $E(u)^{-1}$ without additional conditions. Later works on the convergence analysis using Lipchit-type conditions, particularly for the Newton–Gauss method (5), can be found in [10,24] and the references therein.

Next, we address the problems with the implementation of method (1) which constitutes the motivation for this paper. Let $\Delta \in \mathcal{B}(T_1, T_2)$ and let $\Delta^\# \in \mathcal{B}(T_2, T_1)$ be an OI of Δ.

Suppose $\Delta_1^\#(u) = (I + \Delta^\#(\Delta - E(u)))^{-1} \Delta^\#$ is an OI. A criterion for $\Delta_1^\#$ to be an OI is $\|\Delta^\#(E(u) - \Delta)\| \leq 1$ (see Lemma 2). Then, (2) becomes

$$x_{n+1} = x_n - \Delta_1^\#(x_n) Y(x_n). \tag{7}$$

But the main problem with the implementation of (2) of (7) still remains. This problem requires the invertibility of Δ_2, $\Delta_2(u) = I + \Delta^\#(\Delta - E(u))$. This inversion can be avoided. Let m be a fixed natural number. Define the operators

$$H = H(u) = \Delta^\#(\Delta - E(u))$$

and

$$L = L_m(u) = I + H + H^2 + \cdots + H^m.$$

Then, we can consider the replacement of (7) given as

$$x_{n+1} = x_n - L\Delta^{\#}Y(x_n). \tag{8}$$

By letting $m \to +\infty$ in the definition of L, we have that

$$E(x_n)^{\#} = \lim_{m \to +\infty} L_m(x_m)\Delta^{\#}.$$

Thus, it is worth studying the convergence of (8) instead of (2), since we avoid the inversion of the operator Δ_2. Let us provide examples of possible choices for the operator Δ. First, consider the case when the operator $E = Y'(u)$ is invertible. Moreover, let $T_1 = T_2 = \mathbb{R}^i$, i is a positive integer, and J denotes the Jacobian of the operator F. Then, choose $\Delta = J(x_0)$ in the semi-local convergence case of $\Delta = J(x^*)$ in the local case, where $x^* \in \Omega$ is assumed to be a solution of the equation $Y(u) = 0$. The selection $\Delta = J(\bar{u})$ has been used in [43,44], for $\bar{u} \in \Omega$. In the setting of a Banach space for $E = Y'(u)$, the operator Δ can be chosen to be $\Delta = Y'(x_n)$ (semi-local case) or $\Delta = Y'(x^*)$ (local case). Numerous selections for Δ connected to OI or generalized inverses (GI) can also be found in [5,11,13,31] and the references therein. Other selections for Δ are also possible provided that they satisfy the convergence conditions (C_5) and (C_6) of Section 3. The convergence analysis relies on the relaxed generalized continuity used to control the derivative Y' and majorizing sequences for the iterates $\{x_n\}$ (see also Section 2). The results in this article specialize immediately to solve nonsingular equations if $E(u)^{\#}$ is replaced by $E(u)^{-1}$.

The rest of the article provides the preliminaries in Section 2; the convergence of (8) is in Section 3; and the applications are in Section 4. The article's concluding remarks appear in Section 5.

2. Preliminaries

We reproduce standard results on OI and GI to make the article as self-contained as possible. More properties can be found in [5,11–13,31]. Let $\Delta \in \mathcal{B}(T_1, T_2)$. An operator $B \in \mathcal{B}(T_2, T_1)$ is said to be an inner inverse (II) of Δ if $\Delta B \Delta = \Delta$, and an OI of Δ if $B\Delta B = B$. It is well known that II and bounded OI always exist. The zero is always an OI. So, we consider only nonzero outer inverses. Suppose the operator B is either an inverse or an OI of Δ. Then, ΔB and $B\Delta$ are linear idempotents (algebraic projectors). Suppose that B is an inverse of E, then for $N(\bar{E})$, $N(B\Delta) = N(\Delta)$ and $R(\Delta) = R(\Delta B)$. Consequently, the following decompositions hold $T_1 = N(\Delta) + R(B\Delta)$ and $T_2 = R(\Delta) + N(\Delta B)$. Since, B is an OI of Δ if and only if Δ is an inverse of B, it follows that $T_1 = R(B) \oplus N(B\Delta)$ and $T_2 = N(B) \oplus R(\Delta B)$. If B is an inner and an outer inverse of Δ, then B is called a GI of Δ. Moreover, there exists a unique GI $B = \Delta_{P,Q}^{+}$ satisfying $\Delta B \Delta = \Delta$, $B\Delta B = B$, $B\Delta = I - P$ and $\Delta B = Q$, where P is a given projection of T_1 into $N(\Delta)$ and Q a given projection of T_2 into $R(\Delta)$. In the special case when T_1 and T_2 are Hilbert spaces, and P, Q are orthogonal projections. Then, $\Delta_{P,Q}^{+}$ is the Moore–Penrose inverse of Δ.

We need the following six auxiliary Lemmas, the proof of which can be found in Section 2 in [31].

Lemma 1. *Let* $\Delta \in \mathcal{B}(T_1, T_2)$. *If* $\Delta^{\#}$ *is a bounded OI of* Δ. *Then, the following assertions hold*

$$T_1 = R(\Delta^{\#}) \oplus N(\Delta^{\#}\Delta)$$

and

$$T_2 = N(\Delta^{\#}) \oplus R(\Delta\Delta^{\#}).$$

Lemma 2 (Banach Perturbation-Like Lemma). *Let $\Delta \in \mathcal{B}(T_1, T_2)$ and $\Delta^\# \in \mathcal{B}(T_2, T_1)$ be an OI of Δ. Let also $B \in \mathcal{B}(T_1, T_2)$ be such that $\|\Delta^\#(B - \Delta)\| < 1$. Then, $B^\# := (I + \Delta^\#(B - \Delta))^{-1}\Delta^\#$ is a bounded OI of B so that $N(B^\#) = N(\Delta^\#)$, $R(B^\#) = R(\Delta^\#)$,*

$$\|B^\# - \Delta^\#\| \leq \frac{\|\Delta^\#(B - \Delta)\Delta^\#\|}{1 - \|\Delta^\#(B - \Delta)\|}$$

$$\leq \frac{\|\Delta^\#(B - \Delta)\| \, \|\Delta^\#\|}{1 - \|\Delta^\#(B - \Delta)\|}$$

and

$$\|B^\# \Delta\| \leq \frac{1}{1 - \|\Delta^\#(B - \Delta)\|}.$$

Lemma 3. *Let $\Delta, B \in \mathbb{B}(T_1, T_2)$ and let $\Delta^\#$ and $B^\# \in \mathbb{B}(T_2, T_1)$ be OI of Δ, and B, respectively. Then, $B^\#(I - \Delta\Delta^\#) = 0 \Leftrightarrow N(\Delta^\#) \subset N(B^\#)$.*

Lemma 4. *Let $\Delta \in \mathcal{B}(T_1, T_2)$. Suppose that T_1 and T_2 have topological decompositions $T_1 = N(\Delta) \oplus M$, $T_2 = R(\Delta) \oplus S$. Let $\Delta^+ (= \Delta^+_{M,S})$ stand for the GI of Δ connected to these decompositions. Let B satisfy $\|\Delta^+(B - \Delta)\| < 1$, and $(I + (B - \Delta)\Delta^+)B$ sends $N(\Delta)$ to $R(\Delta)$. Then, the following assertions hold:*

$$B^+ := B^+_{R(\Delta^+), N(\Delta^+)} \text{ exists,}$$

$$B^+ = \Delta^+(I + B_0\Delta^+)^{-1} = (I + \Delta^+ B_0)^{-1}\Delta^+,$$

$$R(B^+) = R(\Delta^+), N(B^+) = N(\Delta^+)$$

and

$$\|B^+ \Delta\| \leq \frac{1}{\|\Delta^+(B - \Delta)\|},$$

where $B_0 = B - \Delta$.

Lemma 5. *Let $\Delta \in \mathcal{B}(T_1, T_2)$ and Δ^+ be the GI as given in the Lemma 4. Let $B \in \mathcal{B}(T_2, T_1)$ satisfy $\|\Delta^\#(B - \Delta)\| \leq 1$ and $R(B) \subseteq R(\Delta)$. Then, the conclusions of the Lemma 4 hold and $R(B) = R(\Delta)$.*

Lemma 6. *Let $\Delta \in \mathcal{B}(T_1, T_2)$ and let Δ^+ be bounded GI of Δ. Let $B \in \mathcal{B}(T_2, T_1)$ satisfy $\|\Delta^+(B - \Delta)\| < 1$. Let $B^\# := (I + \Delta^+(B - \Delta))^{-1}\Delta^+$. Then, $B^\#$ is a GI of $B \Leftrightarrow \dim N(B) = \dim N(\Delta)$, and $\operatorname{codim} R(B) = \operatorname{codim} R(\Delta)$.*

Define the parameter

$$r = \|\Delta^\#(\Delta - E(x))\|, \forall x \in \Omega. \tag{9}$$

We need some estimates.

Lemma 7. *Let $\Delta \in \mathcal{B}(T_1, T_2)$ and let $\Delta^\# \in \mathcal{B}(T_2, T_1)$ be an OI of Δ. Let $E(x) \in \mathcal{B}(T_1, T_2)$ with $r \in [0, \frac{1}{2})$. Then, $\Delta_1^\#$ is a bounded OI of $E(x)$. Moreover, the following estimates hold.*

$$\|I - L\| \leq \frac{r(1 - r^m)}{1 - r} = b < 1, \tag{10}$$

the operator $L^{-1} \in \mathcal{B}(T_2, T_1)$ and

$$\|L^{-1}\| \leq \frac{1}{1 - b} = \bar{b}, \tag{11}$$

where $\Delta_1^\#$, L are as defined in the introduction.

Proof. The operator $\Delta_1^\#$ is a bounded OI of $E(x)$ by Lemma 2 for $B = E(x)$. Moreover, we have in turn by the definition of L:

$$\begin{aligned}\|I - L\| &= \|H + H^2 + \cdots + H^m\| \\ &\leq \|H\| + \|H\|^2 + \cdots + \|H\|^m = \frac{\|H\|(1 - \|H\|^m)}{1 - \|H\|} \\ &\leq \frac{r(1 - r^m)}{1 - r} = b < 1,\end{aligned}$$

by the choice of r. It is followed by the Lemma 2 that $H^{-1} \in \mathcal{B}(T_2, T_1)$ and $\|H^{-1}\| \leq \frac{1}{1-b} = \bar{b}$. □

3. Semi-Local Convergence

The convergence of the method (8) is shown using scalar majorizing sequences.

Definition 1. *Let $\{x_n\}$ be a sequence in T_1. Then, real sequence $\{p_n\}$ satisfying*

$$\|x_{n+1} - x_n\| \leq p_{n+1} - p_n, \ \forall n \geq 0$$

is called a majorizing sequence for $\{x_n\}$. If the sequence $\{p_n\}$ converges, then also $\{x_n\}$ converges, and for $x^* = \lim_{n \to \infty} x_n$ and $p^* = \lim_{n \to \infty} p_n$, we have

$$\|x^* - x_n\| \leq p^* - p_n.$$

Therefore, the convergence of the sequence $\{x_n\}$ relates to that of $\{p_n\}$.

Let $M = [0, +\infty)$.

Some conditions are required in the convergence of (8).

Suppose that

(C_1) There exists parameters $\kappa \geq 0, r \in [0, \frac{1}{2})$, a point $x_0 \in \Omega, \Delta \in \mathcal{B}(T_1, T_2)$ having outer inverse $\Delta^\#$ such that $\|L\Delta^\# Y(x_0)\| \leq \kappa$.

(C_2) There exists function $\phi_0 : M \to M$ which is continuous and nondecreasing such that the equation $\phi_0(t) - 1 = 0$ admits a smallest positive solution r_0. Take $M_0 = [0, r_0)$.

(C_3) There exists functions $\phi : M_0 \to M, \phi_1 : M_0 \to M$. Define the real sequence $\{s_n\}$ for $s_0 = 0, s_1 = \kappa$ as

$$s_{n+1} = s_n + e_n(s_n - s_{n-1}), \tag{12}$$

where $e_n = (1 + r + \ldots + r^m)\left[\int_0^1 \phi\big((1 - \theta)(s_n - s_{n-1})\big)\, d\theta + \phi_1(s_{n-1}) + \bar{b}r^{m+1}\right]$, $n = 0, 1, 2, \ldots$.

The sequence $\{s_n\}$ is proven to be majorizing for $\{x_n\}$ (see Theorem 1). However, some conditions for this sequence are needed first.

(C_4) There exists $r \in [\kappa, r_0)$ such that for all $n = 0, 1, 2, \cdots, s_n \leq r$.

By this condition and (12) that $0 \leq s_n \leq s_{n+1} \leq r$ and there exists $s^* \in [\kappa, r]$ such that $\lim_{n \to +\infty} s_n = s^*$.

The functions ϕ_0, ϕ and ϕ_1 connect to the operators on the method (8).

(C_5) $\|\Delta^\#(Y'(u) - \Delta)\| \leq \phi_0(\|u - x_0\|)$ for all $u \in \Omega$. Set $\Omega_0 = \Omega \cap E(x_0, r_0)$, where $E(x_0, r_0) = \{x \in X : \|x - x_0\| < r_0\}$. We shall also denote by $E[x_0, r_0]$ the closure of $E(x_0, r_0)$.

(C_6) $r = \|\Delta^\#(\Delta - E(u))\| < \frac{1}{2}, \|\Delta^\#(Y'(\tilde{u}) - Y'(u))\| \leq \phi(\|\tilde{u} - u\|)$ and $\|\Delta^\#(Y'(u) - E(u))\| \leq \phi_1(\|u - x_0\|)$ for all $u, \tilde{u} \in \Omega_0$.

(C_7) The equation $e(t) - 1 = 0$ has a smallest solution in $(0, s^*]$, where $e(t) = (1 + r + \cdots + r^m) \left[\int_0^1 \phi((1-\theta)t) \, d\theta + \phi_1(t) + \bar{b} r^{m+1} \right]$. Denote such solution by $\bar{s}$
and
(C_8) $E[x_0, s^*] \subset \Omega$.

Next, the convergence is established for (8).

Theorem 1. *Suppose that the conditions* (C_1)–(C_8) *hold. Then, the sequence* $\{x_n\}$ *produced by the method* (8) *converges to a unique solution* $x^* \in E[x_0, s^*] \cap \{x_0 + R(\Delta^\#)\}$ *of the equation* $\Delta^\# Y(x_0) = 0$. *Moreover, the following assertion holds*

$$\|x^* - x_n\| \leq s^* - s_n. \tag{13}$$

Proof. Mathematical induction on n shall establish the estimates

$$\|x_{n+1} - x_n\| \leq s_{n+1} - s_n. \tag{14}$$

Since

$$\|x_1 - x_0\| = \|E(x_0)^\# Y(x_0)\| \leq \kappa = s_1 = s_1 - s_0 < s^*,$$

the assertion (13) holds if $n = 0$ and $x_1 \in E(x_0, s^*)$. It follows by (9) (for $x = x_1$) and Lemma 7 that $\Delta_1(x_1)^\#$ is an outer inverse of $E(x_1)$ and $\|\Delta_1(x_1)^\# A\| \leq \bar{b}$ and $N(\Delta_1(x_1)^\#) = N(\Delta^\#)$. Suppose that for $i = 1, 2, \cdots, n$; $\|x_i - x_{i-1}\| \leq s_i - s_{i-1}$ and $N(\Delta_1(x_{n-1})^\#) = N(\Delta^\#)$. Then, we have

$$\begin{aligned}\|x_n - x_0\| &\leq \|x_n - x_{n-1}\| + \cdots + \|x_1 - x_0\| \\ &\leq s_n - s_{n-1} + \cdots + s_1 - s_0 = s_n < s^*,\end{aligned}$$

and $N(\Delta_1(x_n)^\#) = N(\Delta_1(x_{n-1})^\#) = N(\Delta^\#)$. Hence, by the Lemma 3, it follows that

$$\Delta_1(x_n)^\# \left(I - E(x_{n-1}) \Delta_1(x_{n-1})^\# \right) = 0.$$

Then, by the method (8)

$$\begin{aligned}Y(x_n) &= Y(x_n) - Y(x_{n-1}) - \Delta L^{-1}(x_n - x_{n-1}) \\ &= Y(x_n) - Y(x_{n-1}) - Y'(x_{n-1})(x_n - x_{n-1}) \\ &\quad + (Y'(x_{n-1}) - A_{n-1})(x_n - x_{n-1}) + (A_{n-1} - \Delta L^{-1})(x_n - x_{n-1}) \\ &= Y(x_n) - Y(x_{n-1}) - Y'(x_{n-1})(x_n - x_{n-1}) \\ &\quad + (Y'(x_n) - A_{n-1} - A_{n-1})(x_n - x_{n-1}) \\ &\quad + (A_{n-1} L - \Delta) L^{-1}(x_n - x_{n-1}).\end{aligned} \tag{15}$$

But, we have by the definition of L

$$\begin{aligned}A_{n-1} L - \Delta &= A_{n-1}(I + H + \cdots + H^m) - \Delta \\ &= A_{n-1} - \Delta + (-\Delta + \Delta + A_{n-1})(I + H + \cdots + H^m) \\ &= A_{n-1} - \Delta + \Delta(H + \cdots + H^m) - (\Delta - H)(H + \cdots + H^m) \\ &= A_{n-1} - \Delta + \Delta H + \Delta(H^2 + \cdots + H^m) \\ &\quad - (\Delta - A_{n-1})(H + \cdots + H^m) \\ &= \Delta(H^2 + \cdots + H^m) - \Delta(\Delta - A_{n-1})(H + \cdots + H^m).\end{aligned}$$

So,

$$\Delta^\# (A_{n-1} L - \Delta) = -H^{m+1}, \tag{16}$$

where we also used $A_{n-1} - \Delta + \Delta H = 0$ by the definition of H. Using the induction hypotheses and the conditions (C_5), (C_6), (14), (15), (11), we have in turn that

$$\begin{aligned}
\|\Delta^\# Y(x_n)\| &\leq \int_0^1 \phi((1-\theta)\|x_n - x_{n-1}\|)\, d\theta \, \|x_n - x_{n-1}\| \\
&\quad + \phi_1(\|x_{n-1} - x_0\|)\|x_n - x_{n-1}\| + \bar{b}r^{m+1}\|x_n - x_{n-1}\| \\
&\leq \left[\int_0^1 ((1-\theta)(s_n - s_{n-1}))\, d\theta + \phi_1(s_{n-1}) + \bar{b}r^{m+1}\right] \\
&\quad \times (s_n - s_{n-1}).
\end{aligned} \qquad (17)$$

Hence, by (8), Lemma 7 and (17)

$$\begin{aligned}
\|x_{n+1} - x_n\| &\leq (1 + r + \cdots + r^m)\left[\int_0^1 \phi((1-\theta)(s_n - s_{n-1}))\, d\theta \right. \\
&\quad \left. + \phi_1(s_{n-1}) + \bar{b}r^{m+1}\right](s_n - s_{n-1}) = s_{n+1} - s_n
\end{aligned}$$

and

$$\begin{aligned}
\|x_{n+1} - x_0\| &\leq \|x_{n+1} - x_n\| + \|x_n - x_0\| \\
&\leq s_{n+1} - s_n + s_n - s_0 = s_{n+1} < s^*.
\end{aligned}$$

The induction is completed. Thus, we have for any n

$$\|x_{n+1} - x_n\| \leq s_{n+1} - s_n,$$

$$\|x_n - x_0\| \leq s_n \leq s^*$$

$$\|\Delta^\#(E(x_{n+1}) - \Delta)\| < 1,$$

and

$$\Delta_1(x_{n+1})^\# := \left(I + \Delta^\#(E(x_{n+1}) - \Delta)\right)^{-1}\Delta^\#$$

is an OI of $E(x_{n+1})$. The sequence $\{s_n\}$ is complete as convergent and majorizes $\{x_n\}$. So, the sequence $\{x_n\}$ is also complete in T_1. Then, it is convergent to a $x^* \in E[x_0, s^*]$. By the definition

$$\Delta_1(x_n)^\# = \left(I + \Delta^\#(E(x_n) - A)\right)^{-1}\Delta^*, \text{for all } n$$

and

$$\begin{aligned}
0 &= \lim_{n\to\infty}\left(I + \Delta^\#(E(x_n) - A)\right)(x_n - x_{n-1}) \\
&= \lim_{n\to\infty} \Delta^\# Y(x_n) = \Delta^\# Y(x^*).
\end{aligned} \qquad (18)$$

Thus, x^* solves $\Delta^\# Y(x) = 0$. Using Lemma 2, we have $R(\Delta_1(x_n)^\#) = R(\Delta^\#)$ for all $n = 0, 1, 2, \cdots$. So, $x_{n+1} - x_n = -\Delta_1(x_n)^\# Y(x_n) \in R(\Delta^\#)$ and from Lemma 1, we obtain $R(\Delta^\#) = R(\Delta^\# \Delta)$, so $x_{n+1} \in x_n + R(\Delta^\#)$. Thus, $x_n \in x_0 + R(\Delta^\#)$ for all n. Suppose that $w \in E[x_0, s^*] \cap \{x_0 + R(\Delta^\#)\}$ solves the equation $\Delta^\# Y(x) = 0$. Then, we have $w - x^* \in R(\Delta^\#)$ and $\Delta^\# E(w - x_n) = \Delta^\# E(w - x_0) + \Delta^\# E(x_n - x_0) = w - x_n$, for all $n = 0, 1, 2, \ldots$. Then, (11), as in (16) and using (C_7)

$$\begin{aligned}
\|w - x_{n+1}\| &= \|w - x_n + \Delta_1(x_n)^{\#}Y(x_n) - \Delta_1(x_n)^{\#}Y(w)\| \\
&\leq (1 + r + \cdots + r^m)\left[\int_0^1 \phi((1-\theta)\|w - x_n\|)\,d\theta \right.\\
&\quad \left. + \phi_1(\|x_n - x_0\|) + \bar{b}r^{m+1}\right]\|w - x_n\| \\
&\leq d\|w - x_n\| \leq d^{n+1}\|x_0 - w\| < \bar{b} \leq s^*,
\end{aligned} \qquad (19)$$

where $d = (1 + r + \cdots + r^m)\left[\int_0^1 \phi((1-\theta)\|w - x_0\|)\,d\theta + \phi_1(s^*) + \bar{b}r^{m+1}\right] \in [0, 1)$. Therefore, we conclude $x^* = \lim_{n \to +\infty} x_n = w$. Finally, from (14) and the triangle inequality, we obtain for $j = 0, 1, 2, \ldots$

$$\begin{aligned}
\|x_{n+j} - x_n\| &\leq \|x_{n+j} - x_{n+j-1}\| + \|x_{n+j-1} - x_{n+j-2}\| + \cdots + \|x_{n+1} - x_n\| \\
&\leq s_{n+j} - s_{n+j-1} + s_{n+j-1} - s_{n+j-2} + \cdots + s_{n+1} - s_n \\
&= s_{n+j} - s_n.
\end{aligned}$$

By letting $j \to +\infty$ in (19), we show the assertion (13). □

Remark 1.

(i) The results of the Theorem 1 specialize for the Newton method with OI defined by $x_{n+1} = x_n - Y'(x_n)^{\#}Y(x_n)$, for solving Equation (5). Simply, take $E(x) = Y'(x)$ and $\phi_1 = 0$.

(ii) Under the conditions $(C_1) - (C_8)$, further suppose that the operator $\left(I + \Delta^+(\Delta - E(x))\right)^{-1} E(x)$ sends $N(A)$ to $R(A)$ provided that for $x \in \Omega$, the inverse of

$$I + \Delta^+(E(x) - \Delta) \quad \text{exists.} \qquad (20)$$

Then, by Lemma 4, $E(x_n)^{\#} := \left(I + \Delta^+(E(x_n) - \Delta)\right)^{-1}\Delta^+$ is a GI. Thus, the proof of Theorem 1 establishes the convergence of method (8) for GI.

(iii) By the Lemma 6, the condition (20) can be exchanged by rank $(E(x)) \leq \text{rank}(E(x_0))$ for $\Delta = E(x_0)$ and if T_1 and T_2 are finite dimensional. In general Banach spaces, the condition (20) can be switched by the stronger $R(E(x)) \subset R(E(x_0))$ (for $\Delta = E(x_0)$) (see Lemma 5) or by the conditions of the Lemma 6.

4. Examples

The example considers method (4) with $Y'(x)^+ = Y'(x)^{-1}$ for the case $\Delta = I$, which is independent of x_0. It is also compared with method (8) for $\Delta = Y'(x_0)$. In this case, the methods (4) and (8) become Newton's method

$$x_{n+1} = x_n - Y'(x_n)^{-1}Y(x) \qquad (4)'$$

and

$$x_{n+1} = x_n - LY'(x_0)^{-1}Y(x) \qquad (8)',$$

respectively.

We shall solve the system

$$\begin{aligned}
F_1(u, v) &= u - 0.1\sin u - 0.3\cos v + 0.4 \\
F_2(u, v) &= v - 0.2\cos u + 0.1\sin v + 0.3.
\end{aligned}$$

If $F = (F_1, F_2)$. Then, we can write

$$Y(z) = 0 \text{ for } z = (u, v)^T.$$

Consequently, we obtain

$$Y'((u,v)) = \begin{bmatrix} 1 - 0.1\cos(u) & 0.3\sin(v) \\ 0.2\sin(u) & 0.1\cos(v) + 1 \end{bmatrix}.$$

Example 1. Method ($8'$): Set $m = 1$ and $\Delta = I$. We have that

$$\begin{aligned} L_1(x) &= I + (I - Y'(x)), \\ P_1(x) &= x - (I + (I - Y'(x)))Y(x), \\ x_{j+1} &= P_1(x_j). \end{aligned} \tag{21}$$

Example 2. Method ($8'$): Set, $m = 2$ and $\Delta = I$. It follows that

$$\begin{aligned} L_2(x) &= I + (I - Y'(x)) + (I - Y'(x))^2, \\ P_2(x) &= x - L_2(x)Y(x), \\ x_{j+1} &= P_2(x_j). \end{aligned} \tag{22}$$

Example 3. Method ($8'$): Set $m = 3$ and $\Delta = I$. Then, we have

$$\begin{aligned} L_3(x) &= I + (I - Y'(x)) + (I - Y'(x))^2 + (I - Y'(x))^3, \\ P_3(x) &= x - L_3(x)Y(x), \\ x_{j+1} &= P_3(x_j). \end{aligned} \tag{23}$$

Example 4. Method ($8'$): Set $m = 4$ and $\Delta = I$. Then, we have

$$\begin{aligned} L_4(x) &= I + (I - Y'(x)) + (I - Y'(x))^2 + (I - Y'(x))^3 + (I - Y'(x))^4, \\ P_4(x) &= x - L_4(x)Y(x), \\ x_{j+1} &= P_4(x_j). \end{aligned} \tag{24}$$

Example 5. Method ($8'$): Set $m = 5$ and $\Delta = I$. Then, we have

$$\begin{aligned} L_5(x) &= I + (I - Y'(x)) + (I - Y'(x))^2 + (I - Y'(x))^3 + (I - Y'(x))^4 + (I - Y'(x))^5, \\ P_5(x) &= x - L_5(x)Y(x), \\ x_{j+1} &= P_5(x_j). \end{aligned} \tag{25}$$

Example 6. Method ($8'$): Set $m = \overline{1,5}$ and $\Delta = Y'(x_0)$. It follows that

$$\begin{aligned} x_{n+1} &= x_n - L\Delta^{-1}Y(x_n), \\ H &= \Delta^{-1}(\Delta - Y'(x)), \\ L &= I + \sum_{j=1}^{m} H^j. \end{aligned} \tag{26}$$

Definition 2. *Let $\{x_n\}$ be a sequence. Then, the computational order of convergence (COC) is for $\theta_n = x_n - x^*$* [4]

$$\overline{h}_n = \frac{\ln |\theta_{n+1}/\theta_n|}{\ln |\theta_n/\theta_{n-1}|}.$$

Definition 3. Let $\{x_n\}$ be a sequence. Then, the approximate computational order of convergence (ACOC) is for $\widehat{\theta}_n = x_n - x_{n-1}$

$$\widehat{h}_n = \frac{\ln |\widehat{\theta}_{n+1}/\widehat{\theta}_n|}{\ln |\widehat{\theta}_n/\widehat{\theta}_{n-1}|}.$$

The Tables 1–5 demonstrate that the cheaper-to-implement method (8) is behaving the same as Newton's method for a large enough m.

Table 1. Iterations to obtain error tolerance $\varepsilon = 10^{-9}$ for initial point $x_0 = (1,1)$, where $\|I - Y'(x_0)\| = 0.3129 < 1$.

Method	Iterations	CPU Time	Method	Iterations	CPU Time
(4)' Newton	4	10.82×10^{-6}	(4)' Newton	4	10.82×10^{-6}
(21), $m=1$	6	6.94×10^{-6}	(26), $m=1$	8	13.063×10^{-6}
(22), $m=2$	5	6.922×10^{-6}	(26), $m=2$	6	12.255×10^{-6}
(23), $m=3$	4	5.946×10^{-6}	(26), $m=3$	5	9.089×10^{-6}
(24), $m=4$	4	6.324×10^{-6}	(26), $m=4$	5	9.198×10^{-6}
(25), $m=5$	4	6.836×10^{-6}	(26), $m=5$	4	8.743×10^{-6}

Table 2. Iterations to obtain error tolerance of $\varepsilon = 10^{-9}$ for initial point $x_0 = (0,0)$, where $\|I - Y'(x_0)\| = 0.1414 < 1$.

Method	Iterations	CPU Time	Method	Iterations	CPU Time
(4)' Newton	3	7.215×10^{-6}	(4)' Newton	3	7.215×10^{-6}
(21), $m=1$	5	5.122×10^{-6}	(26), $m=1$	3	4.256×10^{-6}
(22), $m=2$	4	5.8×10^{-6}	(26), $m=2$	3	5.862×10^{-6}
(23), $m=3$	3	5.503×10^{-6}	(26), $m=3$	3	5.575×10^{-6}
(24), $m=4$	3	5.771×10^{-6}	(26), $m=4$	3	5.825×10^{-6}
(25), $m=5$	3	5.895×10^{-6}	(26), $m=5$	3	5.973×10^{-6}

Table 3. Iterations to obtain error tolerance of $\varepsilon = 10^{-9}$, for $x_0 = (-15, -15)$, where $\|I - Y'(x_0)\| = 0.257 < 1$.

Method	Iterations	CPU Time	Method	Iterations	CPU Time
(4)' Newton	5	13.454×10^{-6}	(4)' Newton	5	13.454×10^{-6}
(21), $m=1$	7	7.184×10^{-6}	(26), $m=1$	9	12.015×10^{-6}
(22), $m=2$	5	10.195×10^{-6}	(26), $m=2$	7	13.245×10^{-6}
(23), $m=3$	5	7.352×10^{-6}	(26), $m=3$	6	9.378×10^{-6}
(24), $m=4$	5	7.883×10^{-6}	(26), $m=4$	6	9.829×10^{-6}
(25), $m=5$	5	8.636×10^{-6}	(26), $m=5$	5	8.936×10^{-6}

Table 4. Iterations to obtain error tolerance of $\varepsilon = 10^{-12}$, for $x_0 = (-15, -15)$, where $\|I - Y'(x_0)\| = 0.257 < 1$.

Method	Iterations	CPU Time	Method	Iterations	CPU Time
(4)' Newton	7	16.719×10^{-6}	(4)' Newton	7	16.719×10^{-6}
(21), $m=1$	8	15.677×10^{-6}	(26), $m=1$	12	24.742×10^{-6}
(22), $m=2$	7	20.052×10^{-6}	(26), $m=2$	8	27.178×10^{-6}
(23), $m=3$	7	14.711×10^{-6}	(26), $m=3$	8	20.43×10^{-6}
(24), $m=4$	7	15.357×10^{-6}	(26), $m=4$	7	19.2×10^{-6}
(25), $m=5$	7	16.49×10^{-6}	(26), $m=5$	7	17.538×10^{-6}

Table 5. COC versus ACOC with $x_0 = (-15, -15)$, $\varepsilon = 10^{-12}$.

Method	COC	ACOC
(2) Newton	1.8624	1.9697
(21), $m = 1$	0.863	1
(22), $m = 2$	0.2695	1.0438
(23), $m = 3$	1.9714	2.3569
(24), $m = 4$	1.8354	1.9453
(25), $m = 5$	1.8642	1.9661
(26), $m = 1$	0.9065	1.0118
(26), $m = 2$	0.5912	0.999
(26), $m = 3$	0.7321	0.9926
(26), $m = 4$	1.933	2.0151
(26), $m = 5$	1.8679	1.9578

5. Conclusions

We developed a semi-local Kantorovich-like analysis of Newton-type methods for solving singular nonlinear operator equations using outer or generalized inverses. These methods do not use inverses as in earlier studies but a sum of operators. This sum converges to the inverse and makes the implementation of these methods easier than the ones using inverses. The analysis of the methods relies on the concept of generalized continuity for the operators involved and majorizing sequences. Examples complement the theory. Due to its generality, this article's technique can be applied on other method with inverses along the same lines [6,14,19,32,39,43,45–49]. It is worth noting that the method (8) should be used for sufficiently small m. Otherwise, if m is very large, it may be as expensive to implement as method (4).

Author Contributions: Conceptualization, I.K.A., S.G., S.R. and M.I.A.; Methodology, I.K.A., S.G., S.R. and M.I.A.; Software, I.K.A., S.G., S.R. and M.I.A.; Validation, I.K.A., S.G., S.R. and M.I.A.; Formal analysis, I.K.A., S.G., S.R. and M.I.A.; Investigation, I.K.A., S.G., S.R. and M.I.A.; Resources, I.K.A., S.G., S.R. and M.I.A.; Data curation, I.K.A., S.G., S.R. and M.I.A.; Writing—original draft, I.K.A., S.G., S.R. and M.I.A.; Writing—review & editing, I.K.A., S.G., S.R. and M.I.A.; Visualization, I.K.A., S.G., S.R. and M.I.A.; Supervision, I.K.A., S.G., S.R. and M.I.A.; Project administration, I.K.A., S.G., S.R. and M.I.A.; Funding acquisition, I.K.A., S.G., S.R. and M.I.A. All authors have read and agreed to the published version of the manuscript.

Funding: This research received no external funding.

Data Availability Statement: Data is contained within the article.

Acknowledgments: We would like to express our sincere graduate to Mykhailo Havdiak.

Conflicts of Interest: The authors declare no conflicts of interest.

References

1. Yamamoto, T. A convergence theorem for Newton-like algorithms in Banach spaces. *Numer. Math.* **1987**, *51*, 545–557. [CrossRef]
2. Adly, S.; Ngai, H.V.; Nguyen, V.V. Newton's method for solving generalized equations: Kantorovich's and Smale's approaches. *J. Math. Anal. Appl.* **2016**, *439*, 396–418. [CrossRef]
3. Artacho, F.J.A.; Dontchev, M.; Gaydu, A.L.; Geoffroy, M.H.; Veliov, V.M. Metric regularity of Newton's iteration. *SIAM J. Control Optim.* **2011**, *49*, 339–362. [CrossRef]
4. Argyros, I.K. *The Theory and Applications of Iteration Methods with Applications, Engineering Series*, 2nd ed.; CRC Press, Taylor and Francis Publ.: Boca Raton, FL, USA, 2022.
5. Ben-Israel, A. On applications of generalized inverses in nonlinear analysis. In *Theory and Application of Generalized Inverses of Matrices*; Boullion, T.L., Odell, P.L., Eds.; Mathematics Series 4; Texas Technological College: Lubbock, TX, USA, 1968; pp. 183–202.
6. Cibulka, R.; Dontchev, A.; Preininger, J.; Roubal, T.; Veliov, V. *Kantorovich-Type Theorems for Generalized Equations, Research Report 2015-16*; Vienna University of Technology: Vienna, Austria, 2015.
7. Dokov, S.P.; Dontchev, A.L. Robinson's Strong Regularity Implies Robust Local Convergence of Newton's Method. In *Optimal Control (Gainesville, FL, 1997), Applied Optimization*; Kluwer: Dordrecht, The Netherlands, 1998; Volume 15, pp. 116–129.

8. Deuflhard, P. *Newton Algorithms for Nonlinear Problems: Affine Invariance and Adaptive Algorithms*; Springer Series in Computational Mathematics; Springer: Berlin/Heidelberg, Germany, 2004; Volume 35.
9. Kelley, C.T. *Solving Nonlinear Equations with Iterative Methods, Solvers and Examples in Julia, Fundamentals of Algorithms*; SIAM: Philadelphia, PA, USA, 2023.
10. Li, C.; Ng, K.F. Convergence analysis of the Gauss–Newton method for convex inclusion and convex-composite optimization problems. *J. Math. Anal. Appl.* **2012**, *389*, 469–485. [CrossRef]
11. Nashed, M.Z. On the perturbation theory for generalized inverse operators in Banach spaces. In *Functional Analysis Methods in Numerical Analysis*; Nashed, M.Z., Ed.; Lecture Notes in Mathematics; Springer: Berlin/Heidelberg, Germany; New York, NY, USA, 1979; Volume 701, pp. 180–195.
12. Nashed, M.Z. Inner, outer, and generalized inverses in Banach and Hilbert spaces. *Nemer. Funct. Anal. Optim.* **1987**, *9*, 261–325. [CrossRef]
13. Nashed, M.Z. A new approach to classification and regularization of ill-posed operator equations. In *Inverse and Ill-Posed Problems*; Engl, H.W., Groetsch, C.W., Eds.; Notes and reports in mathematics in science and engineering; Academic Press: New York, NY, USA, 1987; Volume 4, pp. 53–75.
14. Pollock, S.; Rebholz, L.G. Anderson acceleration for contraction and noncontractive operators. *IMA Numer. Anal.* **2021**, *41*, 2841–2872. [CrossRef]
15. Rockafellar, R.T. *Convex Analysis*; Princeton Mathematics Series; Princeton University Press: Princeton, NJ, USA, 1970; Volume 28.
16. Argyros, I.K.; George, S. On a unified convergence analysis for Newton-type methods solving generalized equations with the Aubin property. *J. Complex.* **2024**, *81*, 101817. [CrossRef]
17. Ben-Israel, A.; Greville, T.N.E. *Generalized Inverses: Theory and Applications*; John Wiley and Sons: New York, NY, USA, 1974.
18. Bian, W.; Chen, X.; Kelley, C.T. Anderson acceleration for a class of nonsmooth fixed-point problems. *SIAM J. Sci. Comp.* **2021**, *43*, S1–S20. [CrossRef]
19. Canes, E.; Kremlin, G.; Levitt, A. Convergence analysis of direct minimization and self-consistent iterations. *SIAM J. Sci. Comp.* **2021**, *42*, 243–274.
20. Dontchev, A.L. Local analysis of a Newton-type method based on partial linearization. In *The Mathematics of Numerical Analysis (Park City, UT, 1995), Lectures in Applied Mathematics*; AMS: Providence, RI, USA, 1996; Volume 32, pp. 295–306.
21. Dontchev, A.L.; Rockafellar, R.T. Newton's method for generalized equations: Asequential implicit function theorem. *Math. Program.* **2010**, *123*, 139–159. [CrossRef]
22. Dontchev, A.L.; Rockafellar, R.T. Convergence of inexact Newton methods for generalized equations. *Math. Program.* **2013**, *139*, 115–137. [CrossRef]
23. Ferreira, O.P. A robust semi-local convergence analysis of Newtons method for cone inclusionproblems in Banach spaces under affine invariant majorant condition. *J. Comput. Appl. Math.* **2015**, *279*, 318–335. [CrossRef]
24. Ferreira, O.P.; Goncalves, M.L.N.; Oliveira, P.R. Local convergence analysis of the Gauss–Newton method under a majorant condition. *J. Complex.* **2011**, *27*, 111–125. [CrossRef]
25. Ferreira, O.P.; Goncalves, M.L.N.; Oliveira, P.R. Convergence of the Gauss–Newton method for convex composite optimization under a majorant condition. *SIAM J. Optim.* **2013**, *23*, 1757–1783. [CrossRef]
26. Ferreira, O.P.; Silva, G.N. Inexact Newton's Method to Nonlinear Functions with Valuesin a Cone. *arXiv* **2015**, arXiv:1510.01947.
27. Ferreira, O.P.; Silva, G.N. Local Convergence Analysis of Newton's Method for Solving Strongly Regular Generalized Equations. *arXiv* **2016**, arXiv:1604.04568.
28. Ferreira, O.P.; Svaiter, B.F. Kantorovich's majorants principle for Newton's method. *Comput. Optim. Appl.* **2009**, *42*, 213–229. [CrossRef]
29. Háussler, W.M. A Kantorovich-type convergence analysis for the Gauss–Newton–Method. *Numer. Math.* **1986**, *48*, 119–125. [CrossRef]
30. Josephy, N. *Newton's Method for Generalized Equations and the PIES Energy Model*; University of Wisconsin-Madison: Madison, WI, USA, 1979.
31. Nashed, M.Z.; Chen, X. Convergence of Newton-like methods for singular operators using outer inverses. *Numer. Math.* **1993**, *66*, 235–257. [CrossRef]
32. Proinov, P.D. New general convergence theory for iterative processes and its applications to Newton–Kantorovich type theorems. *J. Complex.* **2010**, *25*, 3–42. [CrossRef]
33. Rheinboldt, W.C. A unified convergence theory for a class of iterative process. *SIAM J. Numer. Anal.* **1968**, *5*, 42–63. [CrossRef]
34. Robinson, S.M. Extension of Newton's method to nonlinear functions with values in a cone. *Numer. Math.* **1972**, *19*, 341–347. [CrossRef]
35. Robinson, S.M. Normed convex processes. *Trans. Amer. Math. Soc.* **1972**, *174*, 127–140. [CrossRef]
36. Robinson, S.M. Strongly regular generalized equations. *Math. Oper. Res.* **1980**, *5*, 43–62. [CrossRef]
37. Argyros, I.K.; George, S.; Shakhno, S.; Regmi, S.; Havdiak, M.; Argyros, M.I. Asymptotically Newton–Type Methods without Inverses for Solving Equations. *Mathematics* **2024**, *12*, 1069. [CrossRef]
38. Argyros, I.K.; George, S.; Regmi, S.; Argyros, C.I. Hybrid Newton-like Inverse Free Algorithms for Solving Nonlinear Equations. *Algorithms* **2024**, *17*, 154. [CrossRef]

39. Deuflhard, P.; Heindl, G. Affine invariant convergence theorems for Newton's method and extensions to related methods. *SIAM J. Numer. Anal.* **1979**, *16*, 1–10. [CrossRef]
40. Kantorovich, L.V.; Akilov, G. *Functional Analysis in Normed Spaces*; Fizmatgiz: Moscow, Russia, 1959.
41. Silva, G.N. Kantorovich's theorem on Newton's method for solving generalized equationsunder the majorant condition. *Appl. Math. Comput.* **2016**, *286*, 178–188.
42. Yamamoto, T. Uniqueness of the solution in a Kantorovich-type theorem of Haussler for the Gauss–Newton Method. *Jpn. J. Appl. Math.* **1989**, *6*, 77–81. [CrossRef]
43. Ezquerro, J.A.; Gutierrez, J.M.; Hernandez, M.A.; Romero, N.; Rubio, M.J. The Newton algorithm: From Newton to Kantorovich. *Gac. R. Soc. Mat. Esp.* **2010**, *13*, 53–76. (In Spanish)
44. Ezquerro, J.A.; Hernandez-Veron, M.A. Domain of global convergence for Newton's algorithm from auxiliary points. *Appl. Math. Lett.* **2018**, *85*, 48–56. [CrossRef]
45. Catinas, E. The inexact, inexact perturbed, and quasi-Newton algorithms are equivalent models. *Math. Comp.* **2005**, *74*, 291–301. [CrossRef]
46. Candelarion, G.; Cordero, A.; Torregrosa, J.R.; Vassileva, M.P. Generalized conformable fractional Newton-type method for solving nonlinear systems. *Numer. Algorithms* **2023**, *93*, 1171–1208. [CrossRef]
47. Erfanifar, R.; Hajariah, M.A. A new multi-step method for solving nonlinear systems with high efficiency indices. *Numer. Algorithms* **2024**. [CrossRef]
48. Gutierrez, J.M.; Hernandez, M.A. Newtons method under weak Kantorovich conditions. *IMA J. Numer. Anal.* **2000**, *20*, 521–532. [CrossRef]
49. Singh, S. A third order iterative algorithm for inversion of cumulative beta distribution. *Numer. Algor.* **2023**, *94*, 1331–1353.

Disclaimer/Publisher's Note: The statements, opinions and data contained in all publications are solely those of the individual author(s) and contributor(s) and not of MDPI and/or the editor(s). MDPI and/or the editor(s) disclaim responsibility for any injury to people or property resulting from any ideas, methods, instructions or products referred to in the content.

Article

An Accelerated Dual-Integral Structure Zeroing Neural Network Resistant to Linear Noise for Dynamic Complex Matrix Inversion

Feixiang Yang, Tinglei Wang and Yun Huang *

College of Computer Science and Engineering, Jishou University, Jishou 416000, China;
2021401395@stu.jsu.edu.cn (F.Y.); wtl@stu.jsu.edu.cn (T.W.)
* Correspondence: huangyun@jsu.edu.cn; Tel.: +86-139-0744-7310

Abstract: The problem of inverting dynamic complex matrices remains a central and intricate challenge that has garnered significant attention in scientific and mathematical research. The zeroing neural network (ZNN) has been a notable approach, utilizing time derivatives for real-time solutions in noiseless settings. However, real-world disturbances pose a significant challenge to a ZNN's convergence. We design an accelerated dual-integral structure zeroing neural network (ADISZNN), which can enhance convergence and restrict linear noise, particularly in complex domains. Based on the Lyapunov principle, theoretical analysis proves the convergence and robustness of ADISZNN. We have selectively integrated the SBPAF activation function, and through theoretical dissection and comparative experimental validation we have affirmed the efficacy and accuracy of our activation function selection strategy. After conducting numerous experiments, we discovered oscillations and improved the model accordingly, resulting in the ADISZNN-Stable model. This advanced model surpasses current models in both linear noisy and noise-free environments, delivering a more rapid and stable convergence, marking a significant leap forward in the field.

Keywords: dynamic complex matrix inversion; zeroing neural network; linear noise; activation function; residual fluctuations

MSC: 34A55

Citation: Yang, F.; Wang, T.; Huang, Y. An Accelerated Dual-Integral Structure Zeroing Neural Network Resistant to Linear Noise for Dynamic Complex Matrix Inversion. *Axioms* **2024**, *13*, 374. https://doi.org/10.3390/axioms13060374

Academic Editor: Feliz Manuel Minhós

Received: 7 April 2024
Revised: 15 May 2024
Accepted: 31 May 2024
Published: 2 June 2024

Copyright: © 2024 by the authors. Licensee MDPI, Basel, Switzerland. This article is an open access article distributed under the terms and conditions of the Creative Commons Attribution (CC BY) license (https://creativecommons.org/licenses/by/4.0/).

1. Introduction

Matrix inversion is a fundamental and crucial problem encountered in various domains [1–5], including mathematics and engineering, chaotic systems [1–3], and robotic dynamics [5]. Numerous methods exist for solving this problem, primarily categorized into two approaches. The first is numerical computation methods, such as Newton's iterative method [6,7], which, though fundamentally serial in nature, suffer from slow computation speed and high resource consumption, rendering them ineffective for efficiently computing the inverse of high-dimensional matrices. Another approach is neural-network-based methods, inherently parallel in computation, such as gradient neural networks (GNNs) [8–11], renowned for their high computational accuracy and exponential convergence. However, GNNs have their own set of challenges and limitations, particularly when it comes to handling dynamic or time-varying data.

Introduced 20 years ago, the ZNN model proposed by Zhang et al. [12] is a specialized neural network architecture that is more adaptive and efficient for solving real-time matrix inversion problems. However, ZNNs are only applicable in ideal noise-free environments. In reality, various types of noise exist, impairing ZNNs' convergence to theoretical values. Dynamic matrix inversion encompasses two domains: dynamic real matrix inversion and dynamic complex matrix inversion. According to PID control theory [13], the Integration-Enhanced Zhang Neural Network model (IEZNN) [14], proposed by Jin et al., restricts noise interference and is employed to address dynamic real matrix inversion problems, demonstrating commendable noise restriction capabilities and convergence performance through theoretical analysis and experimental validation.

The applications of dynamic matrix inversion in the complex domain span various scientific and engineering disciplines [15–19]. Mathematical models in the complex domain are crucial for describing phenomena such as control systems [16], signal processing [17], and optical systems [18]. Therefore, this paper focuses on the problem of dynamic complex matrix inversion.

Expanding upon previous research on zeroing neural network (ZNN) models, Zhang et al. proposed a complex-valued ZNN (CVZNN) to address DCMI problems [20]. Xiao et al. introduced a complex-valued noise-tolerant ZNN (CVNTZNN) model [21] aimed at restricting real-world noise interference, inspired by the noise reduction principle of integral-based zeroing neural networks. However, the CVNTZNN model struggles to effectively restrict linear noise. Recently, Hua et al. introduced the dual-integral structure zeroing neural network (DISZNN) model [22]. Leveraging its inherent dual-integral structure, the DISZNN model demonstrates superior performance in restricting linear noise for DCMI problems, as evidenced by theoretical analysis based on Laplace transforms. Moreover, numerous studies suggest that integrating activation functions (AFs) into ZNN models enhances noise tolerance and convergence performance [23–31]. Therefore, this paper proposes an accelerated dual-integral structure zeroing neural network (ADISZNN) by combining AFs with the DISZNN model to enhance its noise restriction capabilities against linear noise and accelerate convergence. It is noteworthy that the DISZNN model is restructured in this study, and the convergence and robustness of the ADISZNN model are theoretically analyzed and demonstrated in a different manner.

This article delineates the following scholarly contributions: The integration of DISZNN with a novel activation function has culminated in the development of an accelerated dual-integral structure zeroing neural network (ADISZNN). This model utilizes a dual-integral structure and activation function, demonstrating improved convergence speed. This means that the model's computed results can more quickly approach the theoretical inverse of the target matrix. Oscillatory fluctuations observed in the steady-state residual error of ADISZNN, particularly with the SBPAF activation function, have been identified and mitigated through targeted enhancements. Theoretical analyses, supported by results from three comparative numerical experiments, confirm the outstanding convergence and robustness of the enhanced stable ADISZNN model. To our knowledge, no prior work has introduced an accelerated dual-integral structure zeroing neural network capable of linear noise cancellation in the context of dynamic complex matrix inversion.

The article is structured into five methodical sections. Section 2 delves into the DCMI problem, presenting the design formulation and procedural details of the ADISZNN model. Section 3 offers a theoretical exposition and validation of ADISZNN's convergence and robustness, utilizing Lyapunov's theorem and supported by graphical analyses, with the SBPAF function selected for the model's activation. In Section 4, we conducted three sets of numerical comparison experiments. The article concludes with a summary of the findings in Section 5.

2. Problem Formulation, Design Formula, and ADISZNN Model

2.1. Consideration of the DCMI Problem

The dynamic complex matrix inverse problem can be described as follows:

$$\mathbf{A}(t)\mathbf{X}(t) = \mathbf{I}, \quad \text{or} \quad \mathbf{X}(t)\mathbf{A}(t) = \mathbf{I} \in \mathbb{C}^{n \times n}, \tag{1}$$

where $\mathbf{A}(t) \in \mathbb{C}^{n \times n}$ is a nonsingular and smooth dynamic complex coefficient matrix with rank n, and $\mathbf{X}(t)$ represents the real-time solution of Equation (1), obtained through the ADISZNN model, where $\mathbf{I} \in \mathbb{C}^{n \times n}$ denotes the identity matrix. Our aim is to compute $\mathbf{X}(t)$ such that Equation (1) holds true at any given time $t \in [0, +\infty)$. Hence, we have $\mathbf{X}^*(t) = \mathbf{A}^{-1}(t)$.

As complex numbers consist of real and imaginary parts, Equation (1) can be rewritten as

$$[\mathbf{A}_{\text{re}}(t) + j\mathbf{A}_{\text{im}}(t)][\mathbf{X}_{\text{re}}(t) + j\mathbf{X}_{\text{im}}(t)] = \mathbf{I}, \quad (2)$$

where $[\mathbf{A}_{\text{re}}(t) + j\mathbf{A}_{\text{im}}(t)][\mathbf{A}_{\text{re}}(t) + j\mathbf{A}_{\text{im}}(t)]$ is the expansion of the complex matrix $\mathbf{A}(t)$, and $\mathbf{A}_{\text{re}}(t)$ and $\mathbf{A}_{\text{im}}(t)$ are, respectively, the real and imaginary parts of the given matrix $\mathbf{A}(t)$. Similarly, $\mathbf{X}_{\text{re}}(t)$ and $\mathbf{X}_{\text{im}}(t)$ are, respectively, the real and imaginary parts of the state solution $\mathbf{X}(t)$, where the imaginary unit is denoted as $j = \sqrt{-1}$.

2.2. Design Formula

To compute the dynamic complex matrix inversion, a function is devised to measure the real-time error in Equation (1), as follows:

$$\mathbf{E}(t) = \mathbf{A}(t)\mathbf{X}(t) - \mathbf{I}. \quad (3)$$

Its derivative with respect to time t is given by

$$\dot{\mathbf{E}}(t) = \dot{\mathbf{A}}(t)\mathbf{X}(t) + \mathbf{A}(t)\dot{\mathbf{X}}(t). \quad (4)$$

The design formula of the integration-enhanced zeroing neural network model is as follows [14]:

$$\dot{\mathbf{E}}(t) = -s_0(\mathbf{E}(t)) - s_1 \int_0^t \mathbf{E}(\tau)d\tau \quad (5)$$

where design parameters $s_0 > 0$ and $s_1 > 0$ are adjusted for the rate. By combining Equations (4) and (5), we can derive the following formula:

$$\mathbf{A}(t)\dot{\mathbf{X}}(t) = -\dot{\mathbf{A}}(t)\mathbf{X}(t) - s_0(\mathbf{A}(t)\mathbf{X}(t) - \mathbf{I}) - s_1 \int_0^t (\mathbf{A}(\tau)\mathbf{X}(\tau) - \mathbf{I})d\tau. \quad (6)$$

In actuality, a wide array of noise phenomena are consistently present across numerous practical applications. Examples include the superfluous movements observed in robotic arm operations, as discussed in [32], and the chaotic dynamics within permanent magnet synchronous motor (PMSM) systems, as explored in [33], among others. To more accurately reflect real-world conditions, we introduce noise into Equation (6), thereby obtaining the following equation:

$$\mathbf{A}(t)\dot{\mathbf{X}}(t) = -\dot{\mathbf{A}}(t)\mathbf{X}(t) - s_0(\mathbf{A}(t)\mathbf{X}(t) - \mathbf{I}) - s_1 \int_0^t (\mathbf{A}(\tau)\mathbf{X}(\tau) - \mathbf{I})d\tau + \mathbf{N}(t). \quad (7)$$

2.3. Dual-Integral Structure ZNN Model Design

The DISZNN model proposed by Hua et al. [22] has demonstrated significant efficacy in the restriction of noise, particularly linear noise. The model for DISZNN is as follows:

$$\dot{\mathbf{E}}(t) = -s_0^3 \int_0^t \int_0^\delta \mathbf{E}(\tau)d\tau d\delta - 3s_0^2 \int_0^t \mathbf{E}(\delta)d\delta - 3s_0 \mathbf{E}(t) \quad (8)$$

in which $s_0 \in \mathbb{R}^+$ is the design parameter, the single-integral term restricts noise, while the double-integral term not only restricts noise but also accelerates convergence speed.

2.4. ADISZNN Model Design

It has been mentioned in many papers [23–31] that adding an activation function to some ZNN-like models can accelerate the convergence of the error function and enhance the model's ability to restrict noise. Therefore, we modified the ZNN model by adjusting its design formula to

$$\dot{\mathbf{E}}(t) = -\alpha \Phi(\mathbf{E}(t)) \quad (9)$$

in which, $\Phi(\cdot)\colon \mathbb{C}^{n \times n} \to \mathbb{C}^{n \times n}$ is an activation function.

To provide a more intuitive description of the model's evolution, we set

$$\Theta(t) = \dot{\mathbf{E}}(t) + \alpha\Phi(\mathbf{E}(t)) \tag{10}$$

Letting
$$\Theta(t) = -\lambda \int_0^t \Theta(\tau)d\tau, \tag{11}$$

where $\lambda > 0$.

We define
$$\mathbf{Y}(t) = \Theta(t) + \lambda \int_0^t \Theta(\tau)d\tau, \tag{12}$$

and substituting Equation (10) into Equation (12), we can obtain
$$\begin{aligned}\mathbf{Y}(t) &= \dot{\mathbf{E}}(t) + \alpha\Phi(\mathbf{E}(t)) + \lambda \int_0^t (\dot{\mathbf{E}}(t) + \alpha\Phi(\mathbf{E}(\tau)))d\tau \\ &= \dot{\mathbf{E}}(t) + \alpha\Phi(\mathbf{E}(t)) + \lambda\mathbf{E}(t) + \lambda\alpha \int_0^t \Phi(\mathbf{E}(\tau))d\tau.\end{aligned} \tag{13}$$

Similarly, we let
$$\mathbf{Y}(t) = -\lambda \int_0^t \mathbf{Y}(\tau)d\tau, \tag{14}$$

combining Equations (13) and (14), we can obtain the following equation:
$$\begin{aligned}&\dot{\mathbf{E}}(t) + \alpha\Phi(\mathbf{E}(t)) + \lambda\mathbf{E}(t) + \lambda\alpha \int_0^t \Phi(\mathbf{E}(\tau))d\tau \\ &= -\lambda \int_0^t (\dot{\mathbf{E}}(\tau) + \alpha\Phi(\mathbf{E}(\tau))) + \lambda\mathbf{E}(\tau) \\ &\quad + \lambda\alpha \int_0^\tau \Phi(\mathbf{E}(\delta))d\delta)d\tau \\ &= -\lambda\mathbf{E}(t) - \alpha\lambda \int_0^t \Phi(\mathbf{E}(\tau))d\tau \\ &\quad - \lambda^2 \int_0^t \mathbf{E}(\tau)d\tau - \lambda^2\alpha \int_0^t \int_0^\tau \Phi(\mathbf{E}(\delta))d\delta d\tau.\end{aligned} \tag{15}$$

Thus, we obtain the ADISZNN model,
$$\begin{aligned}\dot{\mathbf{E}}(t) = &-\alpha\Phi(\mathbf{E}(t)) - 2\lambda\mathbf{E}(t) - 2\lambda\alpha \int_0^t \Phi(\mathbf{E}(\tau))d\tau \\ &- \lambda^2 \int_0^t \mathbf{E}(\tau)d\tau - \lambda^2\alpha \int_0^t \int_0^\tau \Phi(\mathbf{E}(\delta))d\delta d\tau.\end{aligned} \tag{16}$$

Therefore, the ADISZNN model form with noise can be reformulated as
$$\begin{aligned}\dot{\mathbf{E}}(t) = &-\alpha\Phi(\mathbf{E}(t)) - 2\lambda\mathbf{E}(t) - 2\lambda\alpha \int_0^t \Phi(\mathbf{E}(\tau))d\tau \\ &- \lambda^2 \int_0^t \mathbf{E}(\tau)d\tau - \lambda^2\alpha \int_0^t \int_0^\tau \Phi(\mathbf{E}(\delta))d\delta d\tau \\ &+ \mathbf{N}(t).\end{aligned} \tag{17}$$

Furthermore, since we already know that $\mathbf{E}(t) = \mathbf{A}(t)\mathbf{X}(t) - \mathbf{I}$ and $\dot{\mathbf{E}}(t) = \dot{\mathbf{A}}(t)\mathbf{X}(t) + \mathbf{A}(t)\dot{\mathbf{X}}(t)$, we can further derive the ADISZNN model incorporating noise:

$$\begin{aligned}\mathbf{A}(t)\dot{\mathbf{X}}(t) = &- \dot{\mathbf{A}}(t)\mathbf{X}(t) - \alpha\Phi(\mathbf{A}(t)\mathbf{X}(t) - \mathbf{I}) \\ &- 2\lambda(\mathbf{A}(t)\mathbf{X}(t) - \mathbf{I}) \\ &- 2\lambda\alpha \int_0^t \Phi(\mathbf{A}(\tau)\mathbf{X}(\tau) - \mathbf{I})d\tau \\ &- \lambda^2 \int_0^t (\mathbf{A}(\tau)\mathbf{X}(\tau) - \mathbf{I})d\tau \\ &- \lambda^2\alpha \int_0^t \int_0^\tau \Phi(\mathbf{A}(\delta)\mathbf{X}(\delta) - \mathbf{I})d\delta d\tau \\ &+ \mathbf{N}(t)\end{aligned} \qquad (18)$$

3. Theoretical Analyses

In previous research on DISZNN [22], theoretical analysis of convergence and robustness was demonstrated using Laplace transform methods. However, in this paper, we employ a different approach, based on the Lyapunov principle, for proof. In this section, we primarily discuss and demonstrate the convergence and robustness of the ADISZNN model based on the Lyapunov principle, and analyze and apply lemmas to select the activation function. To better represent the Frobenius norm of $\mathbf{E}(t)$, we introduce $\|\mathbf{E}(t)\|_F = \|\mathbf{A}(t)\mathbf{X}(t) - \mathbf{I}\|_F$.

3.1. Convergence

The convergence of the ADISZNN model in the absence of noise is proven in this subsection.

Theorem 1. *(Convergence) In the absence of noise, using the ADISZNN model (16) to solve the DCMI problem, as t tends to infinity, the Frobenius norm of the error $\mathbf{E}(t)$ approaches zero; that is,*

$$\lim_{t \to \infty} \|\mathbf{E}(t)\|_F = 0.$$

The proof of Theorem 1 is as follows.

Proof of Theorem 1. We rewrite Equation (18) in the absence of noise interference as

$$\begin{aligned}\dot{\mathbf{E}}(t) = &- \alpha\Phi(\mathbf{E}(t)) - 2\lambda\mathbf{E}(t) - 2\lambda\alpha \int_0^t \Phi(\mathbf{E}(\tau))d\tau \\ &- \lambda^2 \int_0^t \mathbf{E}(\tau)d\tau - \lambda^2\alpha \int_0^t \int_0^\tau \Phi(\mathbf{E}(\delta))d\delta d\tau.\end{aligned} \qquad (19)$$

To provide a clearer proof, let $\mathbf{a}_{xy}(t)$, $\mathbf{x}_{xy}(t)$, $\mathbf{e}_{xy}(t)$, $\theta_{xy}(t)$, and $v_{xy}(t)$, respectively, represent the xyth subelements of $\mathbf{A}(t)$, $\mathbf{X}(t)$, $\mathbf{E}(t)$, $\Theta(t)$, and $\mathbf{Y}(t)$.

Firstly, considering that the equation

$$\mathbf{Y}(t) = \dot{\mathbf{E}}(t) + \alpha\Phi(\mathbf{E}(t)) + \lambda \int_0^t (\dot{\mathbf{E}}(t) + \alpha\Phi(\mathbf{E}(t))) \qquad (20)$$

under the condition of no noise interference for the ADISZNN model can be transformed into the following form:

$$\mathbf{Y}(t) = -\lambda \int_0^t \mathbf{Y}(\tau)d\tau, \qquad (21)$$

the element-wise item of (21) is

$$v_{xy}(t) = -\lambda \int_0^t v_{xy}(\tau)d\tau, \qquad (22)$$

its derivative is

$$\dot{v}_{xy}(t) = -\lambda v_{xy}(t). \qquad (23)$$

Assuming a Lyapunov function $\epsilon(t) = v_{xy}^2(t)$, its derivative form is as follows:

$$\dot{\epsilon}(t) = 2\dot{v}_{xy}(t)v_{xy}(t). \tag{24}$$

Substituting (23) into (24) yields

$$\dot{\epsilon}(t) = -2\lambda v_{xy}^2(t). \tag{25}$$

Since $\epsilon(t)$ is positive definite, its derivative $\dot{\epsilon}(t)$ is negative definite, thus $\epsilon(t)$ is asymptotically stable. Therefore, we obtain the equation

$$\lim_{t \to \infty} |\epsilon(t)| = \lim_{t \to \infty} |v_{xy}^2(t)| = \lim_{t \to \infty} |v_{xy}(t)| = 0. \tag{26}$$

So, based on Equations (20) and (26), we have the following: As $t \to \infty$, $|v_{xy}| = |\dot{\mathbf{e}}_{xy}(t) + \alpha\Phi(\mathbf{e}_{xy}(t)) + \lambda \int_0^t (\dot{\mathbf{e}}_{xy}(\tau) + \alpha\Phi(\mathbf{e}_{xy}(\tau)))d\tau| = 0$. Considering $\theta_{xy}(t) = \dot{\mathbf{e}}_{xy}(t) + \alpha\Phi(\dot{\mathbf{e}}_{xy}(t))$

and we have

$$\theta_{xy}(t) = -\lambda \int_0^t \theta_{xy}(\tau)d\tau, \quad t \to \infty, \tag{27}$$

thus,

$$\lim_{t \to \infty} \left| \theta_{xy}(t) + \lambda \int_0^t \theta_{xy}(\tau)d\tau \right| = 0,$$

it is easy to obtain that

$$\lim_{t \to \infty} |\theta_{xy}(t)| = \lim_{t \to \infty} \left| -\lambda \int_0^t \theta_{xy}(\tau)d\tau \right| = 0.$$

Taking the derivative of the above equation, we obtain

$$\lim_{t \to \infty} |\dot{\theta}_{xy}(t)| = \lim_{t \to \infty} |-\lambda\theta_{xy}(t)| + \Delta, \quad \Delta \to 0,$$

in which Δ is the small error in the derivative of $\theta(t)$.

Let us assume another Lyapunov function:

$$\dot{\rho}(t) = 2\dot{\theta}_{xy}(t)\theta_{xy}(t) = -2\lambda\theta_{xy}^2(t). \tag{28}$$

According to the Lyapunov principle, $\rho(t) \geq 0$, $\dot{\rho}(t) \leq 0$, we can obtain

$$\lim_{t \to \infty} |\theta_{xy}(t)| = 0.$$

Because of $\theta_{xy}(t) = \dot{\mathbf{e}}_{xy}(t) + \alpha\Phi(\mathbf{e}_{xy}(t))$,

$$\lim_{t \to \infty} |\dot{\mathbf{e}}_{xy}(t) + \alpha\Phi(\mathbf{e}_{xy}(t))| = 0, \tag{29}$$

is obtained, thus, $\dot{\mathbf{e}}_{xy}(t) = -\alpha\Phi(\mathbf{e}_{xy}(t))$.

Clearly, we obtain

$$\lim_{t \to \infty} |\mathbf{e}_{xy}(t)| = 0.$$

Therefore, its matrix form is as follows:

$$\lim_{t \to \infty} \|\mathbf{E}(t)\|_F = 0. \tag{30}$$

Thus, Theorem 1 is proven. □

3.2. Robustness

In the presence of linear noise $\mathbf{N}(t)$ in matrix form, the ADISZNN model can still asymptotically approach the theoretical solution. Its effectiveness and convergence in handling DCMI problems will be analyzed and demonstrated.

Theorem 2. *(Robustness) In the presence of linear noise, using the ADISZNN model (17) to solve the DCMI problem, as t tends to infinity, the Frobenius norm of the error $\mathbf{E}(t)$ approaches zero; that is,*

$$\lim_{t\to\infty} \|\mathbf{E}(t)\|_F = 0.$$

Proof of Theorem 2. The linear noise is expressed as

$$\mathbf{N}(t) = \mathcal{A}t + \mathcal{B},$$

where $\mathcal{A}$ and $\mathcal{B}$ are constant matrices, and their elements can be written as

$$n_{xy}(t) = a_{xy}t + b_{xy}.$$

According to Theorem 1, and Equations (20) and (21), the ADISZNN model in the presence of linear noise can be transformed into the following form:

$$\mathbf{Y}(t) = -\lambda \int_0^t \mathbf{Y}(\tau)d\tau + \mathbf{N}(t), \tag{31}$$

with elements as in

$$v_{xy}(t) = -\lambda \int_0^t v_{xy}(\tau)d\tau + n_{xy}(t). \tag{32}$$

Differentiating v_{xy} twice, we can obtain

$$\ddot{v}_{xy}(t) = -\lambda \dot{v}_{xy}(t) + \ddot{n}_{xy}(t), \tag{33}$$

Taking the first and second derivatives of the noise separately, we obtain $\dot{n}_{xy}(t) = a_{xy}$ and $\ddot{n}_{xy}(t) = 0$. Then,

$$\ddot{v}_{xy}(t) = -\lambda \dot{v}_{xy}(t).$$

Assuming the Lyapunov equation to be

$$\vartheta(t) = \dot{v}_{xy}^2(t),$$

therefore,

$$\dot{\vartheta}(t) = 2\ddot{v}_{xy}(t)\dot{v}_{xy}(t) = -\lambda \dot{v}_{xy}^2(t),$$

Since $\vartheta(t) \geq 0$ is positive definite and its derivative $\dot{\vartheta}(t) \leq 0$ is negative definite, $\vartheta(t)$ is globally asymptotically stable, and we obtain

$$\lim_{t\to\infty} |\vartheta(t)| = \lim_{t\to\infty} \left|\dot{v}_{xy}^2(t)\right| = \lim_{t\to\infty} |\dot{v}_{xy}(t)| = 0. \tag{34}$$

By combining (32) and (34), we obtain the following equation:

$$\lim_{t\to\infty} |\dot{v}_{xy}(t)| = \lim_{t\to\infty} |-\lambda v_{xy}(t) + \dot{n}_{xy}(t)|.$$

Substituting $\dot{n}_{xy}(t) = a$ into it, we obtain

$$\lim_{t\to\infty} |-\lambda v_{xy}(t) + a| = 0,$$

thus, concluding that
$$\lim_{t\to\infty}|\lambda v_{xy}(t)|=|a|,$$
then, we obtain
$$\lim_{t\to\infty}|v_{xy}(t)|=\left|\frac{a}{\lambda}\right|.$$
So, we can derive that as $t\to\infty$,
$$|v_{xy}(t)|=\left|\dot{\mathbf{e}}_{xy}(t)+\alpha\Phi(\mathbf{e}_{xy}(t))\right|+\lambda\int_0^t\left(\dot{\mathbf{e}}_{xy}(\tau)+\alpha\Phi(\mathbf{e}_{xy}(\tau))\right)d\tau=\left|\frac{a}{\lambda}\right|. \tag{35}$$
Let
$$\theta_{xy}(t)=\dot{\mathbf{e}}_{xy}(t)+\alpha\Phi(\mathbf{e}_{xy}(t)) \tag{36}$$
then, we have
$$|v_{xy}(t)|=\left|\theta_{xy}(t)+\lambda\int_0^t\theta_{xy}(\tau)d\tau\right|=\left|\frac{a}{\lambda}\right|.$$
therefore, we can deduce that
$$\lim_{t\to\infty}\left|\theta_{xy}(t)+\lambda\int_0^t\theta_{xy}(\tau)d\tau\right|=0,$$
then, we draw
$$\lim_{t\to\infty}|\dot{\theta}_{xy}(t)|=\lim_{t\to\infty}|-\lambda\theta_{xy}(t)|.$$

Clearly, $\lambda>0$, and $\dot{\theta}$ and θ have opposite signs, thus
$$\lim_{t\to\infty}|\theta_{xy}(t)|=0.$$
Furthermore,
$$\theta_{xy}(t)=\dot{\mathbf{e}}_{xy}(t)+\alpha\Phi(\mathbf{e}_{xy}(t)),$$
which means that we can obtain
$$\lim_{t\to\infty}|\theta_{xy}(t)|=\lim_{t\to\infty}|\dot{\mathbf{e}}_{xy}(t)+\alpha\Phi(\mathbf{e}_{xy}(t))|=0,$$
so, $\dot{\mathbf{e}}_{xy}(t)=-\alpha\Phi(\mathbf{e}_{xy}(t))$.
According to the Lyapunov theorem, we can obtain
$$\lim_{t\to\infty}|\mathbf{e}_{xy}(t)|=0.$$
The corresponding matrix form is as follows:
$$\lim_{t\to\infty}\|\mathbf{E}(t)\|_F=0. \tag{37}$$

Thus, Theorem 2 is proven. □

3.3. Selection of Activation Function

For the ADISZNN model, different activation functions will result in different degrees of convergence in the model solution. To maintain generality in our discussion, we consider the three most common types of activation functions: linear-like activation functions [26], sigmoid-like activation functions [27], and sign-like activation functions [34–36]. Here, we take the linear activation function (LAF), smooth bi-polar sigmoid activation function (SBPSAF), and signal bi-power activation function (SBPAF) as examples. They are defined as follows:

- LAF:
$$\Phi_1(x) = x \tag{38}$$
- SBPSAF:
$$\Phi_2(x) = \frac{1}{2}x^{r_1} + \frac{1+e^{-r_2 x}}{1-e^{-r_2 x}}(1 - \frac{e^{-r_2 x}}{1+e^{-r_2 x}}), \tag{39}$$
where $r_1 > 0, r_2 > 0$.
- SBPAF:
$$\Phi_3(x) = (k_1|x|^\eta + k_2|x|^w)sign(x) + k_3 x, \tag{40}$$
where $sign(\cdot)$ is a symbolic function and the design parameters are $k_1 > 0, k_2 > 0, k_3 > 0$, $0 < \eta < 1$, and $w > 0$.

However, determining whether an activation function is suitable is a challenging task. Ref. [35] elucidates a concept within the Lyapunov stability framework, suggesting that the rate of convergence of a system is positively correlated with the magnitude of its derivative near the origin. Specifically, the larger the derivative, the faster the system converges. To illustrate this, Figure 1 in the paper depicts the derivative curves for three activation functions: $\Phi_1(x)$ LAF, $\Phi_2(x)$ SBPSAF, and $\Phi_3(x)$ SBPAF. It is observed that near the origin, the derivative of SBPAF exceeds that of LAF, and similarly, the derivative of LAF surpasses that of SBPSAF. Based on this observation, it can be inferred that the ADISZNN model employing the SBPAF activation function may converge in a shorter time compared to the model using the LAF activation function. Likewise, the model with the LAF activation function is likely to converge faster than the one with the SBPSAF activation function.

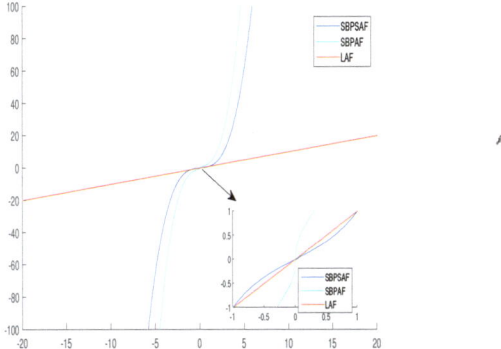

Figure 1. Three sorts of activation functions presented: linear activation function (LAF) $\Phi_1(x)$ (red solid line), smooth bi-polar sigmoid activation function (SBPSAF) $\Phi_2(x)$ (sky blue solid line), and signal bi-power activation function (SBPAF) $\Phi_3(x)$ (blue solid line).

Therefore, in this article, we will use SBPAF as the activation function adopted by ADISZNN.

4. Simulation and Comparative Numerical Experiments

4.1. Comparison Experiments of Activation Functions

In this section, to further validate the correctness of our activation function selection, we compare the ADISZNN models using three different activation functions.

In this example, a two-dimensional dynamic complex matrix **A** is presented as follows:

$$\mathbf{A}(t) = \begin{bmatrix} j\sin(3t) & j\cos(3t) \\ -j\cos(3t) & j\sin(3t) \end{bmatrix} \in \mathbb{C}^{2\times 2}. \tag{41}$$

For convenience, this matrix only contains the imaginary part. To verify the correctness of the ADISZNN model, the theoretical inverse of the above dynamic complex matrix is obtained through mathematical calculation:

$$\mathbf{A}^{-1}(t) = \begin{bmatrix} -j\sin(3t) & j\cos(3t) \\ -j\cos(3t) & -j\sin(3t) \end{bmatrix} \in \mathbb{C}^{2\times 2}. \qquad (42)$$

Figure 2 delineates the computational and convergence trajectories of the ADISZNN model across various activation functions, all in the absence of noise. A discernible observation from this figure is that models utilizing the LAF and SBPSAF activation functions achieve near-simultaneous steady-state error close to zero at approximately 2.3 s. In stark contrast, the ADISZNN model equipped with the SBPAF activation function demonstrates a markedly swifter convergence, reaching near-zero error within a mere 0.6 s—a rate that is roughly threefold faster than its counterparts.

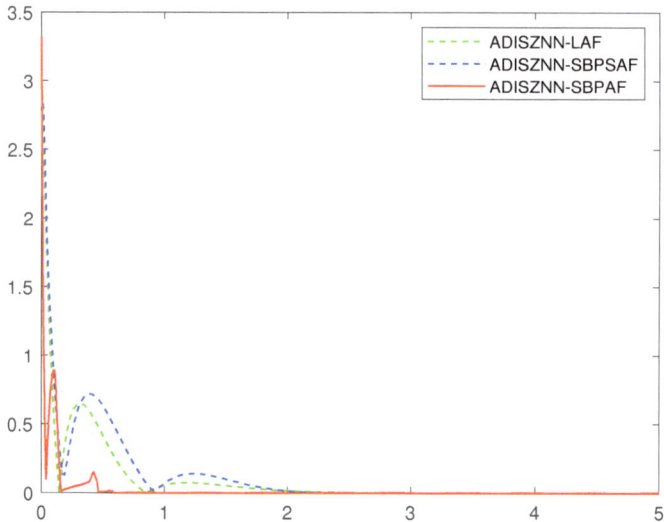

Figure 2. Comparative graph of the computation and convergence processes of ADISZNN with three different activation functions without noise interference; the design parameters are $\lambda = 4$ and $\alpha = 4$: ADISZNN-LAF (green dashed line), ADISZNN-SBPSAF (blue dashed line), ADISZNN-SBPAF (red solid line).

Figure 3, on the other hand, captures the ADISZNN model's performance under the influence of linear noise, with each subplot showcasing the model's behavior when driven by the LAF, SBPSAF, and SBPAF activation functions, respectively. For the readers' ease, a comparative analysis of these models is tabulated in Table 1. The table underscores a significant finding: the proximity of the activation function's derivative to the origin is positively correlated with the model's convergence efficiency. Notably, the ADISZNN model harnessing SBPAF exhibits the most rapid convergence. Nonetheless, it is important to note that models incorporating SBPSAF and SBPAF show a relatively diminished robustness when compared to the LAF-equipped model.

Table 1. Comparison of ADISZNN model adopting LAF, SBPSAF, and SBPAF.

AF	LAF	SBPSAF	SBPAF
Derivative near 0 point	Large	Normal	Larger
Convergence	Fast	Normal	Faster
Robustness	Strong	Weak	Normal

These experiments not only confirm the enhanced convergence speed of the ADISZNN model employing the SBPAF activation function proposed in this paper but also validate the appropriateness of the chosen activation function.

Next, we will compare and analyze the convergence performance of the ADISZNN model using the signal bi-power activation function with the DISZNN model without using any activation function under the condition of linear matrix noise interference.

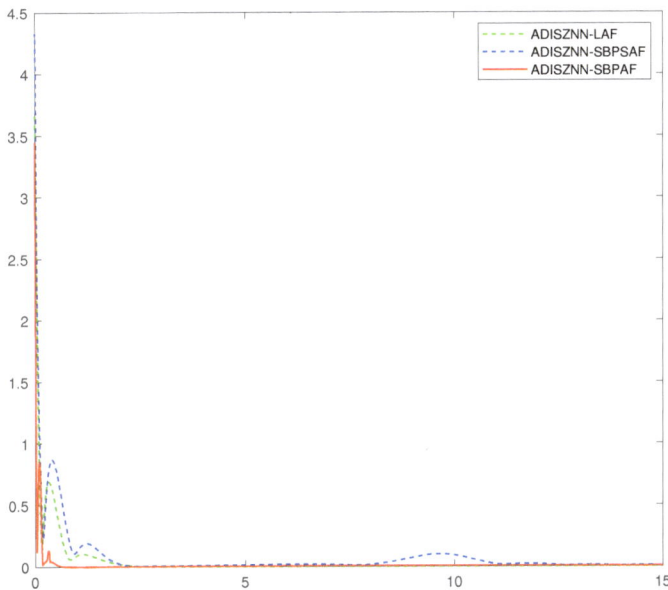

Figure 3. Comparative graph of the computation and convergence processes of ADISZNN with three different activation functions under linear noise $\mathbf{N} = [0.8 + 4t]^{2\times 2}$; the design parameters are $\lambda = 4$ and $\alpha = 4$: ADISZNN-LAF (green dashed line), ADISZNN-SBPSAF (blue dashed line), ADISZNN-SBPAF (red solid line).

4.2. Comparison Experiments between DISZNN and ADISZNN

The DISZNN model is rewritten as follows:

$$\dot{\mathbf{E}}(t) = -s_0^3 \int_0^t \int_0^\delta \mathbf{E}(\tau) d\tau d\delta - 3s_0^2 \int_0^t \mathbf{E}(\delta) d\delta - 3s_0 \mathbf{E}(t) \tag{43}$$

where $s_0 \in \mathbb{R}^+$ is a design parameter.

The error results of the DISZNN model and the ADISZNN model using SBPAF are shown in Figure 4. Under the condition without noise interference, for any initial value of the dynamic complex matrix $\mathbf{X}(0) \in [-(2+2j), 2+2j]^{2\times 2}$ the error of the DISZNN model converges almost completely to 0 around 2.8 s. When the SBPAF activation function is introduced, the error of the ADISZNN model converges almost completely to 0 within 0.6 s. Therefore, the convergence speed of the ADISZNN model is significantly faster than that of DISZNN.

To compare the tolerance of ADISZNN and DISZNN to noise, a common linear noise $\mathbf{N} = [0.8 + 4t]^{2\times 2}$ is introduced. Their numerical experimental comparison is shown in Figure 5, where the design parameters are set as $s_0 = 4$, $\lambda = 4$, and $\alpha = 4$. Under the interference of linear noise, both DISZNN and ADISZNN can still make the residual $||\mathbf{E}(t)||_F$ close to 0 within approximately 2.8 s and 0.6 s, respectively, which is nearly the same as the case without noise interference. This demonstrates that ADISZNN and DISZNN possess inherent tolerance to linear noise.

However, during the experimental process, we observed that the residual plot of the ADISZNN model with the signal bi-power activation function exhibits oscillatory fluctuations after reaching the magnitude of 10^{-3} at 0.6 s. This indicates a decrease in the precision of the model's computations, as it fails to maintain stable convergence at the 10^{-3} magnitude level. This implies a reduction in the robustness of the ADISZNN model. The residual plots of the ADISZNN model with noise interference and the comparison of residuals between the DISZNN and ADISZNN models without noise interference are shown in Figures 6 and 7, respectively. In the next subsection, we will discuss the stable version (high-precision version) of the ADISZNN model.

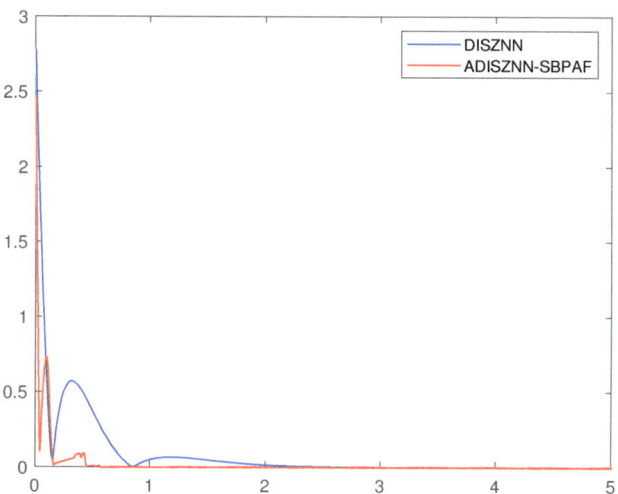

Figure 4. Convergence comparison of ADISZNN and DISZNN without noise interference; the design parameters are $s_0 = 4$ $\lambda = 4$ and $\alpha = 4$: ADISZNN-SBPAF (red solid line) and DISZNN (blue solid line).

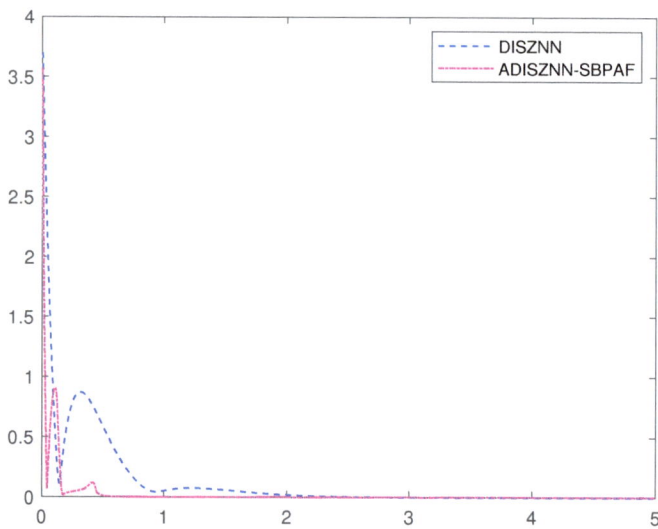

Figure 5. Convergence comparison of ADISZNN and DISZNN, under linear noise $\mathbf{N} = [0.8 + 4t]^{2\times 2}$: ADISZNN-SBPAF (pink dotted line) and DISZNN (blue dashed line).

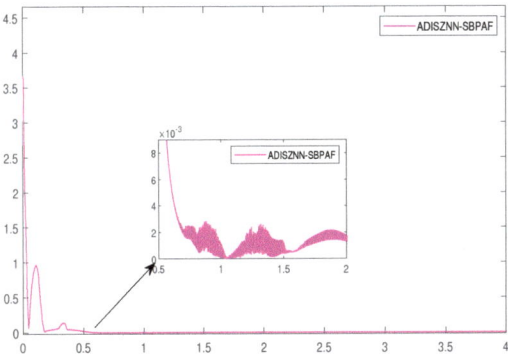

Figure 6. The amplified residual errors of ADISZNN under linear noise $\mathbf{N} = [0.8 + 4t]^{2\times 2}$, with design parameters $\alpha = 4$, $\lambda = 4$, $k_1 = 1$, $k_2 = 1$, $k_3 = 1$, $\eta = 1/3$, and $omega = 3$.

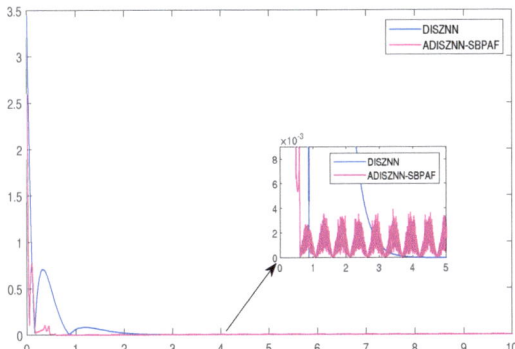

Figure 7. The amplified residual errors of DISZNN and ADISZNN under no noise, with design parameters $\alpha = 4$, $\lambda = 4$, $k_1 = 1$, $k_2 = 1$, $k_3 = 1$, $\eta = 1/3$, $\omega = 3$, and $s_0 = 4$.

4.3. The Stable ADISZNN Model

In this subsection, we propose an improved version of the ADISZNN-SBPAF model to address the oscillation phenomenon (or precision degradation phenomenon). According to the table in experiment 1, we observe that not only can ADISZNN with the signal bi-power activation function accelerate the convergence compared to the DISZNN model, but also the ADISZNN model with the linear activation function (LAF) can similarly accelerate convergence and exhibit stronger robustness.

Based on this observation, we innovatively propose a stable version of the ADISZNN model: When the error of the ADISZNN model using SBPAF approaches zero (i.e., reaches the order of 10^{-3}), we transition the model to use LAF. This transition alters the calculation and convergence of $||\mathbf{A}(t)\mathbf{X}(t) - \mathbf{I}||_F$, transforming the ADISZNN-SBPAF model into the ADISZNN-LAF model. The convergence performance of this approach is illustrated in the Figures 8–10.

The residual plots in Figures 9 and 10, respectively, depict the effects of our improvement on the stable version of the ADISZNN model compared to the unstable version (For the reader's enhanced comprehension, Figure 8 illustrates the comparison of amplified residual errors between the stable and unstable variants of ADISZNN in the absence of noise). While this enhancement results in a slight increase in the convergence time, it strengthens the model's resistance to noise and improves its robustness. Additionally, the computational accuracy is elevated from the order of 10^{-3} to 10^{-4}, thereby enhancing the convergence performance of the model.

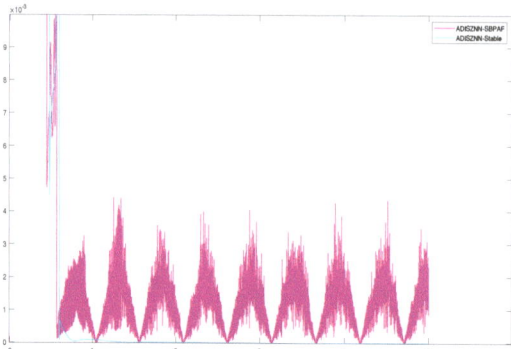

Figure 8. Comparison of the amplified residual errors of stable ADISZNN and unstable ADISZNN under no noise, with design parameters $\alpha = 4$, $\lambda = 4$, $k_1 = 1$, $k_2 = 1$, $k_3 = 1$, $\eta = 1/3$, $\omega = 3$, and $s_0 = 4$.

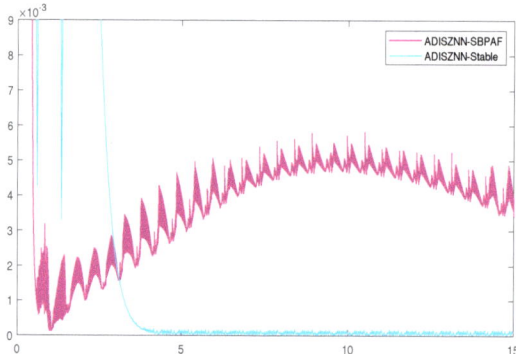

Figure 9. The detailed residual errors of ADISZNN-Stable and ADISZNN-SBPAF, with noise of $[0.8 + 4t]^{2 \times 2}$.

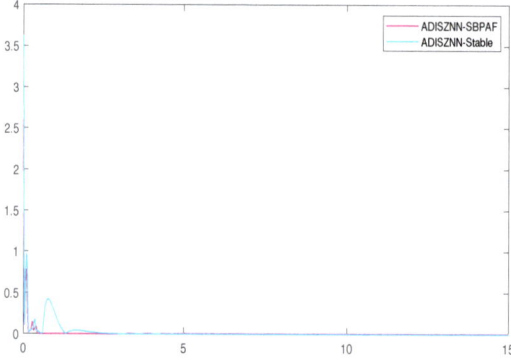

Figure 10. Residual errors of ADISZNN-Stable and ADISZNN-SBPAF with noise of $[0.8 + 4t]^{2 \times 2}$.

In Figure 11, a comparison between the stable version of the ADISZNN model and the original DISZNN model is presented. Compared to the original DISZNN model, the stable version of the ADISZNN model exhibits significant improvements. When the computed solution $\mathbf{X}(t)$ of the model converges to a theoretical state approximation $\mathbf{A}(t)^{-1}$, the convergence time of the stable ADISZNN model is reduced from 2.8 s to 1.9 s. Moreover, the convergence curve of the stable ADISZNN model appears smoother and more refined. Both models achieve a computational accuracy of 10^{-4} when fully converged. These results indicate that the improved stable version of the ADISZNN model not only enhances the convergence speed but also maintains robustness comparable to that of the DISZNN model.

To underscore the merits of the ADISZNN-Stable model, Figures 12 and 13 depict comparative trajectory plots of the DISZNN alongside the ADISZNN-Stable model under conditions of linear noise. Additionally, Figure 14 presents an analysis of residual errors, contrasting the performance of the DISZNN with that of the ADISZNN-Stable model in an environment devoid of noise.

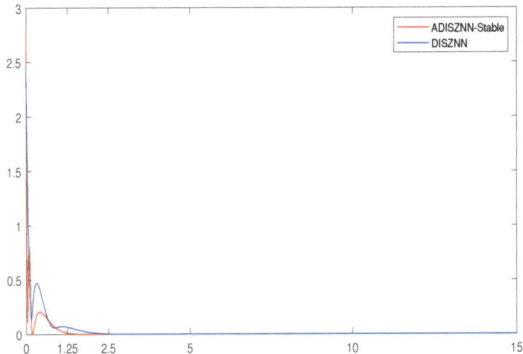

Figure 11. The comparison of the residual errors of stable ADISZNN and DISZNN under linear noise of $[0.8 + 4t]^{2 \times 2}$, with design parameters $\alpha = 4$, $\lambda = 4$, $k_1 = 1$, $k_2 = 1$, $k_3 = 1$, $\eta = 1/3$, $\omega = 3$, and $s_0 = 4$.

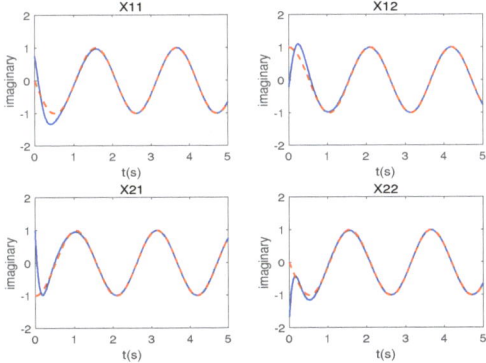

Figure 12. Trajectory analysis for problem (41) under linear noise of $[0.8 + 4t]^{2 \times 2}$; the red line points represent the theoretical solution, while the blue line points show the DISZNN model's solutions.

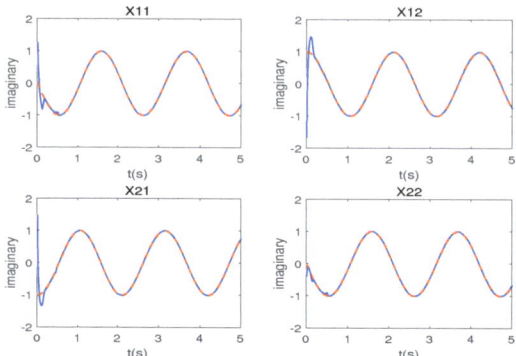

Figure 13. Trajectory analysis for problem (41) under linear noise of $[0.8 + 4t]^{2\times 2}$; the red line points represent the theoretical solution, while the blue line points show the ADISZNN-Stable model's solutions.

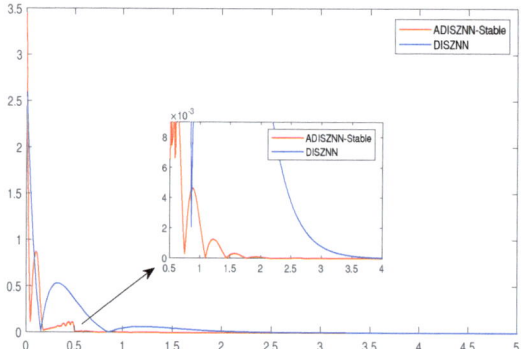

Figure 14. Comparison of the amplified residual errors of stable ADISZNN and DISZNN under no noise, with design parameters $\alpha = 4$, $\lambda = 4$, $k_1 = 1$, $k_2 = 1$, $k_3 = 1$, $\eta = 1/3$, $\omega = 3$, and $s_0 = 4$.

5. Conclusions

This article introduces a novel enhancement to the DISZNN model through the integration of an activation function, culminating in an accelerated dual-integral structure ZNN model. This model exhibits enhanced resilience against linear noise interference, particularly pertinent for dynamic complex matrix inversion challenges. The paper unfolds with the following key contributions: initially, the design formula for a single-integral structure and the DISZNN model are presented and analyzed; subsequently, the architecture of the ADISZNN model is designed, with a theoretical examination of its convergence and robustness; thirdly, both experimental and theoretical analyses are employed to assess the influence of various activation functions on the ADISZNN's convergence efficacy, thereby substantiating the efficacy of our selected activation function; fourthly, comparative tests under linear noise conditions between the ADISZNN and DISZNN models underscore the ADISZNN's superior convergence capabilities, albeit with the caveat that the ADISZNN model utilizing the SBPAF activation function exhibits oscillatory behavior, potentially compromising its robustness. In light of these findings, we propose refinements to the ADISZNN-SBPAF model, yielding a more stable iteration of the ADISZNN. Comparative experimentation facilitates the identification of the optimal ZNN configuration. Future inquiries are suggested to investigate the potential applications of the ADISZNN model within the engineering sector. This paper presents the ADISZNN model, which has certain limitations, specifically detailed in Appendix A.

Author Contributions: Conceptualization, Y.H. and F.Y.; methodology, T.W. and Y.H.; software, F.Y. and Y.H.; validation, F.Y. and Y.H.; formal analysis, F.Y.; investigation, T.W.; resources, Y.H.; data curation, F.Y.; writing—original draft preparation, F.Y.; writing—review and editing, Y.H.; visualization, F.Y.; supervision, Y.H.; project administration, F.Y.; funding acquisition, Y.H. All authors have read and agreed to the published version of the manuscript.

Funding: This work was funded by the National Natural Science Foundation of China under Grant No. 62062036, Grant No. 62066015 and Grant No. 62006095, and the College Students' Innovation Training Center Project at Jishou University under Grant No. JDCX20231012.

Institutional Review Board Statement: Not applicable.

Informed Consent Statement: Not applicable.

Data Availability Statement: Data are contained within the article.

Conflicts of Interest: The authors declare no conflicts of interest.

Abbreviations

The following abbreviations are used in this article:

ZNN	Zeroing neural network
GNN	Gradient neural network
DNSZNN	Dual noise-suppressed ZNN
DISZNN	Dual-integral structure zeroing neural network
CVZNN	Complex-valued ZNN
IEZNN	Integral-enhanced ZNN
CVNTZNN	Complex-valued noise-tolerant ZNN
ADISZNN	Accelerated dual-integral structure zeroing neural network
DRMI	Dynamic real matrix inversion
DCMI	Dynamic complex matrix inversion
AF	Activation function
LAF	Linear activation function
SBPAF	Signal bi-power activation function
SBPSAF	Smooth bi-polar sigmoid activation function

Appendix A. Limitation

1. The ADISZNN model and the ADISZNN-Stable model proposed in this paper currently do not handle discontinuous noise.
2. This paper restricts the inversion of matrices to be non-singular, smooth, dynamic, and complex. The problem of inverting singular or non-smooth matrices is not addressed in this paper.

References

1. Jin, J.; Chen, W.; Ouyang, A.; Yu, F.; Liu, H. A time-varying fuzzy parameter zeroing neural network for the synchronization of chaotic systems. *IEEE Trans. Emerg. Top. Comput. Intell.* **2023**, *8*, 364–376. [CrossRef]
2. Zhang, R.; Xi, X.; Tian, H.; Wang, Z. Dynamical analysis and finite-time synchronization for a chaotic system with hidden attractor and surface equilibrium. *Axioms* **2022**, *11*, 579. [CrossRef]
3. Rasouli, M.; Zare, A.; Hallaji, M.; Alizadehsani, R. The synchronization of a class of time-delayed chaotic systems using sliding mode control based on a fractional-order nonlinear PID sliding surface and its application in secure communication. *Axioms* **2022**, *11*, 738. [CrossRef]
4. Gao, R. Inverse kinematics solution of Robotics based on neural network algorithms. *J. Ambient Intell. Humaniz. Comput.* **2020**, *11*, 6199–6209. [CrossRef]
5. Hu, Z.; Xiao, L.; Li, K.; Li, K.; Li, J. Performance analysis of nonlinear activated zeroing neural networks for time-varying matrix pseudoinversion with application. *Appl. Soft Comput.* **2021**, *98*, 106735. [CrossRef]
6. Ramos, H.; Monteiro, M.T.T. A new approach based on the Newton's method to solve systems of nonlinear equations. *J. Comput. Appl. Math.* **2017**, *318*, 3–13. [CrossRef]

7. Andreani, R.; Haeser, G.; Ramos, A.; Silva, P.J. A second-order sequential optimality condition associated to the convergence of optimization algorithms. *IMA J. Numer. Anal.* **2017**, *37*, 1902–1929.
8. Zhang, Y. Revisit the analog computer and gradient-based neural system for matrix inversion. In Proceedings of the 2005 IEEE International Symposium on, Mediterrean Conference on Control and Automation Intelligent Control, Limassol, Cyprus, 27–29 June 2005; IEEE: Piscataway, NJ, USA, 2005; pp. 1411–1416.
9. Zhang, Y.; Chen, K.; Tan, H.Z. Performance analysis of gradient neural network exploited for online time-varying matrix inversion. *IEEE Trans. Autom. Control* **2009**, *54*, 1940–1945. [CrossRef]
10. Zhang, Y.; Shi, Y.; Chen, K.; Wang, C. Global exponential convergence and stability of gradient-based neural network for online matrix inversion. *Appl. Math. Comput.* **2009**, *215*, 1301–1306. [CrossRef]
11. Xiao, L.; Li, K.; Tan, Z.; Zhang, Z.; Liao, B.; Chen, K.; Jin, L.; Li, S. Nonlinear gradient neural network for solving system of linear equations. *Inf. Process. Lett.* **2019**, *142*, 35–40. [CrossRef]
12. Zhang, Y.; Ge, S. A general recurrent neural network model for time-varying matrix inversion. In Proceedings of the 42nd IEEE International Conference on Decision and Control (IEEE Cat. No. 03CH37475), Maui, HI, USA, 9–12 December 2003; IEEE: Piscataway, NJ, USA, 2003; Volume 6, pp. 6169–6174.
13. Johnson, M.A.; Moradi, M.H. *PID Control*; Springer: Heidelberg, Germany, 2005.
14. Jin, L.; Zhang, Y.; Li, S. Integration-enhanced Zhang neural network for real-time-varying matrix inversion in the presence of various kinds of noises. *IEEE Trans. Neural Networks Learn. Syst.* **2015**, *27*, 2615–2627. [CrossRef]
15. Golub, G.H.; Van Loan, C.F. *Matrix Computations*; JHU Press: Baltimore, MD, USA, 2013.
16. Ogata, K. Control systems analysis in state space. In *Modern Control Engineering*; Pearson Education, Inc.: Hoboken, NJ, USA, 2010; pp. 648–721.
17. Smith, S. *Digital Signal Processing: A Practical Guide for Engineers and Scientists*; Newnes: Boston, UK, 2003.
18. Saleh, B.E.; Teich, M.C. *Fundamentals of Photonics*; John Wiley & Sons: Hoboken, NJ, USA, 2019.
19. Trefethen, L.N.; Bau, D. *Numerical Linear Algebra*; Siam: Philadelphia, PA, USA, 2022; Volume 181.
20. Zhang, Y.; Li, Z.; Li, K. Complex-valued Zhang neural network for online complex-valued time-varying matrix inversion. *Appl. Math. Comput.* **2011**, *217*, 10066–10073. [CrossRef]
21. Xiao, L.; Zhang, Y.; Zuo, Q.; Dai, J.; Li, J.; Tang, W. A noise-tolerant zeroing neural network for time-dependent complex matrix inversion under various kinds of noises. *IEEE Trans. Ind. Inform.* **2019**, *16*, 3757–3766. [CrossRef]
22. Hua, C.; Cao, X.; Xu, Q.; Liao, B.; Li, S. Dynamic Neural Network Models for Time-Varying Problem Solving: A Survey on Model Structures. *IEEE Access* **2023**, *11*, 65991–66008. [CrossRef]
23. Dai, J.; Jia, L.; Xiao, L. Design and analysis of two prescribed-time and robust ZNN models with application to time-variant Stein matrix equation. *IEEE Trans. Neural Netw. Learn. Syst.* **2020**, *32*, 1668–1677. [CrossRef]
24. Li, S.; Chen, S.; Liu, B. Accelerating a recurrent neural network to finite-time convergence for solving time-varying Sylvester equation by using a sign-bi-power activation function. *Neural Process. Lett.* **2013**, *37*, 189–205. [CrossRef]
25. Lan, X.; Jin, J.; Liu, H. Towards non-linearly activated ZNN model for constrained manipulator trajectory tracking. *Front. Phys.* **2023**, *11*, 1159212. [CrossRef]
26. Liao, B.; Zhang, Y. From different ZFs to different ZNN models accelerated via Li activation functions to finite-time convergence for time-varying matrix pseudoinversion. *Neurocomputing* **2014**, *133*, 512–522. [CrossRef]
27. Xiao, L. A nonlinearly activated neural dynamics and its finite-time solution to time-varying nonlinear equation. *Neurocomputing* **2016**, *173*, 1983–1988. [CrossRef]
28. Yang, Y.; Zhang, Y. Superior robustness of power-sum activation functions in Zhang neural networks for time-varying quadratic programs perturbed with large implementation errors. *Neural Comput. Appl.* **2013**, *22*, 175–185. [CrossRef]
29. Liao, B.; Zhang, Y. Different complex ZFs leading to different complex ZNN models for time-varying complex generalized inverse matrices. *IEEE Trans. Neural Netw. Learn. Syst.* **2013**, *25*, 1621–1631. [CrossRef]
30. Xiao, L.; Tan, H.; Jia, L.; Dai, J.; Zhang, Y. New error function designs for finite-time ZNN models with application to dynamic matrix inversion. *Neurocomputing* **2020**, *402*, 395–408. [CrossRef]
31. Lv, X.; Xiao, L.; Tan, Z.; Yang, Z. Wsbp function activated Zhang dynamic with finite-time convergence applied to Lyapunov equation. *Neurocomputing* **2018**, *314*, 310–315. [CrossRef]
32. Li, Z.; Liao, B.; Xu, F.; Guo, D. A New Repetitive Motion Planning Scheme With Noise Suppression Capability for Redundant Robot Manipulators. *IEEE Trans. Syst. Man Cybern. Syst.* **2020**, *50*, 5244–5254. [CrossRef]
33. Liao, B.; Han, L.; Cao, X.; Li, S.; Li, J. Double integral-enhanced Zeroing neural network with linear noise rejection for time-varying matrix inverse. *CAAI Trans. Intell. Technol.* **2023**, *9*, 197–210. [CrossRef]
34. Zhang, M. A varying-gain ZNN model with fixed-time convergence and noise-tolerant performance for time-varying linear equation and inequality systems. *Authorea Prepr.* **2023**. Available online: https://www.techrxiv.org/doi/full/10.36227/techrxiv.16988404.v1 (accessed on 4 April 2024).

35. Zhang, Z.; Deng, X.; Qu, X.; Liao, B.; Kong, L.D.; Li, L. A varying-gain recurrent neural network and its application to solving online time-varying matrix equation. *IEEE Access* **2018**, *6*, 77940–77952. [CrossRef]
36. Han, L.; Liao, B.; He, Y.; Xiao, X. Dual noise-suppressed ZNN with predefined-time convergence and its application in matrix inversion. In Proceedings of the 2021 11th International Conference on Intelligent Control and Information Processing (ICICIP), Dali, China, 3–7 December 2021; IEEE: Piscataway, NJ, USA, 2021; pp. 410–415.

Disclaimer/Publisher's Note: The statements, opinions and data contained in all publications are solely those of the individual author(s) and contributor(s) and not of MDPI and/or the editor(s). MDPI and/or the editor(s) disclaim responsibility for any injury to people or property resulting from any ideas, methods, instructions or products referred to in the content.

Article

An Efficient Anti-Noise Zeroing Neural Network for Time-Varying Matrix Inverse

Jiaxin Hu, Feixiang Yang and Yun Huang *

College of Computer Science and Engineering, Jishou University, Jishou 416000, China
* Correspondence: huangyun@jsu.edu.cn; Tel.: +86-139-0744-7310

Abstract: The Time-Varying Matrix Inversion (TVMI) problem is integral to various fields in science and engineering. Countless studies have highlighted the effectiveness of Zeroing Neural Networks (ZNNs) as a dependable approach for addressing this challenge. To effectively solve the TVMI problem, this paper introduces a novel Efficient Anti-Noise Zeroing Neural Network (EANZNN). This model employs segmented time-varying parameters and double integral terms, where the segmented time-varying parameters can adaptively adjust over time, offering faster convergence speeds compared to fixed parameters. The double integral term enables the model to effectively handle the interference of constant noise, linear noise, and other noises. Using the Lyapunov approach, we theoretically analyze and show the convergence and robustness of the proposed EANZNN model. Experimental findings showcase that in scenarios involving linear, constant noise and noise-free environments, the EANZNN model exhibits superior performance compared to traditional models like the Double Integral-Enhanced ZNN (DIEZNN) and the Parameter-Changing ZNN (PCZNN). It demonstrates faster convergence and better resistance to interference, affirming its efficacy in addressing TVMI problems.

Keywords: time-varyingmartix inversion (TVMI); zeroing neural network (ZNN); anti-noise property; varying parameters; double integral

MSC: 34A34; 34A55

Citation: Hu, J.; Yang, F.; Huang, Y. An Efficient Anti-Noise Zeroing Neural Network for Time-Varying Matrix Inverse. *Axioms* **2024**, *13*, 540. https://doi.org/10.3390/axioms13080540

Academic Editor: Mourad Sini

Received: 11 July 2024
Revised: 1 August 2024
Accepted: 6 August 2024
Published: 9 August 2024

Copyright: © 2024 by the authors. Licensee MDPI, Basel, Switzerland. This article is an open access article distributed under the terms and conditions of the Creative Commons Attribution (CC BY) license (https://creativecommons.org/licenses/by/4.0/).

1. Introduction

The problem of time-varying matrix inversion (TVMI) often arises in various scientific and engineering fields. For instance, in the field of image processing, TVMI is used in real-time image restoration and denoising algorithms to enhance image quality and accuracy [1]. In the field of robotics, TVMI is applied to motion control and path planning in dynamic environments to ensure that robots can adjust and execute complex tasks in real time [2]. In the field of signal processing, TVMI is used for real-time filtering and signal recovery, especially when dealing with time-varying signals and systems [3,4]. In robotic kinematics, TVMI is used to solve kinematic inverse problems to achieve precise control and operation of robotic arms [5], among other applications. Currently, the methods to solve matrix inversion problems primarily fall into the following two categories: numerical algorithms and neural network algorithms. Numerical algorithms are essentially serial processes and are primarily suitable for small-scale and constant matrices. For example, the authors of [6] employed the iteration method to solve matrix inversion; however, the iterative process is highly complex and time-consuming [7]. Unlike traditional numerical methods, neural network methods have advantages such as parallel processing capabilities and distributed storage [8], which have been widely studied. For example, Gradient-based Recurrent Neural Networks (GNNs) [9] are used for static matrix inversion, significantly improving computational efficiency. However, many studies have reported that GNNs struggle to capture changes in variable coefficient matrices and are primarily designed for time-invariant problems [10], rendering them unsuitable for dynamic situations [11].

To effectively address the problem of the TVMI, Zhang and colleagues introduced a novel ZNN model [12] that leverages the time derivative of the error function to achieve exponential decay of the error over an indefinitely long period, effectively solving time-varying problems [13]. Furthermore, numerous scholars have continuously innovated and improved upon the ZNN framework, proposing derivatives of the ZNN models for time-varying problems. For example, the author of [14] proposed a Finite-Time ZNN (FTZNN) model that achieves finite-time convergence for the TVMI problem through a new design formula, significantly improving convergence performance compared to existing recurrent neural networks (such as GNNs) and the original ZNN model. The authors of [15] introduced the Classical Complex-Valued Noise-Tolerant ZNN (CVNTZNN) model, which was developed to address the Dynamic Complex Matrix Inversion (DCMI) problem; the authors explored the performance of the CVNTZNN model in various noise environments. Another study [16] proposed a Fixed-Time Convergent and Noise-Tolerant ZNN (FTCNTZNN) model, demonstrating superior fixed-time convergence and robustness in both noiseless and noisy environments when solving the TVMI problem.

As research has progressed, scholars have faced key issues such as convergence, robustness, and stability when using ZNN models to solve TVMI problems [17–19]. In terms of improving convergence, studies have shown that the design parameters of a ZNN have a significant impact on convergence speed [20]. Traditional ZNN models typically use fixed convergence parameters, and while these models can achieve effective convergence [21], the fixed parameters often require multiple additional experiments to adjust and find approximately optimal parameters. This process is inefficient and difficult to implement in practical applications. In practical applications, convergence parameters generally correspond to the inverse of inductance or capacitance in circuits [22], meaning that convergence parameters are time-varying in hardware systems. Moreover, because larger design parameter values result in better convergence, recent studies have explored various variable-parameter ZNN models to solve the TVMI problem more quickly. For example, the authors of [23] proposed a novel Exponential-enhanced-type Varying-Parameter ZNN (EVPZNN) model that significantly improves convergence speed compared to traditional Fixed-Parameter ZNN (FPZNN) [10]. In [24], P.S. Stanimirovic and others introduced a new segmented varying-parameter approach to establish a Complex Varying-Parameter ZNN (CVPZNN) that adapts to changes in the problem by dynamically adjusting parameters, thereby achieving faster convergence speeds.

In terms of improving robustness, noise resistance is a key factor to consider, as external noise is inevitable in real-life scenarios, (e.g., constant noise, linear noise, and random noise) and can affect the stability of systems [25,26]. In recent years, two types of noise-resistant ZNN models have been developed to address computational problems. One approach incorporates integral items into the design formula of the ZNN, and the other adds Activation Functions (AFs) to the ZNN. For example, in PID control methods [27], it is noted that integral terms can effectively eliminate noise, reducing system error continuously. Jin et al. proposed an Integrated Enhanced ZNN (IEZNN) model [28] that introduces integral terms into the design formula to compensate for the original ZNN's deficiencies in handling noise. Although it shows good robustness in solving TVMI problems, its ability to suppress linear noise is not ideal. Therefore, the Double Integral-Enhanced ZNN (DIEZNN) model proposed by Liao et al. [29] further introduces double integral terms to improve the suppression of linear noise. Moreover, in reference [30], researchers examined the employment of a ZNN alongside fuzzy adaptive activation functions to tackle time-varying linear matrix problems. This strategy effectively boosts robustness against external noise by integrating activation functions. Xiao et al. [31] introduced a Versatile AF (VAF), and Jin et al. [16] proposed a Novel AF (NAF), both of which also enhance the model's noise suppression capabilities.

To solve the TVMI problem more efficiently, this paper introduces a novel efficient anti-noise zeroing neural network (EANZNN) model. This model accelerates convergence through the use of time derivatives of error functions designed with time-varying parameters and incorporates double integral terms to suppress noise. It is worth noting that the EANZNN model employs an innovative time-varying segmentation function as a parameter, which is more flexible than the fixed parameter in the DIEZNN model. Furthermore, via theoretical analysis and simulation tests, this work shows that under the same settings, the EANZNN model performs better in resolving the TVMI issue than both the DIEZNN model and the Parameter-Changing ZNN (PCZNN) model [32].

The remainder of this paper is divided into the following four sections. Section 2 provides a detailed description of the TVMI problem and introduces the design of the PCZNN, DIEZNN, and EANZNN models. Section 3 rigorously analyzes the convergence and robustness of the EANZNN model. Section 4 compares the performance of the EANZNN and PCZNN models in handling the TVMI problem under linear and constant noise and in noise-free environments through experiments. Finally, Section 5 presents a comprehensive summary of the work. The following represent the noteworthy contributions of this study.

- Unlike previous ZNN models, the novel EANZNN model designed in this paper employs an innovative piecewise time-varying parameter that includes an upper bound. This design accelerates the model's convergence speed while maintaining good convergence performance. Additionally, a double integral term is introduced to solve TVMI problems under constant and linear noise, enhancing the model's convergence speed and noise resistance.
- Theoretical analysis based on Lyapunov stability theory rigorously demonstrates that the EANZNN model possesses excellent convergence and robustness when addressing the TVMI problem.
- Experimental results show that under noise-free conditions, the EANZNN model achieves a faster convergence speed in solving the TVMI issue compared to the DIEZNN and PCZNN models. Under constant and linear noise conditions, the EANZNN model not only converges faster but also demonstrates superior robustness.

2. TVMI Description and Model Design

This section describes the time-varying matrix inversion (TVMI) problem. Subsequently, it introduces the relevant models and elaborates on the design process of the EANZNN model, which includes double integral terms. The importance of this paper stems from our proposed EANZNN model's ability to efficiently and precisely solve the TVMI problem.

2.1. Description of TVMI

The TVMI problem can be mathematically formulated as follows:

$$A(t)U(t) = I \in \mathbb{R}^{n \times n}, \quad \text{or} \quad U(t)A(t) = I, \tag{1}$$

where $A(t) \in \mathbb{R}^{n \times n}$ represents a known time-varying, non-singular, smooth coefficient matrix; $U(t) \in \mathbb{R}^{n \times n}$ stands for an unknown invertible matrix; and I signifies a unit matrix of suitable dimensions. The aim of this paper is to use the designed model to solve for $U(t)$ in Equation (1), with the theoretical solution of $U^*(t) = A^{-1}(t) \in \mathbb{R}^{n \times n}$.

2.2. Relevant Model Design

A ZNN, as a specialized type of recurrent neural network, is typically used to address time-varying problems. Its design process can generally be divided into the following three steps [33]:

1. First, define an appropriate error function based on the specific problem to be solved;
2. Design an evolution formula that ensures the error function converges to zero;
3. Substitute the defined error function into the evolution formula to obtain the corresponding ZNN model.

According to the design steps of the ZNN, to solve the online TVMI problem (1), we first define the error function for TVMI (1) as follows:

$$E(t) = A(t)U(t) - I. \quad (2)$$

To ensure the convergence of $A(t)$ towards its theoretical inverse denoted by $U^{-1}(t)$, it is necessary for the error function ($E(t) \in \mathbb{R}^{n \times n}$) to iteratively approach zero, meaning that each element of the error function is $e_{ij}(t) \to 0$ for all $i,j \in \{1, \cdots, n\}$. To achieve this goal and improve the model's performance, Xiao et al. [32] designed a method using power-type time-varying parameters instead of traditional fixed parameters. Compared to fixed parameters, this design achieves super-exponential convergence and accelerates the convergence speed. Due to $t \in [0, +\infty)$, the design formula is expressed as follows:

$$\dot{E}(t) = -\lambda(t)E(t), \quad (3)$$

and the time-varying parameter ($\lambda(t)$) is defined as

$$\lambda(t) = \begin{cases} pe^t, & 0 < p \le 1 \\ p^t + 2pt + p, & p > 1. \end{cases} \quad (4)$$

Next, the time derivative of $E(t)$ in Equation (2) is computed to obtain $\dot{E}(t) = \dot{A}(t)U(t) + A(t)\dot{U}(t)$. Substituting Equation (2) and $\dot{E}(t)$ into Equation (3), the PCZNN model proposed by Xiao et al. [32] to solve the TVMI problem is derived as follows:

$$A(t)\dot{U}(t) = -\dot{A}(t)U(t) - \lambda(t)(A(t)U(t) - I). \quad (5)$$

In real-world situations, external noise interference is inevitably encountered, often characterized by random noise and linear noise. Therefore, Liao et al. [29] introduced a DIEZNN model with double integration to effectively suppress noise, as outlined below.

$$\begin{aligned}A(t)U(t) = & -A(t)U(t) - (2u+1)(A(t)U(t) - I) \\ & - (u^2 + 2u)\int_0^t (A(\sigma)U(\sigma) - I)\,d\sigma \\ & - u^2 \int_0^t \int_0^\sigma (A(\tau)U(\tau) - I)\,d\tau\,d\sigma.\end{aligned} \quad (6)$$

Please note that $u > 0$ is a parameter used to adjust the convergence speed.

2.3. EANZNN Model Design

In this section, a novel efficient anti-noise zeroing neural network (EANZNN) model is proposed. To track the inversion process, we initially establish an error function that mirrors the one defined in Equation (2). On this basis, inspired by the design methodology detailed in references [32,34], we design the error function ($Y(t)$) to satisfy the following two equations:

$$\begin{cases} Y(t) = \dot{E}(t) + \lambda(t)E(t), \\ Y(t) = -\int_0^t \lambda(\sigma)Y(\sigma)\,d\sigma. \end{cases} \quad (7)$$

If the time-varying design parameter ($\lambda(t)$) continues to increase, it may exceed the feasible range or the target limits, which may lead to solution failure. To address this issue, an upper bound is established for the growth of $\lambda(t)$. Specifically, once t exceeds t_0, $\lambda(t)$ is fixed at a constant value ($\lambda(t_0)$) no longer increases with t. The explicit definition of $\lambda(t)$ is provided below.

$$\lambda(t) = \begin{cases} pe^t, & \text{if } 0 < p \leq 1 \text{ and } t \leq t_0, \\ p^t + 2pt + p, & \text{if } p > 1 \text{ and } t \leq t_0, \\ \lambda(t_0), & \text{if } t > t_0. \end{cases} \tag{8}$$

where t_0 is defined as 20 s in this document.

Combining the above equations, it can be further deduced that

$$\begin{aligned} Y(t) &= \dot{E}(t) + \lambda(t)E(t) \\ &= -\int_0^t \lambda(\sigma)\left(\dot{E}(\sigma) + \lambda(\sigma)E(\sigma)\right) d\sigma \\ &= -\lambda(t)E(t) - \int_0^t (\lambda^2(\sigma) - \dot{\lambda}(\sigma))E(\sigma) d\sigma. \end{aligned} \tag{9}$$

Equation (9) is restated as

$$\dot{E}(t) = -2\lambda(t)E(t) - \int_0^t (\lambda^2(\sigma) - \dot{\lambda}(\sigma))E(\sigma) d\sigma. \tag{10}$$

Similarly to the error function ($Y(t)$), we can construct the new error function ($G(t)$) as

$$\begin{cases} G(t) = \dot{E}(t) + 2\lambda(t)E(t) + \int_0^t (\lambda^2(\sigma) - \dot{\lambda}(\sigma))E(\sigma) d\sigma, \\ G(t) = -\int_0^t \lambda(\sigma)G(\sigma) d\sigma, \end{cases} \tag{11}$$

similarly obtaining

$$\begin{aligned} \dot{E}(t) &+ 2\lambda(t)E(t) + \int_0^t \left(\lambda^2(\sigma) - \dot{\lambda}(\sigma)\right)E(\sigma) d\sigma \\ &= -\int_0^t \lambda(\sigma)\left(\dot{E}(\sigma) + 2\lambda(\sigma)E(\sigma) + \int_0^\sigma ((\lambda^2(\tau) - \dot{\lambda}(\tau))E(\tau) d\tau\right) d\sigma \\ &= -\int_0^t \left(\lambda(\sigma)\dot{E}(\sigma) + 2\lambda^2(\sigma)E(\sigma)\right) d\sigma \\ &\quad - \int_0^t \left(\lambda(\sigma)\int_0^\sigma (\lambda^2(\tau) - \dot{\lambda}(\tau))E(\tau) d\tau\right) d\sigma \\ &= -\lambda(t)E(t) - \int_0^t (2\lambda^2(\sigma) - \dot{\lambda}(\sigma))E(\sigma) d\sigma \\ &\quad - \int_0^t \int_0^\sigma \lambda(\sigma)\left((\lambda^2(\tau) - \dot{\lambda}(\tau))E(\tau)\right) d\tau d\sigma. \end{aligned} \tag{12}$$

Therefore, we obtain the design of the EANZNN model as follows:

$$\begin{aligned} \dot{E}(t) = &-3\lambda(t)E(t) - \int_0^t (3\lambda^2(\sigma) - 2\dot{\lambda}(\sigma))E(\sigma) d\sigma \\ &- \int_0^t \int_0^\sigma \lambda(\sigma)\left((\lambda^2(\tau) - \dot{\lambda}(\tau))E(\tau)\right) d\tau d\sigma. \end{aligned} \tag{13}$$

Additionally, under the influence of noise, the design formula for EANZNN is given by

$$\begin{aligned} \dot{E}(t) = &-3\lambda(t)E(t) - \int_0^t (3\lambda^2(\sigma) - 2\dot{\lambda}(\sigma))E(\sigma) d\sigma \\ &- \int_0^t \int_0^\sigma \lambda(\sigma)\left((\lambda^2(\tau) - \dot{\lambda}(\tau))E(\tau)\right) d\tau d\sigma + N(t), \end{aligned} \tag{14}$$

where $N(t) \in \mathbb{R}^{n \times n}$ represents external noise.

Finally, we incorporate the time derivative of $E(t)$ into Equation (14) to obtain the design formulation of EANZNN.

$$\begin{aligned} A(t)\dot{U}(t) = & -\dot{A}(t)U(t) - 3\lambda(t)(A(t)U(t) - I) \\ & - \int_0^t \left(3\lambda^2(\sigma) - 2\dot{\lambda}(\sigma)\right)(A(\sigma)U(\sigma) - I)\,d\sigma \\ & - \int_0^t \int_0^\sigma \lambda(\sigma)\left((\lambda^2(\tau) - \dot{\lambda}(\tau))(A(\tau)U(\tau) - I)\right)d\tau\,d\sigma + N(t). \end{aligned} \qquad (15)$$

By transforming Equation (15), we can obtain the block-diagram form of the noise-disturbed EANZNN model (15) as follows:

$$\begin{aligned} \dot{U}(t) = & (I - A(t))\dot{U}(t) - \dot{A}(t)U(t) - 3\lambda(t)(A(t)U(t) - I) \\ & - \int_0^t \left(3\lambda^2(\sigma) - 2\dot{\lambda}(\sigma)\right)(A(\sigma)U(\sigma) - I)\,d\sigma \\ & - \int_0^t \int_0^\sigma \lambda(\sigma)\left((\lambda^2(\tau) - \dot{\lambda}(\tau))(A(\tau)U(\tau) - I)\right)d\tau\,d\sigma + N(t). \end{aligned} \qquad (16)$$

where $A(t)$ and $\dot{A}(t)$ are the system inputs; $\eta_1(t)$, $\eta_2(t)$, and $\eta_3(t)$ represent $3\lambda(t)$, $3\lambda^2(t) - 2\dot{\lambda}(t)$, and $\lambda(t)\left(\lambda^2(t) - \dot{\lambda}(t)\right)$ respectively; $N(t)$ denotes external noise; and $U(t)$ is the state variable. In robotic control systems, the time-varying matrix inversion problem frequently arises in tasks such as motion control, path planning, and state estimation within dynamic environments. In practical applications, robots need to solve the matrix inverse in real time to accurately execute control commands. However, due to factors such as sensor noise, environmental interference, and computational errors, directly solving the matrix inverse can be challenging. The ZNN model effectively handles time-varying problems by updating the inverse matrix in real time, ensuring timely responses of the robotic control system, even in the presence of noise interference. As shown in Figure 1, the EANZNN model with noise interference can be implemented using summators, multipliers, amplifiers, and integrators to solve $U(t)$.

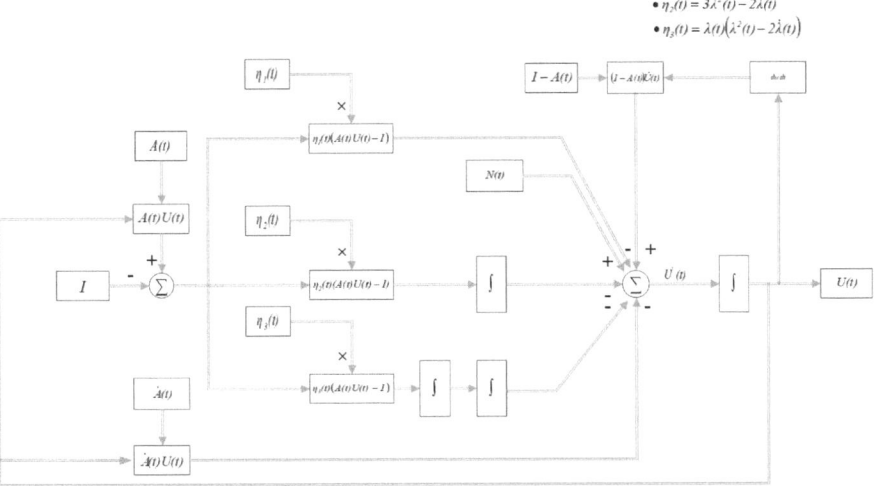

Figure 1. Structure diagram of the EANZNN model (15) for handling noise interference in the TVMI problem.

3. Theoretical Analyses

Theoretical analysis is conducted to examine the convergence and robustness of the EANZNN model (15) with respect to the TVMI problem (Equation (1)), and the following theoretical proof process is provided.

3.1. Convergence

In the primary theoretical analysis, we explore how well the EANZNN model (15) converges when operating in an ideal noise-free setting.

Theorem 1. *Given a matrix ($A(t) \in \mathbb{R}^{n \times n}$), when the EANZNN model (15) resolves the TVMI problem (1) in a noise-free scenario, the state matrix ($U(t) \in \mathbb{R}^{n \times n}$) converges from the initial state ($U(0) \in \mathbb{R}^{n \times n}$) to the theoretical inverse ($A^{-1}(t) \in \mathbb{R}^{n \times n}$). Specifically, as $t \to \infty$, the error norm $\|E(t)\|_F$ tends to zero.*

Proof. According to Section 2.3, we have

$$\begin{cases} G(t) = - \int_0^t \lambda(\sigma) G(\sigma) d\sigma, \\ \dot{G}(t) = -\lambda(t) G(t). \end{cases}$$

Its element-wise form is

$$\begin{cases} g_{ij}(t) = - \int_0^t \lambda(\sigma) g_{ij}(\sigma) d\sigma, \\ \dot{g}_{ij}(t) = -\lambda(t) g_{ij}(t). \end{cases} \quad (17)$$

We design a Lyapunov function as

$$v(t) = g_{ij}^2(t) > 0.$$

Combining Equation (17) ($\dot{g}_{ij}(t) = -\lambda(t) g_{ij}(t)$), we obtain

$$\dot{v}(t) = 2 g_{ij}(t) \dot{g}_{ij}(t) = -2\lambda(t) g_{ij}^2(t).$$

According to the expression of the design parameter ($\lambda(t)$) presented in Section 2.3, it is known that when $t \in [0, +\infty]$, we have $\lambda(t) > 0$. As a result, we obtain $\dot{v}(t) < 0$. Since $v(t)$ is positive and definite and $\dot{v}(t)$ is negative and definite, based on the Lyapunov's asymptotic stability theory [35], we can obtain

$$\lim_{t \to \infty} |g_{ij}(t)| = 0. \quad (18)$$

Similarly, based on the expression for the design parameter ($\lambda(t)$) described in Section 2.3, it is known that as $t \geq t_0$, $\lambda(t)$ is fixed at a constant value, which we denote as ω. Given that $\dot{g}_{ij}(t) = -\lambda(t) g_{ij}(t)$, we can deduce the following:

$$\lim_{t \to \infty} |\dot{g}_{ij}(t)| = \lim_{t \to \infty} |-\omega g_{ij}(t)| = 0. \quad (19)$$

The elemental form of $Y(t)$ in Equation (7) is expressed as $y_{ij}(t) = \dot{e}_{ij}(t) + \lambda(t) e_{ij}(t)$, where y_{ij} and e_{ij} denote the ijth elements of $Y(t)$ and $E(t)$, respectively. Similarly, the element-wise form of $G(t)$ in Equation (11) is $g_{ij}(t) = \dot{e}_{ij}(t) + 2\lambda(t) e_{ij}(t) + \int_0^t (\lambda^2(\sigma) - \dot{\lambda}(\sigma)) e_{ij}(\sigma) d\sigma$. From these equations, we obtain

$$g_{ij}(t) = y_{ij}(t) + \int_0^t \lambda(\sigma) y_{ij}(\sigma) d\sigma.$$

Then, we derive the above equation to obtain

$$\dot{g}_{ij}(t) = \dot{y}_{ij}(t) + \lambda(t)y_{ij}(t).$$

Given that $\lambda(t)$ is fixed at a constant value (ω) for $t \geq t_0$, as $t \to \infty$, we can derive the following equivalent substitution from Equation (19):

$$\lim_{t \to \infty} |\dot{y}_{ij}(t) + \omega y_{ij}(t)| = 0. \tag{20}$$

Based on Equation (20), we can deduce the following:

$$\lim_{t \to \infty} |\dot{y}_{ij}(t)| = \lim_{t \to \infty} |-\omega y_{ij}(t)|.$$

We establish the following Lyapunov function:

$$s(t) = y_{ij}^2(t) > 0.$$

Differentiating the equation provided above, we obtain

$$\dot{s}(t) = 2y_{ij}(t)\dot{y}_{ij}(t) = -2\omega y_{ij}^2(t) < 0.$$

As $t \to \infty$, it can be known that $s(t)$ is positive and definite and $\dot{s}(t)$ is negative and definite. Based on Lyapunov's asymptotic stability theory, we can obtain

$$\lim_{t \to \infty} |y_{ij}(t)| = 0. \tag{21}$$

Subsequently, substituting the expression $y_{ij}(t) = \dot{e}_{ij}(t) + \lambda(t)e_{ij}(t)$ from Equation (21) yields the following equation:

$$\lim_{t \to \infty} |\dot{e}_{ij}(t) + \omega e_{ij}(t)| = 0. \tag{22}$$

Therefore, we have

$$\lim_{t \to \infty} |\dot{e}_{ij}(t)| = \lim_{t \to \infty} |-\omega e_{ij}(t)|.$$

Following the same method, we define the following Lyapunov function:

$$h(t) = e_{ij}^2(t) > 0.$$

By differentiating the preceding equation, we obtain

$$\dot{h}(t) = 2e_{ij}(t)\dot{e}_{ij}(t) = -2\omega e_{ij}^2(t) < 0.$$

Similarly, as $t \to \infty$, it can be known that $h(t)$ is positive and definite and $\dot{h}(t)$ is negative and definite. Based on Lyapunov's theory of asymptotic stability, it follows that

$$\lim_{t \to \infty} |e_{ij}(t)| = 0.$$

Since $\lim_{t \to \infty} |e_{ij}(t)| = 0$, its corresponding matrix form can also be expressed as

$$\lim_{t \to \infty} \|E(t)\|_F = 0.$$

As a result, the demonstration is finished. □

3.2. Robustness

In practical scenarios, external noise interference is common and nearly unavoidable. Therefore, it is essential to consider its impact. This section investigates the robustness of the EANZNN model (15) under the interference of matrix-type external noise ($N(t)$).

Theorem 2. *Given a matrix ($A(t) \in \mathbb{R}^{n \times n}$), when the EANZNN model (15) resolves the TVMI problem (1) under the interference of external constant matrix-type noise ($N(t) = K \in \mathbb{R}^{n \times n}$), the state matrix ($U(t) \in \mathbb{R}^{n \times n}$) converges from the initial state ($U(0) \in \mathbb{R}^{n \times n}$) to the theoretical inverse ($A^{-1}(t) \in \mathbb{R}^{n \times n}$). Specifically, as $t \to \infty$, the error norm ($\|E(t)\|_F$) tends to zero.*

Proof. The noise ($N(t)$) is specified by

$$N(t) = K,$$

where $K \in \mathbb{R}^{n \times n}$ is a constant matrix, and the form of the corresponding element is

$$n_{ij}(t) = k_{ij}.$$

Considering the noise ($N(t)$) described in Equation (15), we have

$$\begin{cases} g_{ij}(t) = -\int_0^t \lambda(\sigma) g_{ij}(\sigma) d\sigma + n_{ij}(t), \\ \dot{g}_{ij}(t) = -\lambda(t) g_{ij}(t) + \dot{n}_{ij}(t). \end{cases}$$

By differentiating $n_{ij}(t)$, we find

$$\dot{n}_{ij}(t) = 0.$$

Therefore, we have

$$\begin{cases} g_{ij}(t) = -\int_0^t \lambda(\sigma) g_{ij}(\sigma) d\sigma + k_{ij}(t), \\ \dot{g}_{ij}(t) = -\lambda(t) g_{ij}(t). \end{cases} \quad (23)$$

Similar to the derivation of Equation (18), we conclude that

$$\lim_{t \to \infty} |g_{ij}(t)| = 0.$$

Similarly, considering that Equation (23) includes $\dot{g}_{ij}(t) = -\lambda(t) g_{ij}(t)$, we have

$$\lim_{t \to \infty} |\dot{g}_{ij}(t)| = \lim_{t \to \infty} |-\omega g_{ij}(t)| = 0. \quad (24)$$

Given that Equation (24) is identical to Equation (19), it can be deduced that

$$\lim_{t \to \infty} |y_{ij}(t)| = 0, \quad (25)$$

due to

$$y_{ij}(t) = \dot{e}_{ij}(t) + \lambda(t) e_{ij}(t).$$

Consequently, substituting this expression into Equation (25), we derive

$$\lim_{t \to \infty} |\dot{e}_{ij}(t) + \omega e_{ij}(t)| = 0.$$

Since the aforementioned equation is identical to Equation (22), we obtain

$$\lim_{t \to \infty} |e_{ij}(t)| = 0.$$

The corresponding matrix form is written as follows:

$$\lim_{t \to \infty} \|E(t)\|_F = 0.$$

As a result, the demonstration is finished. □

Theorem 3. *Given a matrix ($A(t) \in \mathbb{R}^{n \times n}$), when the EANZNN model (15) resolves the TVMI problem (1) under the interference of linear noise ($N(t) = Kt + B \in \mathbb{R}^{n \times n}$), the state matrix ($U(t) \in \mathbb{R}^{n \times n}$) converges from the initial state ($U(0) \in \mathbb{R}^{n \times n}$) to the theoretical inverse ($A^{-1}(t) \in \mathbb{R}^{n \times n}$). Specifically, as $t \to \infty$, the error norm ($\|E(t)\|_F$) tends to zero.*

Proof. The noise ($N(t)$) is specified by

$$N(t) = Kt + B,$$

where $K, B \in \mathbb{R}^{n \times n}$ represents constant matrices, and their corresponding elemental forms are represented as

$$n_{ij}(t) = k_{ij}t + b_{ij}.$$

Considering the linear noise ($N(t)$) described in Equation (15), we have

$$\begin{cases} g_{ij}(t) = -\int_0^t \lambda(\sigma) g_{ij}(\sigma) d\sigma + n_{ij}(t), \\ \dot{g}_{ij}(t) = -\lambda(t) g_{ij}(t) + \dot{n}_{ij}(t). \end{cases}$$

Taking the derivative of $n_{ij}(t)$, we obtain

$$\dot{n}_{ij}(t) = k_{ij}.$$

Therefore, we obtain

$$\begin{cases} g_{ij}(t) = -\int_0^t \lambda(\sigma) g_{ij}(\sigma) d\sigma + n_{ij}(t), \\ \dot{g}_{ij}(t) = -\lambda(t) g_{ij}(t) + k_{ij}. \end{cases} \quad (26)$$

To analyze the limit ($\lim_{t \to \infty} |\dot{g}_{ij}(t)|$) and considering that as $t \to \infty$, $\lambda(t)$ is fixed at a constant value (ω) for $t \geq t_0$, we can rewrite Equation (26) as

$$\begin{cases} g_{ij}(t) = -\int_0^t \omega g_{ij}(\sigma) d\sigma + n_{ij}(t), \\ \dot{g}_{ij}(t) = -\omega g_{ij}(t) + k_{ij}. \end{cases}$$

After differentiating the expression for $\dot{g}_{ij}(t)$ in the aforementioned equation once again, we obtain the following result:

$$\ddot{g}_{ij}(t) = -\omega \dot{g}_{ij}(t).$$

We define the following Lyapunov function:

$$\theta(t) = \dot{g}_{ij}^2(t) > 0.$$

Differentiating the above expression, we obtain

$$\dot{\theta}(t) = 2 \dot{g}_{ij}(t) \ddot{g}_{ij}(t) = -2\omega \dot{g}_{ij}^2(t) < 0.$$

As $t \to \infty$, $\theta(t)$ is positive and definite, and $\dot{\theta}(t)$ is negative and definite. According to Lyapunov's theorem of asymptotic stability, we can derive

$$\lim_{t \to \infty} |\dot{g}_{ij}(t)| = 0.$$

Substituting $g_{ij}(t) = y_{ij}(t) + \int_0^t \lambda(\sigma) y_{ij}(\sigma) d\sigma$ into the above equation, we further obtain

$$\lim_{t \to \infty} |\dot{y}_{ij}(t) + \omega y_{ij}(t)| = 0. \quad (27)$$

Noting that Equation (27) is identical to Equation (20), we can infer

$$\lim_{t\to\infty} |y_{ij}(t)| = 0.$$

Since $y(t) = \dot{e}_{ij}(t) + \lambda(t)e_{ij}(t)$,

$$\lim_{t\to\infty} |\dot{e}_{ij}(t) + \omega e_{ij}(t)| = 0.$$

This equation is similar to Equation (22), from which it follows that

$$\lim_{t\to\infty} |e_{ij}(t)| = 0.$$

The corresponding matrix form is written as follows:

$$\lim_{t\to\infty} \|E(t)\|_F = 0.$$

As a result, the demonstration is finished. □

4. Example Verification

Remark 1. *The experimental data and results presented in this paper were obtained using MATLAB R2021a Version. Initially, the EANZNN model (15) was built in MATLAB, where the design parameter (p) was set, and the initial state matrix ($U(0)$) was randomly generated to handle the given time-varying matrix ($A(t)$). Next, the matrix differential equation was converted into a vector differential equation using the "kron" function (Kronecker product technique) in Matlab, followed by solving the differential equation using the ode45 solver. Through iterative updates, the dynamic system outputs the real-time state solution ($U(t)$). Additionally, the Frobenius norm ($\|\cdot\|_F$) was calculated to obtain real-time data and results of the error function ($E(t)$).*

In this section, we further verify the effectiveness and superiority of the EANZNN model (15) in solving the TVMI problem (1) under noise-free and external noise conditions through three examples. To clearly demonstrate the experimental results and the advantages of the EANZNN model (15), we also compared it with the existing PCZNN model (5) and DIEZNN model (6) under the same conditions, considering the results with different design parameters ($u = p = 0.8$, $u = p = 2$, $u = p = 3$, and $u = p = 15$). These simulations were all conducted on a laptop equipped with a Windows 10 64-bit operating system, Intel Core i7-11800H CPU (2.30 GHz), and 16 GB of memory.

4.1. Experiment 1—Convergence

To validate the effectiveness and convergence of the EANZNN model in solving the TVMI problem, we used simple 2×2 time-varying coefficient matrices ($A(t)$) (28), with random initial values ($U(0)$) and various design parameters. In the experiment, we conducted a comparative analysis of the EANZNN model relative to the PCZNN and DIEZNN models under noise-free conditions.

We considered the following time-varying invertible matrix ($A(t)$) for the TVMI problem:

$$A(t) = \begin{bmatrix} \sin(4t) & \cos(4t) \\ -\cos(4t) & \sin(4t) \end{bmatrix} \in \mathbb{R}^{2\times 2}. \tag{28}$$

Obviously, the theoretical solution ($U^*(t)$) of the corresponding TVMI can be readily computed as

$$U^*(t) = A^{-1}(t) = \begin{bmatrix} \sin(4t) & -\cos(4t) \\ \cos(4t) & \sin(4t) \end{bmatrix} \in \mathbb{R}^{2\times 2}.$$

This inverse serves as a benchmark to evaluate the accuracy of the solutions obtained by the PCZNN, DIEZNN, and EANZNN models for the TVMI problem.

Figure 2 presents the convergence trajectories of the error norm ($\|E(t)\|_F$) when solving the TVMI problem using the PCZNN, DIEZNN, and EANZN models under a noise-free environment. As can be seen, starting from the randomly generated initial state ($U(0) \in [-2,2]^{2\times 2}$), all three models converge to approximately zero. With design parameters of $u = p = 0.8$, as illustrated in Figure 2a, the error norm ($\|E(t)\|_F$) for DIEZNN converges to just above 10^{-3} within 12 s. PCZNN's convergence accuracy stabilizes at around 10^{-4}, while EANZNN exhibits higher precision, achieving a convergence accuracy of 10^{-5} within 3 s and further converging to 10^{-11} within 12 s. Figure 2b shows the results with design parameters of $u = p = 3$. It can be seen that EANZNN significantly outperforms the other two models in terms of convergence speed and precision. Specifically, the error norm ($\|E(t)\|_F$) for EANZNN rapidly decreases to 10^{-3} within 1 s and further improves to approximately 10^{-13} over time. In contrast, PCZNN and DIEZNN only converge to above 10^{-8} within 10 s. Among them, PCZNN stabilizes around 10^{-4}, while DIEZNN converges above 10^{-5}. These comparative results indicate that the proposed EANZNN model demonstrates significant advantages in noise-free environments, not only achieving faster convergence but also reaching higher convergence accuracy in a shorter time, showcasing its superior performance in handling the TVMI problem.

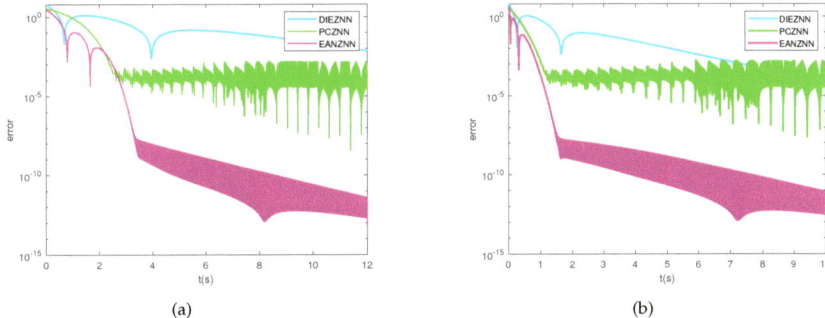

Figure 2. The error norm ($\|E(t)\|_F$) computed for the TVMI of the matrix equation (28) using PCZNN, DIEZNN, and EANZNN under noise-free conditions. (a) u = p= 0.8; (b) u = p = 3.

4.2. Experiment 2—Robustness

Next, to verify the robustness and convergence of the EANZNN model, we conducted further experiments under different noise conditions. Specifically, we solved the TVMI problem in the presence of constant and linear noise. We continued using the time-varying matrix ($A(t)$) (28) defined in the previous experiment and considered different noise intensities and design parameters. Through these experiments, we assessed the performance of the EANZNN model under noise interference and compared it with that of the PCZNN and DIEZNN models.

Although all three models converge under noise-free conditions, it is more important to consider model validation under external noise. Figures 3–5 display the convergence trajectories of the state ($U(t)$) and the error norm ($\|E(t)\|_F$) synthesized by the PCZNN, DIEZNN, and EANZNN models under linear noise conditions ($N(t) = [10 + 10t]^{2\times 2}$). Here, the symbol $[10t + 10]^{2\times 2}$ represents a 2×2 matrix where each element is $10t + 10$, which was used to simulate the impact of linear noise at different times (t). In these figures, the initial state ($U(0)$) is randomly generated as $U(0) \in [-2,2]^{2\times 2}$, and the model parameters are set to $u = 1$ and $p = 1$. The theoretical state solution is depicted by the black dashed line, while the state solutions of the PCZNN, DIEZNN, and EANZNN models are represented by the green solid line, light-blue solid line, and magenta solid line, respectively.

Figure 3a displays the state solution, while Figure 3b illustrates the error norm for PCZNN. From Figure 3a, it can be visually observed that under linear noise conditions

($N(t) = [10+10t]^{2\times 2}$), PCZNN converges to zero in approximately 12 s. Figure 4a and Figure 4b show the state solution and error norm of DIEZNN, respectively. It can be observed from Figure 4b that DIEZNN converges to zero in approximately 15 s and remains stable under this linear noise.

Figure 5a and Figure 5b depict the state solution and the error norm of EANZNN, respectively. It is evident that EANZNN can converge to zero under linear noise conditions ($N(t) = [10+10t]^{2\times 2}$). From Figure 5b, it can be observed that EANZNN converges to zero in approximately 3.5 s with a design parameter of $p = 1$ and remains stable under this linear noise. Therefore, it can be concluded from the aforementioned findings that when subjected to linear noise conditions ($N(t) = [10+10t]^{2\times 2}$), EANZNN exhibits the shortest computation time to resolve the TVMI problem, showcasing its superior convergence and robustness.

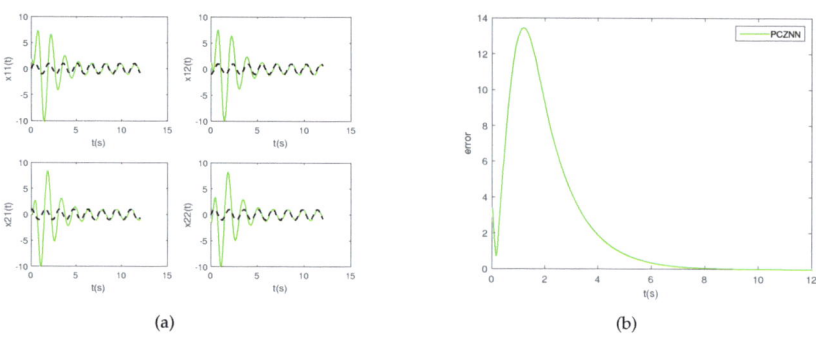

Figure 3. Simulation results of solving the TVMI problem for matrix Equation (28) using PCZNN with $p = 1$ under conditions of linear noise ($N(t) = [10+10t]^{2\times 2}$). (**a**) State $U(t)$; (**b**) error norm $||E(t)||_F$.

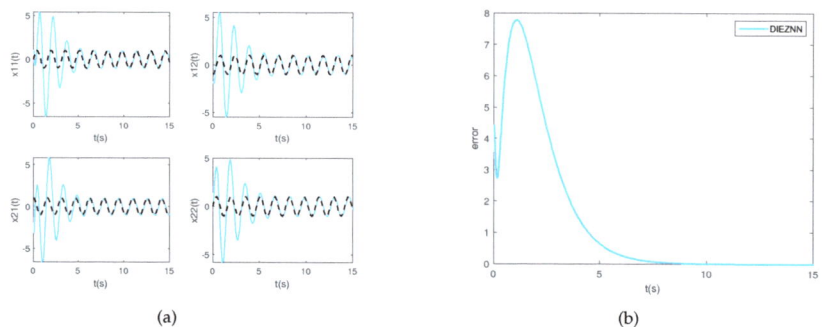

Figure 4. Simulation results of solving the TVMI problem for matrix Equation (28) using DIEZNN with $u = 1$ under conditions of linear noise ($N(t) = [10+10t]^{2\times 2}$). (**a**) State $U(t)$; (**b**) error norm $||E(t)||_F$.

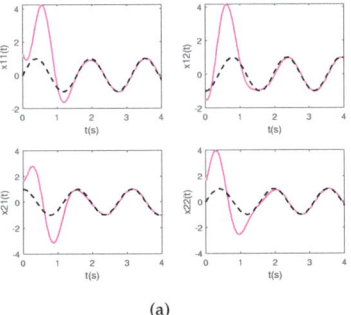
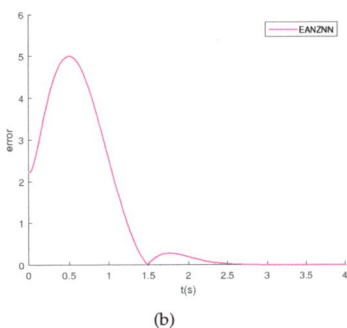

(a)   (b)

Figure 5. Simulation results of solving the TVMI problem for matrix Equation (28) using EANZNN with $p = 1$ under conditions of linear noise ($N(t) = [10 + 10t]^{2 \times 2}$). (**a**) State $U(t)$; (**b**) Error norm $||E(t)||_F$.

Next, several other external noises ($N(t)$) were investigated to further illustrate the superior noise suppression performance of EANZNN.

1. Linear noise: $N(t) = [12t + 0.8]^{2 \times 2}$;
2. Linear noise: $N(t) = [1000t + 100]^{2 \times 2}$;
3. Constant noise: $N(t) = [20]^{2 \times 2}$.

Figure 6a,b show the error norm ($||E(t)||_F$) when solving the TVMI problem under linear noise conditions ($N(t) = [12t + 0.8]^{2 \times 2}$) using the PCZNN, DIEZNN, and EANZNN models. Figure 6a presents the results for $u = p = 2$, where PCZNN does not converge to near zero within 9 s, while DIEZNN converges to approximately 3.12×10^{-3} around 9 s. Compared with these two models, EANZNN converges the fastest, with the error norm ($||E(t)||_F$) starting to be less than 10^{-5} after approximately 6 s. Figure 6b shows the results when the parameters of the three models are $u = p = 15$. It is evident that the error norm ($||E(t)||_F$) of EANZNN is less than 10^{-5} after about 1.8 s, whereas the error norms ($||E(t)||_F$) of the other two models only converge to 10^{-3} or higher.

The error norm ($||E(t)||_F$) of PCZNN, DIEZNN, and EANZNN under linear noise conditions ($N(t) = [1000t + 100]^{2 \times 2}$) is shown in Figure 7. Figure 7a presents the results when the parameters of the three models are $u = p = 2$. PCZNN does not converge to a near-zero value within 9 s, whereas DIEZNN converges to 2.27×10^{-1} within the same time frame and EANZNN converges to 10^{-5}. Figure 7b shows the results when the parameters for the three models are set to $u = p = 15$; in comparison, the error norm $||E(t)||_F$ of EANZNN starts to be less than 10^{-7} after 3 s, while both PCZNN and DIEZNN do not converge to 10^{-5} within 3 s. In summary, when the linear noise increases, the convergence performance of EANZNN far surpasses that of DIEZNN and PCZNN.

Furthermore, Figure 8a,b display the error norm ($||E(t)||_F$) of PCZNN, DIEZNN, and EANZNN under constant noise ($N(t) = [20]^{2 \times 2}$). As illustrated in Figure 8a, under the influence of constant noise ($N(t) = [20]^{2 \times 2}$), for the case of $u = p = 2$, the error norm ($||E(t)||_F$) of the EANZNN model rapidly declines and stabilizes below 1.831×10^{-8} within approximately 3 s. In contrast, the PCZNN and DIEZNN models do not achieve lower error levels within the 9 s observation period, with error norms only converging to above 10^{-3}. With the increase in design parameters, as shown in Figure 8b, when $u = p = 15$, the residuals decrease for all models. However, EANZNN achieves significantly quicker convergence than PCZNN and DIEZNN. Therefore, it is clear that the presented EANZNN exhibits greater convergence performance in resolving the TVMI problem in the presence of constant noise as compared to PCZNN and DIEZNN.

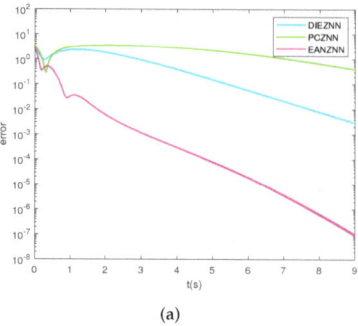
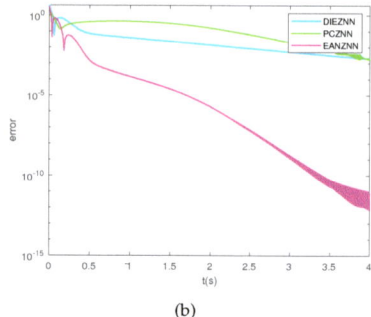

(a)   (b)

Figure 6. Under linear noise ($N(t) = [12t + 0.8]^{2 \times 2}$), the error norm ($\|E(t)\|_F$) for the TVMI of the matrix equation (28) is computed using PCZNN, DIEZNN, and EANZNN. (**a**) $u = p = 2$; (**b**) $u = p = 15$.

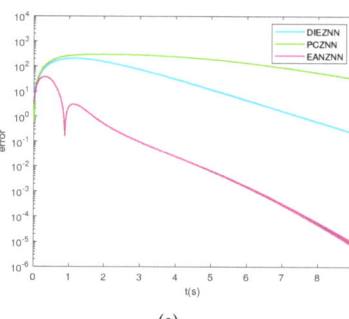
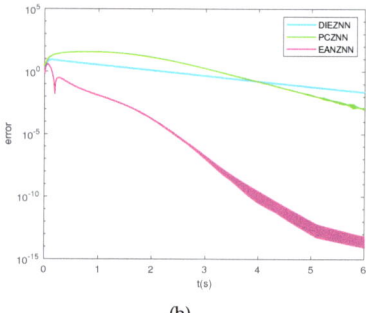

(a)   (b)

Figure 7. Under linear noise ($N(t) = [1000t + 100]^{2 \times 2}$), the error norm ($\|E(t)\|_F$) for the TVMI of the matrix equation (28) is computed using PCZNN, DIEZNN, and EANZNN. (**a**) $u = p = 2$; (**b**) $u = p = 15$.

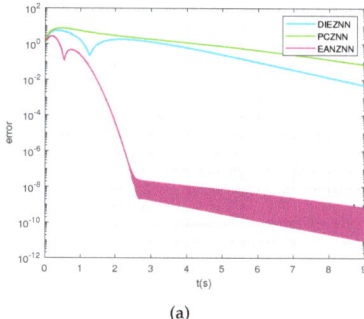
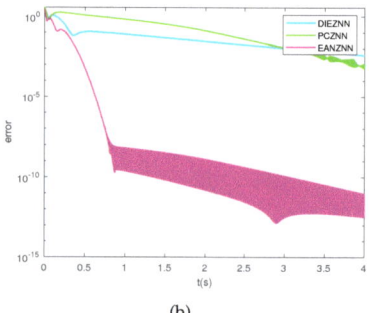

(a)   (b)

Figure 8. Under linear noise ($N(t) = [20]^{2 \times 2}$), the error norm ($\|E(t)\|_F$) for the TVMI of the matrix equation (28) is computed using PCZNN, DIEZNN, and EANZNN. (**a**) $u = p = 2$; (**b**) $u = p = 15$.

4.3. Experiment 3—High-Dimensional Matrix

In order to further illustrate the efficiency and superiority of the constructed EANZNN in computing the TVMI, we consider the following two high-dimensional example equations:

$$A(t) = \begin{bmatrix} 2.1 + \sin(1.5t) & \cos(1.5t) & \frac{\cos(1.5t)}{2} \\ \cos(1.5t) & 2.1 + \sin(1.5t) & \cos(1.5t) \\ \frac{\cos(1.5t)}{2} & \cos(1.5t) & 2.1 + \sin(1.5t) \end{bmatrix}, \tag{29}$$

and

$$A(t) = \begin{bmatrix} 1.1 + \sin(t) & 0.3\cos(t) & 0.2\sin(2t) & 0.1\cos(2t) & 0.2\sin(t) \\ 0.3\cos(t) & 1.2 + \cos(t) & 0.3\sin(t) & 0.2\cos(2t) & 0.1\sin(2t) \\ 0.2\sin(2t) & 0.3\sin(t) & 1.3 + \sin(t) & 0.1\cos(t) & 0.2\cos(2t) \\ 0.1\cos(2t) & 0.2\cos(2t) & 0.1\cos(t) & 1.4 + 0.5\sin(t) & 0.3\sin(2t) \\ 0.2\sin(t) & 0.1\sin(2t) & 0.2\cos(2t) & 0.3\sin(2t) & 1.5 + \cos(t) \end{bmatrix}. \tag{30}$$

Figure 9a illustrates the individual entries of the state solutions ($U(t)$) of the TVMI problem, which were computed using the EANZNN method. The state solutions of $U(t)$ all converge to the theoretical solution within a short period of time, as can be observed. Observing Figure 9b, it is noted that the corresponding error norm ($||E(t)||_F$) synthesized by EANZNN converges to zero in approximately 3 s. This further affirms that the performance of the established EANZNN remains unaffected by variations in matrix dimensions during the resolution of the TVMI problem.

By observing Figure 10, it can be noted that for the inversion of a high-dimensional matrix (29), when $u = p = 2$, the error norm ($||E(t)||_F$) of EANZNN begins to decrease below 10^{-10} after 10 s. Specifically, both PCZNN and DIEZNN fail to converge to 10^{-6} within 14 s, with DIEZNN's error norm reducing to approximately 3.66×10^{-5} at 14 s, while PCZNN's error norm decreases to about 3.19×10^{-2} at the same time. Figure 10b also shows that when the parameters are adjusted to $u = p = 15$, all models' error norms ($||E(t)||_F$) are able to converge to nearly zero. However, EANZNN displays the fastest convergence rate, with its error norm dropping below 1×10^{-8} within 3 s, whereas the error norms of PCZNN and DIEZNN only converge to above 10^{-3} within 3.5 s. This confirms the superior convergence performance of EANZNN compared to PCZNN and DIEZNN when addressing the TVMI problem for high-dimensional matrices.

Similarly, Figure 11 shows the inversion of high-dimensional matrices (30) under noisy conditions using the PCZNN, DIEZNN, and EANZNN models. As shown in Figure 11a, when $u = p = 2$, the error norm ($||E(t)||_F$) for PCZNN does not converge to near zero within 12 s. DIEZNN requires 12 s to reach an error norm of 10^{-3}, while EANZNN achieves the same error norm in just 4 s and further reduces the error norm to approximately 10^{-10} over time. As illustrated in Figure 11b, with increased design parameters $u = p = 15$, the convergence speed significantly accelerates. EANZNN reaches an error norm of 10^{-11} within 3.5 s, whereas PCZNN and DIEZNN only converge to above 10^{-2} within the same time frame. The experimental results indicate that EANZNN outperforms DIEZNN and PCZNN in terms of convergence speed and accuracy, even under noisy high-dimensional matrix conditions.

Based on the simulation results reported above, it is evident that EANZNN demonstrates superior robustness and convergence compared to PCZNN and DIEZNN when tackling the TVMI problem, irrespective of external noise conditions.

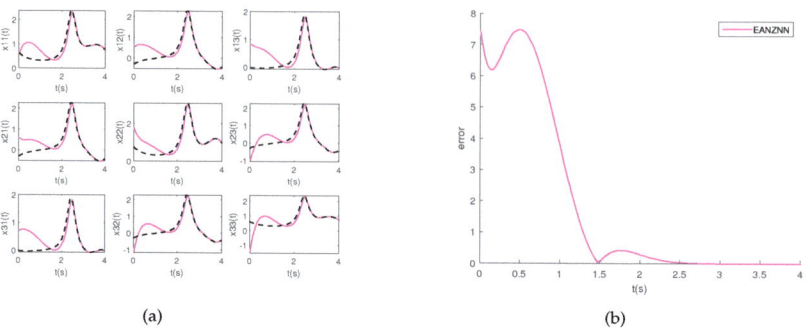

Figure 9. Simulation results of solving the TVMI problem for matrix equation (29) using EANZNN with $p = 1$ under the conditions of linear noise ($N(t) = [10 + 10t]^{3\times3}$). (**a**) State $U(t)$; (**b**) Error norm $||E(t)||_F$.

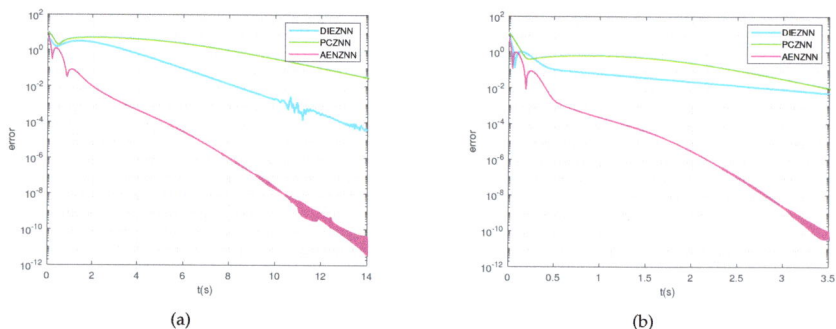

Figure 10. Under the condition of linear noise ($N(t) = [12t + 0.8]^{3\times3}$), the error norm ($||E(t)||_F$) for the TVMI of the matrix equation (29) is computed using PCZNN, DIEZNN, and EANZNN. (**a**) $u = p = 2$; (**b**) $u = p = 15$.

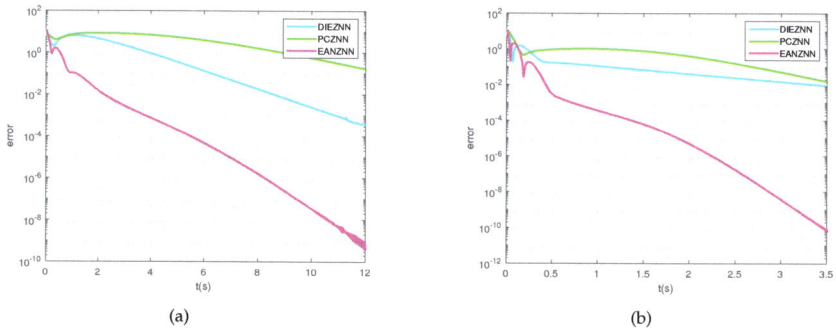

Figure 11. Under the condition of linear noise ($N(t) = [12t + 0.8]^{5\times5}$), the error norm ($||E(t)||_F$) for the TVMI of the matrix equation (30) is computed using PCZNN, DIEZNN, and EANZNN. (**a**) $u = p = 2$. (**b**) $u = p = 15$.

5. Conclusions

To effectively address the TVMI problem, we first investigated the design of segmented time-varying parameters. Based on this, we designed an EANZNN model incorporating double integrals. Additionally, we provided rigorous theoretical proofs of the convergence and robustness of EANZNN. Simulation experiments on matrices of different dimensions and under different noise conditions demonstrated that EANZNN achieves quicker convergence and greater resilience to noise than the DIEZNN and PCZNN models. These results unequivocally showcase the superiority of EANZNN in addressing TVMI challenges. Moving forward, our plan includes further improving the convergence speed of EANZNN through the development of novel nonlinear activation functions.

Author Contributions: Conceptualization, Y.H. and J.H.; methodology, F.Y. and Y.H.; software, J.H. , Y.H. and F.Y.; validation, J.H. and Y.H.; formal analysis, J.H.; investigation, F.Y.; resources, Y.H.; data curation, J.H.; writing—original draft preparation, J.H.; writing—review and editing, Y.H.; visualization, J.H.; supervision, Y.H.; project administration, J.H.; funding acquisition, Y.H. All authors have read and agreed to the published version of the manuscript.

Funding: This work was funded by the National Natural Science Foundation of China under Grant Nos. 62062036, 62066015, and 62006095.

Institutional Review Board Statement: Not applicable.

Informed Consent Statement: Not applicable.

Data Availability Statement: The original contributions presented in the study are included in the article, further inquiries can be directed to the corresponding author.

Conflicts of Interest: The authors declare no conflicts of interest.

Abbreviations

The following abbreviations are used in this manuscript:

TVMI	Time-Varying Matrix Inversion
ZNN	Zeroing Neural Network
EANZNN	Efficient Anti-Noise Zeroing Neural Network
DIEZNN	Double Integral-Enhanced ZNN
PCZNN	Parameter-Changing ZNN
GNN	Gradient-based Recurrent Neural Network
FTZNN	Finite-Time ZNN
DCMI	Dynamic complex matrix inversion
CVNTZNN	Classical Complex-Valued Noise-Tolerant ZNN
FTCNTZNN	Fixed-Time Convergent and Noise-Tolerant ZNN
EVPZNN	Exponential-enhanced-type Varying-parameter ZNN
FPZNN	Fixed-Parameter ZNN
CVPZNN	Complex Varying-Parameter ZNN
AF	Activation Function
IEZNN	Integration-Enhanced ZNN
VAF	Versatile Activation Function
NAF	Novel Activation Function

References

1. Fang, W.; Zhen, Y.; Kang, Q.; Xi, S.D.; Shang, L.Y. A simulation research on the visual servo based on pseudo-inverse of image jacobian matrix for robot. *Appl. Mech. Mater.* **2014**, *494*, 1212–1215. [CrossRef]
2. Xiao, L.; Zhang, Z.; Li, S. Solving time-varying system of nonlinear equations by finite-time recurrent neural networks with application to motion tracking of robot manipulators. *IEEE Trans. Syst. Man Cybern. Syst.* **2018**, *49*, 2210–2220. [CrossRef]
3. Steriti, R.J.; Fiddy, M.A. Regularized image reconstruction using SVD and a neural network method for matrix inversion. *IEEE Trans. Signal Process.* **1993**, *41*, 3074–3077. [CrossRef]
4. Cho, C.; Lee, J.G.; Hale, P.D.; Jargon, J.A.; Jeavons, P.; Schlager, J.B.; Dienstfrey, A. Calibration of time-interleaved errors in digital real-time oscilloscopes. *IEEE Trans. Microw. Theory Tech.* **2016**, *64*, 4071–4079. [CrossRef]
5. Guo, D.; Zhang, Y. Zhang neural network, Getz–Marsden dynamic system, and discrete-time algorithms for time-varying matrix inversion with application to robots' kinematic control. *Neurocomputing* **2012**, *97*, 22–32. [CrossRef]
6. Ramos, H.; Monteiro, M.T.T. A new approach based on the Newton's method to solve systems of nonlinear equations. *J. Comput. Appl. Math.* **2017**, *318*, 3–13. [CrossRef]
7. Jäntschi, L Eigenproblem Basics and Algorithms. *Symmetry* **2023**, *15*, 2046. [CrossRef]
8. Li, X.; Xu, Z.; Li, S.; Su, Z.; Zhou, X. Simultaneous obstacle avoidance and target tracking of multiple wheeled mobile robots with certified safety. *IEEE Trans. Cybern.* **2021**, *52*, 11859–11873. [CrossRef]

9. Zhang, Y.; Li, S.; Weng, J.; Liao, B. GNN model for time-varying matrix inversion with robust finite-time convergence. *IEEE Trans. Neural Netw. Learn. Syst.* **2022** *35*, 559–569. [CrossRef]
10. Zhang, Y.; Ge, S.S. Design and analysis of a general recurrent neural network model for time-varying matrix inversion. *IEEE Trans. Neural Netw.* **2005**, *16*, 1477–1490. [CrossRef]
11. Zhang, Y.; Chen, K.; Tan, H.Z. Performance analysis of gradient neural network exploited for online time-varying matrix inversion. *IEEE Trans. Autom. Control* **2009**, *54*, 1940–1945. [CrossRef]
12. Zhang, Y.; Li, Z. Zhang neural network for online solution of time-varying convex quadratic program subject to time-varying linear-equality constraints. *Phys. Lett. A.* **2009**, *373*, 1639–1643. [CrossRef]
13. Zhang, Y.; Qi, Z.; Qiu, B.; Yang, M.; Xiao, M. Zeroing neural dynamics and models for various time-varying problems solving with ZLSF models as minimization-type and euler-type special cases [Research Frontier]. *IEEE Comput. Intell. Mag.* **2019**, *14*, 52–60. [CrossRef]
14. Xiao, L. A new design formula exploited for accelerating Zhang neural network and its application to time-varying matrix inversion. *Theor. Comput. Sci.* **2016**, *647*, 50–58. [CrossRef]
15. Xiao, L.; Zhang, Y.; Zuo, Q.; Dai, J.; Li, J.; Tang, W. A noise-tolerant zeroing neural network for time-dependent complex matrix inversion under various kinds of noises. *IEEE Trans. Ind. Inform.* **2019**, *16*, 3757–3766. [CrossRef]
16. Jin, J.; Zhu, J.; Zhao, L.; Chen, L. A fixed-time convergent and noise-tolerant zeroing neural network for online solution of time-varying matrix inversion. *Appl. Soft Comput.* **2022**, *130*, 109691. [CrossRef]
17. Guo, D.; Li, S.; Stanimirović, P.S. Analysis and application of modified ZNN design with robustness against harmonic noise. *IEEE Trans. Ind. Inform.* **2019**, *16*, 4627–4638. [CrossRef]
18. Dzieciol, H.; Sillekens, E.; Lavery, D. Extending phase noise tolerance in UDWDM access networks. In Proceedings of the 2020 IEEE Photonics Society Summer Topicals Meeting Series (SUM), Cabo San Lucas, Mexico, 13–15 July 2020; IEEE: New York, NY, USA, 2020; pp. 1–2.
19. Xiao, L.; Tan, H.; Jia, L.; Dai, J.; Zhang, Y. New error function designs for finite-time ZNN models with application to dynamic matrix inversion. *Neurocomputing* **2020**, *402*, 395–408. [CrossRef]
20. Jin, J.; Zhu, J.; Gong, J.; Chen, W. Novel activation functions-based ZNN models for fixed-time solving dynamirc Sylvester equation. *Neural Comput. Appl.* **2022**, *34*, 14297–14315. [CrossRef]
21. Zhang, Y.; Jiang, D.; Wang, J. A recurrent neural network for solving Sylvester equation with time-varying coefficients. *IEEE Trans. Neural Netw.* **2002**, *13*, 1053–1063. [CrossRef]
22. Hu, Z.; Xiao, L.; Dai, J.; Xu, Y.; Zuo, Q.; Liu, C. A unified predefined-time convergent and robust ZNN model for constrained quadratic programming. *IEEE Trans. Ind. Inform.* **2020**, *17*, 1998–2010. [CrossRef]
23. Zhang, Z.; Zheng, L.; Wang, M. An exponential-enhanced-type varying-parameter RNN for solving time-varying matrix inversion. *Neurocomputing* **2019**, *338*, 126–138. [CrossRef]
24. Stanimirović, P.S.; Katsikis, V.N.; Zhang, Z.; Li, S.; Chen, J.; Zhou, M. Varying-parameter Zhang neural network for approximating some expressions involving outer inverses. *Optim. Methods Softw.* **2020**, *35*, 1304–1330. [CrossRef]
25. Han, L.; Liao, B.; He, Y.; Xiao, X. Dual noise-suppressed ZNN with predefined-time convergence and its application in matrix inversion. In Proceedings of the 2021 11th International Conference on Intelligent Control and Information Processing (ICICIP), Dali, China, 3–7 December 2021; IEEE: New York, NY, USA, 2021; pp. 410–415.
26. Xiao, L.; He, Y.; Dai, J.; Liu, X.; Liao, B.; Tan, H. A variable-parameter noise-tolerant zeroing neural network for time-variant matrix inversion with guaranteed robustness. *IEEE Trans. Neural Netw. Learn. Syst.* **2022**, *33*, 1535–1545. [CrossRef] [PubMed]
27. Johnson, M.A.; Moradi, M.H. *PID Control*; Springer: Berlin/Heidelberg, Germany, 2005.
28. Jin, L.; Zhang, Y.; Li, S. Integration-enhanced Zhang neural network for real-time-varying matrix inversion in the presence of various kinds of noises. *IEEE Trans. Neural Netw. Learn. Syst.* **2015**, *27*, 2615–2627. [CrossRef]
29. Liao, B.; Han, L.; Cao, X.; Li, S.; Li, J. Double integral-enhanced Zeroing neural network with linear noise rejection for time-varying matrix inverse. *CAAI Trans. Intell. Technol.* **2024**, *9*, 197–210. [CrossRef]
30. Dai, J.; Yang, X.; Xiao, L.; Jia, L.; Li, Y. ZNN with fuzzy adaptive activation functions and its application to time-varying linear matrix equation. *IEEE Trans. Ind. Inform.* **2021**, *18*, 2560–2570. [CrossRef]
31. Xiao, L.; Zhang, Y.; Dai, J.; Chen, K.; Yang, S.; Li, W.; Liao, B.; Ding, L.; Li, J. A new noise-tolerant and predefined-time ZNN model for time-dependent matrix inversion. *Neural Netw.* **2019**, *117*, 124–134. [CrossRef]
32. Xiao, L.; Tao, J.; Dai, J.; Wang, Y.; Jia, L.; He, Y. A parameter-changing and complex-valued zeroing neural-network for finding solution of time-varying complex linear matrix equations in finite time. *IEEE Trans. Ind. Inform.* **2021**, *17*, 6634–6643. [CrossRef]
33. Jin, L.; Li, S.; Liao, B.; Zhang, Z. Zeroing neural networks: A survey. *Neurocomputing* **2017**, *267*, 597–604. [CrossRef]
34. Liao, B.; Hua, C.; Cao, X.; Katsikis, V.N.; Li, S. Complex noise-resistant zeroing neural network for computing complex time-dependent Lyapunov equation. *Mathematics* **2022**, *10*, 2817. [CrossRef]
35. Nguyen, N.T.; Nguyen, N.T. Lyapunov stability theory. In *Model-Reference Adaptive Control: A Primer*; Springer: Berlin/Heidelberg, Germany, 2018; pp. 47–81.

Disclaimer/Publisher's Note: The statements, opinions and data contained in all publications are solely those of the individual author(s) and contributor(s) and not of MDPI and/or the editor(s). MDPI and/or the editor(s) disclaim responsibility for any injury to people or property resulting from any ideas, methods, instructions or products referred to in the content.

MDPI AG
Grosspeteranlage 5
4052 Basel
Switzerland
Tel.: +41 61 683 77 34

Axioms Editorial Office
E-mail: axioms@mdpi.com
www.mdpi.com/journal/axioms

Disclaimer/Publisher's Note: The title and front matter of this reprint are at the discretion of the Guest Editors. The publisher is not responsible for their content or any associated concerns. The statements, opinions and data contained in all individual articles are solely those of the individual Editors and contributors and not of MDPI. MDPI disclaims responsibility for any injury to people or property resulting from any ideas, methods, instructions or products referred to in the content.

www.ingramcontent.com/pod-product-compliance
Lightning Source LLC
LaVergne TN
LVHW072344090526
838202LV00019B/2478